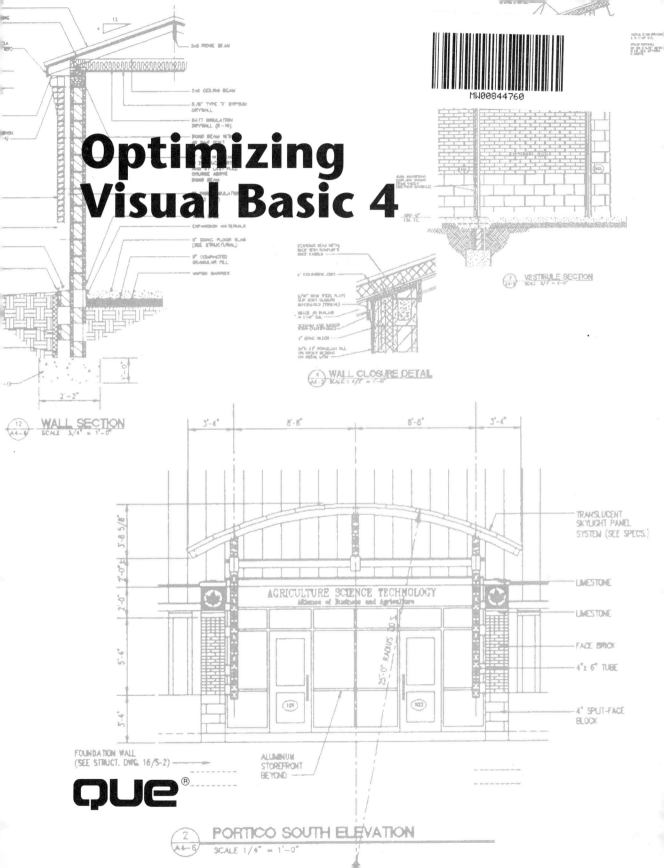

Optimizing
Visual Basic 4

que ®

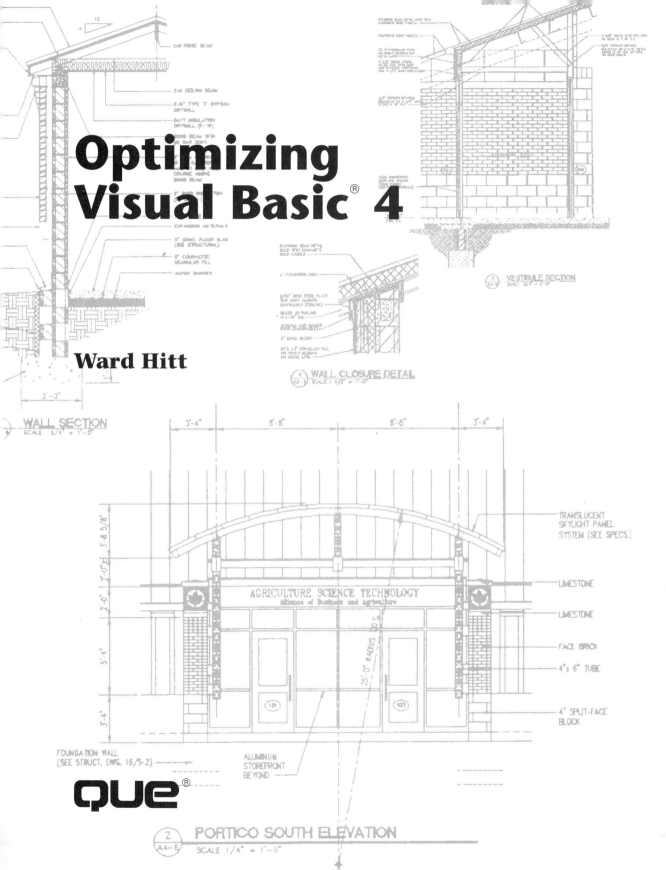

Optimizing
Visual Basic® 4

Ward Hitt

que®

Optimizing Visual Basic 4

Library of Congress Catalog No.: 95-78889

ISBN: 0-7897-0206-1

97 96 95   6 5 4 3 2 1

Interpretation of the printing code: the rightmost double-digit number is the year of the book's printing; the rightmost single-digit number, the number of the book's printing. For example, a printing code of 95-1 shows that the first printing of the book occurred in 1995.

All terms mentioned in this book that are known to be trademarks or service marks have been appropriately capitalized. Que cannot attest to the accuracy of this information. Use of a term in this book should not be regarded as affecting the validity of any trademark or service mark.

Screen reproductions in this book were created using Collage Plus from Inner Media, Inc., Hollis, NH.

Credits

President and Publisher
Roland Elgey

Associate Publisher
Joseph B. Wikert

Editorial Services Director
Elizabeth Keaffaber

Managing Editor
Sandy Doell

Director of Marketing
Lynn E. Zingraf

Senior Series Editor
Chris Nelson

Publishing Manager
Bryan Gambrel

Acquisitions Editor
Fred Slone

Product Director
Stephen L. Miller

Production Editor
Susan Shaw Dunn

Editors
Kelli M. Brooks
Judy Brunetti
Tom Cirtin

Assistant Product Marketing Manager
Kim Margolius

Technical Editor
Russell L. Jacobs

Acquisitions Coordinator
Angela C. Kozlowski

Operations Coordinator
Patricia J. Brooks

Editorial Assistant
Michelle R. Newcomb

Technical Specialist
Cari Skaggs

Book Designer
Kim Scott

Cover Designer
Dan Armstrong

Production Team
Angela D. Bannan, Brian Buschkill,
Jason Carr, Anne Dickerson,
Bryan Flores, John Hulse,
Daryl Kessler, Michelle Lee,
Julie Quinn, Bobbi Satterfield,
Andrew Stone, Jody York

Indexer
Kathy Venable

Composed in *Stone Serif* and *MCPdigital* by Que Corporation

This book is dedicated to my wife, Terri, with gratitude and love.

About the Author

Ward R. Hitt has been programming since 1982. He works as an independent computer consultant, providing Visual Basic development services to corporations and government agencies in the Washington, D.C., area. He is a regular contributor to *Visual Basic Programming Journal* and is a member of *VBPJ*'s Technical Review Board.

In addition to his consulting and writing activities, he develops commercial software in Visual Basic for the home user and programmer markets, which he licenses to various software publishers. His titles include CodeBank, published by Visual Components; Personal Home Inventory from Parsons Technology; and VBDD—The Data Dictionary for Visual Basic, from Progress Software's Crescent Division.

He lives in the Virginia suburbs of Washington, D.C., with his wife, Theresa, and their two children, Katrina and Christopher.

He can be reached via CompuServe at **73361,106** or via the Internet at **73361.106@compuserve.com**.

Acknowledgments

There may have been a time, long ago, when writing a book was a solitary and even lonely endeavor. Not today—and certainly not with this book.

Many people at Que materially participated in the creation of *Optimizing Visual Basic 4*, and you'll find the names of the entire team listed on the credits page. I thank them all. I owe a special debt of gratitude to several individuals at Que. Joe Wikert convinced me to take on this topic and got me started. Fred Slone kept after me with gentle humor to finish the book—it wouldn't have gotten done without him. Steven Miller contributed immeasurably to the substance and flow of the text with ideas and suggestions. Susan Dunn, my production editor, was the ultimate style cop, and did her best to help me turn my prose into something understandable. Judy Brunetti, Tom Cirtin, and Kelli Brooks were the front-line copy editors. Angela Kozlowski kept everything moving smoothly.

My thanks go to Sam Patterson for contributing the Win32 API chapter on short notice. My friend Andrew Brust's advice on VB and Jet tuning was always on target. Frank Moncrief and Jim Fawcette asked the right questions, and got me started on writing about VB in the first place.

Last, but not least, I thank my family: Terri, my wife, and our children, Katrina and Christopher. Without their support, encouragement, and understanding, this book truly would not have been possible.

We'd Like to Hear from You!

As part of our continuing effort to produce books of the highest possible quality, Que would like to hear your comments. To stay competitive, we *really* want you, as a computer book reader and user, to let us know what you like or dislike most about this book or other Que products.

You can mail comments, ideas, or suggestions for improving future editions to the address below, or send us a fax at (317) 581-4663. For the online inclined, Macmillan Computer Publishing has a forum on CompuServe (type **GO QUEBOOKS** at any prompt) through which our staff and authors are available for questions and comments. The address of our Internet site is **http:// www.mcp.com** (World Wide Web).

In addition to exploring our forum, please feel free to contact me personally to discuss your opinions of this book: I'm **76103,1334** on CompuServe, and I'm **smiller@que.mcp.com** on the Internet.

Thanks in advance—your comments will help us to continue publishing the best books available on computer topics in today's market.

Stephen L. Miller
Product Development Specialist
Que Corporation
201 W. 103rd Street
Indianapolis, Indiana 46290
USA

Contents at a Glance

Optimize from the Start

Application Optimization

Database Optimization

Bitwise Optimization

Contents

II Application Optimization   51

4 Faster Forms Architectures   53

III Database Optimization   149

7 Speeding Database Operations   151

8 More Database Speed   185

IV Bitwise Optimization   303

12 Optimizing Graphics and Bitmaps   305

13 Using Components and Subroutines Wisely   357

Introduction

Welcome to *Optimizing Visual Basic 4*, and thanks for purchasing this book. I hope you'll find it useful, and that it helps in some small way as you work to improve your applications.

This book is about Visual Basic, particularly Visual Basic 4. *Optimizing Visual Basic 4* is a general work in the sense that it doesn't focus on any particular type of VB application, like database or graphics programming (although those subjects are covered). But it also isn't a general how-to book. Most all aspects of VB programming are analyzed here, but with a particular view.

This book's viewpoint is optimization: the process of making code faster, leaner, and more effective.

Why Optimize?

Someone asked me the other day, "Why does anyone need to optimize code these days, given the speed of today's 486 and Pentium processors?" Well, CPUs *are* fast and getting faster. But software keeps getting more intensive. My 2-year-old son could write a DOS program that would run very quickly on a Pentium. But who would buy it? Windows 95 has stricter requirements and greater burdens. Of course, many of the old optimization topics, like integer versus floating-point division, are immaterial in almost any situation. Iterating a test 20,000 times to find a tenth-second total difference is not very meaningful.

On the other hand, a tabbed VB form containing 50 controls can take either 2.4 seconds or .33 second to display, depending on how much you choose to optimize it. To locate and read a database record, you can burn 8.9 seconds, 1.2 seconds, or .25 second, depending on your method. Displaying just a few lines of text can require 1.26 seconds or .157 second, with the only difference in the code being an innocuous DoEvents statement (you can also get it down to .028 second—and pretty easily, at that—but that's another story).

Later in the book, in Chapter 6, you'll see a case study involving a 3-D shading graphics subroutine. In its original form, it requires 11.589 seconds to process a small sample bitmap (and, by the way, the subroutine wasn't badly written or purposefully slow). The algorithm is modified in stages through the chapter by applying a defined method of scientific optimization and analysis. The code is tuned step by step, improving performance to 10.13 seconds, then 2.3 seconds, then .508 second, then .329 second. Finally, the paradigm of the algorithm is radically recast for a final speed of .05 second. Mere tuning increased the speed of the algorithm by 35 times. Recasting the algorithm increased the speed by more than 200 times. All without recourse to DLLs, C, or Delphi.

The point of these examples is that CPUs may be faster today, but they're not yet infinitely fast. An 11-second graphics routine isn't usable, but one that takes a twentieth of a second is. An application whose forms takes a third of a second to display seems much faster and friendlier to an end user than one that requires 2 seconds.

Why Not C++?

If you're a Visual Basic programmer, you've no doubt heard *ad nauseum* the C++ mantra, "VB is fine for prototyping, but for a real product you've got to write in C." I've heard it so many times that I get somewhat defensive when I'm asked, "What language do you program in?" The fact is, though, that for 90 percent or more of the real code that's being created today, VB can be just as fast as C. And VB programming is 100 percent, all-the-time, insanely more productive.

But the statement does contain a kernel of truth. VB is, of course, an interpreted language, and thus code-intensive operations in VB will be slower than equivalent C code. And the sad truth is that many VB programs are resource-intensive and low-performance. In the C world, a great deal of time and attention is paid to code optimization. In the VB world, the emphasis is on productivity. Optimization is given a much lower priority than meeting or beating tight development schedules.

In a sense, this is to be expected. Programming projects in each language are geared to the strengths of that language. If a project must be completed quickly, it's done in VB. If it must be as tight and fast as possible, the typical project manager will have the program coded in C, with lots of extra time scheduled for testing and optimization.

There's a large gap in the expectations for programs in VB as opposed to those in C. One of the purposes of this book is to bridge that gap, to bring a greater concern for optimization to the VB world, and to expand the knowledge base relating to VB optimization so that efforts at optimization will be more fruitful, enjoyable, and take less programmer time.

Who Is this Book For?

This book isn't an introductory text, by any stretch of the imagination. In most of the book, I assume that you know at least one way to perform the operations that we are analyzing. So I don't waste your time talking about, for example, code syntax, property values, and so on.

There are exceptions to this general rule for more obscure methods and commands or in discussions of code or control options that directly relate to optimization issues. I always show the code that's used for the benchmark tests, so you can follow along and establish to your satisfaction that the code is written properly.

But if you're looking for a book that will explain how to code a `For...Next` loop, you may want to review other books. There are many fine introductory texts available.

On the other hand, if you want to know whether you should use `For...Next`, `Do Until...Loop`, or some other looping structure, then this book is just the ticket.

How Does this Book Approach Optimization?

Optimization can mean many things to different people. In this book, you'll learn to approach optimization as a process. The nice thing about Visual Basic and Windows programming in general is that it often provides more than one method to do a particular task because of multiple keywords, API calls, and controls that perform similar functions. Beyond that, though, when designing or improving an algorithm or an application, you can often satisfy a user's requirements in radically different ways, according to the approach you choose.

We'll take a journey, you and I, through the different methods available to the VB programmer in this book. We'll see which are easier, which are faster, and which are equal. We'll also investigate the process and nature of optimization itself. Optimization can be seen as an art, or even as black magic. But we'll discover how to apply it as a science.

Optimization goals are set according to need. If your program is too big, optimization will make it smaller. If it's too slow, optimization will make it faster.

What's in this Book?

Optimizing Visual Basic 4 is divided into four sections. Each section contains chapters covering a general optimization topic or area of functionality.

Part I: Optimize from the Start

This section includes chapters on design and interface challenges with VB4 and Windows 95, tools for optimization, and application and database design.

Chapter 1, "Optimization Challenges with Visual Basic 4.0," introduces some of the new VB4 features and challenges, Windows 95's impact on VB programming, and issues related to the transition from 16- to 32-bit programming.

Chapter 2, "Building an Optimization Toolkit," introduces the method and process of optimization that the book proposes, and provides code for profiling application performance, assessing resource usage, and managing reusable code.

Chapter 3, "Designing Optimized Applications," explains pragmatic methods for top-level application database design and explores fundamental aspects of relational database theory.

Part II: Application Optimization

The chapters in this section cover speeding form displays under different architectures, code construct comparisons, and strategies for algorithm improvement.

Chapter 4, "Faster Forms Architectures," analyzes ways to speed form display with MDI and SDI architectures, different control mixes, and methods of manipulating form size and placement.

Chapter 5, "Constructing Optimized VB Code," analyzes scores of different VB key mathematical keywords, text-handling methods, process control structures, variable data types, control properties, and error-handling methods to determine the relative speed of different options.

Chapter 6, "Strategies to Improve Algorithms," demonstrates a step-by-step process of algorithm optimization with a graphic case study.

Part III: Database Optimization

This section analyzes how to speed database functions, including DAO and SQL. It even discusses methods and benefits of eliminating the Jet database engine altogether.

Chapter 7, "Speeding Database Operations," analyzes different DAO (Data Access Object) methods and objects, describes how to apply database optimization principles to your unique databases, and presents a utility program that creates realistic test data sets of any size and complexity.

Chapter 8, "More Database Speed," extends the discussion in Chapter 7 to include data display, editing, relationships, and database validation rules.

Chapter 9, "Improving SQL Performance," analyzes the relative strengths and weaknesses of SQL action and select queries, QueryDefs, and DAOs.

Chapter 10, "Tuning the Jet Engine," discusses options that you can take to change the inner workings of the Jet engine.

Chapter 11, "Eliminating the Jet Engine by Using File I/O," demonstrates two methods that mimic database functionality using the simple sequential file-handling constructs in VB, and assesses the relative speed of file I/O compared to Jet.

Part IV: Bitwise Optimization

This section is dedicated to advanced graphics topics, OLE controls, VBXs and subroutines, and the Windows 32-bit API.

Chapter 12, "Optimizing Graphics and Bitmaps," analyzes the VB graphics methods with various property settings and different control targets. It also compares them to API equivalents, discusses text-printing methods, and analyzes several means of manipulating bitmap graphics.

Chapter 13, "Using Components and Subroutines Wisely," compares the performance of the new OLE Custom Control (OCX) architecture with VBXs and VB code routines, and tests different subroutine architectures, OLE Automation Servers, and inline OLE Servers (OLE DLLs).

Chapter 14, "Exploiting the Windows 32-Bit API," written by Sam Patterson, explores how the 32-bit API differs from the 16-bit API, and demonstrates how various API calls can eliminate controls such as the Common Dialog OCX or enhance code performance.

The CD-ROM

This book shows only the crucial code in the text. Of course, all the related code is on the CD that comes with this book. To find the code for a particular project, look in the directory named after the chapter in which the project is discussed.

The CD also contains Visual CodeBank Limited Edition, a special version of the Visual CodeBank Subroutine Library Generator from Visual Components, Inc. that's in the \Vcb directory. CodeBank is used throughout the book to organize the code and provide access to needed subroutines and functions.

Also included on the CD are two valuable applets to help you manage and optimize your code. Pretty Printer and the Polisher from Aardvark Software are included as an extra bonus that you can use in addition to the CodeBank application. For installation information, refer to the last page of the book.

Benchmarks and Testing Conventions

The benchmarks in this book were timed by using the `BeginTime` and `EndTime` subroutines (discussed in Chapter 2), which use the `GetTickCount()` API call to obtain accurate timing information from the Windows kernel. All benchmarks were run on a 486-66, running Windows 95.

All benchmarks were run in both 32- and 16-bit VB4. While some analysts or authors may focus just on Win32, I believe that 16-bit Windows will need to be supported for some time to come. Fortunately, VB4's conditional compilation makes this less difficult.

Conventions Used in this Book

All program code and commands appear in a special monospace font, as in the following example:

```
Dummy = SetPixel(Picture1.hdc, foo, foobar, &HFF&)
```

Anything that you are required to type appears in monospace boldface, as in the following example: **d:\Windows\Setup.Exe**.

This paragraph format indicates additional information that may help you avoid problems or that should be considered in using the described features.

This paragraph format suggests easier or alternative methods of executing a procedure.

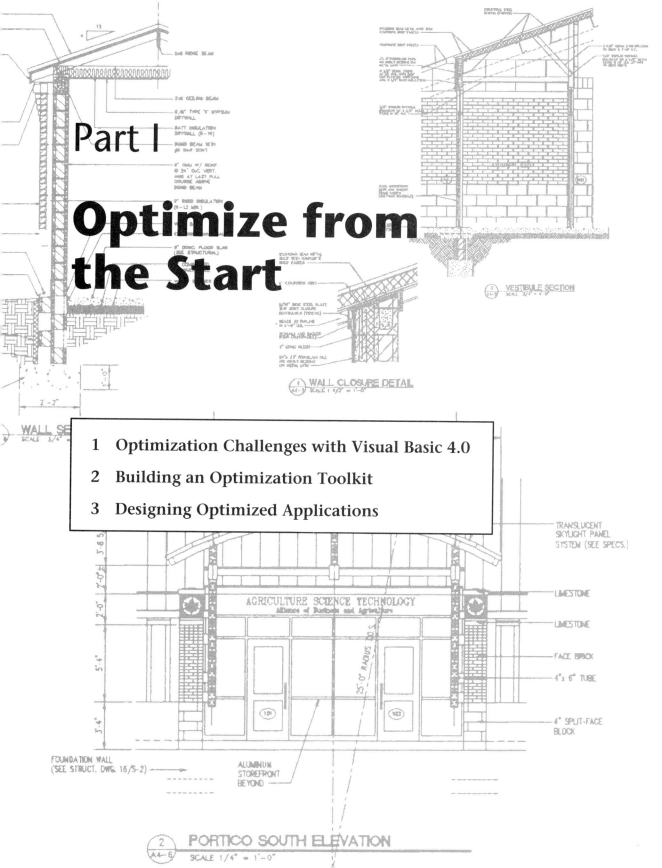

Part I

Optimize from the Start

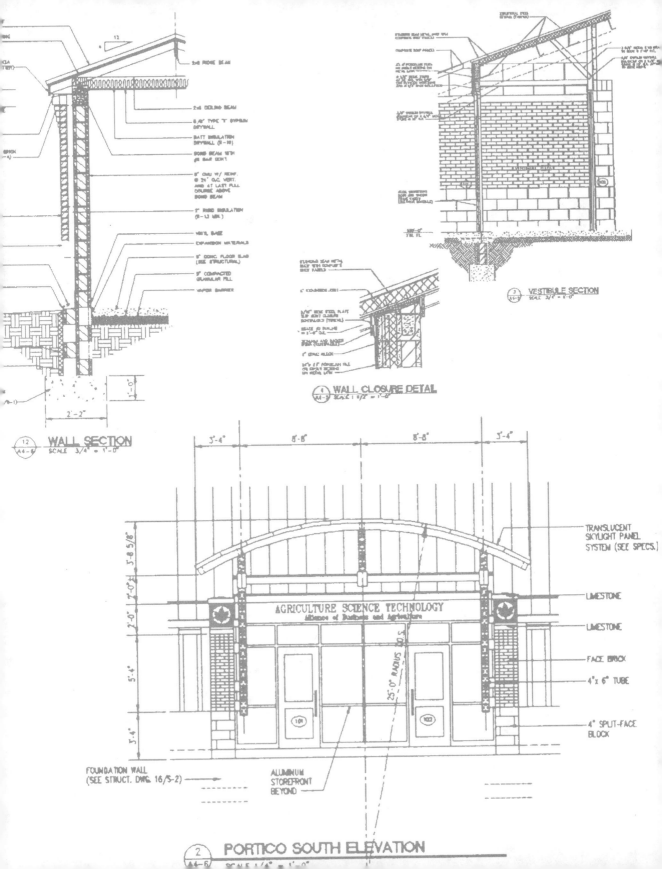

WALL SECTION
SCALE 3/4" = 1'-0"

VESTIBULE SECTION
SCALE 3/4" = 1'-0"

WALL CLOSURE DETAIL
SCALE 1 1/2" = 1'-0"

PORTICO SOUTH ELEVATION
SCALE 1/4" = 1'-0"

2nd RIDGE BEAM

2x6 CEILING BEAM

5/8" TYPE "X" GYPSUM DRYWALL

BATT INSULATION DRYWALL (R-19)

BOND BEAM WITH #5 BAR CONT.

8" CMU W/ REINF. @ 24" O.C. VERT. AND AT LAST FULL COURSE ABOVE BOND BEAM

1" RIGID INSULATION (R-13 MIN.)

VINYL BASE

EXPANSION MATERIALS

8" CONC. FLOOR SLAB (SEE STRUCTURAL)

5" COMPACTED GRANULAR FILL

VAPOR BARRIER

TRANSLUCENT SKYLIGHT PANEL SYSTEM (SEE SPECS.)

LIMESTONE

LIMESTONE

FACE BRICK

4" x 6" TUBE

4" SPLIT-FACE BLOCK

FOUNDATION WALL (SEE STRUCT. DWG 16/S-2)

ALUMINUM STOREFRONT BEYOND

AGRICULTURE SCIENCE TECHNOLOGY
Alliance of Business and Agriculture

25'-0" RADIUS TO S.

101

102

5'-4"   8'-8"   8'-8"   5'-4"

3'-8 5/8"

7'-0"±

2'-0"

5'-4"

5'-4"

1'-0"

2'-2"

Chapter 1

Optimization Challenges with Visual Basic 4.0

You've just written the next killer app in Visual Basic. You're going to top the charts and make a mint. But there's a problem or two. The app is as slow as molasses. Worse, it consumes so many resources that half the time, the app just crashes and burns.

You're facing spending the next year rewriting the project in C++, or ripping out large sections of functionality. You'll lose your market advantage and starve your family.

Not to worry. You can speed up your Visual Basic program substantially without losing a drop of functionality. You can easily reduce memory requirements, slash resource usage, and cut distributable size. And rather than spend a year converting your VB "prototype" into C++, you'll accomplish it all in a matter of hours or days.

In the course of this book, you'll see examples where sections of code are sped up by 200 times or more. You'll learn ways to minimize resource usage and slash megabytes off the distributable size of VB applications. You'll investigate bypassing Visual Basic code bottlenecks by using the Windows API and DLLs. You'll triple or quadruple the speed of database operations and make your forms snap to the screen with an almost audible pop. You'll even make your application sing.

By the time you're through, the only thing that will distinguish your application from one written in C++ will be the VB runtime DLLs that Setup copies to the System directory—and the fact that you brought the program to market in a third of the time.

It's all part of the science of optimization.

This chapter examines the following topics:

- The nature of the optimization process
- New challenges and opportunities with Visual Basic 4
- How to optimize interpreted code
- The OLE paradigm
- Windows 95 interface issues
- 16- and 32-bit development issues

The Optimization Balancing Act

What is optimization, anyway? The American Heritage dictionary defines *optimize* as "to make as perfect or effective as possible." Perfect is a pretty high standard to live up to. I have trouble sometimes with "good enough," let alone "perfect," even with the "as possible" qualifier.

Perfect and even *effective* are pretty vague terms. Is a perfect program one that's infinitely fast, or one that's infinitely small? Is a program more effective if it has a thousand slow features, or 20 fast ones? Is a program perfectly effective if it can perform every known task in the universe, or if it can accomplish one task with infinite ease of use?

In this book, *optimization* is going to be defined as the process of making a program better—faster, smaller, full-functioned, and easier to use and maintain. Not perfect, not as effective as possible, but simply better than it was before you began the process.

I use the term *better*, for all its vagueness, quite deliberately because it's a relational word rather than an absolute term such as *perfect*. B can be better than A, not only because B is fast but because A was slow, relative to each other. I may seem a little pedantic here, but bear with me, because I'm getting to the point: Your efforts at optimization are always specified and measured by the failings of your initial effort.

In this sense, iteration X of your program or algorithm tells you exactly what to do to make it "better." If A is slow, you need to create a faster B. If B is then fast but large, better would be to maintain the speed but shed some fat. So optimization is the iterative process of improving a program, based on the shortcomings of earlier versions.

If you had an infinite amount of time to spend in optimization, maybe you could make a program infinitely better and create perfection. In the real world, though, you're going to have only a certain amount of time to work on optimization. So a critical part of the process of optimization is determining in what sections of your program it's best to spend your time, and when to quit optimizing and ship the product.

Classic Optimization: Execution Speed vs. Resource Consumption

The revised definition is a bit problematic. While you'll review many techniques in this book that simultaneously speed operation and reduce memory and resource consumption, many of the tricks that can make a program faster also increase its size. Conversely, things that decrease a program's size can slow it down.

Suppose that you have a large form, with lots of controls and graphics, that's loading slowly. You could easily speed it up by removing some of the controls and graphics, but that would obviously reduce its functionality.

A Question of Size

Let's consider for a moment the issue of size. Programs consume certain amounts of RAM (which is one issue) but also can consume system resources, a special kind of system memory (which is a whole other issue).

Resource usage is much less of a problem with Windows 95 than Windows 3.x, because Microsoft has moved many of the larger resource structures out of the 64K GDI and user areas to a new, flat, 32-bit area. But resource usage will continue to be an issue, not only because constraints still exist under Windows 95, but also because we'll still be working with Windows 3.x for some time to come. You'll look at this issue in more depth later.

Distributable Size

Size can also refer to *distributable size*, which would include not only the program but also the program's support files: DLLs, databases, help files, and graphics files. This is an issue that we typically pay almost no attention to in our development systems. But if you're distributing shareware systems over telephone lines or trying to compress your distributable onto a certain number of floppy disks, distributable size may be a primary consideration.

Optimization and Programmer Productivity

And then, finally, is the question of time. To implement a given purpose and feature set in a commercially reasonable amount of time, you must achieve a satisfactory productivity level. The amount of time available to produce your product will almost always be less than you really need. After all, if we all had infinite time available, we would write everything in native assembler, tuned for our particular purpose.

Optimization, then, is a balancing act, with priorities determined by the nature and problems of an individual, unique application. The goal of optimization is to define and achieve that balance by implementing the improvements that make the biggest difference in the limited time available.

Overview of Visual Basic 4

This book isn't a general work on Visual Basic 4, so I won't spend a lot of time reviewing the VB4 feature set. But with this latest release of VB, Microsoft has introduced a number of features and improvements that affect the programmer working to optimize code. So it makes sense to take a quick look at some of the major changes that you'll be examining closely later in the book.

VB now supports 32-bit executables that integrate nicely with Windows 95 and Windows NT, while keeping the capability to create 16-bit applications for Windows 3.x operating environments. There's a whole new 32-bit API to learn and a method of conditional compilation to allow you to maintain a single set of code for both 32- and 16-bit applications.

Our much beloved—and well hated—VBXs have been replaced by custom controls based on OLE, Microsoft's object linking and embedding standard, at a significant cost in terms of distributable size and executable speed.

VB has been able to host OLE applications since version 2.0, but with version 4, Visual Basic gains a whole new capability to create OLE Server and OLE Automation applications. OLE-enabled applications now can use VB programs without resorting to the complexities and limitations of DDE (dynamic data exchange).

Major changes have been made in data-access operations. The data control has been significantly improved to the point where it may be ready for serious development work, by itself or with programmatic methods. Data Access Objects (DAOs) have been overhauled and enhanced, and there's better linkage between VB and the Access Jet engine.

And there's been a whole slew of minor improvements and changes. They may not make the Top 10 lists in the advertisements, but they'll provide new opportunities and—in some cases—new challenges for optimization. For example, Multiple Document Interface (MDI) forms may now be preloaded and hidden, which means that you can speed MDI display times significantly. Integer division is no longer always faster than floating-point division, so you'll have to analyze more carefully what type of math you use, based on the data types of the operands.

The PCode Challenge

Nine times out of 10, when Visual Basic programmers think of optimization, they're thinking about enhancing application speed. It's a problematic issue because Visual Basic code is inherently slow, since it's an interpreted language. When Visual Basic "compiles" a project, it actually just converts your text source code into a structure called *PCode*, plus a few instructions to load the runtime DLL at application startup. The runtime DLL then parses the PCode, deciphers it, and executes the instructions by using its own compiled and assembler routines.

Visual Basic's PCode interpreter is very fast, as interpreters go. But interpreted code is always going to be slower than compiled code because of the additional layers of processing that must be executed to generate machine instructions at runtime. Although you can implement just about any task in native VB code, processor-intensive procedures such as JPEG graphics decoding or ZIP file decompression would be unacceptably slow. Of course, this isn't a problem in real development work, thanks to VB's capability to easily integrate DLLs, Windows API calls, and OCX custom controls when fast processor-intensive code is needed.

An even greater challenge is in form display. VB's form engine can be quite slow because VB must interpret PCode to decipher the properties, placement, and nature of the controls on the form before it can display it. This can be a significant problem, and I'll devote Chapter 4 to optimizing form load and display speed.

Other Application Challenges

Fortunately, however, there's another side to this equation. Most applications today aren't code bound—that is, the limiting factor in a VB application's speed isn't typically the code you've written. This is true because of several factors:

■ VB apps run under Windows. Much of what an app does today isn't work coded directly into the application, but rather results from a call to a Windows API function (either explicitly or indirectly by using a VB method or statement, or by setting a VB property value). The Windows API doesn't much care whether it's being called by VB or C++—it'll perform just as quickly with either.

■ Today's machines are very fast. They can execute so many cycles per second that only the most processor-intensive algorithms require all the processor's speed. If, for example, a user is filling out a database form, the time between keystrokes is a sizable fraction of a second. Even an 80-word-per-minute typist won't hit more than about 10 keys a second. VB can interpret and execute a lot of code in that tenth of a second between keystrokes, so the speed of interpreted execution—while important in many algorithms—isn't often the primary performance constraint.

■ When you do run into VB speed limitations, you have a ready-made and wildly popular solution: custom controls. By using custom controls, you can easily implement just about any code-intensive function. VB's component architecture is perhaps one of the primary reasons for its success.

The OLE Control Challenge

Much of VB's popularity can no doubt be attributed to the ease with which it could be extended with VBX custom control components—which has to make you wonder why with VB4 Microsoft has abandoned its hugely successful VBX component architecture in favor of OCXs, otherwise known as OLE custom controls. Microsoft says that the VBX standard simply wasn't robust enough to make the transition to 32 bit.

VBXs were a hastily implemented afterthought, added late in the development of Visual Basic 1.0. Microsoft never released specifications for the VBX host interface, and the only other Microsoft development environment that ever supported VBXs, Visual C++, supported only the first and least functional version. PowerSoft, Clarion, Delphi, and all the other environments that added VBX support were able to do so only by reverse engineering the Visual C++ VBX code.

In any case, they're not supported in 32-bit VB4, and they're clearly on the wane for 16-bit VB, assuming another 16-bit version of VB is ever released. OLE is an integral part of Microsoft's vision for the future, and that may be the final explanation for the change: VBXs just didn't fit the vision.

In their place are OLE custom controls. OCXs are 40K to 90K larger per control than equivalent VBXs due to OLE code overhead. They're somewhat slower in execution than VBXs, and they load more slowly. We'll take a detailed look at OLE custom controls, VBXs, and the alternatives in Chapter 13, "Using Components and Subroutines Wisely."

Other OLE Challenges

OLE controls aren't the only change to VB's OLE support. With version 4, VB now can create OLE Server and OLE Automation executables. Visual Basic has been able to run programs such as Word or Excel for some time as an OLE Host. Now, Word and Excel can return the hospitality by running OLE Server or OLE Automation applications written in VB. Plus, VB itself can run VB OLE objects, which means that you can use VB to create compiled object code routines and then link them to your applications by using OLE. You can establish custom methods and properties for your OLE objects, compile them as OLE DLLs, and register them. For the first time, then, you can create something akin to a callable DLL in VB.

However, there's a significant down side. Performance of OLE Server objects is two to three times slower than native VB code execution. OLE Automation object performance will be examined closely in Chapter 13, "Using Components and Subroutines Wisely."

New Challenges with Windows 95

Visual Basic 4 is an application oriented to the future, and the future is Windows 95. Windows 95 isn't a completely new operating system. Its roots are firmly planted in the past to maintain backward compatibility.

But it's more than just another upgrade, in the sense that Windows 3.1 or even 3.0 was an incremental change. Windows 95 is a radical upgrade. The 32-bit architecture and reliance on OLE are significant departures. The Windows 3.1 API that you've gotten to know so well is history. Although many functions remain similar, most are stored in different libraries than you might expect. Many more are simply gone. Although you can use 3.1-style declares in 16-bit programs (thanks to the thunking layer), for 32-bit functionality you'll have to learn new tricks. It will take some time, because at this point there's little guidance on the changes.

 Windows 95 uses the *thunking layer* to support 16-bit programs. It translates, or *thunks*, 16-bit operations and calls to their 32-bit equivalents on the fly. Although this naturally adds a layer of complexity to execution and thus causes some performance degradation, it's essential for backward compatibility.

Windows 95 also presents a new user interface style. The new style means reworking old assumptions and practices, not only in the way you lay out your applications, but in basic things such as responding to right mouse clicks or providing help support.

Some of the new interface features—such as tabbed forms, which often use many more controls than can fit in an unlayered form—pose significant performance challenges. Although the tabbed dialog metaphor is easy to implement, attractive, and professional in appearance, VB form load and display performance is strongly related to the number of controls on a form.

Dual Development: Windows 3.1 and Windows 95

What makes moving to Windows 95 even more difficult is that for some time, Windows 3.1 will still be with us. We're entering an era of transition. Times of change, while they may be rewarding, can also be trying.

Of course, it's possible to ignore the problem. You could simply write using the 16-bit version of Visual Basic 4. Windows 95 runs 16-bit code, including VB4 16-bit code, very nicely. But most 32-bit operations are twice as fast under Windows 95, because 32-bit code is inherently faster and because 16-bit processes must have their API calls translated to 32 bit on the fly by the thunking layer.

Fortunately, VB4 does have a conditional compilation mechanism that will allow you to maintain one set of code to support both 16-bit Windows 3.1 and 32-bit Windows 95. It's not automatic, but it's better than having to maintain and keep synchronized two separate versions of the same application.

From Here...

For more information about the topics raised in this chapter, read the following chapters:

■ For more information on the process of optimization, see Chapter 2, "Building an Optimization Toolkit," and Chapter 6, "Strategies to Improve Algorithms."

■ For more information on application design, see Chapter 3, "Designing Optimized Applications."

■ For more information about speeding display of Windows 95-style forms, see Chapter 4, "Faster Forms Architectures."

■ For more information about OCXs, VBXs, and OLE Automation, see Chapter 13, "Using Components and Subroutines Wisely."

I

Optimize from the Start

Chapter 2

Building an Optimization Toolkit

This chapter examines the tools you'll need to perform professional optimization. You'll create subroutines to aid in identifying optimization trouble spots, test alternative algorithms, and monitor resources.

Since most VB optimization work involves speeding up code, an essential part of an optimization toolkit is a way to obtain accurate and usable timing information. The `BeginTime` and `EndTime` subroutines provide the solution. In this chapter, you'll see how the routines work, find out when to use them, and learn about their limitations.

The other side of optimization is resource conservation. Windows 95 loosens many of the resource constraints that we face in Windows 3.x, but constraints still exist. Of course, remember also that much of your development effort over the next few years will be dual—for both Windows 95 and 3.x—as the marketplace makes a transition to the new operating system. The `Monitor` subroutine discussed in this chapter provides a method of pinpointing resource usage for both 16- and 32-bit Windows.

This chapter also contains instructions for using Visual CodeBank Limited Edition, a special version of the Visual CodeBank Subroutine Library Generator from Visual Components, Inc. You can find Visual CodeBank on the CD-ROM in the \Vcb directory. CodeBank is used throughout the book to organize the code and provide access to needed subroutines and functions. It is a powerful tool that you can use to help manage reusable code in all your development projects.

In this chapter, you'll learn:

- How the `BeginTime` and `EndTime` routines work, when to use them, and their limitations

- How to use the `Monitor` subroutine to pinpoint resource usage

- How to use Visual CodeBank Limited Edition

Optimization: Tools or Rules?

Before examining the toolkit, let's spend a little time on the reasoning behind it.

The question is natural: Why do we need tools to test different algorithms if we have this book? Can't we derive rules of code craftsmanship that, if followed, will result in the fastest and leanest possible code? Isn't the purpose of this book to provide a set of rules that we can use to optimize, a combination of "how-to" recipes and wizardry secrets that describe the art of optimization?

Well, no, not entirely. Many programmers regard optimization as a black art, as magic to be performed only by wizards with encyclopedic knowledge of VB. In fact, much of this book shows the results of time trials on such things as integer versus floating-point math, or demonstrates reusable subroutines that speed common operations. These areas are where do-this-don't-do-that types of rules can apply. I think of this approach as the *art of optimization*, where programmers apply knowledge and code craftsmanship to creating elegant solutions to optimization problems, based on an ideal understanding of how VB works. Although you often see this type of analysis in writings on optimization ("A \ B is 58 percent faster than A / B"), the art approach takes you only halfway to true optimization.

Most real-world optimization depends on too many factors to be susceptible to dry, analytical rules. Regarding optimization as an art or as an application of rules-based craftsmanship won't always achieve the best results. This book focuses more on method and process: how to construct and measure trials and test sets that accurately reflect the process to be optimized.

The Art of Optimization: A Case Study

Let's look at a simple optimization exercise that will demonstrate the pitfalls of the artistic, craftsmanship approach to optimization.

Craftsmanship and Optimization

The task is to populate a list box with all the records in Table1 that have IDs of 100 or greater. It's not a large list, having only about 20 entries, and only about half of them will meet the criteria.

My first pass at the code is certainly serviceable, but not outstanding:

```
Set MyDyna = MyDb.OpenRecordset("Select * from Table1")
MyDyna.MoveFirst
Do Until MyDyna.EOF
    If MyDyna!Field1 >= 100 Then
        List1.AddItem MyDyna!Field2
    End If
    MyDyna.MoveNext
Loop
```

While this code certainly would work, it's not very well crafted. Even though you need only Field2, the routine selects all the fields from the table. The query retrieves every record in the table, and then loops through the entire dynaset, testing each record to see whether to add it to the list. It's easy to improve this code, simply by restructuring the query. Select only Field2 because that's all that's needed for the list box. Also, use a Where clause to retrieve only the records you want, eliminating the If...Then...End If structure:

```
Set MyDyna = MyDb.OpenRecordset("Select Field2 from Table1 _
        Where Field1 >= 100")
MyDyna.MoveFirst
Do Until MyDyna.EOF
    List1.AddItem MyDyna!Field2
    MyDyna.MoveNext
Loop
```

There! Code craftsmanship and the art of optimization in action! This eliminates two lines of interpreted code, removes a field lookup, and cuts the number of Dynaset.MoveNexts (a notoriously slow method of navigating a database) in half!

There's only one problem, however. The leaner, meaner, optimized code takes an average of 25 percent longer to complete the task as the slow, ugly code. That's as much as a tenth of a second longer! If your form is populated with four list or combo boxes like this, you could burn almost half a second with the new, supposedly improved, algorithm.

What Went Wrong?

Chapter 5, "Constructing Optimized VB Code," looks at database issues in depth, but for now let's take a moment to see what went wrong with the example. First, remember that the code was operating on a very small table. The record has only four fields, and the table has only about 20 records. So the time spent sequentially cycling through the dynaset wasn't that great. When the Jet engine processes a query, it tries to determine the best strategy for fulfilling it. The amount of time Jet thinks about it depends on the complexity of the query and the database structure. Adding the Where clause forced Jet to think about the best way to find the records, increasing the up-front overhead of the query.

Also, because the table wasn't indexed, Jet really couldn't determine a strategy that would work better than sequential searching, so it probably searched through every record itself, applying the same If...Then test that was used in the first algorithm. The increased speed of an SQL sequential search (as opposed to a PCode operation) simply wasn't sufficient to provide greater overall speed, given the small number of records. However, if more records are added to the table, the second method would indeed have been faster (the break-even point on my machine is about 50 records).

Lessons in the Process

Which brings us to the point: Optimization is not an art. Optimization is not magic. Optimization is not the same as craftsmanship. If you think of optimization as an art and proceed on that basis, you may construct some finely crafted code, suitable for framing, but you won't obtain optimal performance.

The Science of Optimization

This book tries to treat optimization as a science. In other words, when we examine code to be optimized, we'll subject it to the same type of analysis an experimental physicist might bring to a theory.

It's probably worth a few moments to review the classic scientific method, since although it's the cornerstone of Western civilization, many of us never learned it. Scientific optimization will succeed or fail based on the fundamental cycle of the scientific method: hypothesis, analysis, and synthesis. In the optimization context, *hypothesis* would refer to alternative code constructs or algorithms. *Analysis* would involve testing the code in realistic settings,

obtaining hard data on code performance or resource usage, and then inter-
preting the data to determine why the results came out the way they did.
Finally, *synthesis* means resolving the results of the analysis to create optimized code, which we then either install in the application or test again
against a new alternative hypothesis.

Quantification

Perhaps the first principle of science is that results must be quantifiable. In
other words, if you can't describe your results by using numbers, you can't
really apply science to your problem. In this sense, pursuing code elegance or
craftsmanship isn't scientific.

Of course, elegance could be measured by line counts, because a more elegant
construct is typically more compact. However, this is a rough measure and
doesn't satisfy the first corollary of quantification: Your measurement must
accurately reflect the issue you're investigating.

In the example in the "Craftsmanship and Optimization" section earlier in
this chapter, the second, slower code was clearly more elegant. The algorithm
had fewer lines of code. Fewer loops would have been required as well, so the
executed line count would have been dramatically smaller. On closer examination, however, it's clear that line counts would be the wrong measurement
for that example. What we were trying to test was algorithm speed, not size.
Since only a loose correlation exists between size and speed in VB, elegance
doesn't matter.

Data Must Be Accurate

The second corollary of quantification is that data must be as accurate as
possible. Although this seems obvious, it's not necessarily easy to accomplish.
The PC clock isn't updated often enough to produce a completely reliable
timing operation, especially on fast operations. Also, if you test different
algorithms using mini-test applications, you may introduce errors because
you aren't duplicating all the real-world conditions that the algorithm will
operate under. Throughout this book, the various chapters on different functional optimization areas will discuss the appropriate test-bed methodology
that you'll need to apply.

Reproducibility and Windows

Scientific analysis must be reproducible to be accepted in the scientific com-
munity. This is basic scientific common sense. If I claim a cure for cancer
but no one can duplicate my results, what good is it? I must have had a bad
sample, improperly applied my tests, or simply faked the data in the search
for fame and fortune.

Optimize from the Start

Reproducibility is even more problematic in the world of Windows. Because Windows is a multitasking operating system, processes may be running behind the scenes that alter your time results. Also, with data optimization, because Jet is an intelligent engine, performance of a given task will improve over the first few times that Jet executes the task. (Chapter 7, "Speeding Database Operations," examines special issues with database optimization reproducibility in more depth.)

It's critical that you repeat any optimization test several times. If the results from a test run vary greatly from the other runs, discard that data and retest. Then average the results of the various valid runs to derive your final results.

Profiling

Probably the most useful function in your optimization toolkit is an accurate timer. With timing functions, you can readily determine what code blocks are slowing your application and which alternative method would provide the best results.

Timer( ) vs. GetTickCount( )

As you may recall from the discussion on quantification, obtaining accurate, hard data is vital when performing speed optimization. Visual Basic contains a function, Timer(), that returns the number of seconds since midnight in sixteenths of a second. However, the timing functions in this book use a Windows API call, GetTickCount(), which has several advantages over Timer(): it returns data to the millisecond, it executes about 70 percent faster than Timer(), and it updates itself more often. Also, GetTickCount() returns the milliseconds elapsed since Windows was last started, rather than the time since midnight. That means it resets itself to 0 every 49.7 days, rather than every 24 hours, so timing runs that begin just before midnight will return valid data without us having to adjust our figures, simplifying the timing algorithm.

The code in listing 2.1 demonstrates the advantages of GetTickCount() over VB's Timer() function. Both functions are executed 30 times and the results are stored in an array. The code then prints the interval since the test began to the debug window. If you want to repeat the test for yourself, you can find the functional code I used on the CD in the \Chap2 subdirectory.

Listing 2.1   TikVsTim.Vbp   The Advantages of *GetTickCount( )* over *Timer( )*

```
Option Explicit
#If Win32 Then
    Private Declare Function GetTickCount Lib "Kernel32" () As Long
#Else
    Private Declare Function GetTickCount Lib "User" () As Long
#End If

Private Sub Command1_Click()
Dim foo As Integer
Dim TickStart As Long, TimerStart As Double
ReDim TickHold(30) As Long
ReDim TimerHold(30) As Double
TickStart = GetTickCount()
TimerStart = Timer
For foo = 1 To 30
    TickHold(foo) = GetTickCount
    TimerHold(foo) = Timer
Next foo
For foo = 1 To 30
    Debug.Print foo, TimerHold(foo) - TimerStart, _
        TickHold(foo) - TickStart
Next foo

End Sub
```

When executed, the in code listing 2.1 will produce output similar to the following:

```
Loop            Timer           GetTickCount
 1              0               0
 2              0               0
 3              0               0
 4              0               0
 5              0               0
 6              0               0
 7              0               15
 8              0               15
 9              0               15
10              0               15
11              0               15
12              0.0625          15
13              0.0625          28
14              0.0625          28
15              0.0625          28
16              0.0625          28
17              0.0625          28
18              0.0625          28
19              0.0625          43
20              0.0625          43
21              0.0625          43
22              0.0625          43
23              0.0625          43
24              0.0625          43
```

25	0.0625	55
26	0.0625	55
27	0.0625	55
28	0.0625	55
29	0.0625	55
30	0.0625	55

As you can see, because `Timer()` updates itself 16 times a second, it's considerably less accurate than the `GetTickCount()` function, which refreshes every 12 to 18 milliseconds.

Code Overview

The timing routines consist of two main subroutines, which also call the generic report printing subroutine from Visual CodeBank, `QuickReport`.

Function of *BeginTime*

The timing engine is initialized by calling the `BeginTime` subroutine, as in

```
BeginTime "Graphics Display Loop Test", 1
```

BeginTime has two parameters: the string caption to use for this time sequence, and the display mode for timer results. Display modes may be 0 for disabled, 1 for interactive detail printing to the debug window, 2 for interactive detail printing to the printer, and 4 to accumulate summaries to be printed on the printer.

Function of *EndTime*

EndTime closes the timing loop and either prints a detail line or increments the summary counters belonging to the current caption. EndTime "remembers" the parameters specified by BeginTime (so you don't have to specify them again) and will format and print the data to the appropriate device.

You can't nest timing calls. You must conclude the current timing function with an EndTime call.

The Routines in Code

Listing 2.2 shows the globals and variable declarations required by the timing routines in every project in this book. Listing 2.3 shows the code for the BeginTime subroutine. Listing 2.4 shows the EndTime subroutine.

Listing 2.2   Required Globals and Variable Declarations

```
#If Win32 Then
    Declare Function GetTickCount Lib "Kernel32" () As Long
#Else
    Declare Function GetTickCount Lib "User" () As Long
#End If
'Printer Fonts
Global gPrnTitRepFontName As String
Global gPrnTitRepFontSize As Integer
Global gPrnTxtRepFontName As String
Global gPrnTxtRepFontSize As Integer
Global gPrnArray(15)
Public Const TIME_DEBUG = 1
Public Const TIME_MSGBOX = 2
Public Const TIME_PRINTER = 3
Global glTimeBegin As Long
Global glTimeEnd As Long
Global gsTimeCaption As String
Global giTimePrintMode As Integer
Type ProfileStorage
    TotalTime As Long
    Iterations As Long
    Caption As String
End Type
Dim StoreTime() As ProfileStorage
```

Listing 2.3   The *BeginTime* Subroutine

```
Public Sub BeginTime(Caption As String, mode As Integer)

gsTimeCaption = Caption
giTimePrintMode = mode
glTimeBegin = GetTickCount()

End Sub
```

Listing 2.4   The *EndTime* Subroutine

```
'Completes profile timing and shows results
Public Sub EndTime()
Static Init As Integer
Dim foo As Integer, foobar As Integer

glTimeEnd = GetTickCount()

Select Case giTimePrintMode
Case 0 'do nothing - disabled
Case 1 'Debug.print Detail
```

(continues)

Listing 2.4   Continued

```
        Debug.Print Format$((glTimeEnd - glTimeBegin) / 1000#,_
            "###0.0000"), gsTimeCaption
    Case 2 'Message Box
        MsgBox gsTimeCaption & Chr$(10) & Format$((glTimeEnd _
            - glTimeBegin) / 1000#, "###0.0000"), , "Time Profile"
    Case 3 'Printer.Print Detail
        If Init = False Then
            Init = True
            gPrnArray(0) = "Profile: " & App.EXEName
            gPrnArray(1) = "Seconds"
            gPrnArray(2) = "Profile Description"
            QuickReport "N", 6, gPrnArray(), "P"
        End If
        Erase gPrnArray()
        gPrnArray(0) = Format$((glTimeEnd - glTimeBegin) / 1000#,_
            "###0.0000")
        gPrnArray(1) = gsTimeCaption
        QuickReport "D", 6, gPrnArray(), "P"
    Case 4 'Printer Stop
        Printer.EndDoc
    End Select

End Sub
```

Resource Monitoring

One of Windows 3.1's greatest limitations was the limited resource space available to programs. Applications doing intensive graphics work could easily exceed the capacity of GDI (Graphic Device Interface) resources, causing application failure and even GPFs. Large applications or multiple applications could exceed the limits of User resources.

The Windows 95 architecture greatly improves the situation but doesn't eliminate resource problems entirely. Also, since many—if not most—programmers will still need to support Windows 3.x for some length of time, resource optimization will still have a high priority.

32- vs. 16-Bit Resources

GDI and User resources in Windows 3.1 and Windows 95 are maintained in separate, fixed 64K data heaps. There are two resource areas: GDI, which is used for bitmapped graphics and printing operations, and User, which tracks window object management and input/output operations. These 16-bit heaps still exist in Windows 95. However, Windows 95 adds 32-bit heaps, which are linked to the 64K heaps. Memory-intensive data structures have been moved from the limited 64K 16-bit heaps to the much larger 32-bit areas.

The *Monitor* Subroutine

The resource optimization projects in this chapter will use a subroutine called Monitor. A number of different tools are available for monitoring resource usage, ranging from the About box in the Windows 3.x Program Manager to floating graphs that update themselves every second. But none of these are integrated with Visual Basic.

What's needed to perform scientific optimization is a routine that provides pinpoint precision. Suppose that you're loading a large bitmap graphic onto a form as a background and then drawing a graph on it by using graphics methods. If you exhaust your GDI resources, you may not be able to tell when and why it happened.

The Monitor subroutine solves this problem by allowing you to check resources at specific points in the code. Monitor checks for available physical RAM, User resources, and GDI resources. It displays the information in the debug window or in a message box, or it prints a report. It will also print or display a user-definable caption showing where in the code you were when the measurements were taken.

Monitor Code

The API calls required to obtain resource and memory allocation information are completely different between the 16- and 32-bit applications, as the code in listing 2.5 shows. The routine therefore uses conditional compilation for the API declares and the calls.

Listing 2.5   Code for the *Monitor* Subroutine

```
Option Explicit
Public Const MON_DEBUG = 1
Public Const MON_MSGBOX = 2
Public Const MON_PRINTER = 3
#If win32 Then
    Declare Sub GlobalMemoryStatus Lib "kernel32" (lpBuffer As
    MEMORYSTATUS)
    Type MEMORYSTATUS
        dwLength As Long            ' sizeof(MEMORYSTATUS)
        dwMemoryLoad As Long        ' percent of memory in use
        dwTotalPhys As Long         ' bytes of physical memory
        dwAvailPhys As Long         ' free physical memory bytes
        dwTotalPageFile As Long     ' bytes of paging file
        dwAvailPageFile As Long     ' free bytes of paging file
        dwTotalVirtual As Long      ' user bytes of address space
        dwAvailVirtual As Long      ' free user bytes
```

(continues)

Listing 2.5 Continued

```
    End Type
    Dim MemStat As MEMORYSTATUS
#Else
    Declare Function GetFreeSystemResources Lib "User" (ByVal
    fuSysResource As Integer) As Integer
    Declare Function GetFreeSpace Lib "Kernel" (ByVal wFlags As
    Integer) As Long
    Const GDI_RESOURCES As Integer = 1
    Const USER_RESOURCES As Integer = 2
#End If

Public Sub Monitor(Caption As String, DisplayMode As Integer)
'DisplayMode    0 = disabled
'               1 = Debug window
'               2 = MsgBox
'               3 = Printer
Dim foo As Integer, foobar As Integer
Dim FreeMem As Long
Dim FreeGDI As Integer
Dim FreeUser As Integer
Dim DisplayStr As String
If DisplayMode = 0 Then Exit Sub
#If win32 Then
    MemStat.dwLength = 32
    Call GlobalMemoryStatus(MemStat)
    FreeMem = MemStat.dwAvailPhys
    FreeGDI = 50 '<<<<<< Need info on updated API calls for Win95
    FreeUser = 50
    DisplayStr = "GDI: " & FreeGDI & "%   User: " & FreeUser & _
        "%   Mem: " & (FreeMem \ 1024) & "K"
#Else
    FreeMem = GetFreeSpace(0)
    FreeGDI = GetFreeSystemResources(GDI_RESOURCES)
    FreeUser = GetFreeSystemResources(USER_RESOURCES)
    DisplayStr = "GDI: " & FreeGDI & "%   User: " & FreeUser & _
        "%   Mem: " & (FreeMem \ 1024) & "K"
#End If
Select Case DisplayMode
Case 1 'Debug.print
    Debug.Print "Free Resources: " & Caption
    Debug.Print DisplayStr
Case 2 'msgbox
    MsgBox Caption & Chr$(10) & Chr$(13) & DisplayStr, 0, _
      "Free Resources"
Case 3 'printer
    Printer.Print "Free Resources: " & Caption;
    Printer.CurrentX = Printer.ScaleWidth / 2
    Printer.Print DisplayStr
End Select
End Sub
```

Here's an example of how the subroutine is called:

```
Monitor "Before Loading Graphic", MON_DEBUG
Picture1.Picture = LoadPicture("c:\bitmaps\castle.Bmp")
Monitor "After Loading Graphic", MON_DEBUG
Picture1.FontName = "Arial"
Picture1.Fontsize = 24
Picture1.Print "This is a Test Bitmap"
Monitor "After Printing Caption", MON_DEBUG
```

Managing Reusable Code with Visual CodeBank

Visual CodeBank LE is a special-edition version of Visual CodeBank, the library generator from Visual Components, Inc. Refer to the ReadMe.Txt file in the root directory of the CD-ROM for instructions on how to install CodeBank on your system. Figure 2.1 shows CodeBank's main form.

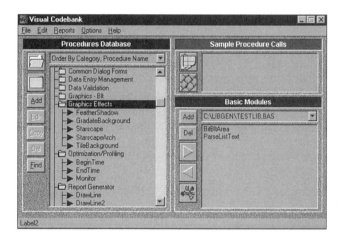

Fig. 2.1
Visual CodeBank's main form consists of three sections.

CodeBank makes managing libraries of reusable subroutines and functions easier. You'll use CodeBank throughout this book when building the sample applications to manage the subroutines' modules. Also, much of the optimized code snippets that you'll see in case studies in the book will become part of the procedure repository that you can use royalty-free in any of your VB applications (for example, the PicClipSub subroutine in the repository is one of the final optimized code examples used in Chapter 13, "Using Components and Subroutines Wisely").

Productivity with Reusable CodeBank Code

Reusable code has always been considered a great way to combine program-mer productivity with application performance. But Visual Basic never provided an effective and easy way to manage code libraries. You could create separate Visual Basic modules for different areas of functionality, but eventually you ended up with multiple declarations (or missing declarations), hand maintenance, or excess code.

CodeBank code libraries are stored in a central MDB repository. CodeBank dynamically creates and maintains customized .BAS modules for each application. The modules contain only the procedures and declarations needed by the application. CodeBank also provides a built-in procedure database containing many useful reusable Visual Basic functions and subroutines, with particular emphasis on optimization procedures.

 The commercial version of CodeBank LE contains hundreds of functions, covering all areas of VB programming.

Add Your Own Subroutines to CodeBank

CodeBank LE not only contains precoded procedures, you can also extend the repository indefinitely by adding your own subroutines and functions. Because CodeBank's procedures are written in VB, you can also copy, enhance, and modify CodeBank's procedures any way you want.

The built-in procedures enhance programmer productivity by eliminating the need to write utility routines. Control replacement functions improve application performance and resource usage by eliminating the need for many commercial VBXs and OCXs (such as ThreeD.Vbx). CodeBank allows you to easily create applications with snazzy features—such as pixelating graphic transitions, rollup containers, elastic forms, or print preview—that previously required either VBXs or extensive manual coding.

The Main CodeBank Form

CodeBank's primary form is divided into three sections. The first section displays the procedure repository organized in an outline tree. The second section contains sample calling syntax for the selected procedure. The third section contains a combo box for the Visual Basic library modules that you've created, plus a list box displaying the procedures contained in the selected library module.

You find the procedure you need by using the category trees, by using a keyword, or by searching alphabetically. Clicking the file folder icon next to a category expands the outline tree to display all procedures associated with that category. Clicking the open folder icon next to an expanded category collapses the category. Clicking the Expand All button (with the open folder icon) expands all categories. Clicking the Collapse All button (with the closed folder icon) collapses all categories.

Maintaining Procedures

Double-clicking an item drills down to an edit form that shows all details of the procedure (see fig. 2.2). Clicking the Add button in the main form calls up the edit form in add mode. Clicking the Copy button in the main form creates a duplicate record of the procedure for easy customization.

Fig. 2.2
The Edit Procedures form is used to maintain procedures.

Each CodeBank record contains the name and Visual Basic source code for the procedure. Each record also contains a full description of the purpose of the procedure, its author and maintenance history, instructions in use of the procedure, generic forms, subprocedures, declarations needed by the procedure, and a sample of the calling syntax.

Specifying Subprocedures

Many CodeBank procedures call other procedures to perform their tasks. When creating a library module, then, you must be sure to include all the procedures needed by each subroutine; otherwise, you'll generate a syntax error when you try to run the project.

Fortunately, CodeBank includes all the called procedures for you. All you need to do is select the procedures called by the procedure you're defining. When you later create your library, CodeBank will remember the sub-procedures needed by this procedure and include them automatically.

To add a called procedure, click the + command button attached to the Sub Procedures Called list box. The Edit Called Procedures form appears (see fig. 2.3). Select the appropriate procedure in the combo control and click OK. Repeat as necessary.

Fig. 2.3
The Edit Called Procedures maintenance form.

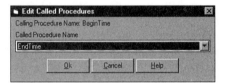

To remove a called procedure, highlight it and click the – button attached to the top of the control.

To change a called procedure, highlight the entry and click the Edit button in the Procedures Database section of the main CodeBank form. Select the new procedure name and click OK.

Declarations and API Calls

Some procedures require API declarations, Const declarations, or public variable declarations to work. This code must be placed in the declaration section of the Visual Basic library module. Figure 2.4 shows the form that you use to make these declarations.

Fig. 2.4
Use the Edit Declares form to make API, Const, or public variable declarations.

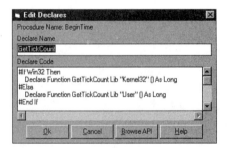

Like it does with called procedures, CodeBank handles the details for you. All you need to do is name the declaration and type the declare code. When you later create your library, CodeBank eliminates duplicate declarations and constructs the declaration section automatically.

To add a declaration, click the + command button attached to the Declarations list box. The Edit Declares form appears. Type the name of the variable, constant, or API or DLL function in the Declare Name text box. In the Declare Code box, type the full declaration code, including type and conditional compilation directives (if needed). Then click OK. Repeat for each declaration.

To remove a declaration, highlight it and click the – button.

To change a declaration, highlight the entry and click the Edit button in the Procedures Database section of the main form. Type the new data and click OK.

Specifying Needed Forms

Some procedures require generic forms such as MsgForm or ArtForm in order to work. These forms must be added to the .VBP file of the project.

CodeBank doesn't modify .MAK files, but it will remind you of the forms you'll need to add when the library is generated, if you've added the forms to the Forms Needed list box.

To add a form, click the + command button attached to the Forms Needed list box. The Edit Forms Required form appears (see fig. 2.5). Type the form path and file name, and then click OK. Repeat for each form.

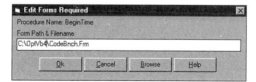

Fig. 2.5
The Edit Forms Required maintenance form.

To remove a form definition, highlight it and click the – button.

To change a form definition, highlight the entry and click the Edit button in the Procedures Database section of the main form. Type the new data and click OK.

Creating a Visual Basic Module

When generating a library, you can select or deselect a procedure with a single click. Adding a procedure to a module list will automatically include any subprocedures, API declarations, and public variables needed by that procedure.

To create a new library module, click the + button and type the path and file name for the module. Then select the procedures you want to include.

When you click the Create Library button (under the arrow buttons in the Basic Modules section), CodeBank generates a complete .BAS module, complete with all the procedures, subprocedures, declarations, and comments you've specified. CodeBank automatically detects and handles duplicated entries.

Now you can simply add the file to your project by choosing Add File from the File menu or by pressing Ctrl+D.

Inserting Procedure Calls into Your Code

When you highlight a procedure in the procedure tree of CodeBank's main form, sample call syntax will appear for that procedure. These sample calls minimize the amount of typing required to implement the CodeBank procedures.

When you click the Clipboard command button (with a paper clip image) in the Sample Procedure Calls section of the main form, the sample call is copied to the Clipboard.

 By default, all the text in the sample call will be copied. However, if you've selected part of the text, just the selected portion will be copied.

From Here...

Examples of the use of the timing procedures presented in this chapter appear throughout the book. For more information on other topics brought up in this chapter, refer to the following chapters:

- For a detailed explanation of the application of scientific optimization procedures to algorithms, including a full case study, see Chapter 6, "Strategies to Improve Algorithms."

- For more information on using API calls with VB, see Chapter 14, "Exploiting the Windows 32-Bit API."

Chapter 3

Designing Optimized Applications

The way many of us approach optimization—for the most part—consists of fiddling, tuning, and conducting endless trials of alternative algorithms and methods in an attempt to speed recalcitrant code or minimize resource usage. The vast majority of classic optimization work is undertaken after a project is functionally complete.

For that reason, most discussions of optimization concentrate on code mechanics. Indeed, most of this book will consist of the same type of analysis.

But some strategic issues can impact speed and memory usage—issues that are best addressed before a line of code is written.

This book isn't for systems analysts, though. We're not going to discuss and contrast seven different application specification methodologies, each named after their creator. I'm not even going to create a Hitt Diagram methodology. Although the most common design mistake is spending too little time in the design stage, it's also true that focusing too much attention on the application's design can lead to "paralysis by analysis." Application design is not an end in itself; its purpose is to enhance productivity through all stages of application development.

So this chapter orients toward the practical: bare, meaty, programmer-oriented specifications that make the coding phase faster and cleaner, and result in a better final product. More specifically, this chapter discusses:

- How application design affects optimization
- How to create clear application specifications
- The advantages of an overview statement

■ How to select a user interface style

■ The different kinds of VB applications

■ How to create an application outline

■ The best way to design forms

■ How to create procedure specifications

■ Relational database design issues

Optimization Begins at the Beginning

One of Visual Basic's virtues is the easy form design made possible by the VB development environment. The *Visual* part of Visual Basic is one of the key reasons for its success.

But it's also a trap. VB invites us to jump into constructing a project early in the design cycle, to construct a working prototype or a semifunctional end-user interface as part of the design phase. Once the prototype form is embedded in a project, a dynamic takes over that makes it hard for us to discard it and start fresh.

All of us have fallen victim to the "Function First, Optimization Second" mind-set. Sometimes, it seems hard enough to make a program work the way we intended without worrying about optimization. So optimization becomes a luxury, to be done at the end of a project—if there's time left, or if some portion of the system is unacceptably slow or resource-intensive.

Optimization by design, though, gives us more time at the end of the project for speeding slow sections of code. Applying code craftsmanship in the writing of the code—writing *optimized code*—leaves us with less overall optimization work to do, and thus provides more time for tightening critical procedures.

Without a road map, we can wander aimlessly through a city. With one, we move directly to our destination. In the same way, clearly defining the goals and stratagems we'll pursue to achieve those goals benefits us in two ways.

Reworked Code Is Slow

We've all written code twice. When code is revisited because of an architectural change or because of a need for additional functionality, the tendency is to layer the new functions on top of the existing code. This way, you preserve your earlier time investment while minimizing the amount of work you need to do to implement the new architecture or function.

But such layered code is almost always slower than code that was written with the larger picture in mind. Reworked code may create additional function calls to layer in a function. The changes may result in *dead code* (routines that are never called) or unused variables. Some of this is inevitable in the maintenance cycle, of course, and the problems can be minimized if you pay attention to potential problems. But if you work with a clear and complete design from the beginning, your code will have fewer missteps, fewer kludges, and fewer awkward reworks.

Faster Development Means More Time to Optimize

Long-distance runners pace themselves at the beginning of a race, with the goal of setting up a good position while saving enough strength for a break-away sprint at the end. In the same way, creating full design specifications delays the start of coding. But it greatly speeds the finish, giving more time to tighten and speed the most important routines.

Creating Clear Specifications

Many methodologies exist for application specification, some with fancy names, almost all resulting in pretty pictures. They have lots of arrows and lines, circles or squares, or even clouds (!). Some automated design systems can cost thousands of dollars per user.

This isn't what I mean when I encourage you to spend time in design. Many of the automated design tools I've seen might be considered overkill for working programmers. A simple legal pad or word processor will do nicely to create a set of specs that achieve the primary purpose of defining a blueprint for code construction. As working programmer/analysts, we want to achieve a balance between design-as-you-go programming and paralysis by analysis.

A balanced specification requires three minimum elements:

- An application overview statement

- A forms outline

- A module specification

The next sections take a closer look at each document. If the application requires a database, a database design or data dictionary should also be created. The section "Optimized Database Design" near the end of this chapter examines database design issues in depth.

Application Overview Statement

The *application overview* is a general summary of the goals and methods of the application. Unlike a database schema that you'll refer to in detail throughout coding, in many ways an application overview is really just a mechanism that forces you to confront a few issues and make a few decisions before beginning your detailed design. It's a technique for focusing thoughts and efforts.

There's no formal methodology for creating such a document. I generally simply write a few paragraphs using a word processor. Several components should be included in the overview, however.

The Mission Statement

The *mission statement* is a paragraph that outlines the goals you intend to achieve with the program. It should address the major functional tasks that the program should perform.

The Users

Perhaps the best single method for focusing your thoughts on the needed functionality and level of complexity is to develop an idea of who your user is going to be. As you develop more detailed aspects of your design, do form layouts, and write code, having an idea of the skills and interests of your typical user will greatly clarify many design questions.

Market Strategy

We don't usually write programs simply for our own use. So before you sit down to write your application, you should have an idea—however vague and subject to modification—of how you're going to sell it.

If you're creating programs for end-user retail sales or shareware, you should have a very good idea of what products compete against your program, and what strategy you'll need to pursue to differentiate your program from the competition. If you can't make a marketing case for your program against the already available software, perhaps you shouldn't write the software.

Even if your program is strictly for internal corporate use, you'll nevertheless have to make an effort to get users to buy into your system and actually start using it.

I don't suggest that you make a full marketing plan here, complete with advertising schedules, marketing budgets, and public relations plans. If you're going to market your software commercially, then of course that will need to be done later. But you should have enough of an idea of the marketing constraints and strategies at this stage to help guide you in making your development decisions.

For example, if you plan to market your software through the shareware market, you'll want to minimize distributable size as much as possible, to make the program easier to download. On the other hand, if you intend to distribute the program commercially through a publishing house or by self-publishing, you may want to increase your use of multimedia—with hooks for video and/or audio help, for instance.

The Operating System Architecture

Until VB4, Visual Basic programmers didn't really have very many decisions to make as far as operating system architectures go. The Windows 3.x environment was the only operating system that could run VB applications in native mode. Things are starting to get a little more complicated, though.

You don't have to write 32-bit applications for Windows 95 and Windows NT. Thanks to the API thunking layer, the 32-bit operating systems will run 16-bit VB quite nicely, converting the 16-bit calls and operations to 32 bit on the fly.

But most code constructs in VB4 run twice as fast in 32-bit mode under Windows 95, compared with 16-bit VB. Although it means more work (since you'll usually want to have both 16- and 32-bit versions), the extra effort is clearly worth it. Not only is the speed issue significant, you'll also give your program a stronger marketing position if you have an application that's native to the user's operating system.

Fortunately, with VB4's dual mode compilers, the level of effort required to target both 16- and 32-bit operating systems is greatly reduced. Most language features perform identically. The biggest difference is in use of API declares and calls, but with VB4's conditional compilation mechanism, you still don't have to maintain two separate versions of your application.

Deciding on an Interface Style

Once you've settled on your application's goals, it's time to begin addressing some more detailed issues. The first major issue is *interface style*.

VB supports two types of Windows form architectures: MDI (Multiple Document Interface) and SDI (Single Document Interface). Both actually allow multiple forms, of course. From the user's point of view, the biggest difference is whether the forms will be contained within a single, master form (MDI), or whether they seem to exist as standalone forms on the desktop (SDI).

If your application is intended to just have one form, your choice is rather obvious. But the converse isn't true. MDI and SDI can be used to provide professional results in multiform applications. VB4 has removed one of the biggest disadvantages of VB3-style MDI: VB4 MDI children can be hidden and/or preloaded. Microsoft Word and Excel are two of the best known MDI programs. Visual Basic itself is a good example of an SDI program.

In some ways, the choice is more of an aesthetic issue than anything else. Many programmers believe that multiform SDI applications seem to scatter their forms across the desktop, making the program feel unconnected. Others believe that MDI programs are harder to control programmatically, because MDI tries to provide default positioning and sizing.

Types of VB Applications

When considering your forms' design and interface style, the biggest single consideration could be the type of application you're creating. In my view, there are four types of VB applications (or, indeed, of applications in general).

Database Management

The first type—and, according to published reports, the most prevalent type of program being written in VB today—is the database management program. This style of program is intended to be used to add, retrieve, and modify database records. Database programs must perform at least two functions: they must allow users to find the information they want, plus view and edit the information once it's found. If they can perform these functions quickly and easily, so much the better.

Drill-Down Interface

One of the most common interface implementations for database management programs is the drill-down style. In this paradigm, each function has its own form. The application starts with a lookup form, which provides a list of record identifiers (such as names). Then, once the user selects a record, the program opens a new edit form, essentially drilling down into the database to uncover the more detailed information.

 I find that drill-down applications are natural MDI applications, particularly for large, multiple-table databases. But I use modal SDI entry forms to ensure that data remains synchronized.

Single Form

A single-form alternative to the drill-down concept always presents the edit form but allows the user to shift the current record by using a data control or by entering a "find" value. The weakness of this concept is that it shows limited information at a time and is suited only for databases with one primary table (although supporting tables, such as list choices, could be displayed in combo boxes).

Grids and Lookup Lists

Grid control interfaces eliminate the edit form by presenting all the information from a record in a single row or line of information. The grid can be scanned, just like a lookup list, and record maintenance can be done on the grid itself. This method has two weaknesses, however:

- It's time-consuming because of all the information that must be displayed in the grid.

- Some users tend to think grids are plain and unappealing.

Grid-style interfaces are naturally MDI because they're easily resizable.

Database Analytic Programs

Analytic programs are the flip side of database management programs: Rather than be concerned with getting information in, they're oriented to extracting information from the database. The raw data is summarized or massaged in some way, and then presented in report or graphical format. Depending on the breadth of analytical choices, either MDI or SDI could be good choices.

Document-Centric Programs

Document-centric programs work on unstructured data. The term *document* in this sense doesn't refer just to classic paper documents, such as letters or contracts. A bitmap image or icon can also be a document. By this definition, Microsoft Word is a document-centric application, but so is Windows Paint or IconWorks, the sample icon-editing program included with VB.

Ideally, document-centric applications should have MDI interfaces. Icon-Works is an SDI example of a document-centric application, so using SDI is possible. But imagine how much of an improvement it would be if IconWorks was rewritten using MDI.

Utility Programs

Utility programs perform highly specific—often system-specific—tasks, such as displaying and printing font samples. Many wouldn't require interfaces at all, were there not a need to launch them and report on completion. They almost invariably require SDI interfaces.

VTOC Form Outlines

VTOC (Visual Table of Contents) Form Outlines documents present a simple, high-level summary of an application's forms. Figure 3.1 shows a simple VTOC for an address book database program. As you can see, forms that are nested, such as drill-down forms, are represented in a tree structure. Common forms, such as File Open dialogs or message boxes, that may be called by many different forms are shown on the right side of figure 3.1.

Fig. 3.1
This VTOC shows the forms hierarchy for a simple AddressBook database program.

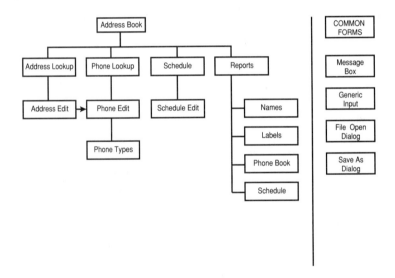

There's nothing really fancy about a VTOC compared with some of the advanced tools available. Its advantage is that it's quick, it's easy to create and modify, and it provides a way to view the application's form components as part of the whole, with a decent idea of how they fit in and what the final scope of work will be.

You don't need any fancy tools to create a VTOC. A legal pad and pencil will do, as will Windows Paint or Visio. The important thing is to create your forms outline before coding, print it out, and tape it to the wall where you can see it while you code. You'll probably find ways to eliminate or combine forms—or preload forms used in multiple places—that might not have been obvious before.

Forms Layout

You don't necessarily have to do a layout for every form. In fact, I've written enough database applications that I pretty much have a settled style into which most needs can fit. So I simply lay things out in VB, using the form-layout capabilities of the Integrated Development Environment (IDE) as a design tool to modify one or another of the form skeletons in my toolkit.

When I'm doing something new or if my design requires corporate approval, however, I'll try to stay away from programming tools until my design is settled. In that case, I'll use pad and pencil, with their flexibility and ease of use, to sketch many different approaches to a design problem. You can sketch a thumbnail of a form more quickly on paper than you can lay one out in VB, so you can test "view" more interface styles that way.

Once I find what I believe is the best approach, I'll then go to VB to lay the form out if I need prior approval before coding, or simply tape the drawing to the wall to refer to later.

Sort of low-tech, isn't it?—especially for a book on optimizing VB. But it has the virtue of working, and I'd rather embarrass myself by admitting that a legal pad is my best design tool than try to feed you a line about using this or that sophisticated and expensive method.

The important thing to remember is that time spent in the design stage pays huge returns. Whether you use a CASE tool costing thousands of dollars or a $1.29 legal pad, you'll achieve greater programmer productivity, faster code, and leaner executables.

Procedure Specifications

Once you've completed your forms design, you'll have a pretty good idea of what VBX or OCX custom controls you might need. Write them down, and then try to whittle the list (if you can). You can easily eliminate cosmetic controls such as THREED.VBX/OCX by using 3-D line-drawing subroutines. If you need a container, use picture boxes. Many custom controls can be eliminated with Visual Basic subroutines. Subroutines for implementing panels and picture command buttons, for example, are included with the CodeBank Limited Edition on the CD that comes with this book. Many more control replacement procedures are available with the full version of CodeBank. And you can easily create many such routines yourself. (For more information on limiting custom control use, see Chapter 13, "Using Components and Sub-routines Wisely.")

You should also list the subroutines and functions to be used in the project. If you use CodeBank to manage your subroutine libraries, you can readily generate a report of the procedures required for the project. If not, use a word processor.

The third element of procedure specifications is particular algorithms or functions that are unique to the application, such as a depreciation or a sales tax algorithm. These should be at least noted at this stage, if not developed in pseudocode. As you develop the procedures more fully, comment the notation.

Optimized Database Design

Since the inclusion of the Jet engine in Visual Basic 3.0, more and more VB programmers have been using VB to create database applications. Some surveys show that as much as 80 percent of the programming done with Visual Basic is database oriented. The chapters in Part III, "Database Optimization," address the optimization of database operations in some detail.

Before you can conduct operations on a database, of course, you must have a database design. The structure of the database is the foundation on which all operations will rest. A good database design lends itself to clean and efficient code implementation. A design that is clumsy, or is built by evolution rather than forethought, will decrease programmer productivity and often results in slower operations.

So it's a good idea to spend a little time reviewing what a relational database is and what makes for a good relational design. Volumes could be—and have been—written on the relational database design theory. It's beyond the scope of this book to thoroughly cover the topic, but the following overview may be helpful to those new to the subject. On the other hand, if you're already familiar with relational database theory and practice, you may want to skim or skip this section.

Relational Theory

Relational databases reflect the rules invented by E.F. Codd in the early 1970s. Database structures until then were rather inefficient—they were based on outdated paradigms that assumed that the storage mechanisms for the data would be decks of paper cards or reels of magnetic tape. Since form follows function, the structures in use at the time reflected the sequential nature of the storage mechanisms.

The invention of the hard disk, with its random-access capabilities, made the old ways of thinking obsolete. Codd's breakthrough was to recognize the data-storage possibilities inherent in fast random access and to create a design paradigm that took advantage of the capabilities of the new technology.

Eliminating Redundancy

The main principle of relational database design is that redundancy in data should be eliminated. Several kinds of redundancy can be addressed.

The most common redundancy is duplicated data. If you're creating a mail-order database, for example, you need to support—at a minimum—two activities: sending catalogs to customers and prospective customers, and processing orders. Obviously, to send catalogs, you need to have a list of customers' names and addresses. To process orders, you need information on the order as well as the customer address. The relational model, quite simply, says that you shouldn't keep the customer address in both lists. Instead, the order list should reference the customer list to get the address.

Another redundancy is more subtle and results from duplication of structures rather than data. Suppose that you're creating an address book database to store information about your friends. Each entry in the address book would need a name, address, and phone number. But these days, people are likely to have more than one phone number. A single person may have separate phone numbers for work, home, fax, modem, pager, and cellular phone.

Now, you could handle this situation by setting up a separate entry item for each type in the list, but then you would have many items devoted to the concept of phone number. If your technologically challenged friends have only a home number, the storage areas for the other phone number types would be wasted. The relational solution is to create a separate list that would contain just phone numbers, with each number identified by the person to whom the number belongs and the type of number it is: fax, pager, and so forth. Each entry would require only as many items as needed to record all the phone numbers.

Virtual Database Structure

Another principle of relational design is that the physical structure of a database isn't related to the use or display of the data. In other words, when the user of your address book application looks up a friend, the friend's name, address, and phone numbers would all appear in the same display form, even though they're on separate lists in the database. This complexity is hidden from the user and—to a degree—from the programmer by the model of the relational database.

SQL

Implementing relational databases is not a trivial task. However, it's made considerably easier by SQL, or Structured Query Language, which is an integral part of the relational design concept. SQL insulates the programmer from many of the mechanics of the database structure, such as indexes. It provides facilities, such as joins, that put related data together automatically.

However, knowledge of database structures is still required, even when using SQL. Plus, there are performance issues and limitations to SQL's use.

Relational Objects

Until now, I've avoided using database jargon in this chapter. The address book example had "lists" of contacts, the phone numbers were "items," and so on. It's time to move from the conceptual, theoretical view of relational database theory, and start getting into the details of the theory.

Relational databases are made up of several types of objects, which then can be made up of other objects.

Tables

The primary storage structure of a relational database is the table. A database can—and almost always does—have more than one table. In the address book example, the database would contain a Friends table and a Phones table.

Rows and Columns

Each table is made up of rows, which are often referred to as *records*. A table will almost always have multiple rows. For example, you would (hopefully) have more than one person in the Friends table.

Each row has multiple columns, or *fields*, that are common to all rows in the table. In other words, every row in the Friends table would have a field for Name, Address, City, and so on.

Indexes

Tables are organized by the use of *indexes*. Indexes provide a rapid means of searching through the tables in the database. Indexes are a type of sort sequence, maintained by the database engine. They are specified by listing the fields by which the table should be ordered.

You can have more than one index in a table. For example, the Friends table might be ordered by Name and then by City.

Relations

A major issue in relational database design is how to handle the connection of data. By their nature, relational databases are disjointed, with information about a single logical concept (such as "friend's address") being scattered about in numerous physical tables. The challenge is to coordinate the information in these various tables so that when the time comes to put the data back together for a report or display, you can easily find all the necessary information.

The challenge is handled by defining connections between structures, called *relations*. Relations are actually the key concept behind the relational model.

Parent/Child

When data is *normalized*, or placed in separate tables to eliminate redundancy, a link between the two tables is established by a *relation*. A relation has two sides: a parent and a child. Child records belong to the parent. A parent can have one child or many children.

In the address book example, the Friends table would be the parent of the Phones table. The link would be set up by establishing a lookup key common to both tables. The lookup key is typically a long integer. When putting records together, the relational engine matches the keys.

This key is typically hidden from the user, so the person entering the data would never know that "John Smith" is internally known as 12345. In this way, if "John Smith" changes his name to "John Doe," the phone numbers remain linked without effort. Plus, if you have more than one "John Smith" in your database, their phone numbers would not be mixed together.

Relation Types

There are several kinds of relations. The simplest type is a one-to-one relationship, where each parent has just one child. This type is rarely implemented, as it doesn't have much value (if any).

One-to-many relationships can have more than one child, as in the address book example.

In many-to-many relationships, a child can have more than one parent. Many-to-many relationships can't be directly established, but rather rely on using a third table as an intermediate parent. This parent has a one-to-many relationship with each table. The child tables are then seen as having a many-to-many relationship with each other.

Ensuring Integrity

With all these types of relations, and with data scattered about in multiple tables, there needs to be some way to enforce the links. Changing a parent table's key field, for example, could *orphan* the parent's children—that is, leave them without a valid parent record. The relational model prevents orphans from resulting by a mechanism called *referential integrity*.

There are several types of referential integrity, each suited to different situations:

■ *Restrictive referential integrity* prevents any changes to the parent key, if that parent has children, and also doesn't allow deletion of the parent record.

■ *Cascading referential integrity* duplicates changes to the parent in the parent's children. If a parent is deleted, the children are also deleted. In the address book example, if you deleted a friend, cascading referential integrity would delete all of the friend's phone numbers automatically.

■ *Nullification referential integrity* typically is only used with deletion. In this case, if a parent is deleted, the child records aren't deleted, but the lookup key in the child is set to null. This is useful in situations where the parent is a pick list, such as a subcategory, where you don't want to lose all data in the corresponding child records just because you are eliminating a subcategory type.

From Here...

For more information on the concepts discussed in this chapter, refer to these chapters:

■ Chapter 4, "Faster Forms Architectures," discusses the optimization of forms architectures and layouts.

■ Chapter 7, "Speeding Database Operations," and Chapter 8, "More Database Speed," provide more information on database operations.

■ For more information on Structured Query Language, see Chapter 9, "Improving SQL Performance."

■ Chapter 13, "Using Components and Subroutines Wisely," covers limiting custom control use.

■ Chapter 14, "Exploiting the Windows 32-Bit API," explains how to use the Windows API to eliminate the Common Dialog OCX.

Part II

Application Optimization

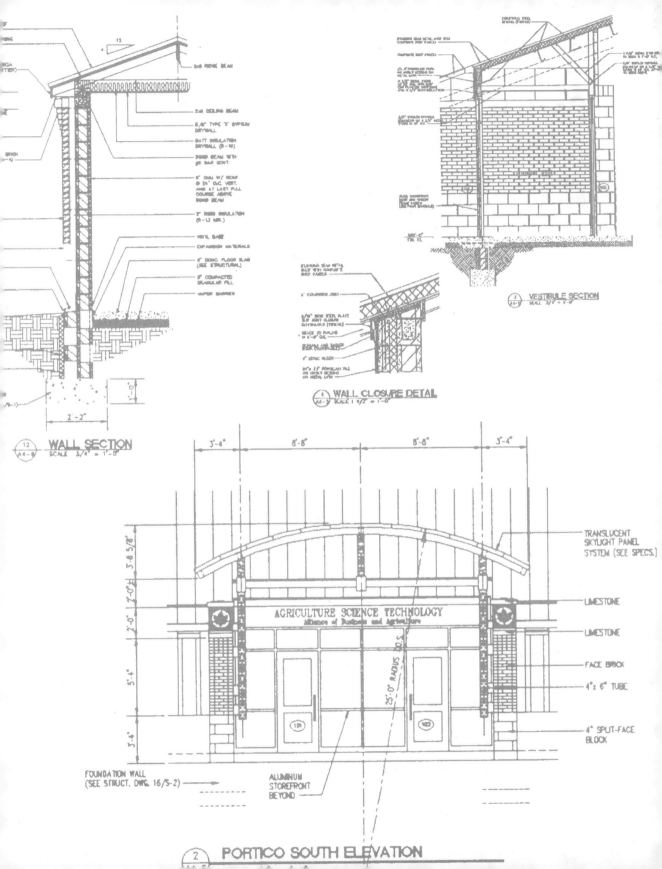

WALL SECTION
⌀12 A4-6 SCALE 3/4" = 1'-0"

2x6 RIDGE BEAM

2x6 CEILING BEAM

5/8" TYPE 'X' GYPSUM DRYWALL

BATT INSULATION DRYWALL (R-19)

BOND BEAM WITH #5 BAR CONT.

8" CMU W/ REINF. @ 24" O.C. VERT. AND AT LAST FULL COURSE ABOVE BOND BEAM

2" RIGID INSULATION (R-13 MIN.)

VINYL BASE

CTP. FINISH ON WALLS

4" CONC. FLOOR SLAB (SEE STRUCTURAL)

4" COMPACTED GRANULAR FILL

VAPOR BARRIER

1'-0"

2'-2"

BRICK

WALL CLOSURE DETAIL
⌀4 M-3 SCALE 1 1/2" = 1'-0"

VESTIBULE SECTION
⌀3 A4-6 SCALE 3/4" = 1'-0"

PORTICO SOUTH ELEVATION
⌀2

3'-4"   5'-8"   5'-8"   5'-4"

TRANSLUCENT SKYLIGHT PANEL SYSTEM (SEE SPECS.)

LIMESTONE

LIMESTONE

FACE BRICK

4" x 6" TUBE

4" SPLIT-FACE BLOCK

AGRICULTURE SCIENCE TECHNOLOGY
Alliance of Business and Agriculture

25'-0" RADIUS TO S.

3'-6 5/8"

2'-0"

5'-4"

3'-4"

FOUNDATION WALL (SEE STRUCT. DWG 16/S-2)

ALUMINUM STOREFRONT BEYOND

101

102

Chapter 4

Faster Forms Architectures

Forms are the most visible part of a Visual Basic program. In fact, forms are the windows that Windows refers to. In Visual Basic 4, forms have been incrementally improved. They have been given a bit of window dressing and a few new options, and some of the default behaviors are a little different.

All in all, though, the basic forms engine remains about the same as in earlier versions of Visual Basic—which is both good and bad. It's good because Visual Basic supports easy creation of either MDI (Multiple Document Interface) or standalone forms. It's bad because form display speed has always been one of Visual Basic's greatest weaknesses. You can use a number of methods, however, to improve form performance in Visual Basic; this chapter examines them.

Forms management also encompasses a number of tricks and techniques to help you get the most from your forms with a minimum of resource usage. We'll look at different ways to set up and use your forms to ride the performance/resource usage curve.

More specifically, in this chapter you'll learn about

- Performance issues with MDI and SDI interface styles

- The speed advantage of preloading forms

- The impact of controls on form display speed

- Benefits of control arrays

- How to reduce control quantities without sacrifice

- How to create controls at runtime

- How to speed form positioning and sizing

MDI or Standalone Forms

As you read in Chapter 3, "Designing Optimized Applications," one of the first choices you'll make as you design your application is the form interface style. In multiform applications, many programmers use the MDI capabilities built into Windows and Visual Basic.

The two styles are no different in resource usage, assuming equivalent functionality. However, using standalone forms has a slight speed advantage.

There will be two test applications in this chapter: FrmTst*X*.Vbp for standalone SDI forms, and MdiTst*X*.Vbp for testing a simple MDI interface. (The *X* in the project name refers to the version number.) As the chapter progresses, the projects will be enhanced with additional features and functionality, and then renamed and saved as FrmTst1.Vbp, FrmTst2.Vbp, and so on. You'll find all the different versions of each test application on the CD, in the \Chap4 subdirectory.

The first test demonstrates display speed for a very simple implementation. Each application has a main form with a toolbar containing two command buttons, and each has two "child" forms with a list box and a command button. Figures 4.1 and 4.2 show the SDI and MDI projects, respectively, in VB design mode.

 NOTE
To place command buttons on an MDI parent form, you must first place a picture box on the form. Only controls with an `Align` property can be placed in an MDI parent's client area, so the picture box, aligned to the top of the form, will serve as a container for the command buttons.

Executable Code Size

The first difference we discover between the two applications is executable size. After compiling in VB4's 16-bit mode, the MDI version of this project is 75 percent larger than the standalone program, requiring 35K of storage compared to just 20K for the standalone version. In 32-bit mode, the difference is even greater, with the MDI version requiring 40K compared to the standalone program's 22K, a difference of 18K or 82 percent.

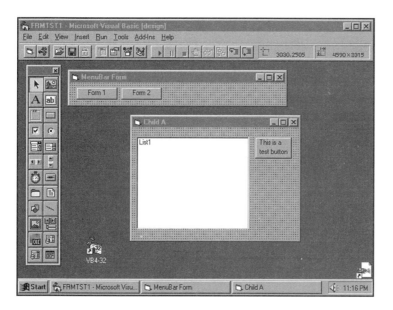

Fig. 4.1
The Single Document Interface (SDI) test project, seen in design mode with one "child" form displayed.

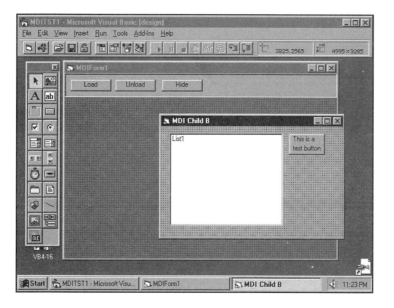

Fig. 4.2
The Multiple Document Interface (MDI) test project, seen in design mode.

Although the size difference isn't terribly substantial, if you're trying to minimize your application's distributable size, it could be a factor worth considering.

Display Speed

MDI child forms are displayed within the MDI parent's client area. The *client area* is the space between the borders, excluding the title bar, menu bar, and any panels or picture boxes that may be placed on the client area. The children are resized automatically to be proportional to the client area. Each form is positioned initially so that the children display in a cascading series.

The MdiTst1 and FrmTst1 projects test load and display times for parent and child forms by using the Show method from the parent form's Load event. Figures 4.3 and 4.4 show how your screen would appear after running the projects.

Fig. 4.3

This is how the SDI project FrmTst1.Vbp appears after execution. Notice that the SDI pseudo-child forms are manually cascaded.

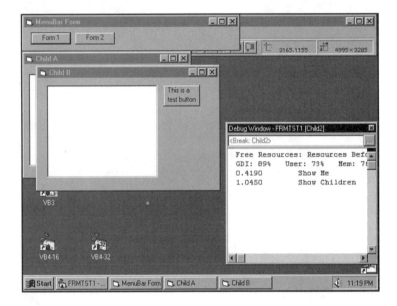

The code in listing 4.1 shows how the forms are displayed in FrmTst1.Vbp.

Listing 4.1   FrmTst1.Vbp   Displaying the Forms in the SDI Project

```
Private Sub Form_Load()

Monitor "Resources Before Showing Forms", MON_DEBUG
BeginTime "Show SDI Main Form ", 1
Me.Move 0, 0
Me.Show
EndTime
DoEvents
BeginTime "Load SDI Children", 1
Child1.Show
```

```
Child2.Show
EndTime
   Monitor "Resources After Showing Forms", MON_DEBUG
```

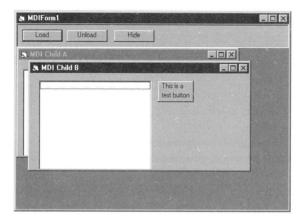

Fig. 4.4
This is how the MDI project MdiTst1.Vbp appears after execution.

To emulate MDI functionality in SDI, we have to position the child forms manually to mimic the cascading behaviors of MDI. In this sample, we just place some simple positioning code in each child form's load events. This is the code for Child A:

```
Private Sub Form_Load()
Me.Move 0, MenuBar.TOP + MenuBar.Height
End Sub
```

This is the positioning code for Child B:

```
Private Sub Form_Load()
Me.Move 360, 360 + MenuBar.TOP + MenuBar.Height
End Sub
```

The code for MdiTst1.Vbp is almost identical to the FrmTst1.Vbp code, as listing 4.2 shows.

Listing 4.2 MdiTst1.Vbp Displaying the Forms in the MDI Project

```
Private Sub MDIForm_Load()
Monitor "Resources Before Form Load", MON_DEBUG
BeginTime "Show Me", 1
Me.Move 0, 0
Me.Show
EndTime
DoEvents
BeginTime "Show Children", 1
```

(continues)

Listing 4.2 Continued

```
MdiChildA.Show
MdiChildB.Show
EndTime
Monitor "Resources After Form Show", MON_DEBUG
End Sub
```

Table 4.1 shows the form display performance results. In 16-bit mode, MDI parent forms take about 10 percent longer to load, whereas child forms take about 5 percent longer.

Table 4.1 Displaying SDI vs. MDI with

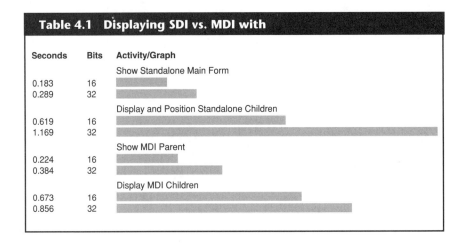

Seconds	Bits	Activity/Graph
		Show Standalone Main Form
0.183	16	
0.289	32	
		Display and Position Standalone Children
0.619	16	
1.169	32	
		Show MDI Parent
0.224	16	
0.384	32	
		Display MDI Children
0.673	16	
0.856	32	

When the projects are compiled and run in 32-bit mode, however, the test tells a slightly different story. MDI parent forms take about 30 percent longer to load, whereas MDI child forms are about 20 percent faster than standalone SDI forms.

Surprisingly, all the forms, when running in 32-bit mode, take substantially longer to load than the same forms running in 16-bit mode. The differences are substantial. On my test system, 32-bit forms are slower to display by 50 percent or more.

Preloading Forms

You can greatly reduce the time required to display your forms by preloading them at startup. The syntax to load a form before displaying it is simple:

```
Load FormName
```

Calling Load like this will place the form into memory but won't make it visible or enabled. If you use this method, make sure that you don't place a Show command or other code in the Load event of the form that will cause it to be displayed.

Of course, a preloaded form consumes as much RAM and resources as one that's visible. Depending on the size of your project, you may want to use this technique selectively—for example, just on the most used forms.

The Speed Advantage of Preloading Forms

Visual Basic still has to do just as much work to display the form, so it takes just as much time when all is said and done. What the preloading method does is split up the work so that part of it occurs at startup, while the user is looking at your splash screen. This will slow startup, which is one of the tradeoffs of preloading forms. However, the overall perceived, or apparent, speed of your application will be greatly increased.

Perceived Speed

Perceived speed is a concept we'll touch on throughout the book. Perceived speed is actually a fairly complex psychological issue. User expectations, motion, color, and many more factors affect it. Rather than try to define it fully here, I'll address different aspects of user perceptions as they affect each optimization task.

When considering form display performance, the primary influence on perceived speed is user expectation. Users expect some delay when a program starts up. Because Visual Basic needs to load not only the .EXE but also the VB runtime DLL, any Visual Basic program will require at least several seconds before it's ready to use. An extra half second or so to preload forms will hardly be noticed. On the other hand, when users click a button or make a menu choice to display a form, they want—and expect—immediate results.

Measuring Display Speed

I'll demonstrate the methods used to preload forms in FrmTst2.Vbp and MdiTst2.Vbp. Note that the forms now have three command buttons, and the buttons actually have some code behind them. Rather than load and display the forms in the Load event, as in the first version of the test projects, the command buttons will be used to test different display scenarios.

The first command button loads but doesn't display the forms. Note that MDI parent forms in VB4 have a new property, called Autoload. You should set this to false; otherwise, the MDI parent will automatically load—but not display—all its child forms when it's loaded.

The Load button loads the forms by using the Load statement:

```
Load Child1
Load Child2
```

The Show button executes the Show method against the child forms:

```
Child1.Show
Child2.Show
```

The Show method functions in two ways, depending on the load state of the form. It simply displays the preloaded form or, if the form isn't loaded yet, loads and then displays the form. Clicking the Show button before loading the child forms establishes baseline timing and resource usage, with .55 second required to load the two child forms—a little more than half a second required to load both the 16-bit SDI and MDI child forms, as table 4.2 shows. In 32-bit mode, MDI forms loaded more quickly than SDI forms, but still far more slowly than 16-bit forms.

Table 4.2   The Baseline *Show* Method for FrmTst2.Vbp and MdiTst2.Vbp

Seconds	Bits	Activity/Graph
		Show SDI Child Forms
0.563	16	
1.168	32	
		Show MDI Children
0.564	16	
0.792	32	

Clicking the Unload button removes the forms from memory and frees the resources used by the forms at a cost of .12 to .67 second (see table 4.3). This code removes the form object using the Unload command:

```
Unload MdiChild1
Unload MdiChild2
Set MdiChild1 = Nothing
Set MdiChild2 = Nothing
```

Table 4.3   Unloading a Form from Memory

Seconds	Bits	Activity/Graph
		Unload SDI Child Forms
0.124	16	
0.673	32	
		Unload MDI Children
0.138	16	
0.237	32	

Clicking the Load button loads the forms without displaying them. This takes a little less than a quarter of a second for 16-bit SDI forms (see table 4.4). Of course, in a normal application, this would be done in the parent form's Load event, so users would never notice the lost time. The code to use is simple:

```
Load Child1
Load Child2
```

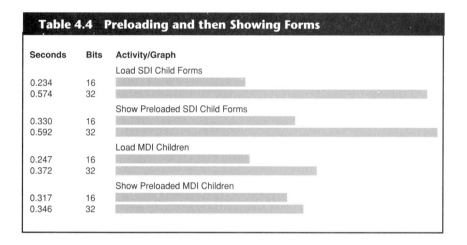

Table 4.4 Preloading and then Showing Forms

Seconds	Bits	Activity/Graph
		Load SDI Child Forms
0.234	16	
0.574	32	
		Show Preloaded SDI Child Forms
0.330	16	
0.592	32	
		Load MDI Children
0.247	16	
0.372	32	
		Show Preloaded MDI Children
0.317	16	
0.346	32	

Now when the Show button is clicked, rather than take half a second to display the forms, the forms appear in about a third of a second. This saves a full tenth of a second per form, a 40 percent speed improvement. More important than the raw statistics, though, is that the speed difference is apparent to users. Run the sample code to try it yourself. The preloaded forms will seem to appear much more quickly.

Of course, when you look at the entire task, you've saved no time. Loading the forms at startup requires .25 second, whereas displaying them requires about .33 second. Loading and displaying all at once requires .55 second, so overall, the program actually lost about a few hundredths of a second. But user perception *has* improved, and where form display is concerned, that's the first priority. When you examine the Hide method in the next section, you'll see how to save even more display time and begin to generate overall time savings.

The *Hide* Method

Hiding forms is one of the best ways to get better performance from VB forms. As users continue working with your application, they may jump from form to form. Often they'll close the form they were working with when they're done with it. Rather than unload the form, you can simply make the form invisible and disabled with the Hide method, as seen in the code beneath the Hide button in the latest iteration of the sample projects (FrmTst2 and MdiTst2):

```
Child1.Hide
Child2.Hide
```

Hiding a form takes about the same length of time as unloading it. But it keeps the form in memory, ready for display, so the next time the form is needed, it will be ready. You "unhide" the form the same way you've displayed the forms before, with the Show method. But in this case, the time not spent loading the form is real time saved, because you're displaying the form twice but only loading it once. In fact, it's better than that. Displaying a form that was hidden is even faster than displaying a preloaded form for the first time, since repositioning isn't needed. The time required to display the two hidden 16-bit forms is less than a quarter of a second, while the 32-bit forms load in a half a second or less (see table 4.5). This is a savings of another tenth of a second, making the overall display speed improvement greater than 50 percent.

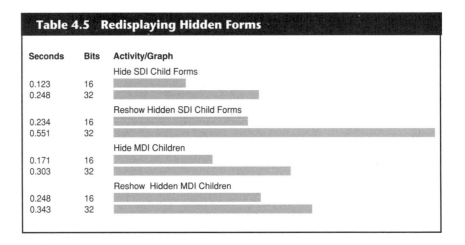

Table 4.5 Redisplaying Hidden Forms

Seconds	Bits	Activity/Graph
		Hide SDI Child Forms
0.123	16	
0.248	32	
		Reshow Hidden SDI Child Forms
0.234	16	
0.551	32	
		Hide MDI Children
0.171	16	
0.303	32	
		Reshow Hidden MDI Children
0.248	16	
0.343	32	

MDI *Hide* and *Load* Enhancements in VB4

The greatest limitation to the Hide method under VB3 was that it couldn't be used with MDI children. Although certain API calls could be used to make MDI children invisible, in my experience they greatly decreased an application's stability.

VB4 has changed all that. MDI children may be unloaded and hidden with the same speed advantage (and resource disadvantage) of standalone SDI forms. While we're on the subject of MDI changes, you can also preload MDI child forms with the Load statement under VB4. Although the Load statement worked with MDI children in VB3, it functioned like the Show method—that is, it would both load and display the MDI child form.

Control Quantity and Speed

Perhaps the greatest single determinant of a form's display speed is the number and type of controls on the form. The more controls, the slower the load and display time. We'll examine the relationship between control quantity and display speed in the FrmTst3.Vbp project.

The form-loading tests we've examined so far showed a reasonable correlation between MDI and SDI performance. For the sake of clarity, through the balance of this chapter I'll just extend the SDI case.

The main form remains the same as before in these examples, with four buttons so we can examine all the different scenarios in the tests. The first child form, Child A, also contains the same controls as before—just a list box and a command button—to provide baseline statistics.

However, to simulate a moderately sized edit screen, I've loaded up Child B with three combo controls, eight text boxes, and four command buttons (see fig. 4.5). And to emulate a large edit form, I've added a new form, Child C, with six combos and 16 text boxes (see fig. 4.6).

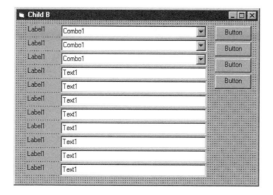

Fig. 4.5
Child B, shown in design mode, contains 26 controls.

As you can see, Child C is densely packed. It has many controls, probably more than would normally be considered usable. However, the number of controls on this form isn't that unusual and will probably become even more typical in the Windows 95 era. This is primarily because of the tabbed edit and display form interface fad. Tabbed forms with multiple entry panels used to be somewhat uncommon but in Windows 95 will probably become more of a norm.

Fig. 4.6
Child C, shown in design mode, contains 52 controls.

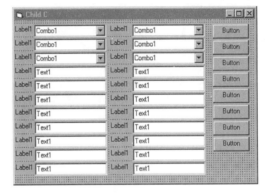

Adding Controls Slows *Show*

Adding controls slows form display significantly. The baseline form, with just two controls, loads in about a third of a second (.316 second). The moderate edit form, with 26 controls, takes more than a second to show, at 1.12 seconds. If you double the number of controls to create 52 combo boxes, text boxes, labels, and control buttons, you come very close to doubling the display time, which now is up to more than 2 seconds, at 2.142 (see table 4.6).

Table 4.6   Using *Show* to Load and Display Baseline, Moderate, and Large Edit Forms

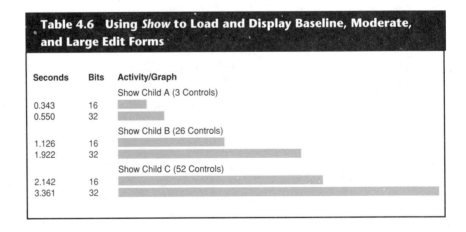

Seconds	Bits	Activity/Graph
		Show Child A (3 Controls)
0.343	16	
0.550	32	
		Show Child B (26 Controls)
1.126	16	
1.922	32	
		Show Child C (52 Controls)
2.142	16	
3.361	32	

Preloading Helps Speed

Two seconds is a long time for a user to wait for a form to display. And we haven't yet scratched the surface of the problem, because the test forms contain empty controls. The database, graphic, or other operations that you eventually would have to add to give these controls meaning would take even more time. Let's look at what you can do to speed up display.

As you saw earlier in this chapter, preloading the forms instead of using the Show method to load and display increased the apparent speed of the forms greatly. It has the same effect after more controls are added, but with an additional twist.

First, let's use the Load button to preload the forms with the Load FormName command. Table 4.7 shows the results. Child A, the baseline form, loads in .22 second. The moderate edit form, Child B, requires .742 second. Child C, with 52 controls, takes 1.4 seconds. If the code is placed in the startup procedure, two-thirds of the task of showing the forms would be accomplished before the application even begins, at a cost of slowing the application's startup by about 2.5 seconds.

Table 4.7   Preloading Forms with Various Numbers of Controls

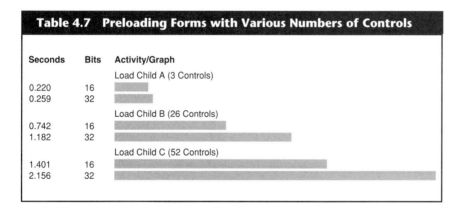

Seconds	Bits	Activity/Graph
		Load Child A (3 Controls)
0.220	16	
0.259	32	
		Load Child B (26 Controls)
0.742	16	
1.182	32	
		Load Child C (52 Controls)
1.401	16	
2.156	32	

Once done, though, the program never has to load the forms again. Now displaying the forms is tremendously improved. As you can see in table 4.8, once it's preloaded, Child B displays in exactly a third of a second, rather than 1.12 seconds. Child C takes barely more time than Child B, at .44 second, instead of more than 2 seconds! The 1 1/2 second difference is more than perceivable—it completely changes the feel of the application.

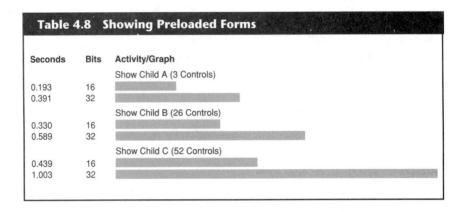

Table 4.8 Showing Preloaded Forms

Seconds	Bits	Activity/Graph
		Show Child A (3 Controls)
0.193	16	
0.391	32	
		Show Child B (26 Controls)
0.330	16	
0.589	32	
		Show Child C (52 Controls)
0.439	16	
1.003	32	

But there's something peculiar here. Child C required 2.14 seconds to load and display using the Show method. Preloading the form with the Load statement and then using Show just to display the form took a total of 1.84 seconds. We saved almost a third of a second in real (not apparent) time. The same thing happened with Child B, but the savings were only about .07 second.

The speed advantage increases even further if you Hide the forms after the first time you Show them. The next time the form is accessed, it displays about six-hundredths of a second faster than the first time it was displayed with Show, as table 4.9 shows.

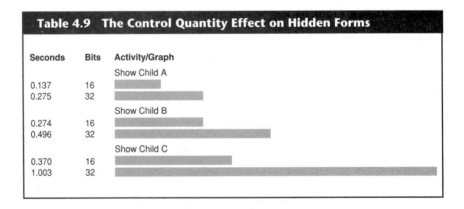

Table 4.9 The Control Quantity Effect on Hidden Forms

Seconds	Bits	Activity/Graph
		Show Child A
0.137	16	
0.275	32	
		Show Child B
0.274	16	
0.496	32	
		Show Child C
0.370	16	
1.003	32	

The perceived time required to display a typical edit form is cut by 75 percent from more than a full second to just a quarter of a second. Display times for forms with large numbers of controls is improved by more than 80 percent, from more than 2 seconds down to .37 second!

However, there is a price. Startup is delayed by more than 2 seconds, and the preloaded forms consume a fair portion of system resources as well as RAM. In the next sections, we'll see if we can do even better.

Control Arrays vs. Individual Controls

In all the examples, the test projects have used forms with a number of controls, all of which were elements of control arrays. A *control array* is a set of controls that share the same name and are differentiated from each other by the Index property.

Control arrays are supposed to consume fewer system resources—although the advantage is slight—and load more quickly. We'll verify that in this section.

To test the speed of control arrays, I added a new form, Child D, to the project (see fig. 4.7). Child D is a copy of Child B, the moderately sized form (refer to fig. 4.5). However, the control arrays were replaced with individual controls, so rather than have Text1(0), Text1(1), and so on, the form has Text1, Text2, Text3, and so on.

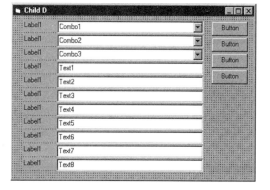

Fig. 4.7
This image shows the Child D form at design time.

By using the Show method to load and display the forms, you can see in table 4.10 that Child B, using control arrays, displays about 30 percent more quickly than Child D, using individual controls.

However, the advantage largely disappears when preloading and then showing the forms. (Table 4.11 shows the performance for the different tasks.) There's no statistically valid difference in the times required to preload the forms. There seems to be about a 5 percent improvement when the forms are initially shown after preloading, but when displaying the forms after they are shown once and then hidden, the display times are identical.

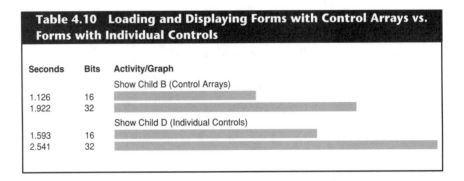

Table 4.10 Loading and Displaying Forms with Control Arrays vs. Forms with Individual Controls

Seconds	Bits	Activity/Graph
		Show Child B (Control Arrays)
1.126	16	
1.922	32	
		Show Child D (Individual Controls)
1.593	16	
2.541	32	

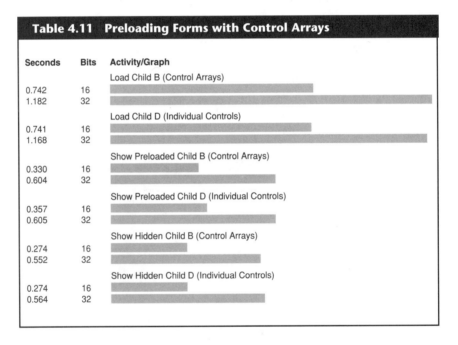

Table 4.11 Preloading Forms with Control Arrays

Seconds	Bits	Activity/Graph
		Load Child B (Control Arrays)
0.742	16	
1.182	32	
		Load Child D (Individual Controls)
0.741	16	
1.168	32	
		Show Preloaded Child B (Control Arrays)
0.330	16	
0.604	32	
		Show Preloaded Child D (Individual Controls)
0.357	16	
0.605	32	
		Show Hidden Child B (Control Arrays)
0.274	16	
0.552	32	
		Show Hidden Child D (Individual Controls)
0.274	16	
0.564	32	

Resource usage is identical with both methods, as far as we can measure. So I haven't really demonstrated a terrific optimizing technique here. However, this once again provides evidence that Visual Basic internally handles preloading with the Load statement differently than loading and displaying with Show. Also, if you do choose to simply Show your forms rather than preload them (perhaps because resources are scarce), control arrays will save time.

Drill-Down Layers

The analysis of control quantity and control arrays leads us to a simple conclusion: The best way to get additional speed improvements in form display times, once preloading and hiding is implemented, is simply to reduce the number of controls on the form. Of course, this is easier said than done. If you're creating a database table edit screen, you pretty much must have at least one control per field.

However, all the fields don't necessarily have to be on the same form. Suppose that you're creating a personnel file record with 25 fields. You could place entry controls for all the fields on the form, perhaps breaking them up in overlaid tabbed panels. With the label captions, you would be creating a form with control quantities equivalent to Child C, with its more than 2-second display time.

But what if you redesigned the application so that the entry form contained only the 10 most referenced fields? You could place the field's employee address information on another form, linked to this one, and open it with a command button. Salary information could be on another form, and performance review and disciplinary information could be on yet another. The initial form might contain just emergency numbers, Social Security information, department, and extension.

When adding or modifying an employee record, the user would click an Address button to call up the subform—in effect, drilling down to the additional detail. If the user didn't need to view or change the address information, the time required to display it would never be used. This method would also lend itself to increased security over sensitive information such as salaries.

Of course, this approach has its disadvantages. Coordinating the data links between the two forms would create a programming problem, although not a substantial one. You couldn't use a data control and bound controls, because data control recordset edits can't be shared across forms. And users would have to perform additional steps and take more time to obtain or enter all the data for an employee. Nevertheless, this technique is valid, and you should consider using it when circumstances warrant and you need more speed.

Virtual Labels

Let's examine other methods to reduce the number of controls on a form—this time, without reducing the amount of information displayed and available.

Of the 56 controls on Child C, six are combo boxes and 16 are text boxes. Because these are the entry areas for the data, we can't really eliminate them. There are also eight command buttons, with the first four representing OK, Cancel, Undo, and Help. (I added the other four buttons to exactly double Child B's controls. I'll leave them for comparison purposes.)

There are also 22 labels, which perform no task other than to describe the entry area. They're essential; otherwise, the user might have no idea what each field meant. It's worth noting that labels can serve as hot keys to allow a user to move the focus to the next control following the label in the tab order, but we're not using that feature here.

What this means is that we could reduce the controls on the form from 56 to 34 by eliminating the labels. And doing so is simple—just use the form's `Print` method to display the caption information in the same location as the labels.

In this instance, it's especially easy because we're using fake captions, all of which say `Label1`. So let's copy Child C to a new form—Child E—and delete all the labels. In Child E's `Paint` event, we place the code shown in listing 4.3.

Listing 4.3 FrmTst3.Vbp Painting Imitation Labels

```
Dim foo As Integer, foobar As Integer
For foo = 0 To 1
    For foobar = 0 To 10
        Me.CurrentX = foo * 2580
        Me.CurrentY = foobar * 360 + 120
        Me.Print "Label1"
    Next foobar
Next foo
```

Now, whenever the form needs to refresh itself, it will paint the imitation labels in the right positions. Figures 4.8 and 4.9 show the design form and the runtime results.

Of course, in a real-world scenario, the labels would need to be meaningful, which can involve a good deal of code. Fortunately, you can use several label-replacing subroutines in CodeBank to simplify the task, including `TagLabelPrint`, `LabelArraySet`, and `LabelArrayPrint`. For now, though, let's just try to emulate Child C to see what effect this change has on performance and resource usage.

Speed

When you run the test application, notice that things are indeed speeded up considerably, as table 4.12 shows. Using the `Show` method on Child C loads and displays it in 2.12 seconds, about the same as before. Child E, however, with the imitation labels, loads and displays in just 1.9 seconds—a savings of almost a quarter of a second!

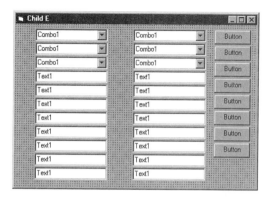

Fig. 4.8
Child E at design
time, with no
labels.

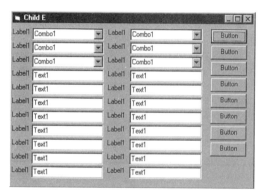

Fig. 4.9
Child E at runtime,
with labels.

II

Application Optimization

Table 4.12	Using *Show* to Load and Display a Virtually Labeled Form	

Seconds	Bits	Activity/Graph
		Show Child C (Standard Labels)
2.129	16	
3.801	32	
		Show Child E (Virtual Labels)
1.909	16	
3.901	32	

The time savings are even more dramatic if you preload the forms. As you can see, the time to load is cut in half to just .75 second, as opposed to 1.5 seconds before removing the label controls (see table 4.13). When the form is displayed with Show, it displays almost a tenth of a second more quickly (see table 4.14). And the savings remain consistent after hiding the form and then redisplaying it (see table 4.15).

Table 4.13 Preloading Forms with Virtual Labels

Seconds	Bits	Activity/Graph
		Preload Child C (Standard Labels)
1.469	16	
2.211	32	
		Preload Child E (Virtual Labels)
0.769	16	
2.032	32	

Table 4.14 Showing Preloaded Forms with Virtual Labels

Seconds	Bits	Activity/Graph
		Show Preloaded Child C (Standard Labels)
0.576	16	
0.975	32	
		Show Preloaded Child E (Virtual Labels)
0.495	16	
0.891	32	

Table 4.15 Showing Hidden Forms with Virtual Labels

Seconds	Bits	Activity/Graph
		Show Hidden Child C (Standard Labels)
0.481	16	
0.971	32	
		Show Hidden Child E (Virtual Labels)
0.392	16	
0.922	32	

A Timing Problem

Now we should look at what has been happening to the overall display times. You may have noticed that as more forms are added to the project, it seems to be taking longer to load each form, even the first ones. Unfortunately, this is true. The larger the project, the slower each task runs because we're running in debug mode with the development tools in memory. In real-world scenarios—for example, when running your application from compiled executables—this effect is minimal or nonexistent.

This highlights an important rule of benchmarking: To produce test results you can rely on, you need to pay attention to the percentage relationships between the time required to perform alternative methods, rather than completely focus on the times themselves. And it's very important to always run your baselines along with the revised code.

Resources

There's another advantage to using virtual controls that this chapter hasn't addressed much: resources. Until now, the alternatives didn't really have any impact on overall user resources. True, preloading forms reduced resources, but the resources would have been used anyway when the form was displayed, so the tests just focused on speed.

The virtual label solution, however, does indeed have a true impact on resources. The eliminated labels will never be used and thus represent a real savings. Loading or displaying Child C reduced available user resources by 7 percent. Child E, with virtual labels, consumed 4 percent. That's a 43 percent improvement! (Which, when you think about it, is sort of strange, since we have only 40 percent fewer controls, and they're supposed to be lightweight, low-resource controls at that. The unexpected discrepancy can be chalked up to rounding error, since the percentage resource figures we get from the API aren't very precise.) Neither method affected the amount of GDI resources available.

Eliminating Other Controls

The forms that we've optimized in this section are pretty standard and somewhat plain, so there aren't a lot of controls to consider eliminating. Future chapters will examine replacing other controls with code based on graphics or other methods.

Runtime Control Creation

Creating virtual labels worked so well to improve performance that it's worth investigating whether you can extend the technique to other controls. Of course, you can't just paint a text box or a combo control on a form. Unlike labels, these controls are interactive. But you can eliminate them from the form design layout and create them at runtime while the form is loading.

Creating Controls in the *Load* Event

To test whether this will save time or resources, copy Child E, with virtual labels and 22 combos and text boxes, to Child F. Next, delete all but one of the combos and text boxes, leaving just the control with index 0. Visual Basic will use this first element of the control array as a model in creating the others when you load the controls. In Child F's Load event, the code in listing 4.4 has been added to create and position the new virtual controls.

Listing 4.4 FrmTst3.Vbp Creating and Positioning New Virtual Controls

```
For foo = 1 To 5
    Load Combo1(foo)
    Combo1(foo).Visible = True
    If foo < 3 Then
        Combo1(foo).Move 540, foo * 360 + 120
    Else
        Combo1(foo).Move 3180, (foo - 3) * 360 + 120
    End If
Next foo
For foo = 1 To 15
    Load Text1(foo)
    Text1(foo).Visible = True
    If foo < 8 Then
        Text1(foo).Move 540, foo * 360 + 1200
    Else
        Text1(foo).Move 3180, (foo - 8) * 360 + 1200
    End If
Next foo
```

Voila! Controls from nowhere! And they're even lined up in two columns, just like Child C and Child E. Figure 4.10 shows the form at design time.

Fig. 4.10
Child F at design time.

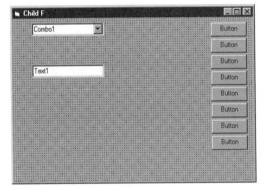

Performance

There's only one little problem: Creating the controls at runtime doesn't help. Sure, the controls appear and, yes, the executable file's size is reduced a little bit, but the form doesn't load and display any faster. Instead, it takes much longer. Loading the form takes almost 50 percent longer than Child E, which has all the controls laid out at design time. Table 4.16 tells the sorry tale.

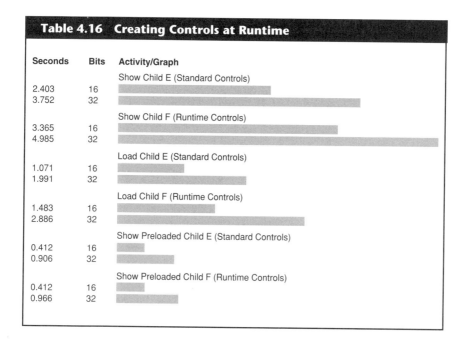

Table 4.16   Creating Controls at Runtime

Seconds	Bits	Activity/Graph
		Show Child E (Standard Controls)
2.403	16	
3.752	32	
		Show Child F (Runtime Controls)
3.365	16	
4.985	32	
		Load Child E (Standard Controls)
1.071	16	
1.991	32	
		Load Child F (Runtime Controls)
1.483	16	
2.886	32	
		Show Preloaded Child E (Standard Controls)
0.412	16	
0.906	32	
		Show Preloaded Child F (Runtime Controls)
0.412	16	
0.966	32	

You do save some resources, though. Resource usage for Child E is between 4 percent and 5 percent, while Child F requires between 3 percent and 4 percent of available user space. (Remember, it's difficult to be more precise because of the way resources are reported.) So if your application is tight for resources and you don't mind slowing your display, you can try this method.

But if you're looking for speed, the lesson here is that the next time someone tells you to load your controls at runtime, just say no. And if you're loading your controls at runtime already, consider changing back.

Positioning and Sizing Forms

When a VB form is displayed from an executable, it appears in the position and size it was in when last edited in design mode. The only exception to this is MDI children, which appear in a cascading position based on the number of forms that have been loaded and with their size determined proportionally to the MDI parent. The parent, however, obeys the same rules as standalone forms, appearing at the same size and place as edited.

This may not be the way you really want your forms to display. Often, I'll center my forms at startup. You might save the placement last chosen by the user in an .INI file and restore them to that position. I usually size my MDI parent forms to occupy 80 percent or sometimes 90 percent of the screen width and height at startup.

Move **Method**

You easily can size the forms by setting the form's Left, Top, Width, and Height properties in the Load event. But a faster way is to use the Move method.

Of course, the Move method isn't exactly a secret. Many of us use Move to position forms, but using it to size the form isn't as commonly practiced. In any case, it might be interesting to try to quantify the speed differences.

Storing System Parameters

The first step is to add some code to FrmMain's Load event to store the screen's width, height, and twip values. This will save you from having to continually check system properties and will save time. Plus, a handy CodeBank subroutine, TwipsPerPixel, does just that, so it's not any effort. The data will be stored in the gTwipsX and gTwipsY global variables.

Cascade Function

Now it's time to move some forms. Let's add four command buttons to the main form to force the forms to move from left to right and back using each method. Then add the code in listing 4.5 to make the forms alternately cascade to the left or right with a height variation, so that we're sure that the forms are forced to actually move (see figs. 4.11 and 4.12).

Listing 4.5 FrmTst4.Vbp Cascading the Forms

```
Case 5 ' Cascade Right
    BeginTime "Cascade Right with Move", 1
    For foo = 1 To Forms.Count - 1
        Forms(foo).Move 360 * (foo - 1), 360 * (foo) _
                + MenuBar.Top + MenuBar.Height
    Next foo
    'Let them Paint
    EndTime
Case 6
    BeginTime "Cascade Left with Left,Top", 1
    'Move them to different position
    For foo = 1 To Forms.Count - 1
        Forms(foo).Left = Screen.Width - (Forms(foo).Width + 360 _
                * (foo - 1))
        Forms(foo).Top = 360 * (foo - 1) + MenuBar.Top _
                + MenuBar.Height
    Next foo
    DoEvents 'let them paint
    EndTime
Case 7
```

```
BeginTime "Cascade Right with Left,Top", 1
For foo = 1 To Forms.Count - 1
    Forms(foo).Left = 360 * (foo - 1)
    Forms(foo).Top = 360 * (foo) + MenuBar.Top + MenuBar.Height
Next foo
'Let them Paint
EndTime
```

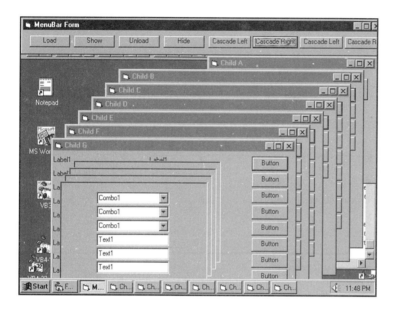

Fig. 4.11
Cascading the
children to the
left.

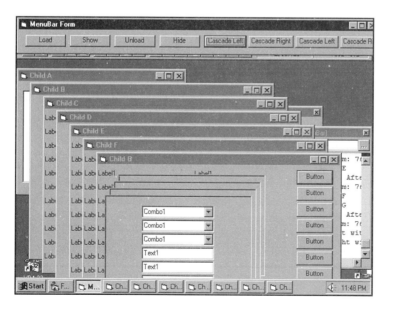

Fig. 4.12
Cascading the
children to the
right.

The results are as expected. The Move method is 1 to 1 1/2 seconds faster than setting the Top and Left properties, as table 4.17 shows.

Table 4.17	Positioning Forms with the	Method
Seconds	**Bits**	**Activity/Graph**
		Cascade Right with Move Method
2.655	16	
7.211	32	
		Cascade Left with Move Method
1.635	16	
7.059	32	
		Cascade Right with Left, Top Properties
3.437	16	
8.802	32	
		Cascade Left with Left, Top Properties
2.115	16	
8.842	32	

 NOTE The CodeBank procedure library has a number of positioning subroutines that you might care to investigate.

Conclusions

You can pursue a number of strategies to reduce form display time. The most effective, from the user's perspective, is preloading forms at startup and then closing them with the Hide method instead of unloading them. VB4 now allows you to use Hide on MDI children.

Be cautious about the number of controls you place on a form. There's almost a straight-line relationship between the number of controls on a form and the length of time it takes to load. By careful planning in the design stage, you can use layered drill-down forms to speed display. You can eliminate controls with graphics methods such as Print and Line.

You need to carefully examine common knowledge. Loading controls at runtime, an often-preached optimization technique, slows form loading considerably. But the commonly suggested Move method *is* significantly faster than setting Top and Left properties.

From Here...

For more information on topics brought up in this chapter, see the following chapters:

- Chapter 3, "Designing Optimized Applications," covers optimization issues in application design.

- Chapter 12, "Optimizing Graphics and Bitmaps," explains how to use and optimize graphics methods such as `Print` and `Line`. You'll also find an interesting case study that optimizes a 3-D caption subroutine in Chapter 6, "Strategies to Improve Algorithms."

- For more details on the effect of controls on form load times, see Chapter 13, "Using Components and Subroutines Wisely."

Chapter 5

Constructing Optimized VB Code

This chapter takes a detailed look at the performance of Visual Basic's most fundamental element: its code. Our objective is to determine the fastest way to achieve a given task in VB code.

You'll cover a lot of ground in this chapter, including the following topics:

- Code craftsmanship and productivity considerations

- CodeBench, the testing utility used throughout the chapter

- Division

- Mathematical operations

- Concatenation

- Text-handling functions, including UCase(), LCase(), Trim(), and Mid()

- Loops and conditionals

- Control property manipulation

- Variable structures

- Error-handling methods

Code Speed and Craftsmanship

There's an old saying that if you ask five programmers how to solve a particular problem, you'll get at least five answers. That's particularly true with VB.

Visual Basic has many more keywords, data types, and code constructs than most languages. When you're addressing even the simplest task, you almost always have alternatives available.

Some alternatives will run more quickly than others, making this an area in which code craftsmanship matters. The results of the tests that are run in this chapter will usually apply universally. For example, if you're dividing two integers, it's always going to be faster to use integer math.

Optimization, however, is still a science, and science is based on doubt. As you'll see in this chapter, the well-known rule that integer division is faster than floating-point math isn't always true. If your operands are doubles and the computer running your program has a floating-point coprocessor, floating-point division can actually be much faster. What hurts isn't the things we don't know, but rather the things that we know that aren't so.

The Productivity Tradeoff

The issues that this chapter addresses don't involve the usual tradeoffs. There isn't any difference in resource usage, for example, between integer and floating-point division. Nor is there any advantage in executable size. The only optimization issue is *speed*.

An opportunity for programmer judgment, however, still arises. Most of the differences we'll see are purely stylistic. Thus, the issue becomes one of speed rather than programmer productivity. Construct A might be marginally faster than construct B. However, if you find that construct B is easier to implement or produces clearer code, you may want to implement the slower construct. Although such a change would be at the expense of theoretical speed, the speed difference may not be detectable in the algorithm you're writing. We'll examine this issue in more detail in the next chapter, "Strategies to Improve Algorithms."

The CodeBench Utility

We'll use the CodeBench utility program to measure and report the performance of the different benchmarks. CodeBench applies the profiling and timing subroutines in our optimization toolkit to the different code constructs, and displays the results in your choice of output formats.

By default, I display the timing results to the debug window. If you're running CodeBench from an executable file, you can have the timing subroutines display each statistic in a message box or printed in report format.

CodeBench Timing

CodeBench's timing subroutines, `BeginTime` and `EndTime`, use the `GetTickCount()` API call to measure time. Note that `GetTickCount()` reports the duration since Windows was started, measured in milliseconds (thousandths of a second). The limit of its precision is 13 milliseconds because the Windows clock updates itself only about that often.

Even with measurements to the millisecond, however, we couldn't measure the speed of an individual line of code. Adding 2+2 takes significantly less than a millisecond. Therefore, to obtain significant measurements, Code-Bench repeats the operation being analyzed by using a `For...Next` loop. Usually we'll need to repeat the operation 1,000 times. Thus, the figures we presented would have an overhead element built in because of the time required to loop. `For...Next` loops are very fast, however. One thousand iterations of a `For...Next` loop require only about 1.2 milliseconds, so the looping overhead is insignificant.

Running CodeBench

All the CodeBench statistics are shown and explained in the relevant code section. The CodeBench project—CodeBnch.Vbp—is on the CD that came with this book, in the \Chap5 directory.

The code samples shown throughout this chapter lie behind the appropriate CodeBench command button (see fig. 5.1). You can, of course, modify or extend the code any way you want to test other scenarios or change the operating assumptions.

You'll probably want to rerun the benchmarks in CodeBench to get a feel for performance issues on your target machines and to double-check the results presented in this chapter against the latest VB runtime DLLs.

> When you run benchmarks under Windows, remember to repeat your test several times; don't rely on a single run. Because Windows is multitasking and Windows 95 is pre-emptively multitasking, Windows possibly may have interfered with the timing process in any single run. Shutting down any running applications before testing will help ensure that the benchmarks are as accurate as possible.

Fig. 5.1
The main screen
in CodeBench.

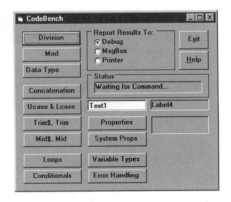

Benchmark Results

In the following sections, you'll review the results of all the different comparisons built into CodeBench. Although this chapter analyzes many different code constructs, it shouldn't be considered a definitive analysis of every VB operation. Such a survey would undoubtedly take several volumes. Instead, CodeBench hits the highlights—commonly used arithmetic operators, string manipulation commands, looping and conditional structures, error-handling methods, and more.

Graphics and database commands are excluded from this analysis because they're handled later in chapters devoted exclusively to those operations. For the same reason, we won't compare VB code with API or DLL calls, and we've already analyzed form management. We also won't learn strategies about implementing the results of the benchmarks in your algorithms; Chapter 6, "Strategies to Improve Algorithms," covers that ground thoroughly.

Each comparison in this chapter includes a table showing the relative speed of the operations being discussed, as well as a bar chart for easy reference. We'll examine the results for both the 16- and 32-bit versions of VB4. The code for each optional algorithm is presented in the discussion. Highlights of the results and the lessons learned from the benchmarks are presented in a summary at the end of each section.

Division Method Optimization

Most of the arithmetic operators are discussed in the following section. Division, however, earns a section of its own because it's the only operator that has more than one built-in method. Visual Basic division can be integer or floating point.

For those of you who may not know, floating-point math includes fractions or decimals, whereas integers are only whole numbers such as 1, 2, and 3. With floating-point division, 3 divided by 2 would equal 1.5; the integer division result, on the other hand, would throw away the "leftover" fraction, so 3 divided by 2 would equal 1.

On older, slower machines, division typing used to make a substantial difference, especially on machines without floating-point coprocessors. Today, the 486DX class and higher machines have built-in floating-point coprocessors, so the speed difference isn't as dramatic—or straightforward—as before. But there's a real difference. Comparisons will be made throughout the book on a 486DX running at 66MHz.

> The DX series chip has a floating-point coprocessor as part of the main CPU.

NOTE

Division with Double Operands

This operation provides our first surprise. As you can see in table 5.1, floating-point math is as much as three times faster than integer math, if you have a floating-point coprocessor.

Table 5.1 Division on Doubles

Seconds	Bits	Activity/Graph
		Floating-Point Division on Doubles
0.069	16	
0.052	32	
		Integer Division on Doubles
0.192	16	
0.082	32	

The code shown in listing 5.1 measures floating-point division. The code clip in listing 5.2 measures integer division on doubles.

Listing 5.1 CodeBnch.Vbp Measuring Floating-Point Division on Doubles

```
BeginTime "Floating Point Division on Doubles", printmode
For foo = 1 To 10000
    a = b / c
```

(continues)

Listing 5.1   Continued

```
    Next foo
    EndTime
```

Listing 5.2   CodeBnch.Vbp   Measuring Integer Division on Doubles

```
    BeginTime "Integer Division on Doubles", printmode
    For foo = 1 To 10000
        a = b \ c
    Next foo
    EndTime
```

Notice that a, b, and c were declared as doubles, and b was initialized to 1,000, whereas c was initialized to 22. The determining factor in this example is that our operands are doubles.

Division with Integer and Long Operands

When we change the data type of the operands, integer division regains its faster status (see table 5.2). In the code segments in listings 5.3 through 5.6, h, i, and j are integers, while k, l, and m are longs. Integer division is slightly faster with longs, and more so with integers.

Listing 5.3   CodeBnch.Vbp   Measuring Floating-Point Division on Integers

```
    BeginTime "Floating Point Division on Integers", printmode
    For foo = 1 To 10000
        h = i / j
    Next foo
    EndTime
```

Listing 5.4   CodeBnch.Vbp   Measuring Floating-Point Division on Longs

```
    BeginTime "Floating Point Division on Longs", printmode
    For foo = 1 To 10000
        k = l / m
    Next foo
    EndTime
```

Listing 5.5 CodeBnch.Vbp Measuring Integer Division on Integers

```
BeginTime "Integer Division on Integers", printmode
For foo = 1 To 10000
    h = i \ j
Next foo
EndTime
```

Listing 5.6 CodeBnch.Vbp Measuring Integer Division on Longs

```
BeginTime "Integer Division on Longs", printmode
For foo = 1 To 10000
    k = l \ m
Next foo
EndTime
```

Table 5.2 Division on Integers and Longs

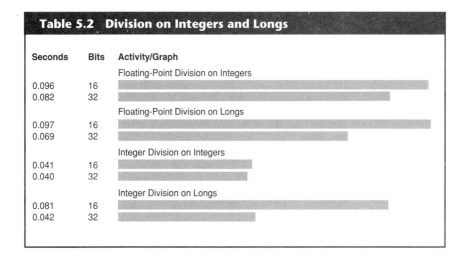

Seconds	Bits	Activity/Graph
		Floating-Point Division on Integers
0.096	16	
0.082	32	
		Floating-Point Division on Longs
0.097	16	
0.069	32	
		Integer Division on Integers
0.041	16	
0.040	32	
		Integer Division on Longs
0.081	16	
0.042	32	

As in the previous floating-point test, the value of i was initialized to 1,000 and j was set to 22. Two things are worth noting in this comparison:

- Integer division is only marginally faster than floating-point division with a coprocessor, except when using integers rather than longs.

- Floating-point division is almost 50 percent slower applied against longs than on doubles in 16-bit VB4.

The bottom line is that floating-point division on doubles, as shown in this test, is now as fast or faster than integer division on longs. This conclusion is especially significant because in most operations, you'll probably need to use longs rather than integers (because of the limited capacity of signed integers).

Division with Variant Operands

Integer division truly outperforms floating-point division only with variants. As in the other examples, w is set to 1,000 while x equals 22. The code for the test is shown in listings 5.7 and 5.8. The results of the test are shown in table 5.3.

Listing 5.7 CodeBnch.Vbp Measuring Floating-Point Division on Variants

```
BeginTime "Floating Point Division on Variants", printmode
For foo = 1 To 10000
    v = w / x
Next foo
EndTime
```

Listing 5.8 CodeBnch.Vbp Measuring Integer Division on Variants

```
BeginTime "Integer Division on Variants", printmode
For foo = 1 To 10000
    v = w \ x
Next foo
EndTime
```

Table 5.3 Division on Variants

Seconds	Bits	Activity/Graph
		Floating-Point Division on Variants
0.205	16	
0.124	32	
		Integer Division on Variants
0.137	16	
0.111	32	

Simulating Division with Multiplication

The following comparison examines how the results might vary if we tried something unusual. Rather than continually divide by a given factor, we divided the divisor by one and then used the result of that division as a multiplication factor. The hypothesis was that by using VB's multiplication, algorithms might provide better performance. This method, however, is handy only in situations where a large set of numbers are being divided by the same factor.

Listings 5.9 through 5.11 show the CodeBench code used for this test.

Listing 5.9   CodeBnch.Vbp   Measuring MultFactor Division on Doubles

```
BeginTime "MultFactor Division on Doubles", printmode
multfactor = 1 / c
For foo = 1 To 10000
    a = b * multfactor
Next foo
EndTime
```

Listing 5.10   CodeBnch.Vbp   Measuring MultFactor Division on Longs

```
BeginTime "MultFactor Division on Longs", printmode
multfactor = 1 / j
For foo = 1 To 10000
    h = i * multfactor
Next foo
EndTime
```

Listing 5.11   CodeBnch.Vbp   Measuring MultFactor Division on Variants

```
BeginTime "MultFactor Division on Variants", printmode
multfactor = 1 / x
For foo = 1 To 10000
    v = w * multfactor
Next foo
EndTime
```

II

Application Optimization

The results were negative, as there was no real improvement in speed (see table 5.4). This is actually very good, because now you don't have to worry about doing this.

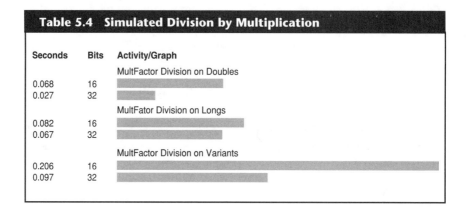

Table 5.4 Simulated Division by Multiplication

Seconds	Bits	Activity/Graph
		MultFactor Division on Doubles
0.068	16	
0.027	32	
		MultFator Division on Longs
0.082	16	
0.067	32	
		MultFactor Division on Variants
0.206	16	
0.097	32	

Mixed Type Division with Double Output

Until now, the analysis has focused on single data type expressions—longs divided by longs, or doubles divided by doubles. This comparison analyzes what happens if we mix data types so that there are both long and double operands in the expression, and then output the results to a double. Listings 5.12 and 5.13 show the code for this comparison.

Listing 5.12 CodeBnch.Vbp Measuring Floating-Point Division on Mixed Types with Double Output

```
BeginTime "Floating Point Division on Mixed Types: Double _
        Output", printmode
For foo = 1 To 10000
    a = i / c
Next foo
EndTime
```

Listing 5.13 CodeBnch.Vbp Measuring Integer Division on Mixed Types with Double Output

```
BeginTime "Integer Division on Mixed Types: Double Output", _
        printmode
For foo = 1 To 10000
    a = i \ c
Next foo
EndTime
```

Remember, floating-point division is significantly faster than integer division, as table 5.5 demonstrates.

Table 5.5		Mixed Type Division with Double Output
Seconds	**Bits**	**Activity/Graph**
		Floating-Point Division on Mixed Types: Double Output
0.082	16	
0.042	32	
		Integer Division on Mixed Types: Double Output
0.151	16	
0.071	32	

Mixed Type Division with Integer Output

If you take the same expressions used in the preceding comparison and output them to a long integer rather than a double, you get very different results. Floating-point math slows down, whereas integer division speeds up. The result is that it takes exactly the same amount of time to evaluate the expression, regardless of the method used (see table 5.6). Listings 5.14 and 5.15 show the code used.

Listing 5.14 CodeBnch.Vbp Measuring Floating-Point Division on Mixed Types with Integer Output

```
BeginTime "Floating Point Division on Mixed Types: Integer _
     Output", printmode
For foo = 1 To 10000
    h = i / c
Next foo
EndTime
```

Listing 5.15 CodeBnch.Vbp Measuring Integer Division on Mixed Types with Integer Output

```
BeginTime "Integer Division on Mixed Types: Integer Output", _
     printmode
For foo = 1 To 10000
    h = i \ c
Next foo
EndTime
```

II

Application Optimization

Table 5.6		Mixed Type Division with Integer Output
Seconds	**Bits**	**Activity/Graph**
		Floating-Point Division on Mixed Types: Integer Output
0.109	16	
0.069	32	
		Integer Division on Mixed Types: Integer Output
0.109	16	
0.068	32	

Mod Division

The Mod operator is a type of division, but rather than return the number of times a divisor will fit into an exponent, Mod returns the amount that would be left over—that is, the remainder. For example, the expression 5 Mod 2 would return 1 because 2 goes into 5 twice with 1 remaining. In other words, the Mod operator essentially stops at the decimal point of the expression.

Mod by Data Type

Unlike division, there's only one type of Mod in VB. However, you obtain different results depending on the data type of the variables being manipulated. As table 5.7 shows, Mod is significantly faster with integers than any other data type. Even variants are processed by Mod more quickly than doubles in 16-bit mode, although the speed advantage isn't apparent in 32-bit VB4. Listings 5.16 through 5.18 show the code involved.

Listing 5.16   CodeBnch.Vbp   Measuring *Mod* on Integers

```
BeginTime "Mod on Integers", printmode
For foo = 1 To 10000
    h = i Mod j
Next foo
EndTime
```

Listing 5.17   CodeBnch.Vbp   Measuring *Mod* on Doubles

```
BeginTime "Mod on Doubles", printmode
For foo = 1 To 10000
    a = b Mod c
Next foo
EndTime
```

Listing 5.18 CodeBnch.Vbp Measuring *Mod* on Variants

```
BeginTime "Mod on Variants", printmode
For foo = 1 To 10000
    v = w Mod x
Next foo
EndTime
```

Table 5.7 *Mod* by Data Type

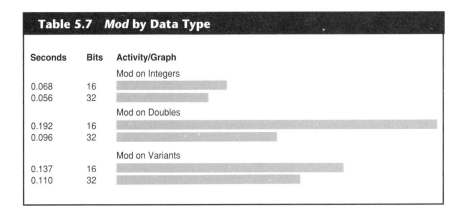

Seconds	Bits	Activity/Graph
		Mod on Integers
0.068	16	
0.056	32	
		Mod on Doubles
0.192	16	
0.096	32	
		Mod on Variants
0.137	16	
0.110	32	

Simulating *Mod* Algorithmically

Although the built-in Mod operator is handy, you could also easily emulate it in code. To do so, use integer division on the operands, and then multiply the whole number result by the divisor. Subtract this value from your original exponent to obtain the Mod result. Listings 5.19 through 5.21 show how I did this.

Listing 5.19 CodeBnch.Vbp Measuring Algorithmic *Mod* on Integers

```
BeginTime "Algorithmic Mod on Integers", printmode
For foo = 1 To 10000
    h = i - ((i \ j) * j)
Next foo
EndTime
```

Listing 5.20 CodeBnch.Vbp Measuring Algorithmic *Mod* on Doubles

```
BeginTime "Algorithmic Mod on Doubles", printmode
For foo = 1 To 10000
    a = b - (Int(b / c) * c)
Next foo
EndTime
```

Listing 5.21 CodeBnch.Vbp Measuring Algorithmic *Mod* on Variants

```
BeginTime "Algorithmic Mod on Variants", printmode
For foo = 1 To 10000
    v = w - ((w \ x) * x)
Next foo
EndTime
```

The reward for all this effort is a Mod emulation for doubles that's twice as fast in 16 bits and 25 percent faster in 32 bits as the built-in VB4 Mod (see table 5.8). Unfortunately, the algorithmic method isn't faster with integers or variants, so be sure to use it only with doubles.

Table 5.8 Simulating *Mod* Algorithmically

Seconds	Bits	Activity/Graph
		Algorithmic Mod on Integers
0.110	16	
0.068	32	
		Algorithmic Mod on Doubles
0.096	16	
0.069	32	
		Algorithmic Mod on Variants
0.247	16	
0.274	32	

Mod on Mixed Data Types

As with the analyses of division, when we mix data types in the expression, Mod speeds are controlled by the type of the output. Integer output is somewhat faster than double output. Table 5.9 shows the exact figures for the code segments shown in listings 5.22 and 5.23.

Listing 5.22   CodeBnch.Vbp   Measuring *Mod* on Mixed Data Types. with Integer Output

```
BeginTime "Mod on Mixed Types: Integer Output", printmode
For foo = 1 To 10000
    h = i Mod c
Next foo
EndTime
```

Listing 5.23   CodeBnch.Vbp   Measuring *Mod* on Mixed Data Types with Double Output

```
BeginTime "Mod on Mixed Types: Double Output", printmode
For foo = 1 To 10000
    a = i Mod c
Next foo
EndTime
```

Table 5.9   *Mod* with Mixed Data Types

Seconds	Bits	Activity/Graph
		Mod on Mixed Types: Integer Output
0.110	16	
0.055	32	
		Mod on Mixed Types: Double Output
0.137	16	
0.069	32	

Algorithmic *Mod* on Mixed Types

Table 5.10 shows the results when you test the algorithmic version of Mod using mixed data types as operands. Listings 5.24 and 5.25 show the code used to get these results.

Listing 5.24   CodeBnch.Vbp   Testing Algorithmic *Mod* on Mixed Types with Integer Output

```
BeginTime "Algorithmic Mod on Mixed Types: Integer Output", _
    printmode
For foo = 1 To 10000
    h = i - (Int(i / c) * c)
Next foo
EndTime
```

II

Application Optimization

Listing 5.25 CodeBnch.Vbp   Testing Algorithmic *Mod* on Mixed Types with Double Output

```
BeginTime "Algorithmic Mod on Mixed Types: Double Output", _
    printmode
For foo = 1 To 10000
    a = i - (Int(i / c) * c)
Next foo
EndTime
```

Table 5.10 *Mod* with Mixed Data Types

Seconds	Bits	Activity/Graph
		Algorithmic Mod on Mixed Types: Integer Output
0.137	16	
0.095	32	
		Algorithmic Mod on Mixed Types: Double Output
0.110	16	
0.085	32	

Mathematical Operations by Data Type

Compared to division and Mod, the results for other mathematical operations are refreshingly consistent. Integer addition, subtraction, and multiplication are always faster than the same operations on doubles, and double mathematics is always faster than variant mathematics. The results for addition are shown in table 5.11, for subtraction in table 5.12, and for multiplication in table 5.13.

The code clips in listings 5.26 through 5.29 show the addition test routines. The code sections in listings 5.30 through 5.33 test subtraction. Listings 5.34 through 5.37 show the test code for multiplication.

Listing 5.26 CodeBnch.Vbp   Measuring Addition on Integers

```
BeginTime "Addition on Integers", printmode
For foo = 1 To 30000
    h = i + j
Next foo
EndTime
```

Listing 5.27   CodeBnch.Vbp   Measuring Addition on Longs

```
BeginTime "Addition on Longs", printmode
For foo = 1 To 30000
    l = k + m
Next foo
EndTime
```

Listing 5.28   CodeBnch.Vbp   Measuring Addition on Doubles

```
BeginTime "Addition on Doubles", printmode
For foo = 1 To 30000
    a = b + c
Next foo
EndTime
```

Listing 5.29   CodeBnch.Vbp   Measuring Addition on Variants

```
BeginTime "Addition on Variants", printmode
For foo = 1 To 30000
    v = w + x
Next foo
EndTime
```

Listing 5.30   CodeBnch.Vbp   Measuring Subtraction on Integers

```
BeginTime "Subtraction on Integers", printmode
For foo = 1 To 30000
    h = i - j
Next foo
EndTime
```

Listing 5.31   CodeBnch.Vbp   Measuring Subtraction on Longs

```
BeginTime "Subtraction on Longs", printmode
For foo = 1 To 30000
    l = k - m
Next foo
EndTime
```

II

Application Optimization

Listing 5.32 CodeBnch.Vbp Measuring Subtraction on Doubles

```
BeginTime "Subtraction on Doubles", printmode
For foo = 1 To 30000
    a = b - c
Next foo
EndTime
```

Listing 5.33 CodeBnch.Vbp Measuring Subtraction on Variants

```
BeginTime "Subtraction on Variants", printmode
For foo = 1 To 30000
    v = w - x
Next foo
EndTime
```

Listing 5.34 CodeBnch.Vbp Testing Multiplication on Integers

```
BeginTime "Multiplication on Integers", printmode
For foo = 1 To 30000
    h = i * j
Next foo
EndTime
```

Listing 5.35 CodeBnch.Vbp Testing Multiplication on Longs

```
BeginTime "Multiplication on Longs", printmode
For foo = 1 To 30000
    l = k * m
Next foo
EndTime
```

Listing 5.36 CodeBnch.Vbp Testing Multiplication on Doubles

```
BeginTime "Multiplication on Doubles", printmode
For foo = 1 To 30000
    a = b * c
Next foo
EndTime
```

Listing 5.37   CodeBnch.Vbp   Testing Multiplication on Variants

```
BeginTime "Multiplication on Variants", printmode
For foo = 1 To 30000
    v = w * x
Next foo
EndTime
```

Table 5.11   Addition by Data Type

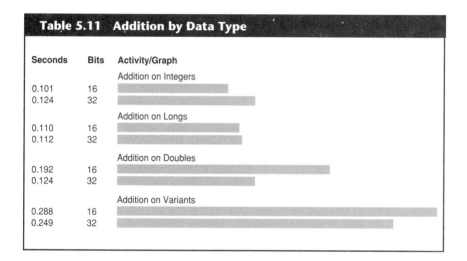

Seconds	Bits	Activity/Graph
		Addition on Integers
0.101	16	
0.124	32	
		Addition on Longs
0.110	16	
0.112	32	
		Addition on Doubles
0.192	16	
0.124	32	
		Addition on Variants
0.288	16	
0.249	32	

Concatenation

Visual Basic provides two concatenation operators: the ampersand (&) and the plus sign (+). The plus sign, of course, does double duty because it's also the addition operator. When using variants, the plus sign can give unexpected results, depending on the data type of the variants being processed. Our optimization test checks whether VB took significant amounts of time deciding whether to add or concatenate with the plus sign, and determines the speed difference between concatenation with strings as opposed to variants.

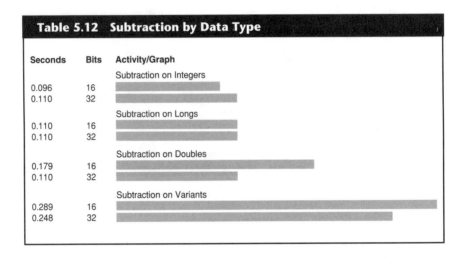

Table 5.12   Subtraction by Data Type

Seconds	Bits	Activity/Graph
		Subtraction on Integers
0.096	16	
0.110	32	
		Subtraction on Longs
0.110	16	
0.110	32	
		Subtraction on Doubles
0.179	16	
0.110	32	
		Subtraction on Variants
0.289	16	
0.248	32	

Table 5.13   Multiplication by Data Type

Seconds	Bits	Activity/Graph
		Multiplication on Integers
0.109	16	
0.109	32	
		Multiplication on Longs
0.152	16	
0.110	32	
		Multiplication on Doubles
0.179	16	
0.109	32	
		Multiplication on Variants
0.302	16	
0.247	32	

Surprisingly, the + operator is slightly faster than the & operator in 16-bit mode, whereas the reverse is true in 32-bit mode, as you can see in table 5.14. The data type of the strings being manipulated is a much stronger indicator of speed: Dynamic string concatenation is always significantly faster than variants, and both are much faster than fixed-length strings.

The variables d, e, f are defined as fixed-length strings, as in

```
Dim d As String * 20, e As String * 10, f As String * 10
```

The code in listings 5.38 through 5.40 tests the & operator. The code in listings 5.41 through 5.43 tests the + operator.

**Listing 5.38 CodeBnch.Vbp Testing Concatenation with the &
Operator on Strings**

```
BeginTime "Concatenation with & Operator on Strings", printmode
For foo = 1 To 10000
    a = b & c
Next foo
EndTime
```

**Listing 5.39 CodeBnch.Vbp Testing Concatenation with the &
Operator on Fixed Strings**

```
BeginTime "Concatenation with & Operator on Fixed Strings", _
    printmode
For foo = 1 To 10000
    d = e & f
Next foo
EndTime
```

**Listing 5.40 CodeBnch.Vbp Testing Concatenation with the &
Operator on Variants**

```
BeginTime "Concatenation with & Operator on Variants", printmode
For foo = 1 To 10000
    x = y & z
Next foo
EndTime
```

**Listing 5.41 CodeBnch.Vbp Testing Concatenation with the +
Operator on Strings**

```
BeginTime "Concatenation with + Operator on Strings", printmode
For foo = 1 To 10000
    a = b + c
Next foo
EndTime
```

II

Application Optimization

Listing 5.42 CodeBnch.Vbp Testing Concatenation with the + Operator on Fixed Strings

```
BeginTime "Concatenation with + Operator on Fixed Strings", _
    printmode
For foo = 1 To 10000
    d = e + f
Next foo
EndTime
```

Listing 5.43 CodeBnch.Vbp Testing Concatenation with the + Operator on Variants

```
BeginTime "Concatenation with + Operator on Variants", printmode
For foo = 1 To 10000
    x = y + z
Next foo
EndTime
```

Table 5.14 Concatenation by Data Type and Operator

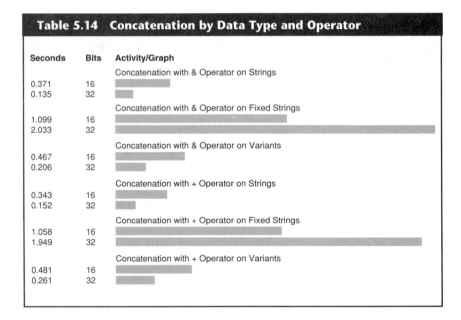

Seconds	Bits	Activity/Graph
		Concatenation with & Operator on Strings
0.371	16	
0.135	32	
		Concatenation with & Operator on Fixed Strings
1.099	16	
2.033	32	
		Concatenation with & Operator on Variants
0.467	16	
0.206	32	
		Concatenation with + Operator on Strings
0.343	16	
0.152	32	
		Concatenation with + Operator on Fixed Strings
1.058	16	
1.949	32	
		Concatenation with + Operator on Variants
0.481	16	
0.261	32	

UCase() and *LCase()*

UCase() and LCase() are handy functions, especially when you're making comparisons between strings that you want to be case-insensitive. But compared to most operations we've analyzed so far, they're very slow.

These functions seem to violate the usual optimization rules: Variants are faster than strings, with fixed-length strings being slowest of all. Even stranger is that 16-bit operations using UCase() and LCase() are four to five times faster than 32-bit operations.

Listings 5.44 through 5.49 show the code used to make the comparisons.

Listing 5.44   CodeBnch.Vbp   Testing *UCase()* on Strings

```
BeginTime "UCase on Strings", printmode
For foo = 1 To 10000
    a = UCase(b)
Next foo
EndTime
```

Listing 5.45   CodeBnch.Vbp   Testing *UCase()* on Fixed Strings

```
BeginTime "UCase on Fixed Strings", printmode
For foo = 1 To 10000
    d = UCase(e)
Next foo
EndTime
```

Listing 5.46   CodeBnch.Vbp   Testing *UCase()* on Variants

```
BeginTime "UCase on Variants", printmode
For foo = 1 To 10000
    x = UCase(y)
Next foo
EndTime
```

Listing 5.47   CodeBnch.Vbp   Testing *UCase()* on Strings

```
BeginTime "LCase on Strings", printmode
For foo = 1 To 10000
    a = LCase(b)
Next foo
EndTime
```

Listing 5.48 CodeBnch.Vbp Testing *LCase()* on Fixed Strings

```
BeginTime "LCase on Fixed Strings", printmode
For foo = 1 To 10000
    d = LCase(e)
Next foo
EndTime
```

Listing 5.49 CodeBnch.Vbp Testing *LCase()* on Variants

```
BeginTime "LCase on Variants", printmode
For foo = 1 To 10000
    x = LCase(y)
Next foo
EndTime
```

UCase() seems to be marginally faster than LCase() with variants and dynamic strings, whereas LCase() is faster with fixed-length strings. Again, though, the major determinant of speed is data type. Table 5.15 shows the results.

Table 5.15 *UCase()* and *LCase()* by Data Type

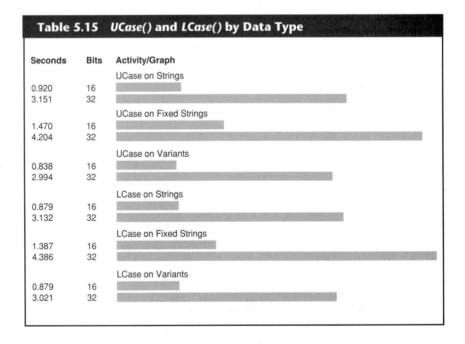

Seconds	Bits	Activity/Graph
		UCase on Strings
0.920	16	
3.151	32	
		UCase on Fixed Strings
1.470	16	
4.204	32	
		UCase on Variants
0.838	16	
2.994	32	
		LCase on Strings
0.879	16	
3.132	32	
		LCase on Fixed Strings
1.387	16	
4.386	32	
		LCase on Variants
0.879	16	
3.021	32	

Trim()

The Trim() function discards leading and trailing spaces from a string and returns the characters in the middle of the string. The function is faster with strings than with variants, and much slower with fixed-length strings. What's more, 32-bit operations are more than twice as fast as 16-bit operations (see table 5.16). Listings 5.50 through 5.52 show the test code used.

Listing 5.50   CodeBnch.Vbp   Testing *Trim$()* on Strings

```
BeginTime "Trim$ on Strings", printmode
For foo = 1 To 10000
    a = Trim$(b)
Next foo
EndTime
```

Listing 5.51   CodeBnch.Vbp   Testing *Trim$()* on Fixed Strings

```
BeginTime "Trim$ on Fixed Strings", printmode
For foo = 1 To 10000
    c = Trim$(e)
Next foo
EndTime
```

Listing 5.52   CodeBnch.Vbp   Testing *Trim()* on Variants

```
BeginTime "Trim on Variants", printmode
For foo = 1 To 10000
    x = Trim(y)
Next foo
EndTime
```

Table 5.16   *Trim()* by Data Type

Seconds	Bits	Activity/Graph
		Trim$() on Strings
0.462	16	
0.138	32	
		Trim$() on Fixed Strings
1.497	16	
2.335	32	
		Trim() on Variants
0.536	16	
0.206	32	

Mid()

The Mid() and Mid$() functions extract a string from within a string. You specify the source string, the starting position for the cut, and (optionally) the length of the string to be cut. If you don't supply a cut length, the function returns all characters from the starting position to the end of the string.

Listings 5.53 through 5.58 show the code used for the tests.

Listing 5.53 CodeBnch.Vbp Testing _Mid$()_ on Strings

```
BeginTime "Mid$ on Strings", printmode
For foo = 1 To 10000
    a = Mid$(b, 5, 6)
Next foo
EndTime
```

Listing 5.54 CodeBnch.Vbp Testing _Mid$()_ on Fixed Strings

```
BeginTime "Mid$ on Fixed Strings", printmode
For foo = 1 To 10000
    d = Mid$(e, 5, 6)
Next foo
EndTime
```

Listing 5.55 CodeBnch.Vbp Testing _Mid()_ on Variants

```
BeginTime "Mid on Variants", printmode
For foo = 1 To 10000
    x = Mid(y, 5, 6)
Next foo
EndTime
```

Listing 5.56 CodeBnch.Vbp Testing _Mid$()_ on Strings Without the Length Parameter

```
BeginTime "Mid$ on Strings without Length Param", printmode
For foo = 1 To 10000
    a = Mid$(b, 5)
Next foo
EndTime
```

Listing 5.57 CodeBnch.Vbp Testing *Mid$()* on Fixed Strings Without the Length Parameter

```
BeginTime "Mid$ on Fixed Strings without Length Param", printmode
For foo = 1 To 10000
    d = Mid$(e, 5)
Next foo
EndTime
```

Listing 5.58 CodeBnch.Vbp Testing *Mid()* on Variants Without the Length Parameter

```
BeginTime "Mid on Variants without Length Param", printmode
For foo = 1 To 10000
    x = Mid(y, 5)
Next foo
EndTime
```

The function works more quickly on strings than variants, and more quickly on variants than fixed-length strings (see table 5.17). 32-bit mode is substantially faster than 16-bit mode. The function is fastest if you don't supply the length to cut, although of course you then get all the characters from the cut point to the end of the string.

Table 5.17 *Mid()* and *Mid$()* by Data Type

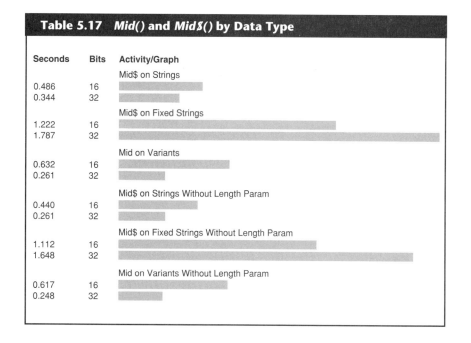

Seconds	Bits	Activity/Graph
		Mid$ on Strings
0.486	16	
0.344	32	
		Mid$ on Fixed Strings
1.222	16	
1.787	32	
		Mid on Variants
0.632	16	
0.261	32	
		Mid$ on Strings Without Length Param
0.440	16	
0.261	32	
		Mid$ on Fixed Strings Without Length Param
1.112	16	
1.648	32	
		Mid on Variants Without Length Param
0.617	16	
0.248	32	

Loops

Visual Basic has two looping constructs: `For...Next` and `Do...Loop`.
`For...Next` loops execute a specified number of times, which is normally
defined in the `For` clause. `Do...Loop` loops can be infinite or can break based
on conditionals: either `Do While` something is true, or `Do Until` something is
true.

You can also create your own looping mechanism by using the `GoTo` statement, although most programming professionals would rightly frown on
code constructs that contain `GoTo`. In optimization, however, breaking the
rules is most definitely allowed—if it's faster.

Fortunately, we don't have to worry about it, because the `GoTo` structure is no
faster than `Do...Loop`, and not nearly as fast as the `For...Next` loop. (The
exact results are seen in tables 5.18 and 5.19.) The `For...Next` structure is
almost three times as fast as the `Do...Loop` structure, mainly because
`Do...Loop` has to maintain a counter within the loop to trigger its exit logic.
A `For...Next` loop that contains an expression is about the same speed as
`Do...Loop`.

Table 5.18 Looping Constructs (16-Bit Mode)	
Seconds	**Activity/Graph**
	For...Next Loop with Integer Counter
0.206	
	For...Next Loop with Incrementing Expression
0.494	
	Do While Loop with Integer Counter
0.591	
	Do Until Loop with Integer Counter
0.577	
	Do Loop with Break on Integer Counter
0.631	
	GoTo Loop with Label and Integer Counter
0.631	
	GoTo Loop with Line Number and Integer Counter
0.632	
	For...Next Loop Step by Ten
0.206	
	Do While Loop Step by Ten
0.593	

Table 5.19	Looping Constructs (32-Bit Mode)

Seconds	Activity/Graph
	For...Next Loop with Integer Counter
0.150	
	For...Next Loop with Incrementing Expression
0.344	
	Do While Loop with Integer Counter
0.439	
	Do Until Loop with Integer Counter
0.412	
	Do Loop with Break on Integer Counter
0.455	
	GoTo Loop with Label and Integer Counter
0.466	
	GoTo Loop with Line Number and Integer Counter
0.467	
	For...Next Loop Step by Ten
0.177	
	Do While Loop Step by Ten
0.441	

The lesson here is that if you're incrementing a variable solely for the purpose of triggering the Do...Loop logic, eliminate it and use the For...Next structure without the redundant expression. Otherwise, if the incrementing is being done for a reason—that is, if the incrementing is performing real work that you would have to do in the For...Next anyway—then using For...Next will produce only a small benefit.

Also note that all these structures are quite fast. To obtain the results in tables 5.18 and 5.19, we looped 100,000 times (see listings 5.59 through 5.67). *Stepping* (incrementing the control variable by values other than one) has no significant effect on speed.

Listing 5.59   CodeBnch.Vbp   Testing a *For...Next* Loop with an Integer Counter

```
BeginTime "For...Next Loop with Integer Counter", printmode
For foo = 1 To 100000
    '
Next foo
EndTime
```

Listing 5.60 CodeBnch.Vbp   Testing a *For...Next* Loop with an Incrementing Expression

```
foobar = 0

BeginTime "For...Next Loop with Incrementing Expression", printmode
For foo = 1 To 100000
    foobar = foobar + 1
Next foo
EndTime
```

Listing 5.61 CodeBnch.Vbp   Testing a *Do While* Loop with an Integer Counter

```
BeginTime "Do While Loop with Integer Counter", printmode
foobar = 0
foo = 0
Do While foo <= 100000
    foo = foo + 1
Loop
EndTime
```

Listing 5.62 CodeBnch.Vbp   Testing a *Do Until* Loop with an Integer Counter

```
BeginTime "Do Until Loop with Integer Counter", printmode
foobar = 0
foo = 0
Do Until foo = 100000
    foo = foo + 1
Loop
EndTime
```

Listing 5.63 CodeBnch.Vbp   Testing a *Do...Loop* with a Break on an Integer Counter

```
BeginTime "Do Loop with Break on Integer Counter", printmode
foobar = 0
foo = 0
Do
    foo = foo + 1
    If foo = 100000 Then Exit Do
Loop
EndTime
```

Listing 5.64 CodeBnch.Vbp   Testing a *GoTo* Loop with a Label and Integer Counter

```
BeginTime "GoTo Loop with Label and Integer Counter", printmode
foobar = 0
foo = 0
StartHere:
    foo = foo + 1
    If foo < 100000 Then GoTo StartHere
EndTime
```

Listing 5.65 CodeBnch.Vbp   Testing a *GoTo* Loop with a Line Number and Integer Counter

```
BeginTime "GoTo Loop with Line Number and Integer Counter", _
    printmode
foobar = 0
foo = 0
100 foo = foo + 1
    If foo < 100000 Then GoTo 100
EndTime
```

Listing 5.66 CodeBnch.Vbp   Testing a *For...Next* Loop Step by 10

```
BeginTime "For...Next Loop Step by Ten", printmode
For foo = 1 To 1000000 Step 10
Next foo
EndTime
```

Listing 5.67 CodeBnch.Vbp   Testing a *Do While* Loop Step by 10

```
BeginTime "Do While Loop Step by Ten", printmode
foobar = 0
foo = 0
Do While foo <= 1000000
    foo = foo + 10
Loop
EndTime
```

II

Application Optimization

Conditionals

The heart of any computer program is logic. The heart of logic is branching, where one action is taken when a condition is true, and another is taken if the condition is false. Visual Basic has five different methods for implementing conditional logic:

- The classic structured mechanism is the `If...Then...Else` construct.

- `If...Then...ElseIf` is a modified `If...Then...Else` that allows the extension of conditions with less code.

- `Select Case` constructs are less flexible than `If...Then...Else` structures because all tests refer to the same value. However, `Select Case` constructs are easier to read and implement, particularly when many conditions apply.

- Somewhat obscure, the `Switch()` function allows you to list up to seven expressions and returns one of the expressions based on a condition expression that evaluates to a value between one and seven.

- The `Choose()` function lets you list seven conditions, each with an associated expression, and returns the first of the expressions whose condition evaluates to true.

Listings 5.68 through 5.72 show the code used to text the conditionals.

Listing 5.68 CodeBnch.Vbp Testing the *If...Else* Conditional

```
BeginTime "If Else", printmode
For foo = 1 To 10000
    If foobar = 1 Then
        h = foobar
    Else
        If foobar = 2 Then
            h = foobar
        Else
            If foobar = 3 Then
                h = foobar
            Else
                If foobar = 4 Then
                    h = foobar
                Else
                    h = 1
                End If
            End If
        End If
    End If
Next foo
EndTime
```

Listing 5.69 CodeBnch.Vbp Testing the _If...ElseIf_ Conditional

```
BeginTime "If ElseIf", printmode
For foo = 1 To 10000
    If foobar = 1 Then
        h = foobar
    ElseIf foobar = 2 Then
        h = foobar
    ElseIf foobar = 3 Then
        h = foobar
    ElseIf foobar = 4 Then
        h = foobar
    Else
        h = 1
    End If
Next foo
EndTime
```

Listing 5.70 CodeBnch.Vbp Testing the _Select Case_ Conditional

```
BeginTime "Select Case", printmode
For foo = 1 To 10000
    Select Case foobar
    Case 1
        h = foobar
    Case 2
        h = foobar
    Case 3
        h = foobar
    Case 4
        h = foobar
    Case Else
        h = 1
    End Select
Next foo
EndTime
```

Listing 5.71 CodeBnch.Vbp Testing the _Switch()_ Conditional

```
BeginTime "Switch", printmode
For foo = 1 To 10000
    h = Switch(foobar = 1, 1, foobar = 2, 2, foobar = 3, 3, _
        foobar = 4, 4, foobar > 4, 1)
Next foo
EndTime
```

II

Application Optimization

Listing 5.72 CodeBnch.Vbp Testing the *Choose()* Conditional

```
BeginTime "Choose", printmode
For foo = 1 To 10000
    h = Switch(foobar, 1, 2, 3, 4, 5)
Next foo
EndTime
```

Table 5.20 shows the results of the benchmark. In VB4, `Switch()` and `Choose()` are abysmally slow. Unless concise code is a desperate concern, they're basically not worth considering.

`If...Then...ElseIf` is the fastest construct in this test, followed closely by `Select Case` and then `If...Then...Else`. These comparisons are true in both 16- and 32-bit modes.

Table 5.20 Conditionals

Seconds	Bits	Activity/Graph
		If...Else
0.151	16	
0.165	32	
		If...ElseIf
0.124	16	
0.110	32	
		Select Case
0.137	16	
0.131	32	
		Switch
14.447	16	
5.525	32	
		Choose
10.740	16	
4.134	32	

Property Assignment and Retrieval

Until now, we've evaluated different code constructs based on manipulation of internal variables. But much of the work we do in Visual Basic consists of retrieving values from controls or setting controls to a value, because controls are our interface to the user. Control values are stored in properties. We'll examine the speed of property assignment and retrieval in many different scenarios, and with several different controls.

The code in listing 5.73 tests text controls. The code in listing 5.74 tests label controls. The code in listing 5.75 tests `Tag` property manipulation with a variety of controls.

Listing 5.73   CodeBnch.Vbp   Testing Text Controls

```
BeginTime "Text Property Assignment with Default Prop", printmode
For foo = 1 To 1000
    cntrl = a
Next foo
EndTime

BeginTime "Text Property Assignment with Explicit Prop", printmode
For foo = 1 To 1000
    cntrl.Text = a
Next foo
EndTime

BeginTime "Text Property Retrieve with Default Prop", printmode
For foo = 1 To 1000
    a = cntrl
Next foo
EndTime

BeginTime "Text Property Retrieve with Explicit Prop", printmode
For foo = 1 To 1000
    a = cntrl.Text
Next foo
EndTime
```

Listing 5.74   CodeBnch.Vbp   Testing Label Controls

```
BeginTime "Caption Property Assignment with Default Prop", _
    printmode
For foo = 1 To 1000
    ltcntrl = a
Next foo
EndTime

BeginTime "Caption Property Assignment with Explicit Prop", _
    printmode
For foo = 1 To 1000
    ltcntrl.Caption = a
Next foo
EndTime

BeginTime "Caption Property Retrieve with Default Prop", printmode
For foo = 1 To 1000
    a = ltcntrl
Next foo
EndTime
```

II

Application Optimization

Listing 5.75 CodeBnch.Vbp Testing Tag Property Manipulation with Various Controls

```
BeginTime "Caption Property Retrieve with Explicit Prop", printmode
For foo = 1 To 1000
    a = ltcntrl.Caption
Next foo
EndTime

BeginTime "Text Tag Property Assignment", printmode
For foo = 1 To 1000
    cntrl.Tag = a
Next foo
EndTime

BeginTime "Label Tag Property Assignment", printmode
For foo = 1 To 1000
    ltcntrl.Tag = a
Next foo
EndTime

BeginTime "Picture Tag Property Assignment", printmode
For foo = 1 To 1000
    pCntrl.Tag = a
Next foo
EndTime

BeginTime "Text Tag Property Retrieve", printmode
For foo = 1 To 1000
    a = cntrl.Tag
Next foo
EndTime

BeginTime "Label Tag Property Retrieve", printmode
For foo = 1 To 1000
    a = ltcntrl.Tag
Next foo
EndTime

BeginTime "Picture Tag Property Retrieve", printmode
For foo = 1 To 1000
    a = pCntrl.Tag
Next foo
EndTime
```

The first lesson, as shown in table 5.21, is that using the default property of a control implicitly is considerably faster than referencing the same property explicitly. When assigning or retrieving the Text property of a text box, the difference is as much as 30 percent. With the label control, retrieving the default caption property is more than three times faster.

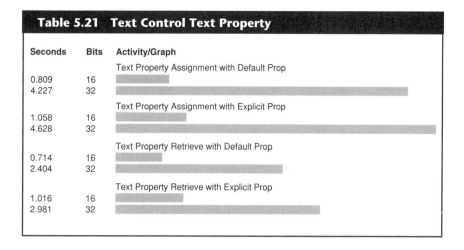

Table 5.21 Text Control Text Property

Seconds	Bits	Activity/Graph
		Text Property Assignment with Default Prop
0.809	16	
4.227	32	
		Text Property Assignment with Explicit Prop
1.058	16	
4.628	32	
		Text Property Retrieve with Default Prop
0.714	16	
2.404	32	
		Text Property Retrieve with Explicit Prop
1.016	16	
2.981	32	

Lightweight controls such as labels are much faster than more powerful heavyweight controls such as text boxes (see table 5.22). Retrieval is twice as fast, while assignment is a whopping six times faster.

When it comes to non-display properties such as the tag, however, there's no substantial difference among controls, even when comparing a heavyweight container control such as a picture box (see table 5.23).

Table 5.22 Label Control Caption Property

Seconds	Bits	Activity/Graph
		Caption Property Assignment with Default Prop
0.124	16	
0.234	32	
		Caption Property Assignment with Explicit Prop
0.302	16	
0.370	32	
		Caption Property Retrieve with Default Prop
0.384	16	
0.248	32	
		Caption Property Retrieve with Explicit Prop
0.811	16	
0.453	32	

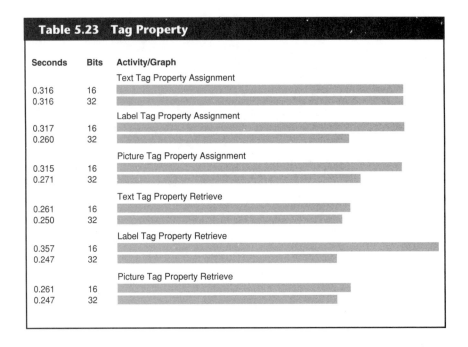

Table 5.23 Tag Property

Seconds	Bits	Activity/Graph
		Text Tag Property Assignment
0.316	16	
0.316	32	
		Label Tag Property Assignment
0.317	16	
0.260	32	
		Picture Tag Property Assignment
0.315	16	
0.271	32	
		Text Tag Property Retrieve
0.261	16	
0.250	32	
		Label Tag Property Retrieve
0.357	16	
0.247	32	
		Picture Tag Property Retrieve
0.261	16	
0.247	32	

Variable Structures

Variables in Visual Basic may not only have a type, such as string or integer, they may also be stored in different kinds of structures. In the most common sense, you simply have a variable such as X. Or variables may be grouped in more complex structures, called *types*, where type X could contain a string variable called Y and an integer called Z. Or the variables could be stored in arrays, where you might have x(0), X(1), and so on. The arrays can be dimensioned to a fixed size or may be redimensioned—even on the fly—into the exact number of elements you need for a particular purpose.

In this section, we'll determine if all variable storage structures are created equal, or if instead storing variables in one structure as opposed to another is faster. The code used for these tests is shown in listings 5.76 through 5.82.

Listing 5.76 CodeBnch.Vbp Testing Assignment to a String

```
BeginTime "Assignment to String", printmode
For foo = 1 To 50
    For foobar = 1 To 100
        b = a
    Next foobar
Next foo
EndTime
```

Listing 5.77   CodeBnch.Vbp   Testing Assignment to a Type Structure

```
BeginTime "Assignment to Type Structure", printmode
For foo = 1 To 50
    For foobar = 1 To 100
        T.TestStr = a
    Next foobar
Next foo
EndTime
```

Listing 5.78   CodeBnch.Vbp   Testing Assignment to a Fixed-Length Array

```
BeginTime "Assignment to Fixed-Length Array", printmode
For foo = 1 To 50
    For foobar = 1 To 100
        FixedArray(foobar) = a
    Next foobar
Next foo
EndTime
```

Listing 5.79   CodeBnch.Vbp   Testing Assignment to a Dynamic Array

```
BeginTime "Assignment to Dynamic Array", printmode
For foo = 1 To 50
    ReDim DynamicArray(0)
    For foobar = 1 To 100
        ReDim Preserve DynamicArray(foobar)
        DynamicArray(foobar) = a
    Next foobar
Next foo
EndTime
```

Listing 5.80   CodeBnch.Vbp   Testing Assignment to a Quasi-Dynamic Array

```
BeginTime "Assignment to Quasi-Dynamic Array", printmode
ReDim DynamicArray(100)
For foo = 1 To 50
    For foobar = 1 To 100
        DynamicArray(foobar) = a
    Next foobar
Next foo
EndTime
```

II

Application Optimization

Listing 5.81   CodeBnch.Vbp   Testing Assignment to a Dynamic Array with *UBound()*

```
BeginTime "Assignment to Dynamic Array With Ubound", printmode
For foo = 1 To 50
    ReDim DynamicArray(0)
    For foobar = 1 To 100
        ReDim Preserve DynamicArray(foobar)
        DynamicArray(UBound(DynamicArray)) = a
    Next foobar
Next foo
EndTime
```

Listing 5.82   CodeBnch.Vbp   Testing Assignment to a Fixed Array with the Next Position Pointer

```
BeginTime "Assignment to Fixed Array With Next Position Pointer", _
    printmode
For foo = 1 To 50
    For foobar = 1 To 100
        x = foobar
        FixedArray(foobar) = a
    Next foobar
Next foo
EndTime
```

In our test, we assign a value to each type of structure. No overhead is associated with type structures, compared to standalone variables. Only a small penalty is associated with fixed-length arrays. Using dynamic arrays, however, takes 10 times as long as the other methods. (The results can be seen in table 5.24.)

The penalty associated with dynamic arrays comes not from the nature of the storage itself, but from the extra time required to take advantage of this feature's resource-conserving attributes. Each time you add a value to a dynamic array, you increment the number of elements in the array by using the ReDim Preserve statement. If you redim the array only once—at the beginning of the array-loading loop—you incur only a 10 percent performance penalty.

Many programmers, however, use the dynamic array technique with the UBound() function to determine the next available array position, as seen in the benchmark shown earlier in listing 5.81. This handy technique has an elegant feel but is the most time-consuming way to store variables, short of writing them to disk. Using a next position pointer with a fixed array, as shown earlier in listing 5.82, resolves the problem and provides the same functionality with much greater speed.

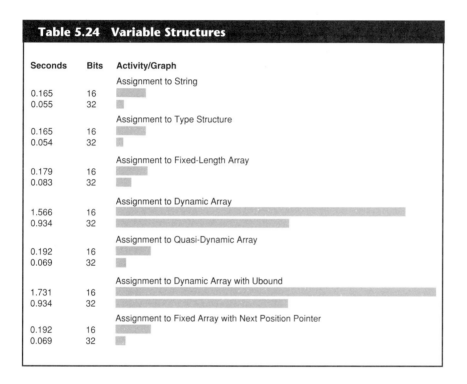

Table 5.24	Variable Structures

Seconds	Bits	Activity/Graph
		Assignment to String
0.165	16	
0.055	32	
		Assignment to Type Structure
0.165	16	
0.054	32	
		Assignment to Fixed-Length Array
0.179	16	
0.083	32	
		Assignment to Dynamic Array
1.566	16	
0.934	32	
		Assignment to Quasi-Dynamic Array
0.192	16	
0.069	32	
		Assignment to Dynamic Array with Ubound
1.731	16	
0.934	32	
		Assignment to Fixed Array with Next Position Pointer
0.192	16	
0.069	32	

Error Handling

There are two fundamental methods to handle errors in Visual Basic: by sending errors to an error handler using the declaration On Error GoTo ErrorHandler, or by passing the error with On Error Resume Next and testing for an error condition after each operation that might generate a trappable error. Listing 5.83 shows the code used for our tests.

There was no performance advantage associated with either method in our comparisons, as seen in table 5.25, but the testing did reveal one interesting aspect of VB performance: The speed with which an error is handled is determined entirely by how deep into the subroutine you are when the error occurs. In other words, an error occurring on the first line of a procedure will be handled much more quickly than the identical error occurring on the 50th line of the procedure.

Listing 5.83   CodeBnch.Vbp   Testing Error Handling

```
For foobar = 0 To 1
    If foobar = 0 Then
        On Error GoTo ErrHandle
        BeginTime "On Error Goto Handler", printmode
    Else
        On Error Resume Next
        BeginTime "On Error Resume Next", printmode
    End If
    For foo = 1 To 1000
        x = x / y
ResumeHere:
    Next foo
    EndTime
Next foobar

For foobar = 0 To 1
    If foobar = 0 Then
        On Error GoTo ErrHandle2
        BeginTime "On Error Goto Handler 2", printmode
    Else
        On Error Resume Next
        BeginTime "On Error Resume Next 2", printmode
    End If
    For foo = 1 To 1000
        x = x / y
ResumeHere2:
    Next foo
    EndTime
Next foobar

For foobar = 0 To 1
    If foobar = 0 Then
        On Error GoTo ErrHandle3
        BeginTime "On Error Goto Handler 3", printmode
    Else
        On Error Resume Next
        BeginTime "On Error Resume Next 3", printmode
    End If
    For foo = 1 To 1000
        x = x / y
ResumeHere3:
    Next foo
    EndTime
Next foobar
Exit Sub 'before hitting err handler again

ErrHandle:
    y = 0
    Resume ResumeHere
ErrHandle2:
    y = 0
    Resume ResumeHere2
ErrHandle3:
    y = 0
    Resume ResumeHere3
```

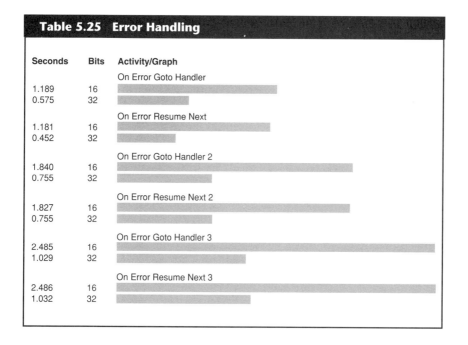

Table 5.25   Error Handling

Seconds	Bits	Activity/Graph
		On Error Goto Handler
1.189	16	
0.575	32	
		On Error Resume Next
1.181	16	
0.452	32	
		On Error Goto Handler 2
1.840	16	
0.755	32	
		On Error Resume Next 2
1.827	16	
0.755	32	
		On Error Goto Handler 3
2.485	16	
1.029	32	
		On Error Resume Next 3
2.486	16	
1.032	32	

From Here...

There's been quite a bit of raw data presented in this chapter. You should use it as a foundation for improving code craftsmanship. But remember, code craftsmanship is not a replacement for the scientific optimization process.

For related information, refer to these chapters:

- See Chapter 2, "Building an Optimization Toolkit," for more information about the timing routines used in CodeBench.

- For more information on how to use the benchmark data presented in this chapter to improve your applications, see Chapter 6, "Strategies to Improve Algorithms."

- For information on using the Windows API to supplement and replace VB's built-in functions, see Chapter 14, "Exploiting the Windows 32-Bit API."

II

Application Optimization

Chapter 6

Strategies to Improve Algorithms

Chapter 5, "Constructing Optimized VB Code," took a close look at the nuts and bolts of code craftsmanship. This chapter examines how to implement some of the lessons you learned. Here, we'll develop overall optimization strategies to apply to individual algorithms. More specifically, in the chapter we will

- Learn the best way to analyze processes to identify candidates for optimization

- Explore ways of analyzing the algorithm and applying experience and scientific tests to the various steps

- Work to tune and finally recast the algorithm through a case study

Using Shade3d as a Test Application

Throughout this chapter, we'll examine a test project called Shade3d. As you may recall, one way to speed the loading of forms in Chapter 4, "Faster Forms Architectures," was to replace label controls with text drawn on the form background by using the Print method. While this worked well, the results were somewhat plain, just like normal labels.

For headlines or headers for form sections, being able to create text with a three-dimensional appearance would be nice. Doing so involves creating the basic text and then applying highlight and shadow colors around the irregular shapes of each letter. The shades should vary depending on whether the text is raised or indented, whether heavy or light shading should be applied, and (of course) what colors are selected.

Shade3d is a simple graphical utility that takes a string of text and applies 3-D shading to it (see fig. 6.1). It's essentially a test bed for the `Emboss3d` subroutine, which hopefully will become reusable in CodeBank.

Fig. 6.1
This is the
Shade3d emboss-
ing screen.

You'll find the full code for the various iterations of Shade3d on the CD that comes with the book, in the \Chap6 directory.

Profiling to Focus Efforts

Optimization, as you know, involves a good amount of work. It can be extremely time-consuming to write and rewrite various code alternatives, devise and run scientific tests, and then apply the results. Most programmers don't have the time to optimize every piece of code in an application. And it's usually not necessary to optimize every section of code. Today's PCs are so fast that, often, inefficient code is simply unnoticeable because the system isn't bound by that code.

Bound Processes

By *bound*, I don't mean *data binding*, as in a data-bound custom control. In optimization jargon, a process is bound by the slowest component of the overall process—as in a bottleneck. If, for example, you print directly to an old dot-matrix printer, the printer most likely is the slowest component in the process, so that process is printer-bound. In other words, the speed of the printer is the limiting factor, controlling how fast the entire process could be. Determining how a process is bound, in this sense, is similar to discovering the critical path in a project-management schedule.

Suppose that you use a keystroke validation subroutine in a database-entry application. This sub would check every keystroke to determine whether it fits the criteria for the database object that will be filled by the input, so that integer fields will receive only numeric entries, and so on. This would be extremely inefficient, compared to checking the entire entry on save or even when focus leaves the control, because it would consume mass quantities of clock cycles with every keypress.

But it doesn't matter, because keystroke validation is performed only when a user types on a keyboard, and it's difficult to write validation code that's slower than even the fastest typist. So when we examine the process of entering text, you aren't code-bound, you're keyboard-bound.

On the other hand, if you display a huge bitmap image or execute some other very slow process with each keystroke, you might be disk-bound, codebound, or graphics-bound.

Identifying Optimization Targets

The first optimization task is determining where to optimize. Generally, we approach this in a top-down fashion, determining general areas of the application that seem suboptimal and narrowing the focus until the culprit or culprits are uncovered.

It's usually pretty easy to find high-level candidates for optimization, such as slow loading forms or a sluggish process. If you can't think of or find any, just ask an end user or beta tester.

The Shade3d test case essentially has three operations: form loading, text entry and sizing, and painting or embossing the shadows. You can run the original Shade3d code from the project, Shade3d.Vbp, in the \Chap6 directory on the CD. Form loading is fast, while text and font-size entry is completely invalidated and would be keyboard-bound anyway. However, applying shading takes just a bit longer than forever.

If we follow the prescriptions in Chapter 4, "Faster Forms Architectures," we might replace our labels with printed text. But why? If we had many controls on the form and the form was loading slowly, then yes, we would do it right away. But form loading isn't slow. The change might take only a few minutes, thanks to the routines in CodeBank, and the form might then load a couple of ticks faster, but for the moment, we have higher priorities. If there's time left in the development schedule later (ha!), we might make the change, but probably more for consistency than any other reason.

Many programmers have trouble learning this optimization lesson: If it ain't broke, don't fix it. Squeezing every nanosecond out of your code isn't necessary—or even helpful. As Bill Donovan, the founder of the OSS (the World War II predecessor to the CIA) used to say, "The perfect is the enemy of the good." Just as you must balance executable speed against resource usage, you must balance optimization efforts against programmer productivity and focus scarce time resources where they'll count the most.

In this case, the place they will count the most is in the emboss procedure. The first change to make is to set up a timing test for the entire process, in order to establish some baseline figures. As you can see in table 6.1, to emboss even a small text item takes almost 12 seconds (more than 26 seconds in 32-bit mode), which is a couple of orders of magnitude (100 times) greater than what you would need to use Emboss3d as a runtime subroutine.

Table 6.1		**The Speed of the Original Shade3d Routine**
Seconds	**Bits**	**Activity/Graph**
		Total Shade Operation
11.907	16	
26.599	32	

Setting Up Profile Tests

I've identified the area of the application that we're going to work on, but we're not yet ready to rework the code. We need to continue to narrow the focus a little further. Once we examine it, the embossing process actually encompasses several steps.

Listing 6.1 shows the original Shade3d code. The Emboss3d subroutine analyzes the graphic text, to find edge points, and applies shadows to make the text appear raised or lowered. Figure 6.2 shows the Shade3d screen with an emboss in progress.

Listing 6.1 Shade3d.Vbp The Original Code for the Project

```
Private Sub Command1_Click(index As Integer)

'Clear the picture control
Picture1.Picture = LoadPicture("")
'Set desired font and size
Picture1.FontSize = Text2
Picture1.Height = Picture1.TextHeight((Text1)) * 1.2
Picture1.Width = Picture1.TextWidth((Text1)) * 1.2
'Show the flat text
Picture1.Print Text1
```

```
DoEvents
'Call the shadow routine
Emboss3d Picture1, Picture2, False, True, &HC0C0C0, _
    &HFFFFFF, &H808080
End Sub

Sub Emboss3d(ctl As Control, CopyCtl As Control, Raised As _
  Integer, Heavy As Integer, Backcolor As Long, LightColor _
  As Long, DarkColor As Long)
Dim Lite As Long, Dark As Long
Dim foobar As Integer, foo As Integer
BeginTime "Emboss3d", TIME_DEBUG
'Adjust colors for shade type
If Raised Then
    Lite = LightColor
    Dark = DarkColor
Else 'Indented
    Lite = DarkColor
    Dark = LightColor
End If

'Init controls
ctl.ScaleMode = 3
ctl.AutoRedraw = True
CopyCtl.ScaleMode = 3
CopyCtl.Height = ctl.Height
CopyCtl.Width = ctl.Width
CopyCtl.Picture = ctl.Image

'Emboss the shades
foobar = 0
Do Until foobar = ctl.ScaleHeight - 1
    foobar = foobar + 1
    foo = 0
    Do Until foo = ctl.ScaleWidth - 1
        foo = foo + 1
        If CopyCtl.Point(foo, foobar) = Backcolor Then
            If Heavy Or Not (Raised) Then
                If CopyCtl.Point(foo - 1, foobar - 1) _
                  <> Backcolor Then
                    ctl.PSet (foo, foobar), Dark
                Else
                    If CopyCtl.Point(foo - 1, foobar) _
                      <> Backcolor Then
                        ctl.PSet (foo, foobar), Dark
                    End If
                End If
            End If
        Else
            If Heavy Or Raised Then
                If CopyCtl.Point(foo, foobar) <> Backcolor Then
                    If CopyCtl.Point(foo - 1, foobar) _
                      = Backcolor Then
                        ctl.PSet (foo - 1, foobar), Lite
```

(continues)

Application Optimization

II

Listing 6.1   Continued

```
                            End If
                            If CopyCtl.Point(foo, foobar - 1) _
                                = Backcolor Then
                                    ctl.PSet (foo, foobar - 1), Lite
                            End If
                        End If
                    End If
                End If
            End If
        Loop
    Loop

    'Restore the scalemode
    ctl.ScaleMode = 1
    CopyCtl.ScaleMode = 1
    EndTime

    End Sub
```

Fig. 6.2

The original
Shade3d emboss-
ing screen with
an emboss in
progress.

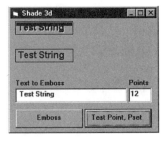

The routine first prints the string to be shaded to the target picture control
with the print method. Then it copies the text's bitmap image to the second
picture box so that it can have an unchanging image for edge finding. Last, it
applies the shading by analyzing each pixel.

A cursory glance at the code in listing 6.1 makes it pretty obvious where the
problem is going to be—in the looping structures that apply the shading. The
embossing code is not only longer than the other code sections, it's also
within a loop that will clearly iterate thousands of times. But it's worth the
effort to profile each step because you never know when you're going to run
into something unexpected. Plus, if it turned out that copying the image took
2 seconds, that might affect what we do in the shading subroutine, even
though the 2 seconds would be only a small part of the problem.

You can see how I applied profiling in Shade3d1.Vbp. Running the project
provides more detailed results, as seen in table 6.2. Things are pretty much as
you might expect: The shading code is where almost all the processing time is
being spent.

Table 6.2 Print, Copy, and Emboss Durations in Shade3d1		
Seconds	**Bits**	**Activity/Graph**
		Print Step on TestString
0.055	16	
0.673	32	
		Setup and Copy Image
0.027	16	
0.091	32	
		Emboss Step on Test String
11.838	16	
26.825	32	

Analyzing the Algorithm

As a result of the profiling test, we can now narrow the optimization focus to the Emboss3d subroutine, and even further to the shade algorithm that loops through the bitmap. The next step, then, will be to begin to analyze what parts of the algorithm are consuming all these cycles.

Breaking Algorithms into Steps

From a functional point of view, when you analyze the emboss algorithm, you can see that three types of operations could be consuming time. Looping and If...Then...Else structures are being used to judge whether each pixel forms part of an edge in the bitmap; the Point method is being used to supply color data on each pixel to the judgment structures; and the PSet method is being used to implement shading when the judgment structures determine that we're at an edge.

Testing the Steps

It's impossible to get more precise time data on the algorithm at this point because all the commands are mixed together. To determine how much time the PSet method is taking, for example, we would have to turn the timer on and off within the loop and accumulate the timings as we go along. However, the timing mechanisms in Windows (and PCs in general) aren't precise enough to measure individual instructions.

The approach to take in this kind of situation is to implement a test case, to obtain additional data. You'll find the code for a Shade3d test in the next version of the project, Shade3d2.Vbp, in the \Chap6 directory. The test case, in this example, needs to accomplish two things:

- Determine the number of times Point and PSet are called.

- Isolate the Point and PSet operations to measure how much time each requires.

The number of iterations is obtained simply by placing incrementing counters in the subroutine. Each time the judgment structures call PSet, PsetCount is incremented to PsetCount + 1. Table 6.3 shows the results of the iterations test.

Table 6.3 *Point* **and** *PSet* **Calls**	
Iterations	**Activity/Graph**
	Point Iterations
8625	
	Pset Iterations
560	

Now we know that Point is being called 15 times as often as PSet. Because PSet is being executed only 560 times, it's possible that it isn't contributing much time to the process. To measure how much time each method requires, we can construct a small piece of test code that will measure the durations (see listing 6.2). To accomplish this, we add an additional button to the form and caption it *Test Point, Pset*. Next, we create two loops that will perform the needed number of iterations of each method. Figure 6.3 shows the test in progress.

Listing 6.2   Shad3d2.Vbp   Measuring Each Method's Duration

```
Picture1.ScaleMode = 3
BeginTime "Test 600 Psets", TIME_DEBUG
For foo = 1 To 100
    For foobar = 1 To 6
        Picture1.PSet (foo, foobar), &H0&
    Next foobar
Next foo
EndTime

BeginTime "Test 10000 Points", TIME_DEBUG
```

```
For foo2 = 1 To 10
    For foo = 1 To 100
        For foobar = 1 To 10
            TestPnt = Picture1.Point(foo, foobar)
        Next foobar
    Next foo
Next foo2
EndTime
```

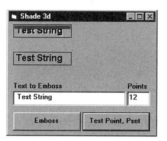

Fig. 6.3
The Shade3d
embossing screen,
running the *Point*
and *PSet* test cycle.

We can't measure the third operation, the judgment loop structures, either because they're linked too tightly to the Point method. But if three operations are in an algorithm and you can measure two of them, obtaining the time required for the third is simply a matter of subtracting the measurements you can obtain from the total time for the algorithm. By applying this technique to the test project, we can infer that the judgment and looping logic requires approximately 3.5 seconds in 16-bit mode and approximately 10 seconds in 32-bit mode (see table 6.4).

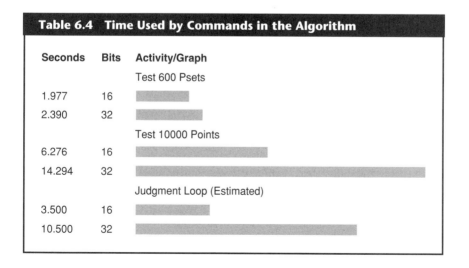

Table 6.4 Time Used by Commands in the Algorithm		
Seconds	**Bits**	**Activity/Graph**
		Test 600 Psets
1.977	16	
2.390	32	
		Test 10000 Points
6.276	16	
14.294	32	
		Judgment Loop (Estimated)
3.500	16	
10.500	32	

Tuning the Algorithm

Since the goal is to reduce the overall time of the process by at least an order of magnitude (10 times) and preferably by two orders of magnitude (100 times), you can see that we're going to have to work on all three functional components of the embossing algorithm. We've gathered enough data; now it's time to try to tune the algorithm. We'll start a new iteration of the project now, called Shade3d3, to implement our changes.

Ordinarily, tuning isn't going to produce improvements greater than an order of magnitude, if it even achieves that. By tuning, I mean applying code craftsmanship to an algorithm to improve the code without changing its fundamental structure. The analysis performed in Chapter 5, "Constructing Optimized VB Code," will help us implement faster code constructs.

Finding Redundant Code

The first tuning step will be to find redundant code. In other words, when the routine is processing in a loop, is any code being executed repeatedly that would always obtain the same result?

Property Lookups

We don't have to look far. The code in the loops refer to the picture control's ScaleWidth and ScaleHeight properties. We know from the analysis in Chapter 5, "Constructing Optimized VB Code," that property lookups are much slower than referencing a variable. So we can eliminate some processing time simply by storing the width and height parameters in variables and looping on those.

This first tuning change is implemented in Shade3d3.Vbp (on the CD in the \Chap6 directory). There will be a number of tuning changes to the Emboss3d algorithm in the Shade3d3 project. With each change, a new version of the subroutine will be added, named Emboss3dA, Emboss3dB, and so on. A command button will be added for each change, so you'll be able to duplicate with precision the effect of each improvement.

The first new subroutine, called Emboss3dA, removes the property lookups from inside the loop, placing them instead in a variable for later reference (see listing 6.3).

Listing 6.3   Shade3d3.Vbp   The *Emboss3dA* Subroutine

```
Sub Emboss3dA(ctl As Control, CopyCtl As Control, Raised As _
Integer, Heavy As Integer, Backcolor As Long, LightColor As Long, _
DarkColor As Long)
Dim Lite As Long, Dark As Long, Dummy As Long, PixCount As Long
Dim foobar As Integer, foo As Integer
Dim PsetCount As Long, PointCount As Long
Dim PicWidth As Long, PicHeight As Long
If Raised Then
    Lite = LightColor
    Dark = DarkColor
Else 'Indented
    Lite = DarkColor
    Dark = LightColor
End If

ctl.ScaleMode = 3
ctl.AutoRedraw = True
CopyCtl.ScaleMode = 3
CopyCtl.Height = ctl.Height
CopyCtl.Width = ctl.Width
CopyCtl.picture = ctl.Image
PicHeight = ctl.ScaleHeight - 1
PicWidth = ctl.ScaleWidth - 1

BeginTime "Tuned Emboss A - No Width / Height Lookup", TIME_DEBUG
foobar = 0
foobar = 0
Do Until foobar = PicHeight
    foobar = foobar + 1
    foo = 0
    Do Until foo = PicWidth
        foo = foo + 1
        If CopyCtl.Point(foo, foobar) = Backcolor Then
            If Heavy Or Not (Raised) Then
                If CopyCtl.Point(foo - 1, foobar - 1) _
                    <> Backcolor Then
                    ctl.PSet (foo, foobar), Dark
                Else
                    If CopyCtl.Point(foo - 1, foobar) _
                        <> Backcolor Then
                        ctl.PSet (foo, foobar), Dark
                    End If
                End If
            End If
        Else
            If Heavy Or Raised Then
                PointCount = PointCount + 1
                If CopyCtl.Point(foo, foobar) <> Backcolor Then
                    If CopyCtl.Point(foo - 1, foobar) _
                        = Backcolor Then
                        ctl.PSet (foo - 1, foobar), Lite
```

(continues)

Listing 6.3   Continued

```
                              End If
                              If CopyCtl.Point(foo, foobar - 1) _
                                 = Backcolor Then
                                   ctl.PSet (foo, foobar - 1), Lite
                              End If
                        End If
                  End If
            End If
      Loop
Loop
ctl.Refresh
ctl.ScaleMode = 1
CopyCtl.ScaleMode = 1
EndTime

End Sub
```

Table 6.5 shows the effect of removing the property lookups from the loop. As you can see, simply removing the lookup saved a full 1.5 seconds in 16-bit mode, and more than 3 seconds in 32-bit mode. Not a bad start!

Table 6.5   Removing *Width* and *Height* Property Lookups

Seconds	Bits	Activity/Graph
		Baseline Emboss Algorithm
11.589	16	
27.001	32	
		Tuned Emboss A - No Width / Height Lookup
10.135	16	
23.676	32	

If...Then Processing

Close examination of the code reveals that nested If...Then constructs cause whole blocks of code to be ignored, depending on whether shading is light versus dark or raised versus indented. We can eliminate these If...Then structures if we change our architecture so that we have different subs for HeavyRaised, HeavyIndented, LightRaised, and LightIndented shading.

But let's think about this. We know from the baseline analysis that the test picture has 127 by 27 pixels, or about 3,400 pixels. When we tested conditionals in Chapter 5, "Constructing Optimized VB Code," we found that 50,000 iterations of If...Then constructs took less than half a second. So we won't save significant amounts of time by making this change. But we will increase the maintenance burden, make implementation of the end product more difficult and less flexible, and be forced to spend considerable time in the implementation process creating and testing the different subroutines. The bottom line is that this change fails to balance projected benefits versus programmer productivity, even though it would save a few nanoseconds.

Testing API Alternatives

Visual Basic was designed to shield the programmer from constant use of the API in order to simplify and speed Windows programming tasks. Some Visual Basic functions and statements represent intricate combinations of API calls, while others are straight VB runtime DLL calls or code. But many have direct Windows API equivalents.

PSet and Point are two examples of this. Point provides the exact functionality of the GetPixel() GDI (Graphics Display Interface DLL) function. PSet is the equivalent of the SetPixel() GDI function.

When you find API equivalents for a command, it's always worth checking out. A direct call to the API, while less stable and more error-prone than going through the VB "wrapper," will usually be faster. Sometimes API equivalents are faster just by a bit, but sometimes you hit pay dirt and save a lot of cycles.

To test SetPixel() and GetPixel(), we add the declarations to Shade3d3.Bas and then copy the code used earlier to provide Point and PSet timings (in listing 6.2). The code is called by a command button captioned *Test Point, Pset*, as before. We had SetPixel paint red, however, to verify that the change was working. This code tests SetPixel():

```
BeginTime "Test 600 SetPixels", TIME_DEBUG
For foo = 1 To 100
    For foobar = 1 To 6
        Dummy = SetPixel(Picture1.hdc, foo, foobar, &HFF&)
    Next foobar
Next foo
Picture1.refresh
EndTime
```

While the PSet method automatically refreshes the picture control, you must add a Picture1.Refresh statement to the SetPixel() code to get the changes to display.

This code tests `GetPixel()`:

```
BeginTime "Test 10000 GetPixels", TIME_DEBUG
For foo2 = 1 To 10
    For foo = 1 To 100
        For foobar = 1 To 10
            TestPnt = GetPixel(Picture1.hdc, foo, foobar)
        Next foobar
    Next foo
Next foo2
EndTime
```

Sure enough, we saved time, as tables 6.6 and 6.7 show. In fact, we saved a lot of time. `GetPixel()` is twice as fast as `Point`, whereas `SetPixel()` is almost 10 times faster than `PSet`!

Table 6.6   _Point_ vs. _GetPixel()_

Seconds	Bits	Activity/Graph
		Test 10000 Points
5.150	16	
14.571	32	
		Test 10000 GetPixels
2.033	16	
5.150	32	

Table 6.7   _PSet_ vs. _SetPixel()_

Seconds	Bits	Activity/Graph
		Test 600 Psets
1.989	16	
2.409	32	
		Test 600 SetPixels
0.164	16	
0.426	32	

Now that we're sure that the API calls will work more quickly, we can take the plunge and change the syntax of the function throughout. When implementing an optimization change, though, be careful not to implement new inefficiencies. In the direct comparison test, for example, the `SetPixel()` call was coded like this:

```
Dummy = SetPixel(Picture1.hdc, foo, foobar, &HFF&)
```

If we implement the API call this way, we would be reintroducing a problem that we've already dealt with, because the `Picture1.Hdc` parameter value creates a property lookup within the loop. To eliminate this in the subroutine, we'll store the `Hdc` for each picture control in a variable. Note that the `Hdc` of a control can and will change regularly, so caching an `Hdc` value generally isn't a good idea. But in a tight subroutine like this, where we do nothing to cause an `Hdc` change, it's acceptable. Listing 6.4 shows the new `Emboss3dB` subroutine.

Listing 6.4   Shade3d3.Vbp   The *Emboss3dB* Subroutine

```
Sub Emboss3dB(ctl As Control, CopyCtl As Control, Raised As _
Integer, Heavy As Integer, Backcolor As Long, LightColor As Long,_
DarkColor As Long)
Dim Lite As Long, Dark As Long, Dummy As Long, PixCount As Long
Dim foobar As Integer, foo As Integer
Dim PsetCount As Long, PointCount As Long
Dim PicWidth As Long, PicHeight As Long
Dim CtlHdc As Long, CopyCtlHdc As Long
If Raised Then
    Lite = LightColor
    Dark = DarkColor
Else 'Indented
    Lite = DarkColor
    Dark = LightColor
End If

ctl.ScaleMode = 3
ctl.AutoRedraw = True
CopyCtl.ScaleMode = 3
CopyCtl.Height = ctl.Height
CopyCtl.Width = ctl.Width
CopyCtl.picture = ctl.Image
PicHeight = ctl.ScaleHeight - 1
PicWidth = ctl.ScaleWidth - 1
BeginTime "Tuned Emboss B - SetPixel and GetPixel", TIME_DEBUG
CtlHdc = ctl.hdc
CopyCtlHdc = CopyCtl.hdc
For foobar = 1 To PicHeight
    For foo = 1 To PicWidth
        If GetPixel(CopyCtlHdc, foo, foobar) = Backcolor Then
            If Heavy Or Not (Raised) Then
                If GetPixel(CopyCtlHdc, foo - 1, foobar - 1) _
```

(continues)

Listing 6.4 Continued

```
                     <> Backcolor Then
                        Dummy = SetPixel(CtlHdc, foo, foobar, Dark)
                 Else
                    If GetPixel(CopyCtlHdc, foo - 1, foobar) _
                       <> Backcolor Then
                          Dummy = SetPixel(CtlHdc, foo, foobar, Dark)
                    End If
                 End If
             End If
         Else
             If Heavy Or Raised Then
                 If GetPixel(CopyCtlHdc, foo, foobar) _
                    <> Backcolor Then
                    If GetPixel(CopyCtlHdc, foo - 1, foobar) _
                       = Backcolor Then
                          Dummy = SetPixel(CtlHdc, foo - 1, _
                                  foobar, Lite)
                    End If
                    If GetPixel(CopyCtlHdc, foo, foobar - 1) _
                       = Backcolor Then
                          Dummy = SetPixel(CtlHdc, foo, foobar _
                                  - 1, Lite)
                    End If
                 End If
             End If
         End If
     Next foo
 Next foobar
 ctl.Refresh
 ctl.ScaleMode = 1
 CopyCtl.ScaleMode = 1
 EndTime

 End Sub
```

We expected a pretty fair performance increase from this change, based mainly on the PSet versus SetPixel() statistics. But the additional improvement of caching the Hdc makes the subroutine truly fly. After this change, the time required to process the shading dropped down to half a second in 16-bit mode and 1.2 seconds in 32-bit mode (see table 6.8)! That's more than 20 times faster than the original subroutine.

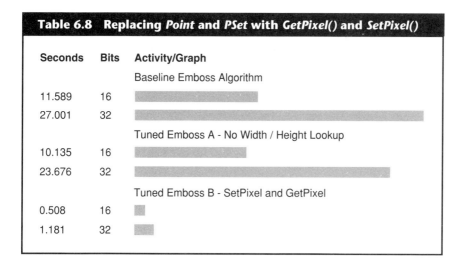

Table 6.8   Replacing *Point* and *PSet* with *GetPixel()* and *SetPixel()*

Seconds	Bits	Activity/Graph
		Baseline Emboss Algorithm
11.589	16	
27.001	32	
		Tuned Emboss A - No Width / Height Lookup
10.135	16	
23.676	32	
		Tuned Emboss B - SetPixel and GetPixel
0.508	16	
1.181	32	

Trade Memory for Speed

We can't be satisfied yet, though, because the routine still isn't quite fast enough for real-time processing. After all, the test string is just 11 characters, and the size is just 14 points. A typical headline could very well be larger in both respects. And even if it weren't, 1.2 seconds is a long time for a user to wait.

We can try one more thing. One reason that the Point (now GetPixel()) operations take so long is because the routine needs to check not only the point it's on, but also the surrounding pixels. This is how it determines whether it has found an edge and thus needs to add a shadow pixel. Thus, we end up looking at three pixels for almost every pixel in the bitmap.

One way to change this would be to make a single pass through the data, storing the results in an array of longs, and then make all future comparisons to the array rather than to the actual bitmap. The storage requirements for the array for the test case would be about 13K (3,300 bytes times 4), and the number of GetPixel() calls would be reduced by two-thirds. Listing 6.5 shows how I modified the judgment code to use the storage array rather than look at the bitmap.

Listing 6.5   Shade3d4.Bas   Using the Storage Array in the Judgment Code

```
Sub Emboss3dC(ctl As Control, CopyCtl As Control, Raised As _
Integer, Heavy As Integer, Backcolor As Long, LightColor As Long, _
DarkColor As Long)
Dim Lite As Long, Dark As Long, Dummy As Long, PixCount As Long
Dim foobar As Integer, foo As Integer
Dim PsetCount As Long, PointCount As Long
Dim PicWidth As Long, PicHeight As Long, CtlHdc As Long
If Raised Then
    Lite = LightColor
    Dark = DarkColor
Else 'Indented
    Lite = DarkColor
    Dark = LightColor
End If

ctl.ScaleMode = 3
ctl.AutoRedraw = True
CopyCtl.ScaleMode = 3
CopyCtl.Height = ctl.Height
CopyCtl.Width = ctl.Width
CopyCtl.picture = ctl.Image
PicHeight = ctl.ScaleHeight - 1
PicWidth = ctl.ScaleWidth - 1
BeginTime "Tuned Emboss C - Store Pixels to Array", TIME_DEBUG
ReDim PicPixels(PicWidth, PicHeight) As Long
CtlHdc = CopyCtl.hdc
For foobar = 0 To PicHeight
    For foo = 0 To PicWidth
        PicPixels(foo, foobar) = GetPixel(CtlHdc, foo, foobar)
    Next foo
Next foobar
CtlHdc = ctl.hdc
For foobar = 1 To PicHeight
    For foo = 1 To PicWidth
        If PicPixels(foo, foobar) = Backcolor Then
            If Heavy Or Not (Raised) Then
                If PicPixels(foo - 1, foobar - 1) <> Backcolor Then
                    Dummy = SetPixel(CtlHdc, foo, foobar, Dark)
                Else
                    If PicPixels(foo - 1, foobar) <> Backcolor Then
                        Dummy = SetPixel(CtlHdc, foo, foobar, Dark)
                    End If
                End If
            End If
        Else
            If Heavy Or Raised Then
                If PicPixels(foo, foobar) <> Backcolor Then
                    If PicPixels(foo - 1, foobar) = Backcolor Then
                        Dummy = SetPixel(CtlHdc, foo - 1, foobar, _
                        Lite)
                    End If
```

```
                            If PicPixels(foo, foobar - 1) = Backcolor Then
                                Dummy = SetPixel(CtlHdc, foo, foobar - 1, _
                                Lite)
                            End If
                        End If
                    End If
                End If
            Next foo
        Next foobar
        ctl.Refresh
        ctl.ScaleMode = 1
        CopyCtl.ScaleMode = 1
        EndTime

    End Sub
```

Sure enough, the revised algorithm provides another performance boost.
Table 6.9 shows the new test results. We've now succeeded in reducing the
amount of time from more than 13 seconds to less than 2 seconds—almost
seven times faster than the original code. Another advantage of this method
is that it eliminates the need for the second picture box, since we're now
storing the image in a memory array.

Table 6.9   Storing Bitmapped Pixel Color Values in an Array

Seconds	Bits	Activity/Graph
		Baseline Emboss Algorithm
11.589	16	
27.001	32	
		Tuned Emboss A - No Width / Height Lookup
10.135	16	
23.676	32	
		Tuned Emboss B - SetPixel and GetPixel
0.508	16	
1.181	32	
		Tuned Emboss C - Store Pixels to Array
0.329	16	
0.618	32	

II

Application Optimization

Recasting the Algorithm

Despite our best tuning efforts, we've succeeded in speeding the algorithm only seven times. That falls far short of the two orders of magnitude that we'd really like to see for this to be a real-time callable subroutine. At this point, though, we couldn't do much more tuning to speed things up. This situation will happen.

It's possible, of course, that our whole approach to the problem was wrong. We might still achieve something out of all this effort, but it's time to think about recasting the algorithm.

Recasting means, essentially, rethinking the whole approach to the problem. When we tuned the algorithm, we tried to make the initial approach satisfy the goals by improving the code. When recasting, on the other hand, we need to be more radical. There are several recasting options:

- Throw the code away and abandon the effort.

- Redefine the way in which the results are integrated into the application.

- Redefine the goal and declare victory.

- Come up with a fresh approach.

Before recasting, it's best to step back from the project and take a deep breath. Put the code away and do something else for a while. Get some perspective. Get a good night's sleep.

An inspiration may come to you, or you may have to do some thinking and research. Talk to a fellow programmer, or get on a forum and look for similar projects or algorithms. Give your mind a chance to let inspiration strike.

Abandon the Function

Sometimes, in programming as in life, what we want just isn't what we get. Maybe implementing 3-D bitmap text in Visual Basic code just isn't viable. Maybe—just maybe—the flat text really looks better after all; it's neat and clean, and nobody complains about it.

If a function isn't crucial to your application (and our case study certainly isn't) and you can't get it to work as quickly as it should, it's much better to simply give it up and move on. In this case, you'd certainly get more complaints about forms taking 15 seconds to display than compliments about your neat 3-D text.

Change Your Integration Method

On the other hand, it's sometimes possible to save your work by revising the application design to accommodate the performance of the algorithm. In the Shade3d example, perhaps you could just use the code as a design-time utility. By adding a save button to the code and using the SavePicture subroutine, you can easily incorporate the results into your project's forms as bitmap files. You could store them in Picture or Image controls, either loaded from disk at runtime or compiled in at design time. With VB4, you can even load them from a resource file, so they use no resources until they're loaded.

Change the Paradigm

Or you might get lucky and find a fresh approach that satisfies all your goals.

There's no structured way to find a new paradigm. There are a couple of hints, though, that have worked for me. Don't think about the algorithm—think about the task. Look for examples of similar functionality in other programs, and imagine how they might work. Most of all, seek a simple approach.

The rethought Emboss3d paradigm is a case in point. What if we just used the Print method to display the text several times, with slight offsets and in different colors to achieve the 3-D look, rather than look at each bit individually?

No doubt you thought this through and found the same solution as I did, and probably much more quickly, too. Listing 6.6 shows how I implemented the subroutine.

Listing 6.6   Shade3d4.Vbp   Using the *Print* Method

```
Sub Text3d(Ctl As Control, Raised As Integer, Heavy As Integer, _
Textcolor As Long, LightColor As Long, DarkColor As Long, _
Caption As String, Fontsize As String)
Dim Lite As Long, Dark As Long

If Raised Then
    Lite = LightColor
    Dark = DarkColor
Else 'Indented
    Lite = DarkColor
    Dark = LightColor
End If

Ctl.ScaleMode = 3
Ctl.Fontsize = Val(Fontsize)
Ctl.AutoRedraw = True
```

(continues)

Listing 6.6 Continued

```
Ctl.ForeColor = Lite
Ctl.CurrentX = 0
Ctl.CurrentY = 0
Ctl.Print Caption
Ctl.ForeColor = Dark
Ctl.CurrentX = 2
Ctl.CurrentY = 2
Ctl.Print Caption
Ctl.ForeColor = Textcolor
Ctl.CurrentX = 1
Ctl.CurrentY = 1
Ctl.Print Caption
End Sub
```

As it turns out, the revised method works great, as you can see in table 6.10. (Fig. 6.4 shows the form used with the revised algorithm.) And rather than take one-half to three-quarters of a second to process, it does the entire task in about a twentieth of a second! Compared to our initial effort, the revised algorithm is more than 200 times faster—which means that we not only met our initial, wildly unrealistic, goal of two orders of magnitude improvement, we exceeded it.

Table 6.10 Using the *Print* Method

Seconds	Bits	Activity/Graph
		Baseline Emboss Algorithm
11.589	16	
27.001	32	
		Tuned Emboss A - No Width / Height Lookup
10.135	16	
23.676	32	
		Tuned Emboss B - SetPixel and GetPixel
0.508	16	
1.181	32	
		Tuned Emboss C - Store Pixels to Array
0.329	16	
0.618	32	
		Text3d - Overlaid Print Method
0.055	16	
0.068	32	

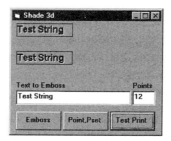

Fig. 6.4
The form for the
Shade3d4 project,
where the
algorithm was
recast.

It seems a shame to throw away the code for the `Emboss3d` subroutine,
though. And I didn't. The Shade3d routine in Visual CodeBank Limited Edition is based on our work, but acts against any picture. It's ideal for converting irregular shapes to a three-dimensional appearance, as long as you use it
in a design-time utility and save the results for later use.

From Here...

For more information on some of the topics brought up in this chapter, refer
to these chapters:

- Chapter 5, "Constructing Optimized VB Code," provides information
  on the speeds of different VB code methods.

- Chapter 12, "Optimizing Graphics and Bitmaps," explains graphics
  methods.

- Consult Chapter 14, "Exploiting the Windows 32-Bit API," for more
  details on the Windows API.

II

Application Optimization

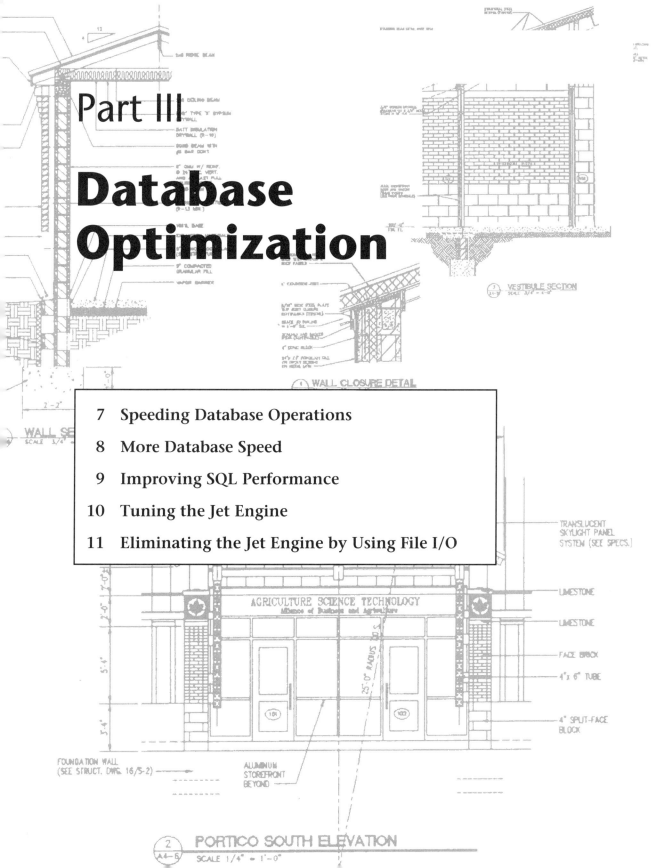

Part III

Database Optimization

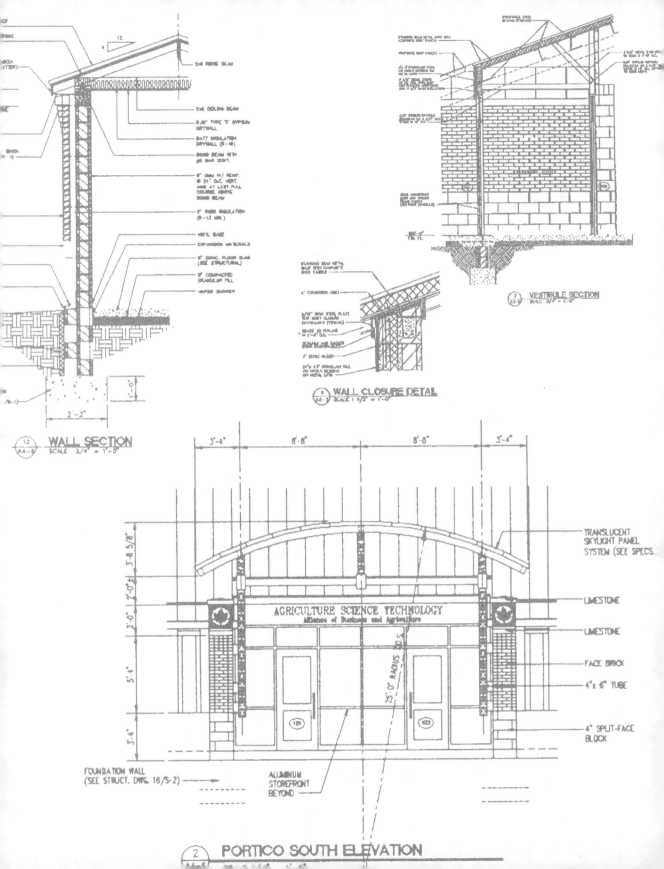

WALL SECTION
12 A4-6
SCALE 3/4" = 1'-0"

2x8 PRIME BEAM

2x6 CEILING BEAM

5/8" TYPE "X" GYPSUM
DRYWALL

BATT INSULATION
DRYWALL (R-19)

BOND BEAM WITH
#6 BAR CONT.

8" CMU W/ REINF.
@ 24" O.C. VERT.
AND AT LAST FULL
COURSE ABOVE
BOND BEAM

2" RIGID INSULATION
(R-13 MIN.)

VINYL BASE

EXPANSION MATERIALS

5" CONC. FLOOR SLAB
(SEE STRUCTURAL)

5" COMPACTED
GRANULAR FILL

VAPOR BARRIER

2'-2"
1'-0"

VESTIBULE SECTION
3
A4-6
SCALE 3/4" = 1'-0"

WALL CLOSURE DETAIL
4
A4-6
SCALE 1 1/2" = 1'-0"

PORTICO SOUTH ELEVATION
2

5'-4"   8'-8"   8'-8"   5'-4"

3'-8 5/8"

7'-0"±

2'-0"

5'-4"

3'-4"

AGRICULTURE SCIENCE TECHNOLOGY
Alliance of Business and Agriculture

25'-0" RADIUS TO S.

101   102

TRANSLUCENT
SKYLIGHT PANEL
SYSTEM (SEE SPECS.)

LIMESTONE

LIMESTONE

FACE BRICK

4" x 6" TUBE

4" SPLIT-FACE
BLOCK

FOUNDATION WALL
(SEE STRUCT. DWG. 16/S-2)

ALUMINUM
STOREFRONT
BEYOND

Chapter 7

Speeding Database Operations

The Jet (Joint Engine Technology) engine included with Visual Basic is a marvel. It contains a built-in database language, SQL (Structured Query Language). It can connect not only with native Access format files, but also with an almost infinite array of ISAM (Indexed Sequential Access Method) and ODBC (Open DataBase Connectivity) databases. It will lock pages to manage multiuser operations, has transaction logging and rollback capability, and can be linked directly to form and control objects.

But power and flexibility never comes without a price. Jet operations can be very slow. If you're not careful, the user can spend outrageous amounts of time staring at the image of an hourglass.

In the next few chapters, we'll conduct in-depth analyses of database operations with Visual Basic. This is probably one of the more important optimization topics, for several reasons.

VB developers, for one, spend a lot of time developing database-oriented programs. Some surveys have shown that up to 80 percent of VB developers use it primarily to create database programs. This is quite different from the original conception of VB as a development environment that would be handy for small utility programs. The focus on database issues has grown since Microsoft included the Jet engine (shared by Visual Basic and Access) with version 3.0.

Database optimization is even more critical because we're talking about operations that are intrinsically slow. Rather than execute internal CPU clock cycles at the speed of light, database operations cause real-world actions to have to be performed. Disks spin. Magnetic heads float to appropriate, narrowly defined physical positions to read and write. A single write action can cause a flurry of activity as fields are verified, related records are checked, table indexes are updated, and locking constructs are set and released. Masses of data can be affected. A division calculation will affect—at most—a few bytes of data. A query can return many, many megabytes worth of records.

The bottom line is that by making your data operations more efficient, you can cut the time required to perform many program tasks by seconds, or even tens of seconds.

This chapter covers the following topics:

- Optimization issues with Jet
- How and why to create realistic test sets
- Using the TestSet utility program
- How to speed loading of lookup lists
- Fastest methods to create data subsets
- Locating individual records
- Speeding up writes

Jet Engine Optimization Quirks

Jet optimization, unfortunately, isn't straightforward. One of the nicer features of the Jet engine is that it tries to optimize its response to your requests. When you ask Jet to list all left-handed widgets, for example, it parses and evaluates your expression, checks for the presence of indexes in the database that might help fulfill the request, looks at the size of the table or tables it needs, and finally arrives at a strategy that it hopes will fulfill your request quickly. Then it does the work.

While this is great, it also means that there are few easy rules of thumb to use in guiding optimization. Results can differ wildly by changes in small details of your query or database structure. You may recall the query optimization example in Chapter 2, "Building an Optimization Toolkit." The more elegant, seemingly efficient Select query, which used a Where clause to create a subset of records, performed more slowly than manually cycling through a dynaset containing all the records from the table. Far from being an unusual example, this is a typical Jet optimization problem. Jet doesn't respect a rational world view. There are no rules, because there are so many combinations and permutations that rules simply wouldn't work. Extensive, realistic testing is the only way to optimize Jet database operations.

Creating Realistic Data Test Sets

Perhaps the greatest—and most common—error that programmers make when creating and testing their code is to use small, well-crafted data test sets. These test sets are essential for testing program logic but worthless for optimization.

Let's look at a simple example. Suppose that you're creating a shipping and invoicing program for a mail-order vendor. Your code would have several tax conditions and algorithms: one for taxable in-state sales (perhaps with different rates based on city, county, or ZIP codes), one for out-of-state non-taxable orders, and one for tax-exempt customers. To test the code, you would just need a database with at least three customers.

The danger lies in using the same database that you crafted to exercise the code to optimize your data operations. Inevitably, since you're creating them manually, your test data sets will be small. Your system response will seem pretty snappy during the testing. You might even conclude that data optimization isn't necessary, or leave it until last—when it will probably be too late, due to time constraints and the volume of embedded code based on a given data access method.

The rude awakening will come when you implement the true, 20,000-record customer data set and discover that operations are a tad, uh, *slow*. The tax calculations may work perfectly, but no one will ever know, because users would rather stick with the old DOS system rather than wait three minutes to enter an order. (This is actually a true story. It happened to an acquaintance of mine, who really should have known better, since he worked for one of the leading vendors of VB add-on tools. The only way he saved his job was because he owned the place.)

The TestSet Utility

Creating relational database structures is simple with VB. You can easily add and remove indexes, fields, relations, and tables by using one of the utilities supplied with VB, including VisData and the Data Manager. However, this accomplishes only half the job. The biggest difficulty in creating a realistic database test set is generating enough test records to mirror the expected quantities in the end user's database.

The TestSet utility generates whatever quantity of semi-randomized data you may need to have to create a completely realistic data set (see fig. 7.1). You can interactively specify the database to create records for, specify the numbers of records to be added to each table, and even define a randomization mask for each field in the database to add realism.

Fig. 7.1

The main form of the TestSet utility.

You can examine the project and run TestSet by loading the TestSet.Vbp project in the \Chap7 directory on the CD-ROM provided with this book.

Selecting a Database

The first step in creating records is to select a database. You can enter the database path and name directly into the text box labeled Database Path/Name, or you can click the Browse button to open the File Open dialog box.

Ordinarily, I create two databases to act as my test cases. First, I create one with a small number of records. This dataset is used for logic testing, where I want to make sure that my algorithms work properly. I manually customize it as necessary to ensure that I have an adequate logic test. I then create another version of the same database by copying the first test set to another name, using Explorer. Then I add sufficient records to the second test set to mirror my expected usage.

I go to the trouble to create two databases because I don't want to have to process huge numbers of records to test every algorithm. On the other hand, I don't want to try optimizing my database operations on a small sample. Fortunately, TestSet allows me to easily create all the data I need.

Once you specify the database name, you can open it by clicking the Open button. The program doesn't open the database automatically, so you can have more control over the process.

Notice that a Repair button is associated with the database. I often include a Repair button on all my main forms for the implementation and debugging cycles because I find that VB, on rare occasions, will corrupt Access databases when it halts a program prematurely in design mode. Having the repair feature instantly available saves time and helps keep me from going completely nuts.

When you click the Open button, TestSet opens the database and scans the Tabledef structure of the database. This may take a few moments because TestSet counts the records in each table. The more records you have, the longer it will take. Finally, TestSet lists the tables in the left list box, followed by the number of records currently in each table.

Specifying Record Quantity

To add records to a table, double-click the desired table in the Table Name list box. A simple InputBox dialog will pop up (see fig. 7.2). Enter the number of records you want to add to the table. (This number is the additional records, not the total number of records you want to end up with.) If you want to have 2,000 records in a table and you already have 500, for example, enter **1500**. Repeat this step for each table that you want to add records to.

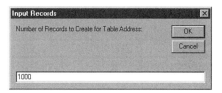

Fig. 7.2
Specifying records to add to a table.

Random Field Creation Parameters

You can perform one more step before you begin to add records; however, it's optional. TestSet by default generates random data for each field, but you may specify a randomization mask for any field (see fig. 7.3). The mask is similar to a simple format string.

Fig. 7.3
Specifying field masks in the TestSet utility.

To create a randomization mask, click a table listing in the main TestSet form (refer to fig. 7.1). The right list box fills with the field names associated with the table. If you double-click a field, an input box will pop up. Enter **#** to reserve space for a numeral, **X** to reserve an uppercase letter, or **x** for a random lowercase letter. Any other character is regarded as a literal and is duplicated exactly.

You can use the mask to make fields look more reasonable. For example, an address field will look more like an address if you use numbers followed by words, as in **#### Xxxxxxxx Xx**. A state abbreviation could be masked as **XX**. A CompanyName field might be masked as **Xxxxxx Xxxxx, Inc.**

The results will still be nonsense words, of course, and will be more heavily loaded with consonants than is typical of English, but will generally appear more pleasant and reasonable than purely random data.

Generating Records

You're now ready to generate your test data. Click Create in the main form to generate the records specified. The screen should appear as in figure 7.4.

Fig. 7.4

Generating records in the TestSet utility.

If you didn't define a mask, TestSet fills string fields completely with random uppercase letters, creates 160-character random memo fields, and fills numeric fields with a random number between 1 and 30,000.

NOTE Child fields—that is, those that are relationally linked to values in other tables—will be filled with the values in those tables. All records for tables that contain parent fields will be generated before the child tables are created. For more information on relations in Jet, see Chapter 3, "Designing Optimized Applications."

The DataBench Utility: Selecting Appropriate Data Access Objects

Now that you have a realistic test set, you can test alternative methods of data access against it with DataBench. DataBench is handy for deciding data access strategies before you begin to code, or for assessing different methods when tuning your code. Figure 7.5 shows the basic form.

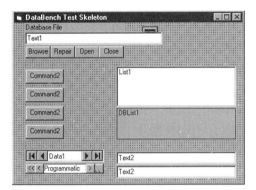

Fig. 7.5
The DataBench utility's main form.

DataBench is a code skeleton that already contains most of the overhead code and controls you may need for data access. When you want to test alternatives, simply plug the code to be benchmarked into the Command1 click event and run the utility. The next few sections test a number of examples using DataBench.

Testing Data Access Objects

Visual Basic's Professional and Enterprise editions (which are highly recommended for serious programming) provide a number of different methods for data access. Unlike the Standard Edition, which allows data operations only through data controls, the more advanced editions of Visual Basic give you direct access to your database using data access objects (DAOs). There are several types of DAO recordsets: tables, dynasets, and snapshots. Data controls are another representation of recordset objects, and can also be one of any of the recordset types.

Which all brings us to the question: Which type of recordset is the most efficient?

The tests throughout this chapter use two sample datasets: TestSet.Mdb and TestSet2.Mdb. These databases are the foundation of a simple address book or customer database. They have an identical structure, with three tables: Address, Phones, and PhoneType. Address contains a person's name, company, and address. Each address record is relationally linked to records in the Phones table in a one-to-many relationship. The Phones table is also a child of the PhoneType table, which contains a short list of valid kinds of phone numbers, such as Home, Cellular, Fax, and so on.

TestSet.Mdb is a small implementation with just 100 address records; the TestSet2.Mdb dataset, on the other hand, has 2,000 records.

Reading Records into a List Box

The first test will demonstrate the simplest data operation: reading data from one table. I modified the DataBnch.Vbp project and saved it in a project called DataBn01.Vbp, which reads 25 records in a test For...Next loop, and DataBn02.Vbp, which reads and lists all address records in the opened database.

DataBn01 displays the names from the address table in a list box, as typically would be done if you were creating a simple lookup and drill-down interface. The program tests four styles of data access: table reads, dynasets, snapshots, and a data control set to the dynaset type (see fig. 7.6).

Fig. 7.6

A loaded list of address records in DataBn02.

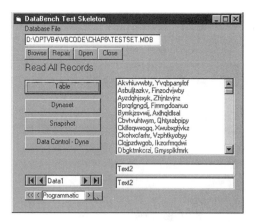

Listings 7.1 through 7.4 show the simple code I used to create equivalent operations. (Notice that the table index is set to NameKey, to get the names in alphabetical order, whereas the dynasets and snapshots must use an order by clause in the SQL statement that creates them.) Listing 7.1 shows the table option; listing 7.2 shows the code used to test dynasets; the code in listing 7.3 loads the list from a snapshot; and the code in listing 7.4 loads the list with a data control.

Listing 7.1   DataBn01.Vbp   The Table Option

```
Select Case Index 'Test Options
Case 0
    List1.Clear
    BeginTime "Load Simple List From Table", TIME_DEBUG
    'Operation
    Set MyTbl = MyDb.OpenTable("Address")
    MyTbl.Index = "NameKey"
    MyTbl.MoveFirst
    For foo = 1 To 25
        List1.AddItem MyTbl!LastName & ", " & MyTbl!Firstname
        MyTbl.MoveNext
    Next foo
    EndTime
    MyTbl.Close
    DoEvents
```

Listing 7.2   DataBn01.Vbp   Testing Dynasets

```
Case 1
    List1.Clear
    BeginTime "Load Simple List From Dynaset", TIME_DEBUG
    'Operation
    Set MyDyna = MyDb.CreateDynaset("Select * from Address order _
        by LastName, FirstName")
    MyDyna.MoveFirst
    For foo = 1 To 25
        List1.AddItem MyDyna!LastName & ", " & MyDyna!Firstname
        MyDyna.MoveNext
    Next foo
    EndTime
    MyDyna.Close
    DoEvents
```

Listing 7.3   DataBn01.Vbp   Loading the List from a Snapshot

```
Case 2
    List1.Clear
    BeginTime "Load Simple List From Snapshot", TIME_DEBUG
    'Operation
    Set MySnap = MyDb.CreateSnapshot("Select * from Address _
        order by LastName, FirstName")
    MySnap.MoveFirst
    For foo = 1 To 25
        List1.AddItem MySnap!LastName & ", " & MySnap!Firstname
        MySnap.MoveNext
    Next foo
    EndTime
    MySnap.Close
    DoEvents
```

III

Database Optimization

Listing 7.4 DataBn01.Vbp Loading the List with a Data Control

```
Case 3
    List1.Clear
    BeginTime "Load Simple List From Data Control", TIME_DEBUG
    'Operation
    Data1.DatabaseName = Text1
    Data1.RecordSource = "Address"
    Data1.Refresh
    Data1.Recordset.MoveFirst
    For foo = 1 To 25
        List1.AddItem Data1.Recordset!LastName & ", " & _
            Data1.Recordset!Firstname
        Data1.Recordset.MoveNext
    Next foo
    EndTime
End Select
```

The results shown in tables 7.1, 7.2, and 7.3 are from DataBn01 and DataBn02. (DataBn02, whose code isn't shown, is the same as DataBn01, except that it reads all the records in each table.) There are clear and dramatic differences in speed, even in such a simple test. Whether reading 25, 100, or 2,000 records, operations with the table object are significantly faster than any other method. Snapshots have a slight edge over dynasets, but when you consider that snapshots are static, read-only objects, one would expect better savings. Data controls trail the pack and are two to four times as slow as table object access.

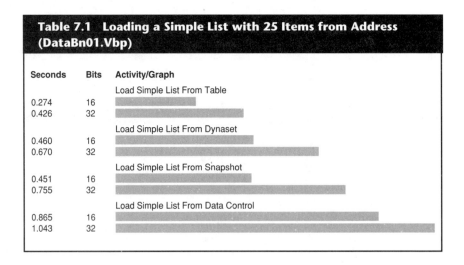

Table 7.1 Loading a Simple List with 25 Items from Address (DataBn01.Vbp)

Seconds	Bits	Activity/Graph
		Load Simple List From Table
0.274	16	
0.426	32	
		Load Simple List From Dynaset
0.460	16	
0.670	32	
		Load Simple List From Snapshot
0.451	16	
0.755	32	
		Load Simple List From Data Control
0.865	16	
1.043	32	

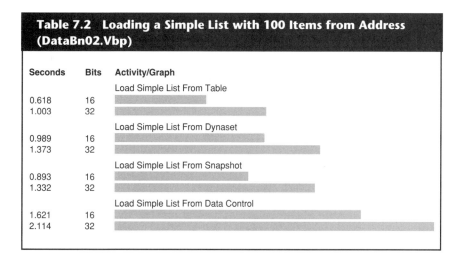

Table 7.2 Loading a Simple List with 100 Items from Address (DataBn02.Vbp)

Seconds	Bits	Activity/Graph
		Load Simple List From Table
0.618	16	
1.003	32	
		Load Simple List From Dynaset
0.989	16	
1.373	32	
		Load Simple List From Snapshot
0.893	16	
1.332	32	
		Load Simple List From Data Control
1.621	16	
2.114	32	

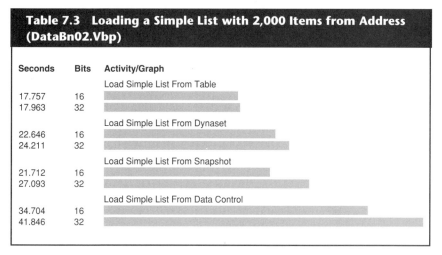

Table 7.3 Loading a Simple List with 2,000 Items from Address (DataBn02.Vbp)

Seconds	Bits	Activity/Graph
		Load Simple List From Table
17.757	16	
17.963	32	
		Load Simple List From Dynaset
22.646	16	
24.211	32	
		Load Simple List From Snapshot
21.712	16	
27.093	32	
		Load Simple List From Data Control
34.704	16	
41.846	32	

The percentage speed advantage of table access diminishes as the number of records increases. This is because a portion of the table recordset's speed advantage comes at the beginning of the operation, when Jet must parse the query and determine an optimum strategy for fulfilling it. As more records are read, this overhead is distributed more broadly. However, close analysis of the data suggests that even if the overhead per record was infinitesimally small (in a huge read operation), table access would still be faster when reading every record.

NOTE

III

Database Optimization

Reading Parent and Children into a List Box

The next example begins to exploit the power of your relational database structure. In addition to reading the parent address record, the program will read the Phones children, if any, that belong to the address record. In the list box, the parent will display, followed by a list of the children phone numbers indented beneath the parent record. For this example, we'll just examine dynasets and tables.

You can find the code for this test in DataBn03.Vbp, in the \Chap7 directory on the CD. Figure 7.7 shows the program running.

Fig. 7.7
Address and phone records in DataBn03.

Reading the data in SQL is pretty easy, of course, because of its join capability. In this case, since we want all parent records, whether or not they have a corresponding child, we use a left join, as seen in listing 7.5. However, it's not so easy to display the data the way we want to. We have a separate record for each join, so we must break them apart for the first indented child and then do control-break processing to detect and display additional phones. We also must test to see whether a child record exists at all, because we might have some parent records without child Phones records.

Listing 7.5   DataBn03.Vbp   Using a Left Join to Get All Parent Records

```
List1.Clear
BeginTime "Load Simple List From Dynaset", TIME_DEBUG
'Operation
Set MyDyna = MyDb.CreateDynaset("Select * from Address, Phones, _
     Address left join Phones on Address.RecordId _
     = Phones.AddressId Order By Address.LastName, _
     Address.FirstName")
MyDyna.MoveFirst
Do Until MyDyna.EOF
   If MyDyna!RecordId <> PrevId Then
        List1.AddItem MyDyna!LastName & ", " & MyDyna!Firstname
        PrevId = MyDyna!RecordId
```

```
            End If
            If MyDyna!PhoneType > "" Then
                List1.AddItem "            " & MyDyna!PhoneType & "-" & _
                MyDyna!PhoneNum
            End If
            MyDyna.MoveNext  .
    Loop
    EndTime
    MyDyna.Close
    DoEvents
```

Table processing is more difficult, as well. In this case, the greater challenge is in getting the data. Display is somewhat less convoluted than the SQL logic, because we don't have to worry about displaying the first record on two lines. To read the child records, we need a second table object, set to the Phones table. As we read each table record, we then Seek a matching Phones record. If we find one, we display it and then sequentially search for more matching records. This will result in extra read operations as we hit the control break, but it can't be helped because the index structures don't create identical orders in the two tables. Listing 7.6 shows the table processing code.

Listing 7.6   DataBn03.Vbp   The Table Processing Code

```
List1.Clear
BeginTime "Load Simple List From Parent & Child Tables", TIME_DEBUG
'Operation
Set MyTbl = MyDb.OpenTable("Address")
MyTbl.Index = "NameKey"
Set MyTbl2 = MyDb.OpenTable("Phones")
MyTbl2.Index = "IdKey"
MyTbl.MoveFirst
Do Until MyTbl.EOF
    List1.AddItem MyTbl!LastName & ", " & MyTbl!Firstname
    MyTbl2.Seek "=", MyTbl!RecordId
    If MyTbl2.NoMatch = False Then
        Do Until MyTbl2.EOF
            If MyTbl2!AddressId <> MyTbl!RecordId Then Exit Do
            List1.AddItem "            " & MyTbl2!PhoneType & "-" & _
                    MyTbl2!PhoneNum
            MyTbl2.MoveNext
        Loop
    End If
    MyTbl.MoveNext
Loop
EndTime
MyTbl.Close
DoEvents
```

Again, table processing emerges as a significant winner, as you can see in tables 7.4 and 7.5. Despite the additional seeks, sequential reads, and extra control-break input, access with tables is 25 percent to 30 percent faster than dynaset joins. That represents almost a full second of improvement with 100 parent records, and 9 seconds with 2,000 records!

Table 7.4 Loading a List with Parent and Child Fields (100 Parent Records)

Seconds	Bits	Activity/Graph
		Load Simple List From Parent and Child Tables
2.499	16	
3.228	32	
		Load Simple List From Joined Dynaset
3.448	16	
4.658	32	

Table 7.5 Loading a List with Parent and Child Fields (2,000 Parent Records)

Seconds	Bits	Activity/Graph
		Load Simple List From Parent and Child Table DAOs
38.234	16	
46.227	32	
		Load Simple List From Joined Dynaset
47.147	16	
52.517	32	

Finding a Subset of Records

Until now, the tests have been somewhat simplistic: get all the records and show them. Now let's take a different approach by trying to locate and display only those records where entries in the LastName field begins with the letter L. This is the kind of operation that SQL was made for.

The test project used in this section is DataBn04.Vbp, which you can find in the \Chap7 directory on the CD. Figure 7.8 shows the program running.

We can obtain a dynaset with just the records we need by simply adding a Where clause to the previous SQL expression. The code uses two comparison methods to perform this operation: one with the Like operator, and one with >= and < operators. In addition to the SQL mechanisms, we also test the FindFirst and FindNext methods on a full table dynaset. To round out the comparison, we use table seeks and sequential processing to test the speed of the operation with table DAOs. To determine the control break for the list of L names, we use the Mid$() function after reading each parent record.

Fig. 7.8
Finding and showing record subsets in DataBn04.Vbp.

The code in listing 7.7 searches for the L records using table DAOs and Seeks.

Listing 7.7   DataBn04.Vbp   Finding L Records by Using Table DAOs and Seeks

```
Select Case Index 'Test Options
Case 0
    List1.Clear
    BeginTime "Find Parent & Child Beginning with 'L' With Table _
        Seeks", TIME_DEBUG
    'Operation
    Set MyTbl = MyDb.OpenTable("Address")
    MyTbl.Index = "NameKey"
    Set MyTbl2 = MyDb.OpenTable("Phones")
    MyTbl2.Index = "IdKey"

    MyTbl.Seek ">=", "L"
    Do Until MyTbl.EOF
        List1.AddItem MyTbl!LastName & ", " & MyTbl!Firstname
        MyTbl2.Seek "=", MyTbl!RecordId
        If MyTbl2.NoMatch = False Then
            Do Until MyTbl2.EOF
                If MyTbl2!AddressId <> MyTbl!RecordId Then Exit Do
                List1.AddItem "            " & MyTbl2!PhoneType & _
                    "-" & MyTbl2!PhoneNum
                MyTbl2.MoveNext
            Loop
        End If
        MyTbl.MoveNext
        If Mid$(MyTbl!LastName, 1, 1) <> "L" Then Exit Do
    Loop
    EndTime
    MyTbl.Close
    DoEvents
```

Listing 7.8 shows how the test program retrieves the L records with a dynaset and `FindFirst`.

Listing 7.8   DataBn04.Vbp   Retrieving the L records with a Dynaset and

```
Case 1
    List1.Clear
    BeginTime "Find Parent & Child Beginning with 'L' With _
    FindFirst/Next On Dynaset", TIME_DEBUG
    'Operation
    Set MyDyna = MyDb.CreateDynaset("Select * from Address, _
        Phones, Address left join Phones on Address.RecordId = _
        Phones.AddressId Order By Address.LastName, _
        Address.FirstName ")
    MyDyna.FindFirst "Address.LastName >= 'L'"
    Do Until MyDyna.EOF
        If MyDyna!RecordId <> PrevId Then
            List1.AddItem MyDyna!LastName & ", " & MyDyna!Firstname
            PrevId = MyDyna!RecordId
        End If
        If MyDyna!PhoneType > "" Then
            List1.AddItem "            " & MyDyna!PhoneType & "-" & _
                MyDyna!PhoneNum
        End If
        MyDyna.FindNext "Address.LastName >= 'L'"
        If MyDyna.NoMatch Then Exit Do
    Loop
    EndTime
    MyDyna.Close
    DoEvents
```

Listing 7.9 shows dynaset operations with an SQL `Where` clause that uses the `Like` operator.

Listing 7.9   DataBn04.Vbp   Dynaset Operations with an SQL Clause That Uses

```
Case 2
    List1.Clear
    BeginTime "Find Parent & Child Beginning with 'L' With _
        Where/Like On Dynaset", TIME_DEBUG
    'Operation
    Set MyDyna = MyDb.CreateDynaset("Select * from Address, _
        Phones, Address left join Phones on Address.RecordId =_
        Phones.AddressId Where Address.LastName Like 'L*'_
        Order By Address.LastName, Address.FirstName ")
    MyDyna.MoveFirst
    Do Until MyDyna.EOF
        If MyDyna!RecordId <> PrevId Then
            List1.AddItem MyDyna!LastName & ", " & MyDyna!Firstname
```

```
                    PrevId = MyDyna!RecordId
                End If
                If MyDyna!PhoneType > "" Then
                    List1.AddItem "              " & MyDyna!PhoneType & "-" & _
                        MyDyna!PhoneNum
                End If
                MyDyna.MoveNext
            Loop
            EndTime
            MyDyna.Close
            DoEvents
```

Listing 7.10 shows an SQL dynaset created with a Where clause using >= and < operators.

Listing 7.10   DataBn04.Vbp   Creating an SQL Dynaset with a   Clause Using >= and <

```
        Case 3
            List1.Clear
            BeginTime "Find Parent & Child Beginning with 'L' With Where _
              >= < On Dynaset", TIME_DEBUG
            'Operation
            Set MyDyna = MyDb.CreateDynaset("Select * from Address, _
                Phones, Address left join Phones on Address.RecordId _
                = Phones.AddressId Where Address.LastName >= 'L' and _
                Address.LastName < 'M' Order By Address.LastName, _
                Address.FirstName ")
            MyDyna.MoveFirst
            Do Until MyDyna.EOF
                If MyDyna!RecordId <> PrevId Then
                    List1.AddItem MyDyna!LastName & ", " & MyDyna!Firstname
                    PrevId = MyDyna!RecordId
                End If
                If MyDyna!PhoneType > "" Then
                    List1.AddItem "              " & MyDyna!PhoneType & "-" &_
                        MyDyna!PhoneNum
                End If
                MyDyna.MoveNext
            Loop
            EndTime
            MyDyna.Close
            DoEvents
    End Select
```

The results show a significant advantage to table processing, despite the additional string manipulation code required (see tables 7.6 and 7.7). Since we can leap directly to the first L record by using a Seek, we save significant time. Table processing is 33 percent to 50 percent faster than using SQL to create dynasets with only the target records. FindFirst and FindNext are the slowest

III

Database Optimization

constructs of all, fully 10 to 20 times slower than table access! Even the relatively slow SQL operations are 5 to 15 times faster than FindFirst and FindNext.

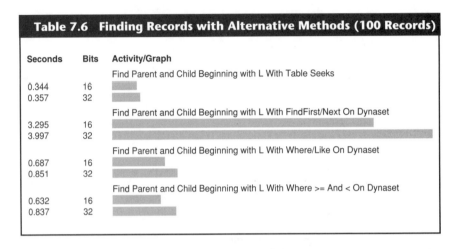

Table 7.6 Finding Records with Alternative Methods (100 Records)

Seconds	Bits	Activity/Graph
		Find Parent and Child Beginning with L With Table Seeks
0.344	16	
0.357	32	
		Find Parent and Child Beginning with L With FindFirst/Next On Dynaset
3.295	16	
3.997	32	
		Find Parent and Child Beginning with L With Where/Like On Dynaset
0.687	16	
0.851	32	
		Find Parent and Child Beginning with L With Where >= And < On Dynaset
0.632	16	
0.837	32	

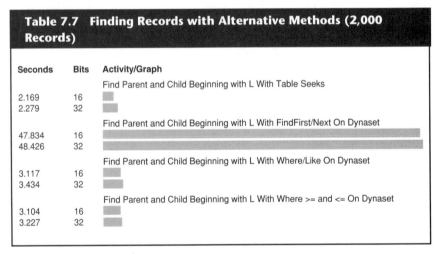

Table 7.7 Finding Records with Alternative Methods (2,000 Records)

Seconds	Bits	Activity/Graph
		Find Parent and Child Beginning with L With Table Seeks
2.169	16	
2.279	32	
		Find Parent and Child Beginning with L With FindFirst/Next On Dynaset
47.834	16	
48.426	32	
		Find Parent and Child Beginning with L With Where/Like On Dynaset
3.117	16	
3.434	32	
		Find Parent and Child Beginning with L With Where >= and <= On Dynaset
3.104	16	
3.227	32	

Finding a Specific Record for Editing

Up to this point, we've examined different alternatives for finding and displaying lists of records as the lookup table part of a drill-down database interface. We'll now examine the other side of the equation: retrieving a specific record for editing. In other words, if the user clicks the list box to edit the *Smith, Mark* record, an edit form would then pop up with text boxes or other controls for entering and modifying the various fields in the record. We would need a mechanism to respond to the user's selection of a record and retrieve the individual record requested.

You can find the test project for this section, DataBn05,Vbp, in the \Chap7 directory. Figure 7.9 shows the routine in operation.

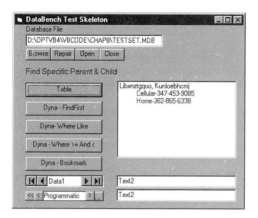

Fig. 7.9
Retrieving a specific record in DataBn05.

As always, we could use several mechanisms. Table seeks are made for pinpoint access. We could also use a FindFirst on a dynaset. Or we could construct an SQL statement whose Where conditions would retrieve the unique record that we need. This section also examines a new type of data retrieval: using a bookmark.

Bookmarks are Jet's answer to record numbers. When a table or dynaset record is first read, it's assigned a unique, random bookmark. You can store the bookmarks in a string array, linked to your display list. If you then want to make a bookmarked record current, you can set the data object's Bookmark property to the saved value.

Bookmarks aren't helpful for initial reads of data objects because they're randomly created each time you refresh a data object. However, they do provide a simple—and speedy—way to use to revisit records, as you would in a drilldown user interface.

Since we're just testing retrieval speed, not display speed, for the sake of simplicity we'll display the found record in the same list box we've been using. Listing 7.11 shows the code that finds parent and child records.

Listing 7.11 DataBn05.Vbp Finding Parent and Child Records

```
Select Case Index 'Test Options
Case 0
    List1.Clear
    BeginTime "Find Specific Parent & Child With Table Seeks", _
        TIME_DEBUG
```

(continues)

III

Database Optimization

Listing 7.11 Continued

```
'Operation
Set MyTbl = MyDb.OpenTable("Address")
MyTbl.Index = "NameKey"
Set MyTbl2 = MyDb.OpenTable("Phones")
MyTbl2.Index = "IdKey"

MyTbl.Seek ">=", "Libxnztgqoo"
List1.AddItem MyTbl!LastName & ", " & MyTbl!Firstname
MyTbl2.Seek "=", MyTbl!RecordId
If MyTbl2.NoMatch = False Then
    Do Until MyTbl2.EOF
        If MyTbl2!AddressId <> MyTbl!RecordId Then Exit Do
        List1.AddItem "           " & MyTbl2!PhoneType & "-" & _
            MyTbl2!PhoneNum
        MyTbl2.MoveNext
    Loop
End If
EndTime
MyTbl.Close
DoEvents
Case 1
    List1.Clear
    BeginTime "Find Specific Parent & Child With FindFirst/Next _
        On Dynaset", TIME_DEBUG
    'Operation
    Set MyDyna = MyDb.CreateDynaset("Select * from Address, _
        Phones, Address left join Phones on Address.RecordId_
        = Phones.AddressId Order By Address.LastName, _
        Address.FirstName ")
    MyDyna.FindFirst "Address.LastName = 'Libxnztgqoo'"
    Do Until MyDyna.EOF
        If MyDyna!RecordId <> PrevId Then
            List1.AddItem MyDyna!LastName & ", " & MyDyna!Firstname
            PrevId = MyDyna!RecordId
        End If
        If MyDyna!PhoneType > "" Then
            List1.AddItem "           " & MyDyna!PhoneType & "-" & _
            MyDyna!PhoneNum
        End If
        MyDyna.FindNext "Address.LastName = 'Libxnztgqoo'"
        If MyDyna.NoMatch Then Exit Do
    Loop
    EndTime
    MyDyna.Close
    DoEvents
Case 2
    List1.Clear
    BeginTime "Find Specific Parent & Child Where/Like On _
        Dynaset", TIME_DEBUG
    'Operation
    Set MyDyna = MyDb.CreateDynaset("Select * from Address, _
        Phones, Address left join Phones on Address.RecordId_
        = Phones.AddressId Where Address.LastName Like _
        'Libxnztgqoo*' Order By Address.LastName, _
        Address.FirstName ")
```

```
        MyDyna.MoveFirst
        Do Until MyDyna.EOF
            If MyDyna!RecordId <> PrevId Then
                List1.AddItem MyDyna!LastName & ", " & MyDyna!Firstname
                PrevId = MyDyna!RecordId
            End If
            If MyDyna!PhoneType > "" Then
                List1.AddItem "          " & MyDyna!PhoneType & "-" _
                    & MyDyna!PhoneNum
            End If
            MyDyna.MoveNext
        Loop
        EndTime
        MyDyna.Close
        DoEvents
    Case 3
        List1.Clear
        BeginTime "Find Specific Parent & Child With Where = On _
            Dynaset", TIME_DEBUG
        'Operation
        Set MyDyna = MyDb.CreateDynaset("Select * from Address, _
            Phones, Address left join Phones on Address.RecordId _
            = Phones.AddressId Where Address.LastName = _
            'Libxnztgqoo' Order By Address.LastName, _
            Address.FirstName ")
        MyDyna.MoveFirst
        Do Until MyDyna.EOF
            If MyDyna!RecordId <> PrevId Then
                List1.AddItem MyDyna!LastName & ", " & MyDyna!Firstname
                PrevId = MyDyna!RecordId
            End If
            If MyDyna!PhoneType > "" Then
                List1.AddItem "           " & MyDyna!PhoneType & "-"_
                    & MyDyna!PhoneNum
            End If
            MyDyna.MoveNext
        Loop
        EndTime
        MyDyna.Close
        DoEvents
    Case 4
        List1.Clear
        'Operation
        BeginTime "Dynaset Setup Time for Bookmark Test", TIME_DEBUG
        Set MyDyna = MyDb.CreateDynaset("Select * from Address, _
            Phones, Address left join Phones on Address.RecordId_
            = Phones.AddressId Order By Address.LastName, _
            Address.FirstName ")
        EndTime
        MyDyna.FindFirst "Address.LastName = 'Libxnztgqoo'"
        StoreBookmark = MyDyna.Bookmark
        MyDyna.MoveFirst

        BeginTime "Find Specific Parent & Child With Bookmark On _
            Dynaset", TIME_DEBUG
```

(continues)

Listing 7.11 Continued

```
        MyDyna.Bookmark = StoreBookmark
        Do Until MyDyna.EOF
            If MyDyna!RecordId <> PrevId Then
                List1.AddItem MyDyna!LastName & ", " & MyDyna!Firstname
                PrevId = MyDyna!RecordId
            End If
            If MyDyna!PhoneType > "" Then
                List1.AddItem "          " & MyDyna!PhoneType & "-" _
                    & MyDyna!PhoneNum
            End If
            MyDyna.FindNext "Address.LastName = 'Libxnztgqoo'"
            If MyDyna.NoMatch Then Exit Do
        Loop
        EndTime
        MyDyna.Close
        DoEvents
    End Select
```

The test results in tables 7.8 and 7.9 show a familiar story: table operations are substantially faster than dynaset SQL operations, whereas Finds are abysmally slow. However, bookmarks are as fast or faster than table seeks, once they are set up. If we assume that the setup is all conducted in the lookup table portion of the operation, bookmarks are a way to achieve table speeds in the edit portion of the interface, while still maintaining the flexibility of a dynaset.

Table 7.8 Finding a Specific Record with Alternative Methods (100 Records)

Seconds	Bits	Activity/Graph
		Find Specific Parent and Child With Table Seeks
0.165	16	
0.164	32	
		Find Specific Parent and Child With FindFirst/Next On Dynaset
0.947	16	
1.072	32	
		Find Specific Parent and Child With Where/Like On Dynaset
0.439	16	
0.537	32	
		Find Specific Parent and Child With Where = On Dynaset
0.440	16	
0.539	32	
		Dynaset Setup Time for Bookmark Test
0.633	16	
0.853	32	
		Find Specific Parent and Child With Bookmark On Dynaset
0.137	16	
0.123	32	

Table 7.9 Finding a Specific Record with Alternative Methods (2,000 Records)		
Seconds	**Bits**	**Activity/Graph**
		Find Specific Parent and Child With Table Seeks
0.234	16	
0.315	32	
		Find Specific Parent and Child With FindFirst/Next On Dynaset
8.391	16	
9.641	32	
		Find Specific Parent and Child With Where/Like On Dynaset
0.586	16	
0.636	32	
		Find Specific Parent and Child With Where = On Dynaset
0.559	16	
0.508	32	
		Dynaset Setup Time for Bookmark Test
7.677	16	
9.737	32	
		Find Specific Parent and Child With Bookmark On Dynaset
0.233	16	
0.515	32	

Finding Records Based on Unindexed Criteria

Usually, when we design our application and database structures, we place table indexes on the fields that we'll use for data retrieval. Indexes speed all database operations, whether the operation is conducted on a table object or a dynaset. Jet usually takes advantage of the indexes underlying SQL data, if they exist, as part of its optimization approach.

However, sometimes you'll need to retrieve records based on criteria that aren't indexed. If you provide users with an SQL search or query-by-example (QBE) mechanism, you may not even know what fields need to be indexed— at least, not with total assurance.

This section reviews what kind of performance hits we might take if we try to access records without an index, and then display a sorted list of the records. We'll obtain a list of Address records by CompanyName. Because table objects have no mechanism for sorting if an index doesn't exist, we need a second list box with its Sort property set to true for the table code to populate.

The test project is DataBn06.Vbp, located in the \Chap7 directory. Figure 7.10 shows the project.

III

Database Optimization

Fig. 7.10

Finding records on
unindexed fields
in DataBn06.

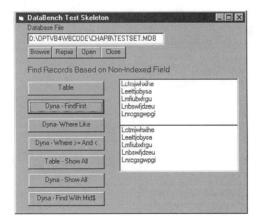

This example won't be reading the child records, so the comparisons will focus more
directly on the unindexed retrieval times. The example also displays all records, just
so we'll have a better case comparison with the simple list displays examined earlier.

Listing 7.12 shows the code that tests the speed of retrieval when finding
unindexed fields.

**Listing 7.12   DataBn06.Vbp   Testing Retrieval Speed in
Unindexed Fields**

```
Select Case Index 'Test Options
Case 0
    List2.Clear
    BeginTime "Find Table Records On Non-Indexed Field", TIME_DEBUG
    Set MyTbl = MyDb.OpenTable("Address")
    MyTbl.MoveFirst
    'Operation
    Do Until MyTbl.EOF
        If Mid$(MyTbl!CompanyName, 1, 1) = "L" Then
            List2.AddItem MyTbl!CompanyName
        End If
        MyTbl.MoveNext
    Loop
    EndTime
    MyTbl.Close
    DoEvents
Case 1
    List1.Clear
    BeginTime "Find Non-Indexed Field With FindFirst/Next On _
        Dynaset", TIME_DEBUG
    Set MyDyna = MyDb.CreateDynaset("Select * from Address Order_
        By CompanyName")
```

```
            MyDyna.FindFirst "CompanyName Like 'L*'"
            'Operation
            Do Until MyDyna.EOF
                List1.AddItem MyDyna!CompanyName
                MyDyna.FindNext "CompanyName Like 'L*'"
                If MyDyna.NoMatch Then Exit Do
            Loop
            EndTime
            MyDyna.Close
            DoEvents
        Case 2
            List1.Clear
            BeginTime "Find Non-Indexed Field With Where/Like On _
            Dynaset", TIME_DEBUG
            'Operation
            Set MyDyna = MyDb.CreateDynaset("Select * from Address Where _
                CompanyName Like 'L*' Order By CompanyName")
            MyDyna.MoveFirst
            Do Until MyDyna.EOF
                List1.AddItem MyDyna!CompanyName
                MyDyna.MoveNext
            Loop
            EndTime
            MyDyna.Close
            DoEvents
        Case 3
            List1.Clear
            BeginTime "Find Non-Indexed Field With Where = On Dynaset", _
                TIME_DEBUG
            'Operation
            Set MyDyna = MyDb.CreateDynaset("Select * from Address Where _
                CompanyName Like 'L*' Order By CompanyName")
            MyDyna.MoveFirst
            Do Until MyDyna.EOF
                List1.AddItem MyDyna!CompanyName
                MyDyna.MoveNext
            Loop
            EndTime
            MyDyna.Close
            DoEvents
        Case 4
            List2.Clear
            BeginTime "Find ALL Table Records On Non-Indexed Field", _
                TIME_DEBUG
            Set MyTbl = MyDb.OpenTable("Address")
            MyTbl.MoveFirst
            'Operation
            Do Until MyTbl.EOF
                List2.AddItem MyTbl!CompanyName
                MyTbl.MoveNext
            Loop
            EndTime
            MyTbl.Close
            DoEvents
        Case 5
            List1.Clear
```

III

Database Optimization

(continues)

Listing 7.12 Continued

```
        BeginTime "Find ALL Dynaset Records on Non-Indexed Field", _
            TIME_DEBUG
        Set MyDyna = MyDb.CreateDynaset("Select * from Address _
            Order By CompanyName")
        MyDyna.MoveFirst
        'Operation
        Do Until MyDyna.EOF
            List1.AddItem MyDyna!CompanyName
            MyDyna.MoveNext
        Loop
        EndTime
        MyDyna.Close
        DoEvents
    End Select
```

Amazingly enough, even though the table object approach has no real intelligence (being simply a brute-force sequential read of every record in the table), it's still faster! In fact, it's more than four times faster than FindFirst and three times faster than SQL using Where logic. Stranger still, displaying *every* table record is twice as fast as SQL retrieval and display of just 4 percent of the records. And strangest of all, reading and displaying every record in a sorted dynaset is faster than retrieving just the records we need. Tables 7.10 and 7.11 show the exact results.

Table 7.10 Finding L Records Based on an Unindexed Field (100 Records)

Seconds	Bits	Activity/Graph
		Find Table Records On Non-Indexed Field
0.288	16	
0.275	32	
		Find Non-Indexed Field With FindFirst/Next On Dynaset
1.198	16	
0.837	32	
		Find Non-Indexed Field With Where/Like On Dynaset
0.934	16	
0.604	32	
		Find Non-Indexed Field With Where = On Dynaset
0.906	16	
0.615	32	
		Find ALL Table Records On Non-Indexed Field
0.481	16	
0.813	32	
		Find ALL Dynaset Records On Non-Indexed Field
0.742	16	
1.195	32	

Table 7.11	Finding L Records Based on an Unindexed Field (2,000 Records)	

Seconds	Bits	Activity/Graph
		Find Table Records On Non-Indexed Field
5.301	16	
3.955	32	
		Find Non-Indexed Field With FindFirst/Next On Dynaset
26.314	16	
11.330	32	
		Find Non-Indexed Field With Where/Like On Dynaset
18.541	16	
6.190	32	
		Find Non-Indexed Field With Where = On Dynaset
17.096	16	
6.135	32	
		Find ALL Table Records On Non-Indexed Field
10.657	16	
18.581	32	
		Find ALL Dynaset Records On Non-Indexed Field
16.934	16	
21.068	32	

If you're a reasonable person, you have to wonder what the heck is going on here. How can displaying all the records be faster than just displaying the records returned by your queries? To examine this further, I created another code section, which created a simple SQL-sorted dynaset with all the records in the table, and then looked through it sequentially using the same brute-force Mid$() logic as the table processing (see listing 7.13). As you can see in table 7.12, even this technique was faster than the query-based methods.

Listing 7.13   DataBn06.Vbp   Finding Records on Unindexed Fields with   on Dynaset

```
Case 6
    List1.Clear
    BeginTime "Find Dynaset Records with Mid$", TIME_DEBUG
    Set MyDyna = MyDb.CreateDynaset("Select * from Address Order _
    By CompanyName")
    MyDyna.MoveFirst
    'Operation
    Do Until MyDyna.EOF
        If Mid$(MyDyna!CompanyName, 1, 1) = "L" Then _
          List1.AddItem MyDyna!CompanyName
        MyDyna.MoveNext
    Loop
    EndTime
    MyDyna.Close
    DoEvents
```

Table 7.12 Finding Records on Unindexed Fields with *Mid$()* on Dynaset		
Seconds	Bits	Activity/Graph
		Find Dynaset Records with Mid$ (100 Records)
0.741	16	
0.700	32	
		Find Dynaset Records with Mid$ (2000 Records)
15.670	16	
9.339	32	

The inescapable conclusion is that Jet SQL processing—although easy to implement, flexible, and very productive for the programmer—simply isn't very efficient. We'll revisit this issue in greater depth in Chapter 9, "Improving SQL Performance," and see if we can find a way to improve SQL operations.

Also, before leaping to any hard-and-fast conclusions, remember that these evaluations are on very limited test sets. While you may take some lessons from these comparisons, situations will vary. In the weird world of Jet operations, you can never be sure that a rule or lesson will apply in your situation unless you test it. This is important, so I'll repeat it:

> *You can never be sure that a rule or lesson will apply in your situation unless you test it!*

Writing Records

We've looked at a number of different data operations, but until now all we've done is read records. It's time to look at the other half of I/O: output. Writing records is inherently slower than reading them because more work is involved. Of course, if you're editing a record, you must first locate and read it. The change must then be made. Before writing the result, record pages must be locked, checked to ensure that the data hasn't been changed since the last read operation, and then written. Indexes must be updated and refreshed.

The first test case, DataBn07.Vbp, looks at a simple Read/Write cycle, where we change one unindexed field. Records are never displayed, as we're just interested in the input/output cycle for now. Figure 7.11 shows the test project running.

We'll run four tests: on a table object, on dynasets, and on two data control recordsets--one based on a table and the other based on a dynaset. Unlike the read tests, we'll isolate the setup of the data object from the timings because we're concerned only with write speed. In the case of the table and dynaset data objects, we use the `Edit` method to buffer the record for changes, make the change, and then issue an `Update` to save the record. For the data controls, we don't need to issue an `Edit`; we'll just use the `UpdateRecord` method to save changes. Listing 7.14 tests the speed of various methods of writing records.

Fig. 7.11
Writing simple records in DataBn07.Vbp.

Listing 7.14   DataBn07.Vbp   Testing the Speed of Writing Methods

```
Select Case Index 'Test Options
Case 0
    Set MyTbl = MyDb.OpenTable("Address")
    MyTbl.Index = "NameKey"
    MyTbl.MoveFirst
    BeginTime "Write Table Records", TIME_DEBUG
    'Operation
    For foo = 1 To 100
        MyTbl.Edit
        MyTbl!TestInt = 10000
        MyTbl.Update
        MyTbl.MoveNext
    Next foo
    EndTime
    MyTbl.Close
    DoEvents
Case 1
    Set MyDyna = MyDb.CreateDynaset("Select * from Address")
    MyDyna.MoveFirst
    BeginTime "Write Dynaset", TIME_DEBUG
    'Operation
```

(continues)

Listing 7.14 Continued

```
        For foo = 1 To 100
            MyDyna.Edit
            MyDyna!TestInt = 15000
            MyDyna.Update
            MyDyna.MoveNext
        Next foo
        EndTime
        MyDyna.Close
        DoEvents
    Case 2
        Data1.RecordSource = "Address"
        Data1.Refresh
        Data1.Recordset.MoveFirst
        BeginTime "Write Data Control", TIME_DEBUG
        'Operation
        For foo = 1 To 100
            Text2(0) = "20000"
            Data1.UpdateRecord
            Data1.Recordset.MoveNext
        Next foo
        EndTime
        DoEvents
    Case 3
        Data2.RecordSource = "Address"
        Data2.Recordset.Index = "NameKey"
        Data2.Refresh
        Data2.Recordset.MoveFirst
        BeginTime "Write Data Control - Table", TIME_DEBUG
        'Operation
        For foo = 1 To 100
            Text2(1) = "25000"
            Data2.UpdateRecord
            Data2.Recordset.MoveNext
        Next foo
        EndTime

        DoEvents
    End Select
```

Again, table updates are faster, but not by much, as table 7.13 shows. This time, rather than be three or four times faster, table operations are only about 20 percent faster. The real story is the terrible performance of data controls, whether dynaset- or table-based. Data control writes are two to three times slower than DAO methods.

Writing Records with Transaction Processing

The speed differences increase when we use transaction processing, which DataBn08.Vbp tests. Transaction processing delays writing changes to the database until you commit the changes with a CommitTrans. The changes then are made all at once. This not only is safer, if you're making changes that depend on each other, but it's also much faster.

Table 7.13		Writing Records (100 Records, 1 Field)
Seconds	**Bits**	**Activity/Graph**
		Write Table Records
1.606	16	
1.691	32	
		Write Dynaset
2.075	16	
2.180	32	
		Write Data Control
4.807	16	
7.527	32	
		Write Data Control--Table
4.201	16	
7.568	32	

The only danger is that you'll run out of transaction space and lose all your changes, so for safety, I generally issue a CommitTrans every hundred records or so. Because that's all this example will be processing, we simply bracket the code from DataBn07.Vbp with BeginTrans and CommitTrans. Figure 7.12 shows the new project running.

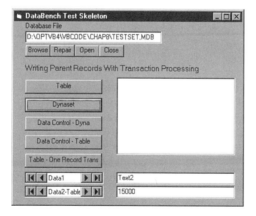

Fig. 7.12
A simple write with transaction processing in DataBn08.Vbp.

Given the nature of transaction processing, you should gain speed only if you're processing many records at a time, in a batch-type process. We'll verify that, though, by issuing a BeginTrans and CommitTrans for every record in the last test run, on a table object. Listing 7.15 shows the code that tests the speed of data writes using transaction processing.

III

Database Optimization

Listing 7.15 DataBn08.Vbp Testing Write Speed Using Transaction Processing

```
Case 0
    Set MyTbl = MyDb.OpenTable("Address")
    MyTbl.Index = "NameKey"
    MyTbl.MoveFirst
    BeginTime "Write Table Records", TIME_DEBUG
    BeginTrans
    'Operation
    For foo = 1 To 100
        MyTbl.Edit
        MyTbl!TestInt = 10000
        MyTbl.Update
        MyTbl.MoveNext
    Next foo
    CommitTrans
    EndTime
    MyTbl.Close
    DoEvents
Case 1
    Set MyDyna = MyDb.CreateDynaset("Select * from Address")
    MyDyna.MoveFirst
    BeginTime "Write Dynaset", TIME_DEBUG
    BeginTrans
    'Operation
    For foo = 1 To 100
        MyDyna.Edit
        MyDyna!TestInt = 15000
        MyDyna.Update
        MyDyna.MoveNext
    Next foo
    CommitTrans
    EndTime
    MyDyna.Close
    DoEvents
Case 2
    Data1.RecordSource = "Address"
    Data1.Refresh
    Data1.Recordset.MoveFirst
    BeginTime "Write Data Control", TIME_DEBUG
    BeginTrans
    'Operation
    For foo = 1 To 100
        Text2(0) = "20000"
        Data1.UpdateRecord
        Data1.Recordset.MoveNext
    Next foo
    CommitTrans
    EndTime

    DoEvents
```

```
  Case 3
      Data2.RecordSource = "Address"
      Data2.Recordset.Index = "NameKey"
      Data2.Refresh
      Data2.Recordset.MoveFirst
      BeginTime "Write Data Control - Table", TIME_DEBUG
      BeginTrans
      'Operation
      For foo = 1 To 100
          Text2(1) = "25000"
          Data2.UpdateRecord
          Data2.Recordset.MoveNext
      Next foo
      CommitTrans
      EndTime
      DoEvents
  Case 4
      Set MyTbl = MyDb.OpenTable("Address")
      MyTbl.Index = "NameKey"
      MyTbl.MoveFirst
      BeginTime "Write Table Records - One Transaction per Record", _
          TIME_DEBUG
      'Operation
      For foo = 1 To 100
          BeginTrans
          MyTbl.Edit
          MyTbl!TestInt = 10000
          MyTbl.Update
          CommitTrans
          MyTbl.MoveNext
      Next foo
      EndTime
      MyTbl.Close
      DoEvents
  End Select
```

Interestingly, as you can see in table 7.14, each operation is sped up by about
the same length of time—about .80 second. This means that table operations
are doubled in speed, while relatively slow data control updates are improved
by only about 20 percent. The single-record transaction experiment showed
no improvement, as expected, and in fact proved to be slower by about 40
percent than writing without transaction processing at all.

The basic survey seems to point to table DAO as generally the fastest method
of batch data operations. But are they the most productive? Are they the
fastest in real-world editing scenarios? Read on; we'll take a deeper look at
data operations issues in Chapter 8, "More Database Speed."

III

Database Optimization

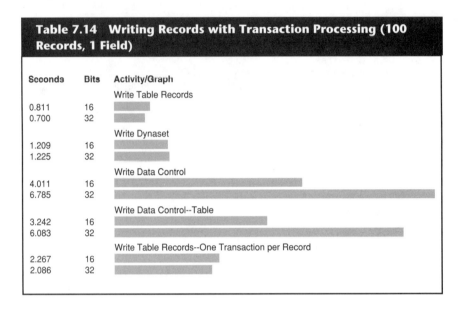

Table 7.14 Writing Records with Transaction Processing (100 Records, 1 Field)

Seconds	Bits	Activity/Graph
		Write Table Records
0.811	16	
0.700	32	
		Write Dynaset
1.209	16	
1.225	32	
		Write Data Control
4.011	16	
6.785	32	
		Write Data Control--Table
3.242	16	
6.083	32	
		Write Table Records--One Transaction per Record
2.267	16	
2.086	32	

From Here...

For more information on some of the subjects brought up in this chapter, refer to the following chapters:

- Chapter 8, "More Database Speed," looks at data operations issues.

- Chapter 9, "Improving SQL Performance," tells how to use SQL to speed up database operations.

Chapter 8

More Database Speed

More speed, power, and control! It seems as though Visual Basic programmers can never get enough. Well, why not? Chapter 7, "Speeding Database Operations," analyzed the speed of various data access objects and methods. This chapter will continue our examination of database issues and take a closer look at some of the more intricate activities we address in database programming.

This chapter examines a number of issues, including

- The best way to display data objects, whether programmatically from DAO recordsets or with data control binding

- New VB4 data control and DAO recordset types

- Advanced database store field validation rules

- Jet's support for referential integrity

Programmatic Methods vs. Bound Data Controls

We saw in Chapter 7, "Speeding Database Operations," that programmatic manipulation of data access objects—and especially table DAOs—provided greater efficiency and throughput, although at the expense of writing detailed code. The tests, however, were more oriented to processing or searching batches of records, and then displaying one or two fields in list controls.

In a sense, we were testing processing of the first half of a drill-down interface: how to display lists of records in a lookup form to the user for selection. In the following sections, we'll examine the other half of a drill-down interface: the edit screen that we would use to display, add, and change records.

Displaying Records

As you may recall from Chapter 4, "Faster Forms Architectures," much of the user's perception of your applications' speed depends on the speed in which your forms display. This is particularly true when a form displays in response to a user's action—for example, when a user clicks or double-clicks a list entry in a lookup form to call up an edit window. We can use the methods in Chapter 4 to cause the form to display quickly. But we also need to make the requested data appear quickly.

Chapter 7, "Speeding Database Operations," covered methods for speeding search and retrieval of the selected record. Now we'll look at the final step: displaying the data in controls on the edit form.

DataBn09.Vbp tests four different methods of displaying data (see fig. 8.1). Ostensibly, the simplest way to display data, of course, is by binding controls to a data control. We'll test raw data control dynaset binding. In VB3, to get a specific record, we had to do an SQL search or FindFirst, both relatively slow operations. VB4, however, allows us to create data-control recordsets from tables and use fast seeks on the resulting recordset.

Fig. 8.1

The DataBn09 project demonstrates loading records with DAOs and data controls.

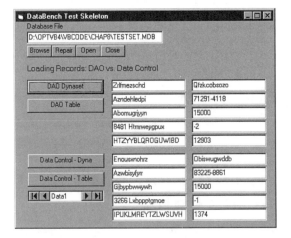

As you saw in Chapter 7, data controls are relatively slow in batch data processing. Plus, data controls and bound controls can lead to other code problems, especially with code needed for dealing with unexpected events and requirements for OCXs. Many programmers refuse to use them at all. So we'll look at the programmatic method of displaying data for dynasets and tables.

Listing 8.1 shows how DataBn09.Vbp programmatically displays dynaset records. The code in listing 8.2 displays records from a table DAO. Listing 8.3 shows the code that loads the record from a data control recordset by using binding. Finally, listing 8.4 shows the code that loads the display controls from a table-type data control recordset.

Listing 8.1   DataBn09.Vbp   Displaying Dynaset Records

```
Select Case Index 'Test Options
Case 0
    Set MyDyna = MyDb.CreateDynaset("Select * from Address _
        Order By LastName")
    MyDyna.MoveFirst
    BeginTime "Load Records Programmatically From Dynaset", _
        TIME_DEBUG
    'Operation
    For foo = 1 To 100
        Text2(0) = MyDyna!LastName
        Text2(1) = MyDyna!FirstName
        Text2(2) = MyDyna!CompanyName
        Text2(3) = MyDyna!Address1
        Text2(14) = MyDyna!Address2
        Text2(15) = MyDyna!City
        Text2(16) = MyDyna!Zip
        Text2(17) = MyDyna!TestInt
        Text2(18) = MyDyna!TestLong
        Text2(19) = MyDyna!RecordId
        DoEvents
        MyDyna.MoveNext
    Next foo
    EndTime
    MyDyna.Close
    'DoEvents
```

Listing 8.2   DataBn09.Vbp   Displaying Records from a Table DAO

```
Case 1
    Set MyTbl = MyDb.OpenRecordset("Address", dbOpenTable)
    MyTbl.Index = "NameKey"
    MyTbl.MoveFirst
    BeginTime "Load Records Programmatically From Table", _
        TIME_DEBUG
    'Operation
    For foo = 1 To 100
        Text2(0) = MyTbl!LastName
        Text2(1) = MyTbl!FirstName
        Text2(2) = MyTbl!CompanyName
        Text2(3) = MyTbl!Address1
        Text2(14) = MyTbl!Address2
```

(continues)

Listing 8.2 Continued

```
            Text2(15) = MyTbl!City
            Text2(16) = MyTbl!Zip
            Text2(17) = MyTbl!TestInt
            Text2(18) = MyTbl!TestLong
            Text2(19) = MyTbl!RecordId
            DoEvents
            MyTbl.MoveNext
        Next foo
        EndTime
        MyTbl.Close
        'DoEvents
```

Listing 8.3 DataBn09.Vbp Using Binding to Load the Record

```
    Case 2
        Data1.DatabaseName = Text1
        Data1.RecordsetType = 1
        Data1.RecordSource = "Select * from Address Order by LastName"
        Data1.Refresh
        BeginTime "Load Records From Data Control Dynaset", TIME_DEBUG
        Data1.Recordset.MoveFirst
        'Operation
        For foo = 1 To 99
            DoEvents
            Data1.Recordset.MoveNext
        Next foo
        EndTime
        'DoEvents
```

Listing 8.4 DataBn09.Vbp Loading the Controls from a Data Control Recordset

```
    Case 3
        Data1.DatabaseName = Text1
        Data1.RecordsetType = 0
        Data1.RecordSource = "Address"
        Data1.Refresh

        BeginTime "Load Records From Data Control Dynaset", TIME_DEBUG
        Data1.Recordset.MoveFirst
        'Operation
        For foo = 1 To 99
            DoEvents
            Data1.Recordset.MoveNext
        Next foo
        EndTime
        'DoEvents
End Select
```

Surprisingly enough, the performance edge that DAO objects consistently gave us in Chapter 7 disappears when displaying many fields of data (see table 8.1). This is due to the overhead of the VB code required to display each DAO field programmatically. Data controls are slow at moving through recordsets but fast at displaying them in bound controls. Dynasets are the slowest performers, but tables are only a second faster. Data control dynasets are more than a second faster than table DAOs, while data control tables speed things by yet another second.

Table 8.1   Reading and Displaying Records: Programmatic DAOs vs. Bound Data Controls (100 Records)

Seconds	Bits	Activity/Graph
		Load Records Programmatically From Dynaset
15.092	16	
24.233	32	
		Load Records Programmatically From Table
14.269	16	
22.834	32	
		Load Records From Data Control Dynaset
13.074	16	
24.883	32	
		Load Records From Data Control Table
11.893	16	
22.979	32	

However, programmers with an unalloyed dislike for data controls (including me, usually) can take heart because the statistical difference is less than 20 percent between like objects. Also, the analysis was conducted on 100 records. The real time differential when displaying a single record in an edit form is just a few hundredths of a second, which probably wouldn't even be perceivable to the end user.

However, we're taking a productivity hit with the programmatic method. As you can easily see in the preceding code listings, programmatic data editing requires a good bit of grunt code to move the data back and forth. We'll address the speed and productivity issues later in this chapter.

Displaying and Saving Records

Of course, typically users won't drill down to a specific record just to view it. They'll call the edit form to add records, or to modify one or another fields in an existing record, and then save their changes. Data controls take care of this automatically, saving the changes when the user or the program

III

Database Optimization

changes the current record. For this programmatic comparison, we'll need to add update code for each field. You can find the changed code in the DataBn10.Vbp project, in the \Chap8 directory on the CD. Figure 8.2 shows the changed project.

Fig. 8.2

The form used to benchmark displaying and saving records with DAOs and data controls in DataBn10.Vbp.

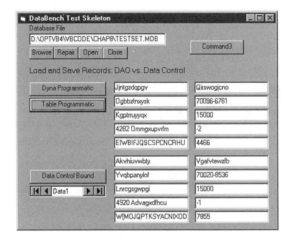

We're taking more and more of a productivity hit with the programmatic method. We've had to add additional code to the form to move the data back and forth from the DAO fields and the form's controls. It may be worth the effort, though, because we save considerable time displaying lookup records with the DAO objects in the lookup form. We also eliminate the convoluted workaround code that's typically needed to make drill-down data-control forms behave properly.

The code in listing 8.5 demonstrates the methods used in displaying and saving records from dynaset-style recordsets.

Listing 8.5 DataBn10.Vbp Displaying and Saving Records from Dynaset-Style Recordsets

```
Select Case Index 'Test Options
Case 0
    Set MyDyna = MyDb.CreateDynaset("Select * from Address _
     Order By LastName")
    MyDyna.MoveFirst
    BeginTime "Load and Save Records Programmatically From _
     Dynaset", TIME_DEBUG
    'Operation
    For foo = 1 To 100
        Text2(0) = MyDyna!LastName
```

```
        Text2(1) = MyDyna!FirstName
        Text2(2) = MyDyna!CompanyName
        Text2(3) = MyDyna!Address1
        Text2(14) = MyDyna!Address2
        Text2(15) = MyDyna!City
        Text2(16) = MyDyna!Zip
        Text2(17) = MyDyna!TestInt
        Text2(18) = MyDyna!TestLong
        Text2(19) = MyDyna!RecordId
        DoEvents
        Text2(17) = "10000"
        MyDyna.Edit
        MyDyna!LastName = Text2(0)
        MyDyna!FirstName = Text2(1)
        MyDyna!CompanyName = Text2(2)
        MyDyna!Address1 = Text2(3)
        MyDyna!Address2 = Text2(14)
        MyDyna!City = Text2(15)
        MyDyna!Zip = Text2(16)
        MyDyna!TestInt = Text2(17)
        MyDyna!TestLong = Text2(18)
        MyDyna!RecordId = Text2(19)
        MyDyna.Update
        MyDyna.MoveNext
    Next foo
    EndTime
    MyDyna.Close
    DoEvents
```

The programmatic methods used for dynasets are only slightly changed for tables, as listing 8.6 shows.

Listing 8.6   DataBn10.Vbp   Programmatic Methods for Dynasets

```
Case 2 'Table
    Set MyTbl = MyDb.OpenTable("Address")
    MyTbl.Index = "NameKey"
    MyTbl.MoveFirst
    BeginTime "Load and Save Records Programmatically From _
     Table", TIME_DEBUG
    'Operation
    For foo = 1 To 100
        Text2(0) = MyTbl!LastName
        Text2(1) = MyTbl!FirstName
        Text2(2) = MyTbl!CompanyName
        Text2(3) = MyTbl!Address1
        Text2(14) = MyTbl!Address2
        Text2(15) = MyTbl!City
        Text2(16) = MyTbl!Zip
        Text2(17) = MyTbl!TestInt
        Text2(18) = MyTbl!TestLong
        Text2(19) = MyTbl!RecordId
```

(continues)

III

Database Optimization

Listing 8.6   Continued

```
        DoEvents
        Text2(17) = "12000"
        MyTbl.Edit
        MyTbl!LastName = Text2(0)
        MyTbl!FirstName = Text2(1)
        MyTbl!CompanyName = Text2(2)
        MyTbl!Address1 = Text2(3)
        MyTbl!Address2 = Text2(14)
        MyTbl!City = Text2(15)
        MyTbl!Zip = Text2(16)
        MyTbl!TestInt = Text2(17)
        MyTbl!TestLong = Text2(18)
        MyTbl!RecordId = Text2(19)
        MyTbl.Update
        MyTbl.MoveNext
    Next foo
    EndTime
    MyTbl.Close
    DoEvents
```

The data control code is considerably more succinct, as listing 8.7 shows.

Listing 8.7   DataBn10.Vbp   The Data Control Code

```
Case 1
    Data1.DatabaseName = Text1
    Data1.RecordSource = "Select * from Address Order By LastName"
    Data1.Refresh
    BeginTime "Load and Save Records From Data Control", TIME_DEBUG
    Data1.Recordset.MoveFirst
    'Operation
    For foo = 1 To 100
        DoEvents
        Text2(10) = "11000"
        Data1.Recordset.MoveNext
    Next foo
    Data1.Recordset.MovePrevious
    DoEvents
    EndTime
    DoEvents
```

The unexpected rears its head, once again, when we run our test. As you can see in table 8.2, the table and dynaset DAOs are suddenly much slower than the data control! In fact, the data control is more than twice as fast as the dynaset DAO, and the table DAO doesn't compare much better.

This is so contrary to our previous experiences that we need to step back and examine this closely.

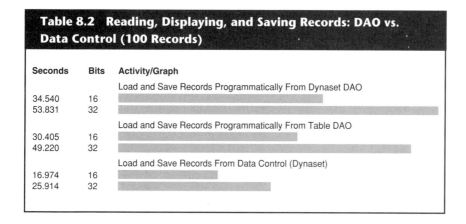

Seconds	Bits	Activity/Graph
		Load and Save Records Programmatically From Dynaset DAO
34.540	16	
53.831	32	
		Load and Save Records Programmatically From Table DAO
30.405	16	
49.220	32	
		Load and Save Records From Data Control (Dynaset)
16.974	16	
25.914	32	

Table 8.2   Reading, Displaying, and Saving Records: DAO vs. Data Control (100 Records)

Speeding Programmatic Saves

We know from previous tests that reading and displaying fields programmatically is just as fast as the same operation with a data control. So we can focus on the logic that writes our changes. We also know that in the analysis of write operations in Chapter 7, "Speeding Database Operations," DAOs were faster than data controls when we changed and saved the TestInt field, just as we're doing here.

When we compare the code, though, one difference stands out: in the DataBn10.Vbp code, we move all our data back and forth from each field to a control, rather than change just the one field in memory as we did in DataBn07.Vbp in Chapter 7. What would happen if we displayed all the fields but wrote out just the changed field? We'll check that in DataBn11.Vbp. Figure 8.3 shows the revised form.

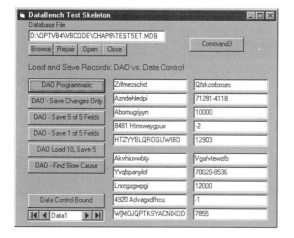

Fig. 8.3
The revised form for DataBn10.

III

Database Optimization

Listing 8.8 shows the data control routines. Listing 8.9 shows dynaset operations.

Listing 8.8 DataBn11.Vbp The Data Control Routines

```
Select Case Index 'Test Options
Case 1
    Data1.DatabaseName = Text1
    Data1.RecordSource = "Select * from Address Order By LastName"
    Data1.Refresh
    BeginTime "Load and Save Records From Data Control", TIME_DEBUG
    Data1.Recordset.MoveFirst
    'Operation
    For foo = 1 To 99
        DoEvents
        Text2(10) = "11000"
        Data1.Recordset.MoveNext
    Next foo
    Data1.UpdateRecord
    DoEvents
    EndTime
    DoEvents
```

Listing 8.9 DataBn11.Vbp Dynaset Operations

```
Case 2
    Set MyDyna = MyDb.CreateDynaset("Select * from Address Order _
    By LastName")
    MyDyna.MoveFirst
    BeginTime "Load and Save Records Programmatically - Just Save _
    Changed Fields", TIME_DEBUG
    'Operation
    For foo = 1 To 100
        Text2(0) = MyDyna!LastName
        Text2(1) = MyDyna!FirstName
        Text2(2) = MyDyna!CompanyName
        Text2(3) = MyDyna!Address1
        Text2(14) = MyDyna!Address2
        Text2(15) = MyDyna!City
        Text2(16) = MyDyna!Zip
        Text2(17) = MyDyna!TestInt
        Text2(18) = MyDyna!TestLong
        Text2(19) = MyDyna!RecordId
        DoEvents
        Text2(17) = "12000"
        MyDyna.Edit
        If MyDyna!LastName <> Text2(0) Then MyDyna!LastName _
        = Text2(0)
        If MyDyna!FirstName <> Text2(1) Then MyDyna!FirstName _
        = Text2(1)
```

```
        If MyDyna!CompanyName <> Text2(2) Then MyDyna!CompanyName _
          = Text2(2)
        If MyDyna!Address1 <> Text2(3) Then MyDyna!Address1 _
          = Text2(3)
        If MyDyna!Address2 <> Text2(14) Then MyDyna!Address2 _
          = Text2(14)
        If MyDyna!City <> Text2(15) Then MyDyna!City = Text2(15)
        If MyDyna!Zip <> Text2(16) Then MyDyna!Zip = Text2(16)
        If MyDyna!TestInt <> Text2(17) Then MyDyna!TestInt _
          = Text2(17)
        If MyDyna!TestLong <> Text2(18) Then MyDyna!TestLong _
          = Text2(18)
        If MyDyna!RecordId <> Text2(19) Then MyDyna!RecordId _
          = Text2(19)
        MyDyna.Update
        MyDyna.MoveNext
    Next foo
    EndTime
    MyDyna.Close
    DoEvents
```

Sure enough, that did it. The dynaset and data control are now roughly equivalent in speed, as you can see in table 8.3.

Table 8.3 Reading, Displaying, and Saving Records: Write Just One DAO Field (100 Records)		
Seconds	**Bits**	**Activity/Graph**
		Load and Save Records Programmatically (Just Save Changed Fields)
17.523	16	
34.178	32	
		Load and Save Records From Data Control
16.659	16	
30.737	32	

This test has some startling implications. When we save a record, Jet saves only the fields that we've touched. It doesn't check for changes, but rather looks only at whether an assignment of any kind has been made—even if the data is the same before and after the save. A more interesting inference is that when Jet reads or writes a record, it actually must perform a number of input/output operations for each field in the record, and some kind of internal transaction logging must be in place to make sure that all required changes have been made to the record.

III

Database Optimization

DAO Saves and Field Touching

Given the flexible nature of Jet databases, with variable-length fields, multitable joined dynasets, and record subsets, this kind of field-by-field architecture makes sense. And it's an architecture that, in many cases, we can exploit in our optimization efforts. But let's test these assumptions further to make sure that we're on the right track.

We saw a real difference between saving one field and saving 10 fields programmatically. If our assumptions are right and field "touching" is the key to I/O speed, then if we save five of our fields, we should get a time roughly equal between our two previous tests. In the following code segment, we'll test this by adding another button to DataBn11.Vbp. The button will load 10 fields but then save just five of them (see listing 8.10). Since we don't use If...Then constructs in this code, we'll also create code that saves just TestInt so that we can compare apples to apples (see listing 8.11).

Listing 8.10   DataBn11.Vbp   Loading 10 Fields and Saving Five

```
Set MyDyna = MyDb.CreateDynaset("Select * from Address Order _
    By LastName")
MyDyna.MoveFirst
BeginTime "Load 10 Fields, Save 5 From Dynaset", TIME_DEBUG
'Operation
For foo = 1 To 100
    Text2(0) = MyDyna!LastName
    Text2(1) = MyDyna!FirstName
    Text2(2) = MyDyna!CompanyName
    Text2(3) = MyDyna!Address1
    Text2(14) = MyDyna!Address2
    Text2(15) = MyDyna!City
    Text2(16) = MyDyna!Zip
    Text2(17) = MyDyna!TestInt
    Text2(18) = MyDyna!TestLong
    Text2(19) = MyDyna!RecordId
    DoEvents
    Text2(17) = "15000"
    MyDyna.Edit
    MyDyna!LastName = Text2(0)
    MyDyna!FirstName = Text2(1)
    MyDyna!Address2 = Text2(14)
    MyDyna!TestInt = Text2(17)
    MyDyna!TestLong = Text2(18)
    MyDyna.Update
    MyDyna.MoveNext
Next foo
EndTime
MyDyna.Close
DoEvents
```

Listing 8.11   DataBn11.Vbp   Testing the Speed of the Dynaset When Writing One Field

```
Set MyDyna = MyDb.CreateDynaset("Select * from Address Order _
    By LastName")
MyDyna.MoveFirst
BeginTime "Load 10 Fields, Save 1 From Dynaset", TIME_DEBUG
'Operation
For foo = 1 To 100
    Text2(0) = MyDyna!LastName
    Text2(1) = MyDyna!FirstName
    Text2(2) = MyDyna!CompanyName
    Text2(3) = MyDyna!Address1
    Text2(14) = MyDyna!Address2
    Text2(15) = MyDyna!City
    Text2(16) = MyDyna!Zip
    Text2(17) = MyDyna!TestInt
    Text2(18) = MyDyna!TestLong
    Text2(19) = MyDyna!RecordId
    DoEvents
    Text2(17) = "15000"
    MyDyna.Edit
MyDyna!TestInt = Text2(17)
MyDyna.Update
    MyDyna.MoveNext
Next foo
EndTime
MyDyna.Close
DoEvents
```

Table 8.4 shows that the five-record save trial is substantially faster, so there is indeed a relationship between the number of fields "touched" and the amount of time required for updates. The only problem is that it seems to save too much time, more than it should if we had a complete understanding of the cause of the problem. If there was a straight-line relationship between the number of fields touched and time required, the "Load 10, Save 5" test should have taken about 26 to 27 seconds. Yet it required only 21. So something additional is happening. We'll need more tests.

Too Fast

Now let's look at the situation from another direction. What happens if we just load five fields, and then save all five or just one? Do we maintain a straight-line relationship, or will we find a point when the process starts accelerating?

The code in listing 8.12 loads and saves five dynaset fields. Listing 8.13 shows the code that saves just one dynaset field.

III

Database Optimization

Table 8.4 Loading and Saving Records: Write 10, 5, and 1 DAO Field(s) (100 Records)

Seconds	Bits	Activity/Graph
		Load and Save Records Programmatically From Dynaset, 10 of 10 Fields
35.991	16	
55.580	32	
		Load 10 Fields, Save 5 From Dynaset
21.082	16	
36.174	32	
		Load 10 Fields, Save 1 From Dynaset
17.194	16	
26.465	32	

Listing 8.12 DataBn11.Vbp Loading and Saving Five Fields

```
Case 3
    Set MyDyna = MyDb.CreateDynaset("Select * from Address Order _
    By LastName")
    MyDyna.MoveFirst
    BeginTime "Load and Save 5 of 5 Fields Programmatically From _
    Dynaset", TIME_DEBUG
    'Operation
    For foo = 1 To 100
        Text2(0) = MyDyna!LastName
        Text2(1) = MyDyna!FirstName
        Text2(2) = MyDyna!CompanyName
        Text2(17) = MyDyna!TestInt
        Text2(18) = MyDyna!TestLong
        DoEvents
        Text2(17) = "13000"
        MyDyna.Edit
        MyDyna!LastName = Text2(0)
        MyDyna!FirstName = Text2(1)
        MyDyna!CompanyName = Text2(2)
        MyDyna!TestInt = Text2(17)
        MyDyna!TestLong = Text2(18)
        MyDyna.Update
        MyDyna.MoveNext
    Next foo
    EndTime
    MyDyna.Close
    DoEvents
```

Listing 8.13   DataBn11.Vbp   Saving Just One Field

```
Case 4
    Set MyDyna = MyDb.CreateDynaset("Select * from Address Order _
    By LastName")
    MyDyna.MoveFirst
    BeginTime "Load and Save 1 of 5 Fields Programmatically _
    - Just Save Changed Fields", TIME_DEBUG
    'Operation
    For foo = 1 To 100
        Text2(0) = MyDyna!LastName
        Text2(1) = MyDyna!FirstName
        Text2(2) = MyDyna!CompanyName
        Text2(17) = MyDyna!TestInt
        Text2(18) = MyDyna!TestLong
        DoEvents
        Text2(17) = "14000"
        MyDyna.Edit
        If MyDyna!LastName <> Text2(0) Then MyDyna!LastName _
        = Text2(0)
        If MyDyna!FirstName <> Text2(1) Then MyDyna!FirstName _
        = Text2(1)
        If MyDyna!CompanyName <> Text2(2) Then MyDyna!CompanyName _
        = Text2(2)
        If MyDyna!TestInt <> Text2(17) Then MyDyna!TestInt _
        = Text2(17)
        If MyDyna!TestLong <> Text2(18) Then MyDyna!TestLong _
        = Text2(18)
        MyDyna.Update
        MyDyna.MoveNext
    Next foo
    EndTime
    MyDyna.Close
    DoEvents
```

The test results show that loading and saving five fields preserves the straight-line relationship (see table 8.5). This actually is very helpful optimization information because it implies that if we want faster form display, we might want to use more child forms. Another strategy could be to load fields that are hidden in inactive tabbed containers only when they're displayed.

Table 8.5   Loading and Saving Records: Load Five, Then Write Five Fields or One (100 Records)

Seconds	Bits	Activity/Graph
		Load and Save 5 of 5 Fields Programmatically From Dynaset
13.294	16	
23.827	32	
		Load and Save 1 of 5 Fields Programmatically (Save Changed Fields)
10.904	16	
18.348	32	

Basic Research

But it doesn't solve our immediate problem, which is why saving 10 fields is so much slower than expected. We have, at this point, no idea what's causing the slowdown. So there's no hypothesis to test.

When you face this kind of optimization problem, you need to acquire some raw data that—let's hope—leads you to a theory. In the next test cycle, we'll add code to DataBn11.Vbp that will chart the time required to save each field (see listing 8.14). We'll always randomize and save TestInt, just to make sure that there's really a changed field in the data. And then we'll see whether the data tells us anything.

Listing 8.14   DataBn11.Vbp   Testing the Time Needed to Save Each Field

```
Case 6 ' Find Slow Field
    Set MyDyna = MyDb.CreateDynaset("Select * from Address Order _
    By LastName")
    Randomize
    'Operation
    For foobar = 1 To 9
        MyDyna.MoveFirst
        BeginTime "Find Slow Field: Case " & Format$(foobar), _
        TIME_DEBUG
        For foo = 1 To 100
            Text2(0) = MyDyna!LastName
            Text2(1) = MyDyna!FirstName
            Text2(2) = MyDyna!CompanyName
            Text2(3) = MyDyna!Address1
            Text2(14) = MyDyna!Address2
            Text2(15) = MyDyna!City
            Text2(16) = MyDyna!Zip
            Text2(17) = MyDyna!TestInt
            Text2(18) = MyDyna!TestLong
            Text2(19) = MyDyna!RecordId
            DoEvents
            Text2(17) = Format$(Rnd * 10000)
            MyDyna.Edit
            MyDyna!TestInt = Text2(17)
            Select Case foobar
            Case 1: MyDyna!LastName = Text2(0)
            Case 2: MyDyna!FirstName = Text2(1)
            Case 3: MyDyna!CompanyName = Text2(2)
            Case 4: MyDyna!Address1 = Text2(3)
            Case 5: MyDyna!Address2 = Text2(14)
            Case 6: MyDyna!City = Text2(15)
            Case 7: MyDyna!Zip = Text2(16)
            Case 8: MyDyna!TestLong = Text2(18)
            Case 9: MyDyna!RecordId = Text2(19)
            End Select
            MyDyna.Update
            MyDyna.MoveNext
```

```
        Next foo
      EndTime
    Next foobar
   MyDyna.Close
   DoEvents
```

Basic research comes through again. Table 8.6 shows that the routine goes along pretty quickly until we get to the RecordId field.

Table 8.6	Finding the Slow Field
Seconds	**Activity/Graph**
20.216	Find Slow Field: Case 1 - LastName
20.078	Find Slow Field: Case 2 - FirstName
17.757	Find Slow Field: Case 3 - CompanyName
17.757	Find Slow Field: Case 4 - Address1
17.744	Find Slow Field: Case 5 - Address2
17.689	Find Slow Field: Case 6 - City
17.716	Find Slow Field: Case 7 - Zip
17.785	Find Slow Field: Case 8 - TestLong
30.790	Find Slow Field: Case 9 - RecordId

If you analyze these results, notice that all the field saves are about the same, except for LastName, FirstName, and RecordId. LastName and FirstName are part of the NameKey index, and index processing apparently adds 2 to 2 1/2 seconds. RecordId is also a key field, but it takes 13 seconds longer to process—almost twice as long as the other fields.

Referential Integrity

What's different about RecordId? It's the parent field in an Jet relation. The speed culprit, then, is referential integrity! Jet is cascading what it thinks is a change down to the associated records in the Phones table!

You can take two lessons from this analysis. First, you probably want to avoid creating relations unless necessary, as you would avoid adding any complexity to a database structure unless needed. Second, you should definitely avoid assigning values to a data object field if the values haven't changed, since Jet apparently doesn't check.

Programmatic PseudoBinding: Productivity and Speed

The analysis to this point has shown that, in the test situation, table DAO objects are significantly faster than data controls for batch processing, searches, and retrieval. Data controls, on the other hand, have a slight edge in speed when displaying and saving data. If you want to stick with DAOs, you have to generate significant code to move data to and from your controls, particularly since it's important that you not assign a value to a field unless it has changed.

But it's possible to have the best of both worlds, with a little help from some CodeBank subroutines. The LoadFields and SaveFields subroutines will examine the tag of each control on the form for a field name, cycling through the form's control collection. Then they programmatically "bind" the control to the data, based on the other parameter provided—the DAO, which can be any type of recordset. The routines will save data only if it has changed. This eliminates all the grunt code that we had to generate to implement programmatic edit forms. Figure 8.4 shows the new form.

Setup is just as easy as binding a data control—you simply fill the Tag property with the field name, as opposed to the data control binding technique of placing the field name in the control's DataField property. You need to make one subroutine call when you want to load and save your data.

Listing 8.15 shows our first pass at the LoadFields and SaveFields subs.

Fig. 8.4

The new form in DataBn12.Vbp.

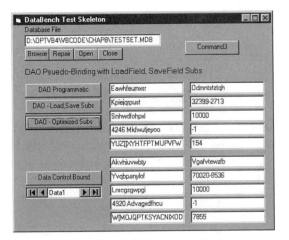

Listing 8.15 DataBn12.Vbp   The *SaveFields* and *LoadFields* Subroutines

```
Public Sub SaveFields0(Rs As Recordset, Frm As Form)
Dim CtlCount As Integer, foo As Integer
Dim CtlTag As String
On Error Resume Next
CtlCount = Frm.Controls.Count - 1
For foo = 0 To CtlCount
    CtlTag = Frm.Controls(foo).Tag
    If CtlTag > "" Then
        If Rs(CtlTag) <> Frm.Controls(foo) Then
            Rs(CtlTag) = Frm.Controls(foo)
        End If
    End If
Next foo
End Sub

Public Sub LoadFields0(Rs As Recordset, Frm As Form)
Dim CtlCount As Integer, foo As Integer
Dim CtlTag As String
On Error Resume Next

CtlCount = Frm.Controls.Count - 1
CtlTag = Frm.Controls(foo).Tag
For foo = 0 To CtlCount
    CtlTag = Frm.Controls(foo).Tag
    If CtlTag > "" Then
        Frm.Controls(foo) = Rs(CtlTag)
    End If
Next foo
End Sub
```

When you run this test, you find what you might have guessed already: The save is dismally slow, as table 8.7 shows. Accessing all those properties is time-consuming. Besides, it turns out that if the data is numeric, you need to convert the values of the control in the subroutine—something that seemed to have been done automatically in the inline code due to a quirk in the VB runtime or parser.

To speed operation of the SaveFields and LoadFields routines, we can introduce a third routine, PseudoBoundSetup, which preloads the "binding" information into a type array. LoadFields and SaveFields then simply cycle through the type array. We also write logic to convert text control values to numeric data, if the recordset field's data type is numeric, preventing us from unintentionally writing data. The revised subroutines execute less code within their loops and examine only "bound controls," so they execute fewer loop cycles. PseudoBoundSetup needs to be executed only once, when loading the form.

III

Database Optimization

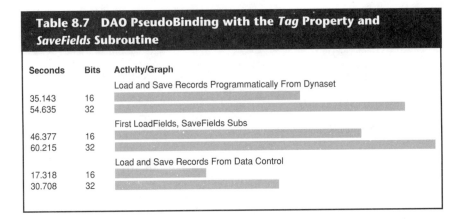

Table 8.7 DAO PseudoBinding with the *Tag* Property and *SaveFields* Subroutine

Seconds	Bits	Activity/Graph
		Load and Save Records Programmatically From Dynaset
35.143	16	
54.635	32	
		First LoadFields, SaveFields Subs
46.377	16	
60.215	32	
		Load and Save Records From Data Control
17.318	16	
30.708	32	

The code in listing 8.16 is used to set up pseudobinding. The revised LoadFields sub in listing 8.17 displays the data. Listing 8.18 shows the SaveFields sub, which writes the values of the controls to the associated recordset fields. Finally, calling the subs is simple, as the code in listing 8.19 demonstrates.

Listing 8.16 DataBn12.Vbp Setting Up Pseudobinding

```
Option Explicit
Type PseudoBound
    Ctl As Control
    Field As String
    Numeric As Integer
End Type
Public Sub PseudoBoundSetup(Rs As Recordset, Frm As Form, BArr() _
  As PseudoBound)
Dim CtlCount As Integer, foo As Integer, foobar As Integer
Dim CtlTag As String
On Error Resume Next
CtlCount = Frm.Controls.Count - 1
foobar = -1
For foo = 0 To CtlCount
    CtlTag = Frm.Controls(foo).Tag
    If CtlTag > "" Then
        foobar = foobar + 1
        If foobar > UBound(BArr) Then ReDim Preserve BArr(foobar) _
          As PseudoBound
        Set BArr(foobar).Ctl = Frm.Controls(foo)
        BArr(foobar).Field = CtlTag
        If Rs(CtlTag).Type <> dbText And Rs(CtlTag).Type _
          <> dbMemo Then
            BArr(foobar).Numeric = True
        Else
            BArr(foobar).Numeric = False
        End If
    End If
Next foo
End Sub
```

Listing 8.17   DataBn12.Vbp   Displaying the Data

```
Public Sub LoadFields(Rs As Recordset, BArr() As PseudoBound)
Dim CtlCount As Integer, foo As Integer
Dim CtlTag As String
On Error Resume Next
CtlCount = UBound(BArr)
For foo = 0 To CtlCount
    BArr(foo).Ctl = Rs(BArr(foo).Field)
Next foo
End Sub
```

Listing 8.18   DataBn12.Vbp   Writing the Control Values to the Recordset Fields

```
Public Sub SaveFields(Rs As Recordset, BArr() As PseudoBound)
Dim CtlCount As Integer, foo As Integer
Dim CtlTag As String
Dim Value As Variant
On Error Resume Next
CtlCount = UBound(BArr)
For foo = 0 To CtlCount
    If BArr(foo).Numeric Then
        Value = Val(BArr(foo).Ctl)
    Else
        Value = BArr(foo).Ctl
    End If
    If Rs(BArr(foo).Field) <> Value Then
        Rs(BArr(foo).Field) = Value
    End If
Next foo

End Sub
```

Listing 8.19   DataBn12.Vbp   Calling the Subroutines

```
Set MyDyna = MyDb.CreateDynaset("Select * from Address Order _
  By LastName")
    MyDyna.MoveFirst
    ReDim BindArray(9) As PseudoBound
    PseudoBoundSetup MyDyna, Me, BindArray()
    BeginTime "Optimized LoadFields, SaveFields Subs", TIME_DEBUG
    'Operation
    For foo = 1 To 100
        LoadFields MyDyna, BindArray()
        DoEvents
        Text2(17) = "13000"
        MyDyna.Edit
        SaveFields MyDyna, BindArray()
```

III

Database Optimization

(continues)

```
Listing 8.19  Continued
          MyDyna.Update
          MyDyna.MoveNext
    Next foo
    EndTime
    MyDyna.Close
    DoEvents
```

The end result: Very little code is required to implement programmatic edit forms. The programmatic method displays and saves information nearly as fast as the data control, with only about a 15 percent speed disadvantage (see table 8.8). Note, however, that the subroutines will bind data only to simple controls that have a single value, such as a check box or text control. Combo or list controls, which require multiple lists of values referenced by a list index, will still have to be loaded manually (although CodeBank has other routines to automate this task). The same is true for option buttons, where the data value is used to set only one group of controls to true. However, despite these limitations, the subs will increase productivity and reduce code size in many situations.

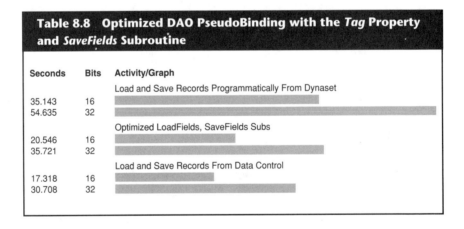

Table 8.8 Optimized DAO PseudoBinding with the _Tag_ Property and _SaveFields_ Subroutine

Seconds	Bits	Activity/Graph
		Load and Save Records Programmatically From Dynaset
35.143	16	
54.635	32	
		Optimized LoadFields, SaveFields Subs
20.546	16	
35.721	32	
		Load and Save Records From Data Control
17.318	16	
30.708	32	

Enhanced Data Controls

We've spent considerable time examining and optimizing DAOs. Now let's turn our attention back to the data control.

Data controls aren't regarded as respectable by many programmers, in large part because of the simplistic and inflexible way they were implemented in VB3. With VB4, Microsoft has gone to great lengths to enhance the functionality of the data control. Just as DAO recordsets can be of any DAO type, data-control recordsets can now be based on tables, dynasets, or snapshots. You can also link a data control to a DAO recordset, essentially cloning the table, dynaset, or snapshot DAO recordset to the data control.

However, there are still problems. Just as in VB3, data controls still require significant additional code to qualify their event processing in edit forms. Because of their fundamental architecture, data controls will never live up to the claim that they enable a codeless data-entry form, except in very simple implementations. Nevertheless, the data control has been significantly enhanced, perhaps even to the point that you might want to consider using it—with, of course, significantly more code.

The following sections analyze various data-control performance issues. Note that in an earlier section, we've already established that table-based data-control recordsets display records more quickly than dynaset data controls.

Saving Data: *UpdateRecord* vs. *Move* Events

You can save changes made to a data control recordset in two ways. The data control will automatically save changes to the current record when the record pointer is changed by a Move method or by the user clicking the data-control navigation keys. Saves are also carried out when the form is unloaded. You have the option of disabling the save in the data-control validate event, but you must write code to do so.

You can also force a save to the current record by using the data-control UpdateRecord method. In DataBn13.Vbp, we test both methods of data-control saves to determine whether either method might have a speed advantage. Figure 8.5 shows the DataBn13 test window.

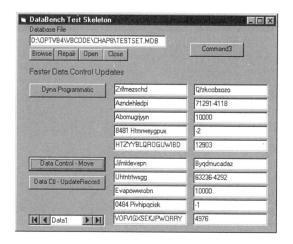

Fig. 8.5
The benchmark test window for the data control UpdateRecord vs. Move events test.

III

Database Optimization

The code in listing 8.20 tests the speed of data control saves by invoking the validate event with the MoveNext method.

Listing 8.20 DataBn13.Vbp . Invoking the Validate Event with the *MoveNext* Method ·

```
Select Case Index 'Test Options
Case 1
    Data1.DatabaseName = Text1
    Data1.RecordSource = "Select * from Address Order By LastName"
    Data1.Refresh
    BeginTime "Load and Save Records From Data Control using _
      Move", TIME_DEBUG
    Data1.Recordset.MoveFirst
    'Operation
    For foo = 1 To 100
        DoEvents
        Text2(10) = "11000"
        Data1.Recordset.MoveNext
    Next foo
    Data1.Recordset.MovePrevious
    DoEvents
    EndTime
    DoEvents
```

Listing 8.21 shows how I tested the UpdateRecord method.

Listing 8.21 DataBn13.Vbp Testing the *UpdateRecord* Method

```
Case 2 'UpdateRecord
    Data1.DatabaseName = Text1
    Data1.RecordSource = "Select * from Address Order By LastName"
    Data1.Refresh
    BeginTime "Load and Save Records From Data Control using _
      UpdateRecord", TIME_DEBUG
    Data1.Recordset.MoveFirst
    'Operation
    For foo = 1 To 100
        DoEvents
        Text2(10) = "12000"
        Data1.UpdateRecord
        Data1.Recordset.MoveNext
    Next foo
    Data1.Recordset.MovePrevious
    DoEvents
    EndTime
    DoEvents
End Select
```

As you can see in table 8.9, the test shows that simply moving the data control's current record pointer is about two-hundredths of a second faster per record than using the validate logic invoked by the Move methods. This probably doesn't represent enough of a savings to be worth worrying about. Effectively, you should feel free to use whatever methodology suits your programming style.

Table 8.9 Data Control *UpdateRecord* vs. *Move* Events (100 Records)		
Seconds	**Bits**	**Activity/Graph**
		Load and Save Records From Data Control - Move Method
14.788	16	
33.057	32	
		Load and Save Records From Data Control - UpdateRecord Method
16.714	16	
32.301	32	

DAO Object-Linked Data Controls

Visual Basic 4's new object-based recordset paradigm creates some interesting possibilities. Data controls are no longer limited to the dynaset model, but can also be tables and snapshots. You can even set a data control to a recordset object, essentially cloning the recordset.

DataBn15.Vbp tests how well a table-type data control performs and compares the performance to a data control whose recordset object has been equated to a DAO table object using Set. This can get confusing, but essentially what we're trying to test is whether there's true link between the types or whether it's all a mirage. Figure 8.6 shows the project.

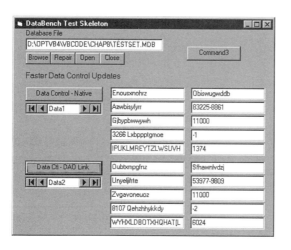

Fig. 8.6
The form for DataBn15.

The code in listings 8.22 and 8.23 shows the methods used to set up the data controls. (Note that the Type property for each data control was set to Table at design time, in the property window.) The code in listing 8.22 tests the speed of a data control table-type recordset, whereas the code in listing 8.23 tests the performance of a data control that's Set to a DAO table recordset.

Listing 8.22   DataBn15.Vbp   Testing the Speed of a Data Control Recordset

```
Select Case Index 'Test Options
Case 1
    Data1.DatabaseName = Text1
    Data1.RecordSource = "Address"
    Data1.Refresh
    Data1.Recordset.Index = "NameKey"
    BeginTime "Data Control - Native Table", TIME_DEBUG
    Data1.Recordset.MoveFirst
    'Operation
    For foo = 1 To 100
        DoEvents
        Text2(3) = Rnd * 10000
        Data1.Recordset.MoveNext
    Next foo
    Data1.Recordset.MovePrevious
    DoEvents
    EndTime
    DoEvents
```

Listing 8.23   DataBn15.Vbp. Testing the Speed of a Data Control Set to a DAO Table Recordset

```
Case 2 'DAO Table
    Set MyTbl = MyDb.OpenRecordset("Address", dbOpenTable)
    MyTbl.Index = "NameKey"
    Set Data2.Recordset = MyTbl
    Data2.Recordset.Index = "NameKey"
    BeginTime "Data Control - DAO Table", TIME_DEBUG
    Data2.Recordset.MoveFirst
    'Operation
    For foo = 1 To 100
        DoEvents
        Text2(10) = Rnd * 10000
        Data2.Recordset.MoveNext
    Next foo
    Data2.Recordset.MovePrevious
    DoEvents
    EndTime
    DoEvents
End Select
```

Performance of the two data controls was almost identical (see table 8.10). The performance also compared favorably to the display speed of a more normal dynaset data control as analyzed earlier. Interestingly enough, when testing these relationships, we observed that all three data objects—the pure table, the data-control table, and the data-control clone of the DAO table—shared identical bookmarks, but like cloned recordsets in VB3, the current records aren't synchronized. The implication is that these recordsets are simply different faces of the same Jet object. This also could mean that you can readily pass bookmarks from a global table to a local data-control table, thus taking advantage of control binding, or mix and match DAO and data-control access methods in any number of ways without speed degradation.

Table 8.10	Data Control Native Table vs. DAO-Linked Table (100 Records)		
Seconds	**Bits**	**Activity/Graph**	
		Data Control - Native Table	
16.412	16		
32.720	32		
		Data Control - DAO Table	
16.467	16		
30.475	32		

Recordsets vs. Explicit Objects

If you worked with DAOs in Visual Basic 3, you're probably familiar with the syntax required to create them. Tables had to be opened with the `OpenTable` method, dynasets with the `CreateDynaset` method, and snapshots with the `CreateSnapshot` method. Visual Basic 4 retains these methods but also allows you to create any of these objects with a single method: `OpenRecordset`.

The new recordset object may be a table object, dynaset, or snapshot, depending on the parameters you specify to the `OpenRecordset` method. Perhaps the nicest thing about this change is the enhanced capability to create reusable code functions and subroutines. In VB3, either we had to have a separate version of our subroutines for each type of DAO, or we had to set up various globals and modes—a messy approach. Now we can pass tables, dynasets, snapshots, and even data controls to a subroutine that has a recordset parameter, greatly simplifying our database code libraries.

III

Database Optimization

In this section, we'll test whether this flexibility has a price tag in terms of performance. DataBn14.Vbp opens, reads, writes, and closes tables and dynasets by using each method.

 The following code uses the dbOpenTable and dbOpenDynaset parameters, two of the new implicit constants in VB4. Like True and False in VB3, implicit constants are predeclared and are now part of the language.

The code in listing 8.24 tests 3.0-style table DAOs. The code in listing 8.25 creates a VB3-style dynaset. Listing 8.26 tests table-type recordsets. Listing 8.27 tests dynaset-type recordsets.

Listing 8.24   DataBn14.Vbp   Testing 3.0-Style Table DAOs

```
Select Case Index 'Test Options
Case 0
    BeginTime "Write Table Records", TIME_DEBUG
    Set MyTbl = MyDb.OpenTable("Address")
    MyTbl.Index = "NameKey"
    MyTbl.MoveFirst
    'Operation
    For foo = 1 To 100
        MyTbl.Edit
        MyTbl!TestInt = 10000
        MyTbl.Update
        MyTbl.MoveNext
    Next foo
    MyTbl.Close
    EndTime
    DoEvents
```

Listing 8.25   DataBn14.Vbp   Creating a VB3-Style Dynaset

```
Case 1
    BeginTime "Write Dynaset", TIME_DEBUG
    Set MyDyna = MyDb.CreateDynaset("Select * from Address")
    MyDyna.MoveFirst
    'Operation
    For foo = 1 To 100
        MyDyna.Edit
        MyDyna!TestInt = 11000
        MyDyna.Update
        MyDyna.MoveNext
    Next foo
```

```
MyDyna.Close
EndTime
DoEvents
```

Listing 8.26   DataBn14.Vbp   Testing Table-Type Recordsets

```
Case 2
    BeginTime "Recordset Table", TIME_DEBUG
    Set MyRsTbl = MyDb.OpenRecordset("Address", dbOpenTable)
    MyRsTbl.Index = "NameKey"
    MyRsTbl.MoveFirst
    'Operation
    For foo = 1 To 100
        MyRsTbl.Edit
        MyRsTbl!TestInt = 12000
        MyRsTbl.Update
        MyRsTbl.MoveNext
    Next foo
    MyRsTbl.Close
    EndTime
    DoEvents
```

Listing 8.27   DataBn14.Vbp   Testing Dynaset-Type Recordsets

```
Case 3
    BeginTime "Recordset Dynaset", TIME_DEBUG
    Set MyRsDyna = MyDb.OpenRecordset("Select * from _
      Address", dbOpenDynaset)
    MyRsDyna.MoveFirst
    'Operation
    For foo = 1 To 100
        MyRsDyna.Edit
        MyRsDyna!TestInt = 13000
        MyRsDyna.Update
        MyRsDyna.MoveNext
    Next foo
    MyRsDyna.Close
    EndTime
    DoEvents
End Select
```

Our analysis, as table 8.11 shows, presents a clear and welcome picture: There's no discernible performance hit from using the new, more flexible recordset objects. So they are indeed two views of the same object, and the 2.5 compatibility layer imposes no meaningful overhead.

III

Database Optimization

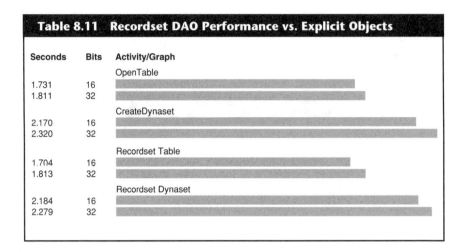

Seconds	Bits	Activity/Graph
		OpenTable
1.731	16	
1.811	32	
		CreateDynaset
2.170	16	
2.320	32	
		Recordset Table
1.704	16	
1.813	32	
		Recordset Dynaset
2.184	16	
2.279	32	

Table 8.11 Recordset DAO Performance vs. Explicit Objects

Field Validation

One of the nicer features of the Jet engine (versions 2.0 and above) is the capability of the database engine to enforce validation rules on field entries. VB4, with its tighter integration with the new Jet features, fully supports field validation. You can set, change, and report database rules for Access-formatted files by simply modifying `Tabledef` properties. The `ValidationRule` property is filled with VBA code, which makes it easy for VB programmers to use.

Once the data dictionary is set, database validation becomes code independent, which means that all programs that maintain the database are forced to obey the same rules (unless someone recklessly redefines the validation settings). Of course, anything that one does in a validation rule in VBA can also be done in straight VB4 code.

The question becomes this: Is there a speed penalty for Jet dictionary validation versus programmatic checking, which may counterbalance the advantages of native data dictionary validation? DataBn16.Vbp tests this issue. The test window has four buttons, each of which will attempt 100 read/writes (see fig. 8.7). The first two buttons will violate field rules and be prevented from changing the entry by the engine or by inline code. The next two buttons will obey the rules to test for a noticeable overhead requirement for successful validation. In each case, we'll modify our TestInt field and test to see whether the value is greater than 12,000.

The code in listing 8.28 uses field validation rules to detect entry errors. The code in listing 8.29 uses programmatic validation to detect entry errors.

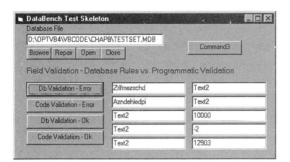

Fig. 8.7
The field valida-
tion window in
DataBn16.Vbp.

**Listing 8.28   DataBn16.Vbp   Detecting Entry Errors with Field
Validation Rules**

```
Case 0
    MyDb.TableDefs("Address").Fields("TestInt").ValidationRule _
        = "(> 12000)"
    Set MyDyna = MyDb.CreateDynaset("Select * from Address Order _
        By LastName")
    MyDyna.MoveFirst
    BeginTime "Database Validation Rules - Entry Error", TIME_DEBUG
    'Operation
    For foo = 1 To 100
        Text2(0) = MyDyna!LastName
        Text2(1) = MyDyna!FirstName
        Text2(17) = MyDyna!TestInt
        Text2(18) = MyDyna!TestLong
        Text2(19) = MyDyna!RecordId
        DoEvents
        Text2(17) = "10000"
        MyDyna.Edit
        MyDyna!LastName = Text2(0)
        MyDyna!FirstName = Text2(1)
        MyDyna!TestInt = Text2(17)
        MyDyna!TestLong = Text2(18)
        MyDyna.Update
        If Err <> 0 Then
            'display field update err
            'Debug.Print Err, Error
        End If
        MyDyna.MoveNext
    Next foo
    EndTime
    MyDyna.Close
    DoEvents
```

Listing 8.29 DataBn16.Vbp Detecting Entry Errors with Programmatic Validation

```
Case 1
    MyDb.TableDefs("Address").Fields("TestInt").ValidationRule = ""
    Set MyDyna = MyDb.CreateDynaset("Select * from Address Order _
      By LastName")
    MyDyna.MoveFirst
    BeginTime "Programmatic Validation Rules - Entry Error", _
      TIME_DEBUG
    'Operation
    For foo = 1 To 100
        Text2(0) = MyDyna!LastName
        Text2(1) = MyDyna!FirstName
        Text2(17) = MyDyna!TestInt
        Text2(18) = MyDyna!TestLong
        DoEvents
        Text2(17) = "10000"
        If (Val(Text2(17)) > 12000) Then
            MyDyna.Edit
            MyDyna!LastName = Text2(0)
            MyDyna!FirstName = Text2(1)
            MyDyna!TestInt = Text2(17)
            MyDyna!TestLong = Text2(18)
            MyDyna.Update
        Else
            'display a message
        End If
        MyDyna.MoveNext
    Next foo
    EndTime
    MyDyna.Close
    DoEvents
```

The code in listing 8.30 tests database field validation overhead when there's no error. The code in listing 8.31 tests programmatic validation overhead when there's no error.

Listing 8.30 DataBn16.Vbp Testing Field Validation Overhead When There Are No Errors

```
Case 2
    MyDb.TableDefs("Address").Fields("TestInt").ValidationRule _
      = "(> 12000)"
    Set MyDyna = MyDb.CreateDynaset("Select * from Address Order _
      By LastName")
    MyDyna.MoveFirst
    BeginTime "Database Validation Rules - Valid Entry", TIME_DEBUG
    'Operation
    For foo = 1 To 100
        Text2(0) = MyDyna!LastName
        Text2(1) = MyDyna!FirstName
        Text2(17) = MyDyna!TestInt
```

```
            Text2(18) = MyDyna!TestLong
            DoEvents
            Err = 0
            Text2(17) = 12002
            MyDyna.Edit
            MyDyna!LastName = Text2(0)
            MyDyna!FirstName = Text2(1)
            MyDyna!TestInt = Text2(17)
            MyDyna!TestLong = Text2(18)
            MyDyna.Update
            If Err <> 0 Then
                'display field update err
                Err = 0
            End If
            MyDyna.MoveNext
        Next foo
        EndTime
        MyDyna.Close
        DoEvents
```

Listing 8.31   DataBn16.Vbp   Testing Programmatic Validation Overhead When There Are No Errors

```
    Case 3
        MyDb.TableDefs("Address").Fields("TestInt").ValidationRule = ""
        Set MyDyna = MyDb.CreateDynaset("Select * from Address Order _
          By LastName")
        MyDyna.MoveFirst
        BeginTime "Programmatic Validation - Valid Entry", TIME_DEBUG
        'Operation
        For foo = 1 To 100
            Text2(0) = MyDyna!LastName
            Text2(1) = MyDyna!FirstName
            Text2(17) = MyDyna!TestInt
            Text2(18) = MyDyna!TestLong
            DoEvents
            Err = 0
            Text2(17) = "14000"
            If (Val(Text2(17)) > 12000) Then
                MyDyna.Edit
                MyDyna!LastName = Text2(0)
                MyDyna!FirstName = Text2(1)
                MyDyna!TestInt = Text2(17)
                MyDyna!TestLong = Text2(18)
                MyDyna.Update
            Else
                'display a message
            End If
            MyDyna.MoveNext
        Next foo
        EndTime
        MyDyna.Close
        DoEvents
```

III

Database Optimization

As might be expected, we do indeed pay a price for database validation (see table 8.12). Database error finding makes the read-write cycle more than twice as long, adding almost 6 seconds per hundred records. No doubt this is because, in large part, Jet must communicate with the application by triggering an error condition. When there's no error, saving a record with Jet validation is equivalent to programmatic validation.

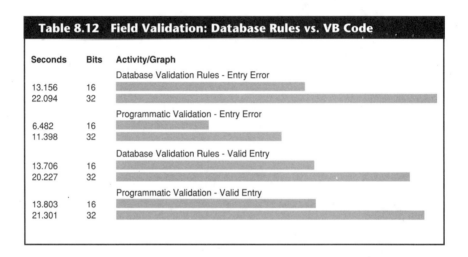

Table 8.12   Field Validation: Database Rules vs. VB Code

Seconds	Bits	Activity/Graph
		Database Validation Rules - Entry Error
13.156	16	
22.094	32	
		Programmatic Validation - Entry Error
6.482	16	
11.398	32	
		Database Validation Rules - Valid Entry
13.706	16	
20.227	32	
		Programmatic Validation - Valid Entry
13.803	16	
21.301	32	

Each validation method has true advantages. Database validation is safer because it will function even when your data is being viewed by other programs. On the other hand, programmatic validation can be executed while the user is filling out the form, so problems can be detected before a save attempt. If a routine or form is performing sluggishly and you need to speed validation performance, consider removing database validation rules.

From Here...

For more information, refer to the following chapters:

- Chapter 7, "Speeding Database Operations," explains how to speed up DAO operations.

- Chapter 9, "Improving SQL Performance," tells how to use SQL to speed up database operations.

Chapter 9

Improving SQL Performance

One of the nicest aspects of Visual Basic's Jet (Joint Engine Technology) engine compared to older database technology is its Structured Query Language, or SQL. SQL lets you accomplish major tasks in a single statement and gives you the power to execute operations regardless of index structures, sorting algorithms, or opening myriad tables. The database engine handles all the nasty details. By using SQL statements, you can greatly enhance your code creation productivity and limit debugging time.

And the news gets better. Jet internally and automatically optimizes your SQL statements, using Rushmore (a method of speeding lookup by using indexes) and other data-optimization technologies. Some SQL statements will run much more quickly than equivalent DAO code. But not always. SQL can also mean a significant performance hit.

This chapter looks at a number of different SQL operations and compares them to equivalent DAO code by using dynaset and table objects on Access format files. We'll also learn about QueryDefs, which are stored and pre-optimized SQL queries, and ascertain their impact on performance.

> SQL is a full data-manipulation language all its own. If you're not familiar with SQL, you should read the Visual Basic SQL documentation and help files to get the most from this chapter.

You'll learn about a number of topics in this chapter, including

- How to speed up performance action queries
- How to summarize data sets with queries

- The benefits and pitfalls of joining tables
- The advantages of QueryDefs

Action Queries

SQL action queries can perform update, deletion, and summary operations on multiple tables or subsets of tables. By using SQL action queries with a single line of code, you can accomplish tasks that might require scores of DAO statements, repeated thousands of times. That doesn't mean, however, that the work doesn't have to be done; it's just performed internally.

Queries vs. DAOs

DataBn17.Vbp, in the \Chap9 directory on the CD that comes with this book, analyzes the performance differences between action queries and DAO operations on dynasets and tables. It sets the value of the TestInt variable on all records in a table to simulate an initialization or other operation. As you can see in the following code, the action query requires just one line of code—an execute operation. By comparison, the DAO operations require 10 lines, four of which must be repeated for every record in the table. Figure 9.1 shows how DataBn17 looks while running.

Fig. 9.1
The main form for the DataBn17 project.

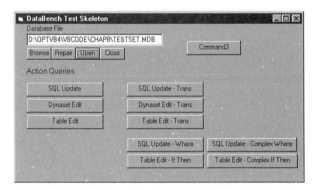

The code section in listing 9.1 uses an action query to update the Address.Mdb database. The code in listing 9.2 uses manual programmatic methods to update a dynaset. The code in listing 9.3 uses programmatic methods on a table DAO.

Listing 9.1   DataBn17.Vbp   Updating the Database with an Action Query

```
Case 0
    BeginTime "Updating With Action Queries", TIME_DEBUG
    'Operation
    MyDb.Execute "Update Address Set TestInt = 10000"
    EndTime
    DoEvents
```

Listing 9.2   DataBn17.Vbp   Updating a Dynaset with Manual Programmatic Methods

```
Case 1
    BeginTime "Programmatic Update on Dynaset", TIME_DEBUG
    Set MyDyna = MyDb.CreateDynaset("Select * from Address Order _
        By LastName")
    MyDyna.MoveFirst
    'Operation
    Do Until MyDyna.EOF
        MyDyna.Edit
        MyDyna!TestInt = 11000
        MyDyna.Update
        MyDyna.MoveNext
    Loop
    EndTime
    MyDyna.Close
    DoEvents
```

Listing 9.3   DataBn17.Vbp   Using Programmatic Methods on a Table DAO

```
Case 2
    BeginTime "Programmatic Update on Table - 100 Records", _
        TIME_DEBUG
    Set MyTbl = MyDb.OpenTable("Address")
    MyTbl.MoveFirst
    'Operation
    Do Until MyTbl.EOF
        MyTbl.Edit
        MyTbl!TestInt = 12000
        MyTbl.Update
        MyTbl.MoveNext
    Loop
    EndTime
    MyTbl.Close
    DoEvents
```

III

Database Optimization

Executing the simple action query—without any judgment or conditions—gives us a baseline for future comparisons. The results aren't too surprising: Action queries are twice as fast as table operations and as much as three times faster than dynaset operations (see tables 9.1 and 9.2). The more records processed, the greater the speed advantage of the query.

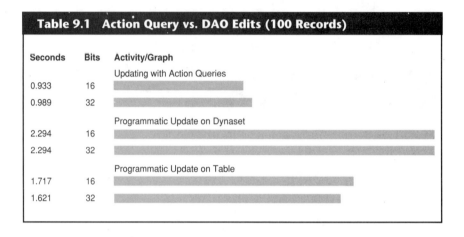

Table 9.1 Action Query vs. DAO Edits (100 Records)

Seconds	Bits	Activity/Graph
		Updating with Action Queries
0.933	16	
0.989	32	
		Programmatic Update on Dynaset
2.294	16	
2.294	32	
		Programmatic Update on Table
1.717	16	
1.621	32	

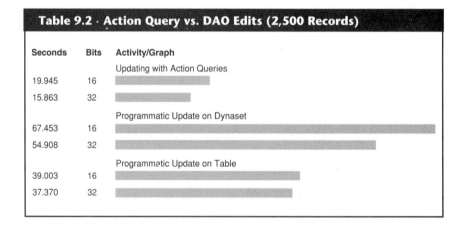

Table 9.2 · Action Query vs. DAO Edits (2,500 Records)

Seconds	Bits	Activity/Graph
		Updating with Action Queries
19.945	16	
15.863	32	
		Programmatic Update on Dynaset
67.453	16	
54.908	32	
		Programmatic Update on Table
39.003	16	
37.370	32	

Using Transactions

The update example didn't take into account the methods we've already reviewed for speeding DAO operations. Because this example is very simple, we don't have the maneuvering room for many code tricks, but we can at least use transactions to speed DAO performance. To keep things fair, we'll also bracket the action query with `BeginTrans` and `CommitTrans` statements.

The code in listing 9.4 adds explicit transaction support to the action query. The code in listing 9.5 adds explicit transaction support to the programmatic dynaset update. The code in listing 9.6 adds explicit transaction support to the table DAO update.

Listing 9.4   DataBn17.Vbp   Adding Explicit Transaction Support to the Action Query

```
Case 3
    BeginTime "Updating With Action Queries - With Transactions", _
        TIME_DEBUG
    BeginTrans
    'Operation
    MyDb.Execute "Update Address Set TestInt = 10000"
    CommitTrans
    EndTime
    DoEvents
```

Listing 9.5   DataBn17.Vbp   Adding Explicit Transaction Support to the Dynaset Update

```
Case 4
    BeginTime "Programmatic Update on Dynaset - With _
        Transactions", TIME_DEBUG
    BeginTrans
    Set MyDyna = MyDb.CreateDynaset("Select * from Address Order _
        By LastName")
    MyDyna.MoveFirst
    'Operation
    Do Until MyDyna.EOF
        MyDyna.Edit
        MyDyna!TestInt = 11000
        MyDyna.Update
        MyDyna.MoveNext
    Loop
    CommitTrans
    EndTime
    MyDyna.Close
    DoEvents
```

Listing 9.6   DataBn17.Vbp   Adding Explicit Transaction Support to the Table DAO Update

```
Case 5
    BeginTime "Programmatic Update on Table - With Transactions", _
        TIME_DEBUG
```

(continues)

III

Database Optimization

Listing 9.6 Continued

```
BeginTrans
Set MyTbl = MyDb.OpenTable("Address")
MyTbl.MoveFirst
'Operation
Do Until MyTbl.EOF
    MyTbl.Edit
    MyTbl!TestInt = 12000
    MyTbl.Update
    MyTbl.MoveNext
Loop
CommitTrans
EndTime
MyTbl.Close
DoEvents
```

As you can see in table 9.3, using transactions speeds up the action query somewhat. But action queries have a profound effect on DAO processing. Table DAO processing is now seen to be just as fast—even a bit faster—than the query! Action queries use a built-in form of transaction processing, which improved the query's performance in the first test.

Table 9.3 Action Query vs. DAO Edits, with Transactions

Seconds	Bits	Activity/Graph
		Updating with Action Queries, with Transactions: 100 Records
0.934	16	
1.215	32	
		Programmatic Update on Dynaset, with Transactions: 100 Records
1.483	16	
1.293	32	
		Programmatic Update on Table, with Transactions: 100 Records
0.893	16	
0.723	32	
		Updating with Action Queries, with Transactions: 2,500 Records
16.563	16	
18.708	32	
		Programmatic Update on Dynaset, with Transactions: 2,500 Records
26.450	16	
26.123	32	
		Programmatic Update on Table, with Transactions: 2,500 Records
15.396	16	
11.374	32	

Of course, all else being equal, you would still want to use the action query because the speed difference between transaction-sped tables and action queries is negligible, whereas the amount of code required is substantial.

Complex Queries

Take a look at a less simple operation. Chances are that you'll only rarely want to change all the records in a table, unless you're initializing a value. But often, multiple records need to be changed based on some condition. For example, if you work in a widget factory and the price of blue paint goes up 200 percent, you may need to increase the price of all your blue widget models. You could do it manually, one unit a time; you could write code to cycle through all the widgets; or you could use an action query with a Where clause.

The next example uses a Where clause to make the update conditions more complex. It tests with one simple condition—that the last name must start with the letter A through L—and with two conditions: that either the last name or the company name must start with A through L. The latter example uses the CompanyName field because it's not part of any index. This demonstrates the flexibility of SQL and how nicely we can ignore indexes with SQL.

This time, we'll just analyze the two best performing types: action queries and table DAO objects. The code in listing 9.7 performs an action query on a subset of records. Listing 9.8 shows how the table DAO update code works with a subset of records. The code in listing 9.9 demonstrates a complex, multifield action query. The code in listing 9.10 implements the complex action with a table DAO.

Listing 9.7   DataBn17.Vbp   Performing an Action Query on a Subset

```
Case 6
    BeginTime "Updating With Action Queries - Where", TIME_DEBUG
    'Operation
    MyDb.Execute "Update Address Set TestInt = 10000 where _
      LastName < 'M'"
    EndTime
    DoEvents
```

Listing 9.8 DataBn17.Vbp   Performing a Programmatic Update on a Table

```
Case 7
    BeginTime "Programmatic Update on Table - If Then", TIME_DEBUG
    BeginTrans
    Set MyTbl = MyDb.OpenTable("Address")
    MyTbl.Index = "NameKeOh,y"
    MyTbl.MoveFirst
    'Operation
    Do Until MyTbl.EOF
        If MyTbl!LastName < "M" Then
            MyTbl.Edit
            MyTbl!TestInt = 12000
            MyTbl.Update
            MyTbl.MoveNext
        Else
            Exit Do
        End If
    Loop
    CommitTrans
    EndTime
    MyTbl.Close
    DoEvents
```

Listing 9.9   DataBn17.Vbp   A Complex, Multifield Action Query

```
Case 8
    BeginTime "Updating With Action Queries - Complex Where", _
      TIME_DEBUG
    'Operation
    MyDb.Execute "Update Address Set TestInt = 10000 where _
      LastName < 'M' or CompanyName < 'M'"
    EndTime
    DoEvents
```

Listing 9.10   DataBn17.Vbp   Implementing the Complex Action with a Table

```
Case 9
    BeginTime "Programmatic Update on Table - Complex If Then", _
      TIME_DEBUG
    BeginTrans
    Set MyTbl = MyDb.OpenTable("Address")
    MyTbl.Index = "NameKey"
    MyTbl.MoveFirst
    'Operation
```

```
Do Until MyTbl.EOF
    If MyTbl!LastName < "M" Or MyTbl!CompanyName < "M" Then
        MyTbl.Edit
        MyTbl!TestInt = 12000
        MyTbl.Update
    End If
    MyTbl.MoveNext
Loop
CommitTrans
EndTime
MyTbl.Close
DoEvents
```

With small data sets, table DAOs have a slight performance edge, even with their additional If...Then processing (see table 9.4). However, the advantage disappears on the larger test database, with the results in table 9.5. In fact, the larger and more complex the operation, the better the SQL action query performs because the Jet overhead of parsing and optimizing the query is spread over more work. In the most significant case, the difference is almost $3\frac{1}{2}$ seconds.

Table 9.4   Updating Table Subsets with Complex Conditions (100 Records)

Seconds	Bits	Activity/Graph
		Updating with Action Queries: Where
0.715	16	
0.960	32	
		Programmatic Update on Table: If...Then
0.618	16	
0.592	32	
		Updating With Action Queries: Complex Where
0.948	16	
1.058	32	
		Programmatic Update on Table: Complex If...Then
0.879	16	
0.824	32	

III

Database Optimization

Seconds	Bits	Activity/Graph

Table 9.5 Updating Table Subsets with Complex Conditions (2,500 Records)

Seconds	Bits	Activity/Graph
		Updating with Action Queries: Where
10.616	16	
9.571	32	
		Programmatic Update on Table: If...Then
11.057	16	
8.020	32	
		Updating With Action Queries: Complex Where
14.310	16	
15.795	32	
		Programmatic Update on Table: Complex If...Then
17.688	16	
14.490	32	

These results simply enforce what I've been saying about data access optimization: You must test your algorithms against your database in the quantities you expect to have, or else you'll have no assurance that you're using the best methods. The results you see in this and other data chapters may apply to your situation, but then again they may not. There are simply too many possible variations in database operations to devise reliable, hard-and-fast rules.

Summary Queries

You'll want to extract information from your databases more often than change them. Access SQL has many aggregate functions that can enable you to summarize and analyze your data in surprisingly sophisticated and powerful ways. To implement summary queries, you must create a dynaset with one or more variables defined to hold the results of the function. You define the variable and call the function in the Select clause of the query—for example:

```
Select Count(*) As Tally from Address
```

By a simple call such as this, you can obtain the total number of records in a table or dynaset without using the MoveLast method, total the values of a field, average a field's values, calculate standard deviations, or perform any number of other operations. (For more information on summary queries, review the VB help file on *Aggregate Functions*.)

The *Count( )* Function

To demonstrate the performance of aggregate or summary queries, let's test one of the simplest functions—Count()—and also analyze the Sum() function.

By using DataBench again, let's construct a test project called DataBn18.Vbp, which you can find on the CD in the \Chap9 directory. Figure 9.2 shows the test project in operation.

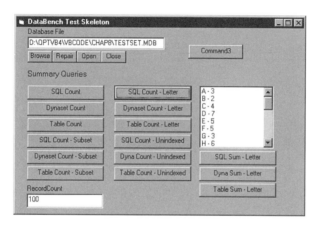

Fig. 9.2
Summary Queries vs. DAO Code (DataBn18.Vbp).

We'll first test the simplest case: how quickly can we determine the total number of records in a table? The code in listing 9.11 uses Count() to return the number of records in the Address table. The code in listing 9.12 uses the MoveLast method to force Jet to return a valid figure in the RecordCount property of the dynaset. The code example in listing 9.13 also uses MoveLast and RecordCount, but this time on a table DAO.

Listing 9.11   DataBn18.Vbp   Returning the Number of Records in the Table

```
Case 0
    BeginTime "Summary Queries - RecordCount", TIME_DEBUG
    'Operation
    Set MyDyna = MyDb.CreateDynaset("Select Count(*) as Tally _
        from Address")
    MyDyna.MoveFirst
    Text2 = MyDyna!Tally
    EndTime
    MyDyna.Close
    DoEvents
```

III

Database Optimization

Listing 9.12 DataBn18.Vbp Using *MoveLast* and *RecordCount* on a Dynaset

```
Case 1
    BeginTime "Dynaset - RecordCount", TIME_DEBUG
    Set MyDyna = MyDb.CreateDynaset("Select * from Address Order _
        By LastName")
    'Operation
    MyDyna.MoveLast
    Text2 = MyDyna.RecordCount
    EndTime
    MyDyna.Close
    DoEvents
```

Listing 9.13 DataBn18.Vbp Using *MoveLast* and *RecordCount* on a Table DAO

```
Case 2
    BeginTime "Table - RecordCount", TIME_DEBUG
    Set MyTbl = MyDb.OpenTable("Address")
    'Operation
    MyTbl.MoveLast
    Text2 = MyTbl.RecordCount
    EndTime
    MyTbl.Close
    DoEvents
```

Unfortunately, the test provides disappointing results for the summary query (see table 9.6). It's far outstripped by the MoveLast operation on table DAOs and is even slower than a dynaset MoveLast when dealing with large numbers of records.

One would have expected better from SQL summary functions. There's one interesting point: The record count for a 2,500-record table is derived just as quickly as for a 100-record table. MoveLast, in the case of table DAOs, is very fast and seems to provide an accurate record count without actually having to touch each record, as dynasets do. Of course, table record counts don't help if you're examining a subset of a table.

As you've seen before, this is only one case, and a very simple one at that. The next test compiicates the picture and checks again.

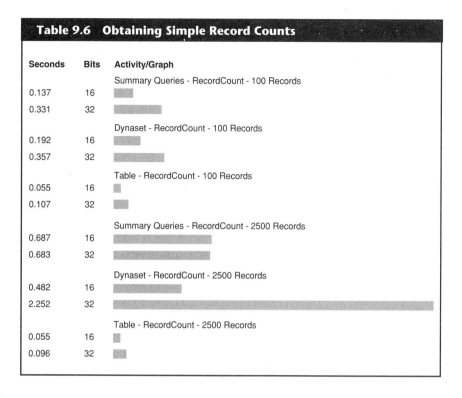

Seconds	Bits	Activity/Graph
		Summary Queries - RecordCount - 100 Records
0.137	16	
0.331	32	
		Dynaset - RecordCount - 100 Records
0.192	16	
0.357	32	
		Table - RecordCount - 100 Records
0.055	16	
0.107	32	
		Summary Queries - RecordCount - 2500 Records
0.687	16	
0.683	32	
		Dynaset - RecordCount - 2500 Records
0.482	16	
2.252	32	
		Table - RecordCount - 2500 Records
0.055	16	
0.096	32	

Table 9.6 Obtaining Simple Record Counts

Complex Summaries

This time, we'll get a count of just a subset of the table's records—those with the LastName field beginning with the letter L. To add this capability to the summary query and dynaset SQL code, we simply add a Where clause. In the case of the table, however, we'll have to add code to loop through the table, counting the L records. To speed things up, let's have the code jump to the beginning of the L's using a seek (because LastName is part of the NameKey index) and terminate processing when the code counts each L record and encounters a control break.

The following code has been added to the DataBn18 project used in the simple Count test in the preceding section. The code in listing 9.14 uses the Count() aggregate function with a Where clause to return a subset of the Address table's records. The code in listing 9.15 uses RecordCount on the Where subset. The code to count records in a table must loop through the table until a control break is reached, as listing 9.16 shows.

III

Database Optimization

Listing 9.14 DataBn18.Vbp Using *Where* to Return a Record Subset

```
Case 3
    BeginTime "Summary Queries - Subset RecordCount - LastName _
        'L'", TIME_DEBUG
    'Operation
    Set MyDyna = MyDb.CreateDynaset("Select Count(*) as Tally _
        from Address where LastName Like 'L*'")
    MyDyna.MoveFirst
    Text2 = MyDyna!Tally
    EndTime
    MyDyna.Close
    DoEvents
```

Listing 9.15 DataBn18.Vbp Using *RecordCount* on the *here* Subset

```
Case 4
    BeginTime "Dynaset - Subset RecordCount - LastName 'L'", _
        TIME_DEBUG
    Set MyDyna = MyDb.CreateDynaset("Select * from Address Where _
        LastName Like 'L*'")
    'Operation
    MyDyna.MoveLast
    Text2 = MyDyna.RecordCount
    EndTime
    MyDyna.Close
    DoEvents
```

Listing 9.16 DataBn18.Vbp Counting Records Until a Control Break Is Reached

```
Case 5
    BeginTime "Table - Subset Count - LastName 'L'", TIME_DEBUG
    Set MyTbl = MyDb.OpenTable("Address")
    MyTbl.Index = "NameKey"
    'Operation
    MyTbl.Seek ">=", "L"
    Do Until MyTbl.EOF
        If MyTbl!Lastname >= "M" Then Exit Do
        foo = foo + 1
        MyTbl.MoveNext
    Loop
    Text2 = foo
    EndTime
    MyTbl.Close
    DoEvents
```

With the added complexity, summary queries start to demonstrate a speed advantage. As you can see in tables 9.7 and 9.8, there's now no significant difference when dealing with your small recordset, whereas table counts were three times faster before. When we test on the larger database, summary queries become 2^1/$_2$ times faster than table operations—a savings of almost a full second—and 25 percent faster than dynaset MoveLasts.

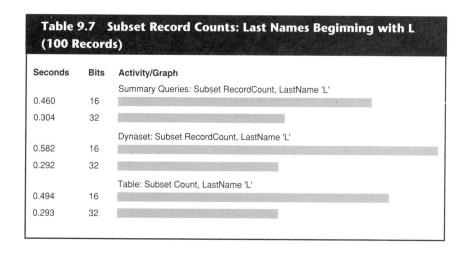

Table 9.7   Subset Record Counts: Last Names Beginning with L (100 Records)

Seconds	Bits	Activity/Graph
		Summary Queries: Subset RecordCount, LastName 'L'
0.460	16	
0.304	32	
		Dynaset: Subset RecordCount, LastName 'L'
0.582	16	
0.292	32	
		Table: Subset Count, LastName 'L'
0.494	16	
0.293	32	

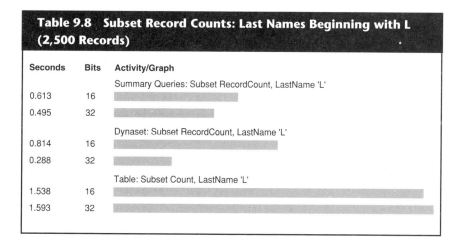

Table 9.8   Subset Record Counts: Last Names Beginning with L (2,500 Records)

Seconds	Bits	Activity/Graph
		Summary Queries: Subset RecordCount, LastName 'L'
0.613	16	
0.495	32	
		Dynaset: Subset RecordCount, LastName 'L'
0.814	16	
0.288	32	
		Table: Subset Count, LastName 'L'
1.538	16	
1.593	32	

III

Database Optimization

Very Complex Counts and Sums

Remember that although the tests have been counting records just to keep things simple, the same performance relationships apply to other types of aggregate functions. You could be totaling the values of a set of records, arriving at averages, or doing whatever, which implies more work—and value—than a simple count.

To prove that, let's test an even more complex scenario by adding some more code to DataBn18.Vbp. This scenario is a straightforward implementation of a common programming task: subtotaling values for all categories or classes of records. A typical use would be to generate a management summary of sales by product, salesman, or region. This project counts the records that begin with each letter, rather than just the L records, and displays the list in a list box. The next test uses the same logic to total the values of the TestInt field using the Sum() function.

To obtain summaries by first letter, add a Group By clause and an additional field to the query. You don't need the Where clause because you're now looking at all the records.

DAO processing gets considerably more difficult. You have to order the dynaset by LastName using the NameKey index for the table. Then read each record in the recordset or table, incrementing the count as you go, until a control break is reached. At the control break, display the data, initialize the counter, and read on.

The code in listing 9.17 shows how I implemented the grouping and aggregate functions in the summary query.

Listing 9.17   DataBn18.Vbp   Implementing the Grouping and Aggregate Functions

```
Case 6
    List1.Clear
    BeginTime "Summary Queries - Count by Letter", TIME_DEBUG
    'Operation
    Set MyDyna = MyDb.CreateDynaset("Select Mid$(LastName,1,1) _
        as firstletter, Count(Address.LastName) as tally _
        from Address group by Mid$(LastName,1,1)")
    MyDyna.MoveFirst
    Do Until MyDyna.EOF
        List1.AddItem MyDyna!FirstLetter & " - " & MyDyna!Tally
        MyDyna.MoveNext
    Loop
    EndTime
    MyDyna.Close
    DoEvents
```

Listing 9.18 demonstrates control-break processing with dynasets.

Listing 9.18 DataBn18.Vbp Control-Break Processing with Dynasets

```
Case 7
    List1.Clear
    BeginTime "Programmatic Dynaset - Count by Letter", TIME_DEBUG
    'Operation
    Set MyDyna = MyDb.CreateDynaset("Select LastName from _
        address order by LastName")
    MyDyna.MoveFirst
    foo = 0
    PrevLetter = Mid$(MyDyna!Lastname, 1, 1)
    Do Until MyDyna.EOF
        If PrevLetter <> Mid$(MyDyna!Lastname, 1, 1) Then
            List1.AddItem PrevLetter & " - " & foo
            PrevLetter = Mid$(MyDyna!Lastname, 1, 1)
            foo = 1
        Else
            foo = foo + 1
        End If
        MyDyna.MoveNext
    Loop
    List1.AddItem PrevLetter & " - " & foo
    EndTime
    MyDyna.Close
    DoEvents
```

The code in listing 9.19 implements control-break processing on the table DAO.

Listing 9.19 DataBn18.Vbp Control-Break Processing with Table DAOs

```
Case 8
    List1.Clear
    BeginTime "Programmatic Table - Count by Letter", TIME_DEBUG
    'Operation
    Set MyTbl = MyDb.OpenTable("Address")
    MyTbl.Index = "NameKey"
    MyTbl.MoveFirst
    foo = 0
    PrevLetter = Mid$(MyTbl!Lastname, 1, 1)
    Do Until MyTbl.EOF
        If PrevLetter <> Mid$(MyTbl!Lastname, 1, 1) Then
            List1.AddItem PrevLetter & " - " & foo
            PrevLetter = Mid$(MyTbl!Lastname, 1, 1)
            foo = 1
        Else
            foo = foo + 1
```

III

Database Optimization

(continues)

```
Listing 9.19  Continued
            End If
            MyTbl.MoveNext
    Loop
    List1.AddItem PrevLetter & " - " & foo
    EndTime
    MyTbl.Close
    DoEvents
```

Tables 9.9 and 9.10 show the test results. Again, the tests indicate that despite the additional code that DAO processing requires, the DAO methods are faster for small recordsets. This is due to the time that Jet must spend compiling and processing the summary query. Given enough records, though, the query becomes as much as two times faster than dynaset operations, although it's less than 20 percent faster than the table DAO method.

Table 9.9 Record Counts by First Letter of Last Names (100 Records)

Seconds	Bits	Activity/Graph
		Summary Queries, Count by Letter
0.755	16	
0.892	32	
		Programmatic Dynaset, Count by Letter
0.715	16	
0.852	32	
		Programmatic Table, Count by Letter
0.481	16	
0.441	32	

Table 9.10 Record Counts by First Letter of Last Names (2,500 Records)

Seconds	Bits	Activity/Graph
		Summary Queries, Count by Letter
6.085	16	
7.580	32	
		Programmatic Dynaset, Count by Letter
12.182	16	
9.517	32	
		Programmatic Table, Count by Letter
7.732	16	
3.885	32	

Next, let's take the same logic applied in the preceding letter-by-letter count example. But rather than count the records, let's add up the values in the TestInt field.

Again, we'll add more code to DataBn18.Vbp. The code in listing 9.20 tests the aggregate query. The code in listing 9.21 tests dynaset control-break processing. The code in listing 9.22 tests table DAO control-break processing.

Listing 9.20 DataBn18.Vbp   Testing the Aggregate Query

```
Case 12
    List1.Clear
    BeginTime "Summary Queries - Sum by Letter", TIME_DEBUG
    'Operation
    Set MyDyna = MyDb.CreateDynaset("Select Mid$(LastName,1,1) _
        as firstletter, Sum(Address.TestInt) as Total from _
        Address group by Mid$(LastName,1,1)")
    MyDyna.MoveFirst
    Do Until MyDyna.EOF
        List1.AddItem MyDyna!FirstLetter & " - " & MyDyna!Total
        MyDyna.MoveNext
    Loop
    EndTime
    MyDyna.Close
    DoEvents
```

Listing 9.21 DataBn18.Vbp   Testing Dynaset Control-Break Processing

```
Case 13
    List1.Clear
    BeginTime "Programmatic Dynaset - Sum by Letter", TIME_DEBUG
    'Operation
    Set MyDyna = MyDb.CreateDynaset("Select LastName, TestInt _
        from address order by LastName")
    MyDyna.MoveFirst
    SubTotals = 0
    PrevLetter = Mid$(MyDyna!Lastname, 1, 1)
    Do Until MyDyna.EOF
        If PrevLetter <> Mid$(MyDyna!Lastname, 1, 1) Then
            List1.AddItem PrevLetter & " - " & SubTotals
            PrevLetter = Mid$(MyDyna!Lastname, 1, 1)
            SubTotals = MyDyna!TestInt
        Else
            SubTotals = SubTotals + MyDyna!TestInt
```

(continues)

Listing 9.21   Continued

```
            End If
            MyDyna.MoveNext
    Loop
    List1.AddItem PrevLetter & " - " & foo
    EndTime
    MyDyna.Close
    DoEvents
```

Listing 9.22   DataBn18.Vbp   Testing Table DAO Control-Break Processing

```
Case 14
    List1.Clear
    BeginTime "Programmatic Table - Sum by Letter", TIME_DEBUG
    'Operation
    Set MyTbl = MyDb.OpenTable("Address")
    MyTbl.Index = "NameKey"
    MyTbl.MoveFirst
    SubTotals = 0
    PrevLetter = Mid$(MyTbl!Lastname, 1, 1)
    Do Until MyTbl.EOF
        If PrevLetter <> Mid$(MyTbl!Lastname, 1, 1) Then
            List1.AddItem PrevLetter & " - " & SubTotals
            PrevLetter = Mid$(MyTbl!Lastname, 1, 1)
            SubTotals = MyTbl!TestInt
        Else
            SubTotals = SubTotals + MyTbl!TestInt
        End If
        MyTbl.MoveNext
    Loop
    List1.AddItem PrevLetter & " - " & foo
    EndTime
    MyTbl.Close
    DoEvents
```

As tables 9.11 and 9.12 show, although Sum() takes longer in all cases than simply counting records, the differences between methods are roughly proportional to the previous test. Table DAO processing is more efficient with small recordsets, but with larger data sets, the query is fastest.

One of the strengths of SQL, and the relational model it supports, is the independence it affords the programmer from the database schema. With SQL, the individual programmer need not know how a table is indexed and, theoretically, need not care (that's the DBA's problem). And the theory works brilliantly. In all the examples above, the code based on SQL would work whether or not there was an index on the last name. The table-driven code, however, would fail completely without the NameKey index, since it's based on control-break processing (which, of course, requires that the names be in order).

Table 9.11 TestInt SubTotals Sum by First Letter of Name (100 Records)

Seconds	Bits	Activity/Graph
		Summary Queries, Sum by Letter
0.851	16	
1.209	32	
		Programmatic Dynaset, Sum by Letter
0.975	16	
1.126	32	
		Programmatic Table, Sum by Letter
0.576	16	
0.536	32	

Table 9.12 TestInt SubTotals Sum by First Letter of Name (2,500 Records)

Seconds	Bits	Activity/Graph
		Summary Queries, Sum by Letter
7.100	16	
9.312	32	
		Programmatic Dynaset, Sum by Letter
20.600	16	
11.425	32	
		Programmatic Table, Sum by Letter
9.587	16	
4.875	32	

III

Database Optimization

But what if you had to analyze fields that weren't part of an index? Would you have no choice but to use SQL? Let's examine that issue by performing another letter-by-letter record count—this time on the CompanyName field, which I've left unindexed.

The SQL code requires no significant changes: Simply substitute the CompanyName field for the LastName field throughout. The table DAO logic, however, must be completely rethought.

There are at least two options. You could use VB's data-definition language to add an index to the table and then use the control-break algorithm. But you may not always be able to add an index. For example, this database may belong to another department, and you might not be allowed to fiddle with the database structure. So in the test code, let's try another approach: have the code read through the records sequentially, and store the values in a temporary holding array, indexed by the ASCII code of the letter being read. After the code reads the table, it outputs the array, in order, converting each element's index to the appropriate letter by using the Chr$() function. It's convoluted and has a lot of code, but it should function.

Listing 9.23 shows how I modified the SQL query. The code in listing 9.24 uses control-break processing on a dynaset ordered by the unindexed CompanyName field. The code in listing 9.25 processes the table DAO sequentially and stores the results in an accumulator array.

Listing 9.23 DataBn18.Vbp The Modified SQL Query

```
Case 9
    List1.Clear
    BeginTime "Summary Queries - Count by Unindexed Letter", _
        TIME_DEBUG
    'Operation
    Set MyDyna = MyDb.CreateDynaset("Select Mid$(CompanyName,1,1) _
        as firstletter, Count(Address.CompanyName) as tally _
        from Address group by Mid$(CompanyName,1,1)")
    MyDyna.MoveFirst
    Do Until MyDyna.EOF
        List1.AddItem MyDyna!FirstLetter & " - " & MyDyna!Tally
        MyDyna.MoveNext
    Loop
    EndTime
    MyDyna.Close
    DoEvents
```

Listing 9.24   DataBn18.Vbp   Control-Break Processing on a Dynaset Ordered by an Unindexed Field

```
Case 10
    List1.Clear
    BeginTime "Programmatic Dynaset - Count by Unindexed Letter", _
        TIME_DEBUG
    'Operation
    Set MyDyna = MyDb.CreateDynaset("Select CompanyName from _
        address order by CompanyName")
    MyDyna.MoveFirst
    foo = 0
    PrevLetter = Mid$(MyDyna!CompanyName, 1, 1)
    Do Until MyDyna.EOF
        If PrevLetter <> Mid$(MyDyna!CompanyName, 1, 1) Then
            List1.AddItem PrevLetter & " - " & foo
            PrevLetter = Mid$(MyDyna!CompanyName, 1, 1)
            foo = 1
        Else
            foo = foo + 1
        End If
        MyDyna.MoveNext
    Loop
    List1.AddItem PrevLetter & " - " & foo
    EndTime
    MyDyna.Close
    DoEvents
```

Listing 9.25   DataBn18.Vbp   Processing the Table DAO Sequentially and Storing the Results

```
Case 11
    List1.Clear
    BeginTime "Programmatic Table - Count by Unindexed Letter", _
        TIME_DEBUG
    ReDim KeepCount(128) As Long
    'Operation
    Set MyTbl = MyDb.OpenTable("Address")
    MyTbl.MoveFirst
    Do Until MyTbl.EOF
        foo = Asc(Mid$(MyTbl!CompanyName, 1, 1))
        KeepCount(foo) = KeepCount(foo) + 1
        MyTbl.MoveNext
    Loop
    For foo = 1 To 128
        If KeepCount(foo) > 0 Then List1.AddItem Chr$(foo) & _
            " - " & KeepCount(foo)
    Next foo
    EndTime
    MyTbl.Close
    DoEvents
```

SQL's ability to handle unindexed conditions doesn't appear to be such a strength, at least as far as performance goes (see tables 9.13 and 9.14). The table DAO method is twice as fast with small recordsets and is almost $2\frac{1}{2}$ seconds faster when processing the large recordset. Interestingly enough, the table DAO to array accumulation code actually was faster than the indexed control-break processing in the preceding example.

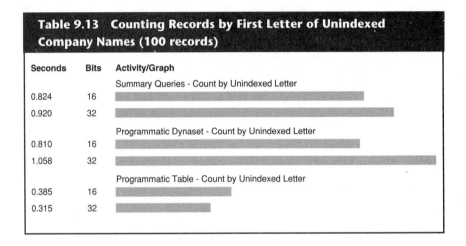

Table 9.13   Counting Records by First Letter of Unindexed Company Names (100 records)

Seconds	Bits	Activity/Graph
		Summary Queries - Count by Unindexed Letter
0.824	16	
0.920	32	
		Programmatic Dynaset - Count by Unindexed Letter
0.810	16	
1.058	32	
		Programmatic Table - Count by Unindexed Letter
0.385	16	
0.315	32	

Table 9.14   Counting Records by First Letter of Unindexed Company Names (2,500 records)

Seconds	Bits	Activity/Graph
		Summary Queries - Count by Unindexed Letter
7.525	16	
7.744	32	
		Programmatic Dynaset - Count by Unindexed Letter
15.491	16	
11.715	32	
		Programmatic Table - Count by Unindexed Letter
5.190	16	
3.145	32	

Some interesting strategies need to be considered when summarizing data. If you're optimizing a particular query, it may very well pay to add indexes and spend some time constructing a table DAO solution, which you then should test versus the SQL solution on realistic recordsets. This last step is critical, of course, because neither method is clearly faster in each situation.

On the other hand, if you're offering an *ad hoc* query mechanism for management information gathering and analysis or whatever purpose, you may find that SQL summaries deliver more than adequate performance, particularly with large recordsets. And the programmer productivity that's possible with SQL is incomparable.

Linking Tables: Joins and Pick Lists

One of the more powerful features of SQL is its join capability. Joins link tables in a meaningful way. As you saw earlier in the discussion of relational database design, the relational model essentially tears data apart in the name of storage and maintenance efficiency. Data that may be repeated from record to record is stored in separate tables, which are then referenced by a record ID or counter field.

A good example of this is the ContactType information in the test database, TestSet.Mdb. The ContactType field in the Address table is a meaningless integer, in good relational form. It points to a record in the ContactType table, which contains the human translation of the integer: 1 is a Friend, 4 is an Employee, and so on.

The challenge is to display this information in a human context because we can't expect users to remember that 1 equals Friend. The relational model and SQL joins were designed for exactly this kind of situation, but are joins always the fastest method? Can they, in fact, provide all the functionality required by a data editing interface? These and other issues are examined later in this chapter. In the following sections, we'll use DataBn19.Vbp as a test project. You can find the project on the CD in the \Chap9 directory. Figure 9.3 shows the project in operation.

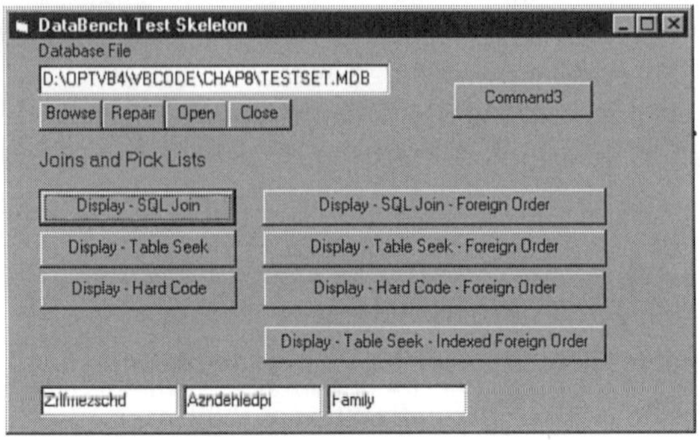

Fig. 9.3

The DataBn19 project tests SQL joins versus programmatic operations.

Simple Joins

The first analysis tests the performance of SQL joins in a simple link and the display of all records in the recordset. You create a dynaset using a left join on the tables to get all the Address records, regardless of whether there's a matching ContactType record. Then display the dynaset records one by one in text boxes to simulate loading a grid or writing a report.

The test compares the performance of the joined dynaset against a table DAO method. The table method displays the address records in order and uses the Seek method to find a match in the ContactType table.

In addition, let's take a look at a hard-coded method for emulating relational tables. In the ContactType example, a relatively small number of categories are pretty static. Although a fully normalized database would always place these categories in a separate table, hard-coding the values would provide similar functionality. This kind of denormalization may be a viable optimization technique under proper conditions—a relatively short list with value sets that don't require frequent changes or additions.

The first test is of a simple join (see listing 9.26).

Listing 9.26   DataBn19.Vbp   A Simple Join

```
Case 0
    BeginTime "Display SQL Join", TIME_DEBUG
    'Operation
    Set MyDyna = MyDb.CreateDynaset("Select LastName, FirstName, _
        TypeName from Address, ContactType, Address Left Join _
        ContactType on Address.ContactType = ContactType.TypeId _
        Order By Address.Lastname, Address.FirstName")
    MyDyna.MoveFirst
    Do Until MyDyna.EOF
        Text2(0) = MyDyna!LastName
```

```
                Text2(1) = MyDyna!FirstName
                Text2(2) = MyDyna!TypeName
                DoEvents
                MyDyna.MoveNext
        Loop
        MyDyna.Close
        EndTime
        DoEvents
```

The code in listing 9.27 programmatically simulates a join with table DAO seeks.

Listing 9.27   DataBn19.Vbp   Programmatically Simulating a Join with Table DAO Seeks

```
    Case 1
        BeginTime "Display Records with Table Seek", TIME_DEBUG
        Set MyTbl = MyDb.OpenTable("Address")
        MyTbl.Index = "NameKey"
        Set MyTbl2 = MyDb.OpenTable("ContactType")
        MyTbl2.Index = "IdKey"
        'Operation
        MyTbl.MoveFirst
        Do Until MyTbl.EOF
            Text2(0) = MyTbl!LastName
            Text2(1) = MyTbl!FirstName
            MyTbl2.Seek "=", MyTbl!ContactType
            If MyTbl2.NoMatch Then
                Text2(2) = ""
            Else
                Text2(2) = MyTbl2!TypeName
            End If
            DoEvents
            MyTbl.MoveNext
        Loop
        MyTbl.Close
        EndTime
        DoEvents
```

The code in listing 9.28 tests the hard-coded relation.

Listing 9.28   DataBn19.Vbp   Testing the Hard-Coded Relation

```
    Case 2
        BeginTime "Display Records with Hard Code", TIME_DEBUG
        Set MyTbl = MyDb.OpenTable("Address")
        MyTbl.Index = "NameKey"
        'Operation
```

(continues)

III

Database Optimization

Listing 9.28 Continued

```
        MyTbl.MoveFirst
        Do Until MyTbl.EOF
            Text2(0) = MyTbl!LastName
            Text2(1) = MyTbl!FirstName
            Select Case MyTbl!ContactType
            Case 1: Text2(2) = "Friend"
            Case 2: Text2(2) = "Customer"
            Case 3: Text2(2) = "Employee"
            Case 4: Text2(2) = "Associate"
            Case 5: Text2(2) = "Family"
            End Select
            DoEvents
            MyTbl.MoveNext
        Loop
        MyTbl.Close
        EndTime
        DoEvents
```

The test results in tables 9.15 and 9.16 show that joins are relatively slow, with both small and large recordsets. You save more than half a second with the table DAO method when you display just 100 records, and 5 seconds when you display 2,500 records. The hard-coded algorithm is even speedier, saving more than 1.2 seconds per 100 records and 16 seconds on 2,500 records.

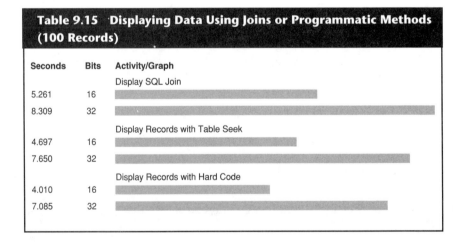

Table 9.15 Displaying Data Using Joins or Programmatic Methods (100 Records)

Seconds	Bits	Activity/Graph
		Display SQL Join
5.261	16	
8.309	32	
		Display Records with Table Seek
4.697	16	
7.650	32	
		Display Records with Hard Code
4.010	16	
7.085	32	

Table 9.16 Displaying Data Using Joins or Programmatic Methods (2,500 Records)		
Seconds	**Bits**	**Activity/Graph**
		Display SQL Join
113.453	16	
187.571	32	
		Display Records with Table Seek
108.220	16	
185.113	32	
		Display Records with Hard Code
97.357	16	
174.579	32	

Complex Joins

Let's complicate the picture and see if the analysis changes. In the preceding example, the data is presented in the table's NameKey index order. But what if you wanted to show the data by category and then by name? In other words, what if you wanted to display Associate records, then Customers, Employees, Friends, and Family?

With the SQL join, code changes are minimal—you simply revise the Order By clause. The table and hard-code algorithms require more extensive changes. To display categories in alphabetical order, you'll loop through the ContactType table in TypeName order, and then loop through the entire Address table once for each ContactType by using the NameKey so that you can display the names in the proper order. The same method will be used for the hard-code example.

The code in listing 9.29 shows how I implemented a foreign key ordered join. The code in listing 9.30 demonstrates the difficulty of foreign key ordering with table DAOs. The code in listing 9.31 shows foreign key ordering with hard-coded relationships.

Listing 9.29   DataBn19.Vbp   A Foreign Key Ordered Join

```
Case 3
    BeginTime "Display SQL Join in Foreign Key Order", TIME_DEBUG
    'Operation
```

(continues)

III

Database Optimization

Listing 9.29   Continued

```
Set MyDyna = MyDb.CreateDynaset("Select LastName, FirstName, _
    TypeName from Address, ContactType, Address Left Join _
    ContactType on Address.ContactType = ContactType.TypeId _
    Order By ContactType.TypeName, Address.Lastname, _
    Address.FirstName")
MyDyna.MoveFirst
Do Until MyDyna.EOF
    Text2(0) = MyDyna!LastName
    Text2(1) = MyDyna!FirstName
    Text2(2) = MyDyna!TypeName
    DoEvents
    MyDyna.MoveNext
Loop
MyDyna.Close
EndTime
DoEvents
```

Listing 9.30   DataBn19.Vbp   Foreign Key Ordering with Table DAOs

```
Case 4
    BeginTime "Display Records with Table Seek - by Foreign Key", _
        TIME_DEBUG
    Set MyTbl = MyDb.OpenTable("Address")
    MyTbl.Index = "NameKey"
    Set MyTbl2 = MyDb.OpenTable("ContactType")
    MyTbl2.Index = "NameKey"
    'Operation
    MyTbl2.MoveFirst
    Do Until MyTbl2.EOF
        MyTbl.MoveFirst
        Do Until MyTbl.EOF
            If MyTbl2!TypeId = MyTbl!ContactType Then
                Text2(0) = MyTbl!LastName
                Text2(1) = MyTbl!FirstName
                Text2(2) = MyTbl2!TypeName
                DoEvents
            End If
            MyTbl.MoveNext
        Loop
        MyTbl2.MoveNext
    Loop
    MyTbl.Close
    EndTime
    DoEvents
```

**Listing 9.31   DataBn19.Vbp   Foreign Key Ordering with
Hard-Coded Relationships**

```
Case 5
    BeginTime "Display Records with Hard Code - by Foreign Key", _
        TIME_DEBUG
    Set MyTbl = MyDb.OpenTable("Address")
    MyTbl.Index = "NameKey"
    'Operation
    For foo = 1 To 5
        'fix alpha order of TypeIds
        Select Case foo
        Case 1
            foobar = 4
            Text2(2) = "Associate"
        Case 2
            foobar = 2
            Text2(2) = "Customer"
        Case 3
            foobar = 3
            Text2(2) = "Employee"
        Case 4
            foobar = 5
            Text2(2) = "Family"
        Case 5
            foobar = 1
            Text2(2) = "Friend"
        End Select
        MyTbl.MoveFirst
        Do Until MyTbl.EOF
            If MyTbl!ContactType = foobar Then
                Text2(0) = MyTbl!LastName
                Text2(1) = MyTbl!FirstName
                DoEvents
            End If
            MyTbl.MoveNext
        Loop
    Next foo
    MyTbl.Close
    EndTime
    DoEvents
```

Tables 9.17 and 9.18 show the test results. Changing the display order slows down the SQL join a little. But dealing with small recordsets seems to have no effect on table access—despite having to cycle through the 100 records five times. Hard-coded access seems to have even been speeded up because the routine isn't constantly rewriting the type.

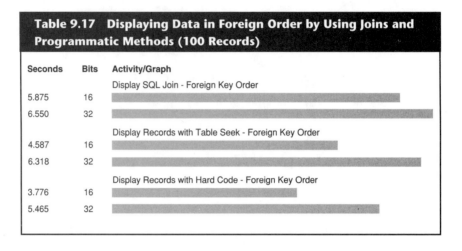

Table 9.17   Displaying Data in Foreign Order by Using Joins and Programmatic Methods (100 Records)

Seconds	Bits	Activity/Graph
		Display SQL Join - Foreign Key Order
5.875	16	
6.550	32	
		Display Records with Table Seek - Foreign Key Order
4.587	16	
6.318	32	
		Display Records with Hard Code - Foreign Key Order
3.776	16	
5.465	32	

Table 9.18   Displaying Data in Foreign Order by Using Joins and Programmatic Methods (100 Records)

Seconds	Bits	Activity/Graph
		Display SQL Join in Foreign Key Order
104.182	16	
147.760	32	
		Display Records with Table Seek
112.051	16	
151.302	32	
		Display Records with Hard Code
95.118	16	
132.018	32	

With large data sets, however, the advantage shifts to joins over table seeks. The join has picked up speed because VB naturally spends less time displaying unchanged assignments to a text box than displaying changed text. The join is now faster than the table method, and the hard-code implementation is faster still. The implication is that when you can do it, hard-coded lists save speed. If lists are large or volatile, you should test both table DAO methods and SQL joins.

Another strategy for database optimization is to change the database structure. In the preceding example, you had to repeatedly read the entire Address table because the ContactType integer wasn't indexed—and wouldn't be in the proper order even if it was. Of course, you might not have the discretion to add an index anyway.

But if you can add an index, you can save significant input/output cycles. You add an index, ContactTypeKey, with ContactType as the first field, followed by last and first names. Now the only problem is that the ContactType integer isn't in alphabetical TypeName order. But you can loop through the ContactTypes table in order and then jump by using a seek to the first matching integer, so that you don't have all that wasteful sequential I/O.

Listing 9.32 shows how I implemented keyed foreign key ordering in DataBn19.Vbp.

Listing 9.32 DataBn19.Vbp Keyed Foreign Key Ordering

```
Case 6
    BeginTime "Display Records with Table Seek - Indexed _
        Foreign Key Order", TIME_DEBUG
    Set MyTbl = MyDb.OpenTable("Address")
    MyTbl.Index = "ContactTypeKey"
    Set MyTbl2 = MyDb.OpenTable("ContactType")
    MyTbl2.Index = "NameKey"
    'Operation
    MyTbl2.MoveFirst
    Do Until MyTbl2.EOF
        'Jump to first appropriate type record
        MyTbl.Seek ">=", MyTbl2!TypeId
        Do Until MyTbl.EOF
            If MyTbl2!TypeId = MyTbl!ContactType Then
                Text2(0) = MyTbl!LastName
                Text2(1) = MyTbl!FirstName
                Text2(2) = MyTbl2!TypeName
                DoEvents
            Else
                Exit Do
            End If
            MyTbl.MoveNext
        Loop
        MyTbl2.MoveNext
    Loop
    MyTbl.Close
    EndTime
    DoEvents
```

The test shows significantly faster results (see table 9.19). Table join simulations now appear to be much faster than SQL joins.

III

Database Optimization

Table 9.19 Displaying Data in Indexed Foreign Order Using Table Methods		
Seconds	**Bits**	**Activity/Graph**
		Display Records with Table Seek - 100 Records
3.447	16	▪
5.716	32	▪
		Display Records with Table Seek - 2500 Records
84.611	16	▬▬▬▬▬▬▬▬
138.022	32	▬▬▬▬▬▬▬▬▬▬

Relational Data Editing

Perhaps the greatest weakness of SQL joins is that they really don't facilitate data editing. Joins don't provide a mechanism for showing alternative choices. They only include the choice that was made or set in the data set, so they're highly productive if you're coding a display mechanism. But when constructing an edit interface, the issue is pick list loading. Whether loading a list box or a combo control, you have to provide the user with some way to display and make choices.

The justification for testing the hard-code method detailed in the preceding example now becomes a little clearer. The best interface analogy to hard-coded values is radio buttons. When you make a few radio buttons available, you're hard-coding the user's choices visually.

The issue, then, that we'll examine is the relative speed of different methods for constructing lists of choices, or pick lists. DataBn20.Vbp, which you'll find on the CD in the \Chap9 directory, tests loading pick lists from SQL dynasets, table DAOs, and hard code. It places the text choice in a combo control and saves the related integer value to the combo's linked ItemData array. Figure 9.4 shows the main form for this project.

We'll repeat each method 10 times to get more significant values because we have only five choices to add to the list. The code in listing 9.33 tests loading a pick list from a dynaset. The code in listing 9.34 loads the list from a table. The code in listing 9.35 loads the list using hard-coded values.

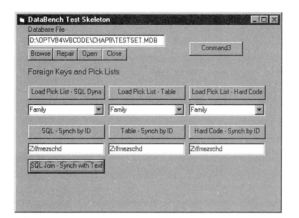

Fig. 9.4
Loading pick lists
in DataBn20.Vbp.

Listing 9.33   DataBn20.Vbp   Loading a Pick List from a Dynaset

```
Case 0
    BeginTime "Load Pick List from SQL Dynaset", TIME_DEBUG
    'Operation
    For foobar = 1 To 10
        Combo1(Index).Clear
        Set MyDyna = MyDb.CreateDynaset("Select * from _
            ContactType Order By TypeName")
        MyDyna.MoveFirst
        Do Until MyDyna.EOF
            Combo1(Index).AddItem MyDyna!TypeName
            Combo1(Index).ItemData(Combo1(Index).ListCount - 1) _
                MyDyna!TypeId
            = MyDyna.MoveNext
        Loop
        MyDyna.Close
    Next foobar
    EndTime
    DoEvents
```

Listing 9.34   DataBn20.Vbp   Loading a Pick List from a Table

```
Case 1
    BeginTime "Load Pick List from Table", TIME_DEBUG
    For foobar = 1 To 10
        Combo1(Index).Clear
        Set MyTbl = MyDb.OpenTable("ContactType")
        MyTbl.Index = "NameKey"
        'Operation
        MyTbl.MoveFirst
        Do Until MyTbl.EOF
```

(continues)

Listing 9.34   Continued

```
                Combo1(Index).AddItem MyTbl!TypeName
                Combo1(Index).ItemData(Combo1(Index).ListCount - 1) _
                    = MyTbl!TypeId
                MyTbl.MoveNext
            Loop
            MyTbl.Close
        Next foobar
        EndTime
        DoEvents
```

Listing 9.35   DataBn20.Vbp   Loading a Pick List Using Hard-Coded Values

```
    Case 2
        BeginTime "Load Pick List from Hard Code", TIME_DEBUG
        For foobar = 1 To 10
            Combo1(Index).Clear
            Combo1(Index).AddItem "Associate"
            Combo1(Index).ItemData(0) = 4
            Combo1(Index).AddItem "Customer"
            Combo1(Index).ItemData(1) = 2
            Combo1(Index).AddItem "Employee"
            Combo1(Index).ItemData(2) = 3
            Combo1(Index).AddItem "Family"
            Combo1(Index).ItemData(3) = 5
            Combo1(Index).AddItem "Friend"
            Combo1(Index).ItemData(4) = 1
        Next foobar
        EndTime
```

As you might expect, loading the pick list from hard code is much faster than other methods, as you can see in table 9.20. Table DAO methods come in a solid second, making them the best choice for larger or less static pick lists. SQL dynasets are by far the slowest choice.

Synchronizing Edit Data

In a data edit task flow, you might first load the pick list and then get the target record. The next issue would be synchronizing the pick list display with the data in the record. In other words, the combo box is needed to display the text that relates to the database record's value.

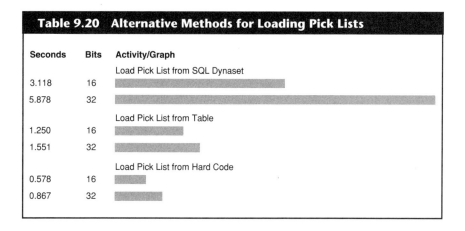

Table 9.20   Alternative Methods for Loading Pick Lists

Seconds	Bits	Activity/Graph
		Load Pick List from SQL Dynaset
3.118	16	
5.878	32	
		Load Pick List from Table
1.250	16	
1.551	32	
		Load Pick List from Hard Code
0.578	16	
0.867	32	

Because DataBn20.Vbp saved the integer value for each pick list text entry in the `ItemData` array, you easily can set the appropriate `ListIndex` value and thus display the matching text by scanning `ItemData` until you find a match. You'll use this method to synchronize 100 table and dynaset records. With the hard-coded example, you can simply set the `ListIndex` to the value you want in a `Select Case` statement.

The last alternative is to obtain the `TypeName` text by joining the records, as you've seen before, and then set the value property of the combo control to equal the text value in the join.

The example in listing 9.36 synchronizes dynaset data using the integer ID. The code in listing 9.37 synchronizes the combo list with the table using the ID. The code in listing 9.38 synchronizes the hard-coded list. The code in listing 9.39 synchronizes joined records using the text value, rather than the ID, in the dynaset.

Listing 9.36   DataBn20.Vbp   Synchronizing Dynaset Data

```
Case 3
    BeginTime "Synchronize SQL Dynaset With Pick List by ID ",_
        TIME_DEBUG
    'Operation
    Set MyDyna = MyDb.CreateDynaset("Select * from Address Order _
        By LastName, FirstName")
    MyDyna.MoveFirst
    Do Until MyDyna.EOF
        Text2(Index - 3) = MyDyna!LastName
        foobar = Combo1(Index - 3).ListCount - 1
        For foo = 0 To foobar
```

(continues)

Listing 9.36   Continued

```
                If Combo1(Index - 3).ItemData(foo) = _
                    MyDyna!ContactType Then
                    Combo1(Index - 3).ListIndex = foo
                    Exit For
                End If
            Next foo
            DoEvents
            MyDyna.MoveNext
    Loop
    MyDyna.Close
    EndTime
    DoEvents
```

Listing 9.37   DataBn20.Vbp   Synchronizing a Combo List

```
    Case 4
        BeginTime "Synchronize Table With Pick List by ID ", TIME_DEBUG
        'Operation
        Set MyTbl = MyDb.OpenTable("Address")
        MyTbl.Index = "NameKey"
        MyTbl.MoveFirst
        Do Until MyTbl.EOF
            Text2(Index - 3) = MyTbl!LastName
            foobar = Combo1(Index - 3).ListCount - 1
            For foo = 0 To foobar
                If Combo1(Index - 3).ItemData(foo) = _
                    MyTbl!ContactType Then
                    Combo1(Index - 3).ListIndex = foo
                    Exit For
                End If
            Next foo
            DoEvents
            MyTbl.MoveNext
        Loop
        MyTbl.Close
        EndTime
        DoEvents
```

Listing 9.38   DataBn20.Vbp   Synchronizing the Hard-Coded List

```
    Case 5
        BeginTime "Synchronize Table With Pick List by Hard Code _
            ID ", TIME_DEBUG
        'Operation
        Set MyTbl = MyDb.OpenTable("Address")
        MyTbl.Index = "NameKey"
```

```
MyTbl.MoveFirst
Do Until MyTbl.EOF
    Text2(Index - 3) = MyTbl!LastName
    Select Case MyTbl!ContactType
    Case 1: Combo1(Index - 3).ListIndex = 4
    Case 2: Combo1(Index - 3).ListIndex = 1
    Case 3: Combo1(Index - 3).ListIndex = 2
    Case 4: Combo1(Index - 3).ListIndex = 0
    Case 5: Combo1(Index - 3).ListIndex = 3
    End Select
    DoEvents
    MyTbl.MoveNext
Loop
MyTbl.Close
EndTime
DoEvents
```

Listing 9.39   DataBn20.Vbp   Synchronizing Joined Dynaset Records Using the Text Value

```
Case 6
    BeginTime "Synchronize SQL Join With Pick List by Text", _
      TIME_DEBUG
    'Operation
    Set MyDyna = MyDb.CreateDynaset("Select * from Address, _
        ContactType, Address Left Join ContactType on _
        Address.ContactType = ContactType.TypeId Order _
        By LastName, FirstName")
    MyDyna.MoveFirst
    Do Until MyDyna.EOF
        Text2(0) = MyDyna!LastName
        Combo1(0) = MyDyna!TypeName
        DoEvents
        MyDyna.MoveNext
    Loop
    DoEvents
    MyDyna.Close
    EndTime
```

Again, hard code is the fastest, whereas dynaset processing is slowest (see table 9.21). But the table DAO and join methods are roughly equivalent when processing 100 records. Of course, if you were trying to edit a single record, the overhead involved in setting up the join would be more significant. But scanning the ItemData array does take time. The larger the list set, the more time you'll need.

III

Database Optimization

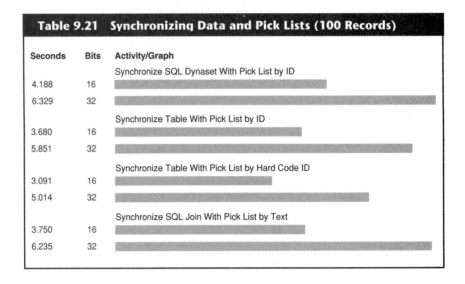

Table 9.21   Synchronizing Data and Pick Lists (100 Records)

Seconds	Bits	Activity/Graph
		Synchronize SQL Dynaset With Pick List by ID
4.188	16	
6.329	32	
		Synchronize Table With Pick List by ID
3.680	16	
5.851	32	
		Synchronize Table With Pick List by Hard Code ID
3.091	16	
5.014	32	
		Synchronize SQL Join With Pick List by Text
3.750	16	
6.235	32	

When you're editing records in the relational model, there are other issues to be concerned about. Saving data can be problematic, as can maintaining parent tables. Loading bound grids pretty much requires use of joins because they act on dynaset recordsets. Then there are reporting issues: With the Crystal Reports report designer, included with the Professional and Enterprise editions of VB, you must use joins and a full relational model. If you write your own reports, you have more flexibility but pay a significant price in programming time.

In any case, the rules for optimization remain the same: Analysis of the challenges and alternatives for particular situations is the key. There are no written-in-stone rules to rely on.

Queries and QueryDefs

QueryDefs are SQL statements that are stored in the database, not in your code. Like any SQL statement, you can use QueryDefs to create dynasets or snapshots, or to execute action queries to update or delete a set of records.

But unlike SQL statements that you pass as text to the Jet engine with the `OpenRecordset` or `CreateDynaset` methods, Jet analyzes and optimizes the way it will fulfill a QueryDef operation when the QueryDef is written to the database. Those familiar with other implementations of SQL will be more familiar with the concept as a *stored procedure*.

How does this improve performance? When you execute a text SQL statement stored in VB code by using the Jet engine, the first thing it does is parse the query to break it down into the necessary steps. Next, Access tries to create a fulfillment strategy that will optimize its handling of the query by using whatever indexes would affect the operation and other internal tricks. Finally, it executes the query. Query parsing and optimization naturally take time. By preprocessing QueryDefs, Jet moves the time required for these steps from runtime to design time.

Of course, you can consider QueryDefs only when you have a standardized query—that is, one that's used in a consistent manner. You can't use them to improve *ad hoc* queries because, by their nature, *ad hoc* queries are generated at runtime.

DataBn21.Vbp, which you'll find on the CD in the \Chap9 directory, analyzes various QueryDefs to determine how much of a performance improvement they offer. Figure 9.5 shows the project running.

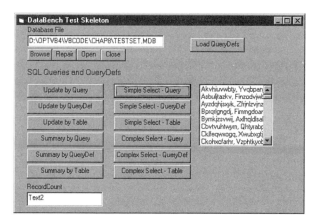

Fig. 9.5
The main form for DataBn21.Vbp.

Action QueryDefs

The first QueryDef analysis will test the speed of an update query that will set all records with a LastName beginning with L to a value. You'll compare the `database.Execute` method's performance by using a text query and then by executing an identically structured QueryDef. To provide a broader context, you'll also run a table DAO method.

The first code clip, in listing 9.40, shows an action query. The code in listing 9.41 executes an action QueryDef. The code in listing 9.42 performs the action with programmatic table DAO processing.

Listing 9.40 DataBn21.Vbp An Action Query

```
Case 0
    BeginTime "Update Query", TIME_DEBUG
    'Operation
    MyDb.Execute ("Update Address Set TestInt = 1111 _
        Where Lastname Like 'L*'")
    DoEvents
    EndTime
    DoEvents
```

Listing 9.41 DataBn21.Vbp An Action QueryDef

```
Case 1
    DoEvents
    BeginTime "Update QueryDef", TIME_DEBUG
    MyDb.Execute ("QdUpdate")
    EndTime
    DoEvents
```

Listing 9.42 DataBn21.Vbp Performing the Action with Programmatic Table DAO Processing

```
Case 2
    BeginTime "Update by Table", TIME_DEBUG
    Set MyTbl = MyDb.OpenTable("Address")
    MyTbl.Index = "NameKey"
    'Operation
    MyTbl.Seek ">=", "L"
    BeginTrans
    Do Until MyTbl.EOF
        If MyTbl!LastName >= "M" Then Exit Do
        MyTbl.Edit
        MyTbl!TestInt = 3333
        MyTbl.Update
        MyTbl.MoveNext
    Loop
    CommitTrans
    EndTime
    MyTbl.Close
    DoEvents
```

As tables 9.22 and 9.23 show, using a QueryDef saves a little time with 100 records, but the table DAO method is faster still. When processing 2,500 records, the QueryDef saves more than half a second over the text query, but the table DAO is still marginally faster.

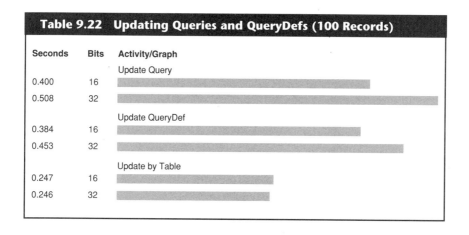

Table 9.22	Updating Queries and QueryDefs (100 Records)	
Seconds	**Bits**	**Activity/Graph**
		Update Query
0.400	16	
0.508	32	
		Update QueryDef
0.384	16	
0.453	32	
		Update by Table
0.247	16	
0.246	32	

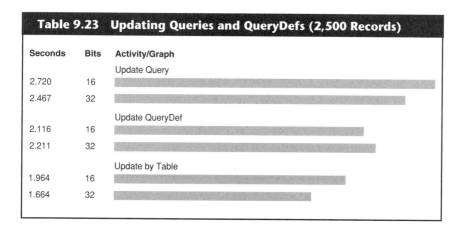

Table 9.23	Updating Queries and QueryDefs (2,500 Records)	
Seconds	**Bits**	**Activity/Graph**
		Update Query
2.720	16	
2.467	32	
		Update QueryDef
2.116	16	
2.211	32	
		Update by Table
1.964	16	
1.664	32	

Summary QueryDefs

Let's turn our attention to summary queries to see what impact QueryDefs have on these statements. The following code counts the records in the Address table by using the Count() aggregate function in a text SQL statement and a QueryDef. It also compares the results to a table record count calculation.

The code in listing 9.43 uses a text query to count the records. The code in listing 9.44 implements the summary query in a QueryDef. The code in listing 9.45 creates the summary data from a table DAO.

Listing 9.43   DataBn21.Vbp   Counting the Records with a Text Query

```
Case 3
    BeginTime "Summary Query - RecordCount", TIME_DEBUG
    'Operation
    Set MyDyna = MyDb.CreateDynaset("Select Count(*) as Tally _
        from Address")
    MyDyna.MoveFirst
    Text2 = MyDyna!Tally
    EndTime
    MyDyna.Close
    DoEvents
```

Listing 9.44   DataBn21.Vbp   Implementing the Summary Query in a QueryDef

```
Case 4
    Set MyQd = MyDb.OpenQueryDef("QdSummary")
    MyQd.SQL = "Select Count(*) as Tally from Address"
    MyQd.Close
    BeginTime "Summary QueryDef - RecordCount", TIME_DEBUG
    'Operation
    Set MyDyna = MyDb.CreateDynaset("QdSummary")
    MyDyna.MoveFirst
    Text2 = MyDyna!Tally
    EndTime
    MyDyna.Close
    DoEvents
```

Listing 9.45   DataBn21.Vbp   Creating Summary Data from a Table DAO

```
Case 5
    BeginTime "Summary by Table - RecordCount", TIME_DEBUG
    Set MyTbl = MyDb.OpenTable("Address")
    'Operation
    MyTbl.MoveLast
    Text2 = MyTbl.RecordCount
    EndTime
    MyTbl.Close
    DoEvents
```

The results are interesting (see tables 9.24 and 9.25). On the 100-record table, QueryDefs provide no advantage over a text summary query. In fact, the speeds are identical. When processing against 2,500 records, however, the QueryDef is four times faster than the text query. Of course, in both cases, the table DAO `RecordCount` property is much faster when determining record counts, as you saw in earlier tests.

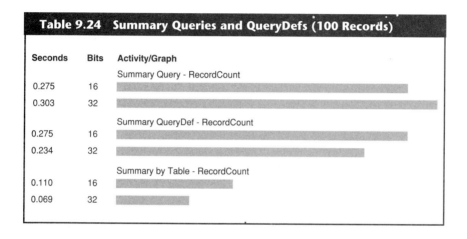

Table 9.24   Summary Queries and QueryDefs (100 Records)

Seconds	Bits	Activity/Graph
		Summary Query - RecordCount
0.275	16	
0.303	32	
		Summary QueryDef - RecordCount
0.275	16	
0.234	32	
		Summary by Table - RecordCount
0.110	16	
0.069	32	

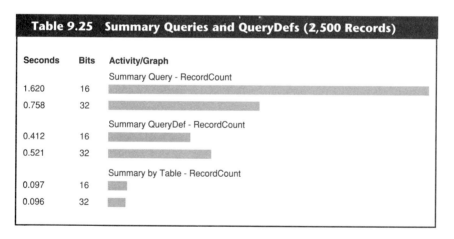

Table 9.25   Summary Queries and QueryDefs (2,500 Records)

Seconds	Bits	Activity/Graph
		Summary Query - RecordCount
1.620	16	
0.758	32	
		Summary QueryDef - RecordCount
0.412	16	
0.521	32	
		Summary by Table - RecordCount
0.097	16	
0.096	32	

Select QueryDefs

You'll test select QueryDefs under two scenarios—first by displaying all records in the table in a list box, and then by using reasonably complex conditions. Again, the SQL operations will be compared against table DAO methods.

The code in listing 9.46 implements a simple text query. The code clip in listing 9.47 shows the dynaset being created by a QueryDef. The code listing 9.48 emulates the select with a table DAO.

Listing 9.46 DataBn21.Vbp Implementing a Simple Text Query

```
Case 6
    List1.Clear
    BeginTime "Simple Select Query", TIME_DEBUG
    'Operation
    Set MyDyna = MyDb.CreateDynaset("Select * from Address _
        order by lastname, firstname")
    MyDyna.MoveFirst
    Do Until MyDyna.EOF
        List1.AddItem MyDyna!LastName & ", " & MyDyna!FirstName
        MyDyna.MoveNext
    Loop
    EndTime
    MyDyna.Close
    DoEvents
```

Listing 9.47 DataBn21.Vbp Creating a Dynaset with a QueryDef

```
Case 7
    List1.Clear
    BeginTime "Simple Select QueryDef", TIME_DEBUG
    'Operation
    Set MyDyna = MyDb.CreateDynaset("QdSelect1")
    MyDyna.MoveFirst
    Do Until MyDyna.EOF
        List1.AddItem MyDyna!LastName & ", " & MyDyna!FirstName
        MyDyna.MoveNext
    Loop
    EndTime
    MyDyna.Close
    DoEvents
```

Listing 9.48 DataBn21.Vbp Emulating the Select with a Table DAO

```
Case 8
    List1.Clear
    BeginTime "Simple Select by Table DAO", TIME_DEBUG
    Set MyTbl = MyDb.OpenTable("Address")
    MyTbl.Index = "NameKey"
    'Operation
    MyTbl.MoveFirst
```

```
Do Until MyTbl.EOF
    List1.AddItem MyTbl!LastName & ", " & MyTbl!FirstName
    MyTbl.MoveNext
Loop
EndTime
MyTbl.Close
DoEvents
```

Tables 9.26 and 9.27 show the results. QueryDefs are 25 percent faster than text queries with small recordsets, but only about 10 percent faster with large recordsets. Tables, however, are much faster—twice as fast with 100 records and almost twice as fast with 2,500 records.

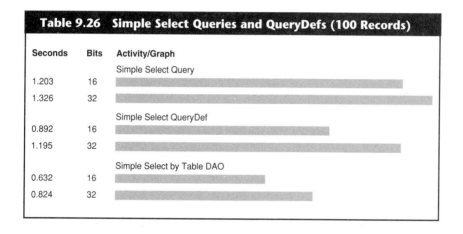

Table 9.26   Simple Select Queries and QueryDefs (100 Records)

Seconds	Bits	Activity/Graph
		Simple Select Query
1.203	16	
1.326	32	
		Simple Select QueryDef
0.892	16	
1.195	32	
		Simple Select by Table DAO
0.632	16	
0.824	32	

Table 9.27   Simple Select Queries and QueryDefs (2,500 Records)

Seconds	Bits	Activity/Graph
		Simple Select Query
20.806	16	
26.522	32	
		Simple Select QueryDef
18.815	16	
23.665	32	
		Simple Select by Table DAO
12.538	16	
17.799	32	

III

Database Optimization

The more complex Select test retrieves those records where the company name and the last name start with the letters A through L. Because the CompanyName field isn't indexed, the table method must sequentially review all the records where the last name meets the criteria.

The code in listing 9.49 tests the complex query. Listing 9.50 shows the QueryDef code. Finally, listing 9.51 shows the table DAO code.

Listing 9.49 DataBn21.Vbp   Testing the Complex Query

```
Case 9
    List1.Clear
    BeginTime "Complex Select Query", TIME_DEBUG
    'Operation
    Set MyDyna = MyDb.CreateDynaset("Select * from Address where _
        CompanyName <= 'L' and Lastname <= 'L' order by lastname,
firstname")
    MyDyna.MoveFirst
    Do Until MyDyna.EOF
        List1.AddItem MyDyna!LastName & ", " & MyDyna!FirstName
        MyDyna.MoveNext
    Loop
    EndTime
    MyDyna.Close
    DoEvents
```

Listing 9.50 DataBn21.Vbp   The QueryDef Code

```
Case 10
    List1.Clear
    BeginTime "Complex Select QueryDef", TIME_DEBUG
    'Operation
    Set MyDyna = MyDb.CreateDynaset("QdSelect2")
    MyDyna.MoveFirst
    Do Until MyDyna.EOF
        List1.AddItem MyDyna!LastName & ", " & MyDyna!FirstName
        MyDyna.MoveNext
    Loop
    EndTime
    MyDyna.Close
    DoEvents
```

Listing 9.51   DataBn21.Vbp   The Table DAO Code

```
Case 11
    List1.Clear
    BeginTime "Complex Select by Table DAO", TIME_DEBUG
    Set MyTbl = MyDb.OpenTable("Address")
    MyTbl.Index = "NameKey"
    'Operation
    MyTbl.MoveFirst
    Do Until MyTbl.EOF
        If MyTbl!LastName >= "M" Then Exit Do
        If MyTbl!LastName <= "L" Then
            List1.AddItem MyTbl!LastName & ", " & MyTbl!FirstName
        End If
        MyTbl.MoveNext
    Loop
    EndTime
    MyTbl.Close
    DoEvents
```

As shown in tables 9.28 and 9.29, the QueryDef is significantly faster than the text query in processing the Select statement with small numbers of records, but the table DAO operation is much faster still. When we process against a larger recordset, however, everything is different. The table operation is the slowest alternative, with text and QueryDef SQL statements being roughly equivalent.

Table 9.28   Complex Select Queries and QueryDefs (100 Records)

Seconds	Bits	Activity/Graph
		Complex Select Query
0.775	16	
0.718	32	
		Complex Select QueryDef
0.563	16	
0.577	32	
		Complex Select by Table DAO
0.398	16	
0.494	32	

III

Database Optimization

Table 9.29		Complex Select Queries and QueryDefs (2,500 Records)
Seconds	Bits	Activity/Graph
		Complex Select Query
6.029	16	
6.331	32	
		Complex Select QueryDef
5.851	16	
6.043	32	
		Complex Select by Table DAO
7.486	16	
9.795	32	

Incremental Jet Optimization and QueryDefs

Earlier I touched on the need to run and rerun optimization tests because of the multitasking nature of Windows. However, an interesting phenomenon raises its head when we test data processes. We know that Jet is an optimizing engine, and the Rushmore technology borrowed from FoxPro can affect processing as well. Apparently, there's an incremental optimization effect with Jet. The more often you run a query, the faster it becomes.

The effect seems to be distinct from the overhead of loading the Jet DLLs, or the beneficial effects of record caching, because if you run other statements (such as a count against a data set) and then run and rerun a `Select` against the records, the `Select` will still get progressively faster for three to four trials before it tops out. The effect can also be seen in table DAO operations. QueryDefs are relatively immune to the effect, as table 9.30 illustrates. You can observe the effect yourself by running just about any of the DataBench routines I've reviewed.

Table 9.30	Jet Incremental Optimization

Seconds	Activity/Graph
	Complex Select Query - 1st Run
0.954	
	Complex Select QueryDef - 1st Run
0.575	
	Complex Select Query - 2nd Run
0.592	
	Complex Select QueryDef - 2nd Run
0.559	

This effect makes optimization and benchmarking rather difficult, as you can imagine—the best you can do is use an average. The bottom line for optimization is that you can't make craftsmanlike judgments about data operations. You should always test your alternatives under the most realistic conditions possible. Generic tests, such as the ones I've discussed, can provide ideas for testing and strategies for optimization but can't provide the whole answer. The unique and individual circumstances of your database structure, table size, application architecture, and patterns of use combine to dictate your optimal solution.

From Here...

For related information, refer to these chapters:

- For information on relational database theory and database design in general, see Chapter 3, "Designing Optimized Applications."

- See Chapter 7, "Speeding Database Operations" and Chapter 8, "More Database Speed," for more information on database optimization.

- For information on tuning the Jet engine, see Chapter 10, "Tuning the Jet Engine."

III

Database Optimization

Chapter 10
Tuning the Jet Engine

As Visual Basic programmers, we often wonder whether we're getting optimal performance from the Jet engine. Chapters 7, 8, and 9 covered just about everything we can do to speed our VB database code. But we're not done yet. In this chapter, we'll reach outside the code and into the Jet engine itself to fine-tune its inner workings.

> The default settings for Jet are pretty good. Often, you'll find that changing the Jet-tuning settings will hurt rather than help performance. Plus, changes that improve performance under one set of conditions may decrease performance in another situation. You should always test your changes, using as realistic a test set as possible, on a machine that mirrors that used by your typical user.

To aid in the analysis, we'll use a version of the DataBench program called DataTune.Vbp that will allow you to test Jet after modifying the parameters for Jet under Windows 3.1. In Windows 95, you'll need to use RegEdit.Exe, the Windows 95 utility, to change the Jet registry settings. You'll get a closer look at the details of modifying Jet parameters in the "How to Tune Jet" section later in this chapter.

We'll look at the following topics in this chapter:

- The parameters that can be changed to tune Jet operations
- The mechanisms or utilities to use to change Jet parameters
- What effect tuning has on performance in a test scenario

Jet-Tuning Parameters

When you read a record using Jet, you don't just read a record. Many things are happening under the hood, so to speak. Pages are locked and unlocked, caches are scanned and populated, and records are buffered. You can control—or at least influence—some of these activities by adjusting Jet's parameters in the Vb.Ini file.

The following sections introduce the different settings available.

MaxBufferSize

The MaxBufferSize parameter controls the amount of RAM, in kilobytes, that Jet uses as a disk cache. It's an integer setting with a minimum value of 18, a maximum value of 4,096, and a default value of 512. The parameter's value must always be an even number, or it will be reduced by one (for example, a value of 511 will yield a 510K buffer). The data stored in the cache reflects the data most often read and written and is different from the data stored in the ReadAheadPages cache.

Of course, memory used as a cache for Jet is memory that isn't available for applications. Often, the additional memory would be better used to speed overall application performance, particularly on PCs running Windows 95 with 8M or less of RAM.

ReadAheadPages

The ReadAheadPages parameter controls the number of sequential 2K data pages that Jet reads into the buffer whenever it reads a record request. In other words, if you're reading a single record and ReadAheadPages is set to 20, Jet will strive to read the next 40K worth of data into the buffer (if the pages aren't already present). The minimum setting for ReadAheadPages is 0, the maximum value is 31, and the default is 16.

Lots of page caching is great if you're performing sequential processing, but it can drag performance down if you're randomly accessing records or accessing records in a different order from that in which they're physically stored on disk.

PageTimeout and LockedPageTimeout

PageTimeout and LockedPageTimeout are like the "Sell By" date on a loaf of bread: they tell Jet whether a data page is fresh enough to use. In other words, in a multiuser environment, if you have a data page cached in RAM, it may or may not reflect the actual data in the database. Jet makes an educated guess, based strictly on the time since last read, whether to use the cached page based on the value in these parameters.

Before Access 2.0, locked and unlocked pages had the same freshness settings. Now, they each have their own parameter. `LockedPageTimeout` and `PageTimeout` have a minimum value of 0, a maximum of more than 2 billion, and a default of 5. (These measurements are in tenths of a second, so the default value of 5 represents a half second.)

> These settings have no effect if you open your database for exclusive use, because there's no possibility that another user could overwrite your data. The cached data is always guaranteed fresh. If you're writing a single-user application, then, you should always open your database with the `OpenDatabase` method's exclusive parameter set to true.

IdleFrequency

The `IdleFrequency` parameter controls when a page is removed from the page cache and is based on the number of move attempts, or record pointer resets, that are executed. In other words, if a page in the cache still hasn't been used after *x* number of `Seeks` or `MoveNexts`, Jet will discard it.

A large value for `IdleFrequency` is generally only better if your application isn't revising data extensively. In other words, your program should be used primarily for viewing data, not modifying it, for changes to this setting to be helpful.

LockRetry and *CommitLockRetry*

`LockRetry` and `CommitLockRetry` are effective only in multiuser operations. What's more, they have an effect only in the event of a data operations failure due to page locking. When you edit a Jet record in a shared database, Jet tries to lock the page (when locking occurs depends on the style of locking you've specified: optimistic or pessimistic). If another user has the page locked, Jet won't return an error immediately. Rather, Jet will try *x* number of times to lock the page before giving up and reporting an error. If you're using transaction processing, Jet will try `LockRetry` multiplied by `CommitLockRetry` times to lock the page—which can become a huge number. The default number of retries is 20, with a minimum of 0 and a maximum of 2 billion.

A lower value for these parameters would result in more errors, but they would be reported to the user more quickly.

How to Tune Jet

Now that you understand the tuning parameters, let's look at how to change them. Under Windows 3.1, the parameters are stored in the .INI file for whatever application is calling the Jet engine. When VB calls in the Jet DLLs, the parameters in the Vb.Ini file are read and applied to the engine. In Windows 95, the settings are stored in the Registry, in the location specified by the DbEngine.DbIniPath parameter.

Before Jet 2.5, if more than one application running on the system is using the Jet engine, the first one that loaded it set its parameters. So, even if you tuned Jet to within an inch of its life, your settings might be ignored. Fortunately, Jet 2.5 and Jet 3.0 support instantiation, so the parameters you set for a session will apply only to that session, as long as you don't change the default settings.

To test the performance impact of changed parameters, let's use a special version of DataBench, called DataTune, that allows you to view and change the .INI file settings for the application (see fig. 10.1). DataTune uses the API calls WritePrivateProfileString() and ReadPrivateProfileString() to adjust the settings. Once they're set, you'll need to restart the application and run a time trial suite to see what effect (if any) your changes had. We'll run tests in 16-bit Windows for this chapter, to give us a feel for the performance considerations. For Windows 95, you'll have to modify the Registry using RegEdit.Exe, a Windows 95 utility. (For information about RegEdit.Exe, refer to a book such as *Special Edition Using Windows 95*, published by Que Corporation.)

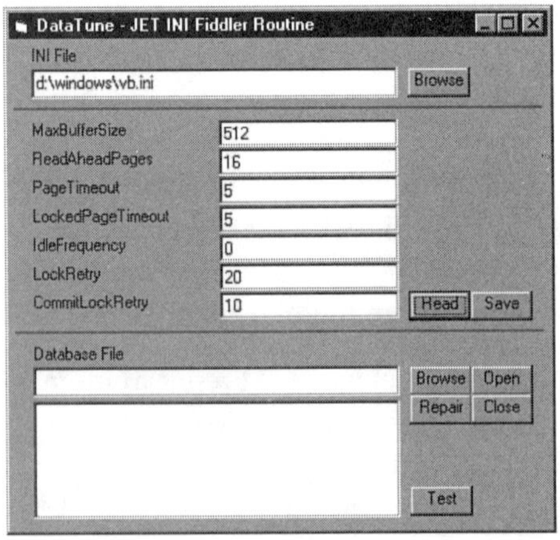

Fig. 10.1
The DataTune
main display form.

You can use two simple procedures to help insulate you from calling the .INI API calls and set up your API calls for 32- or 16-bit mode with conditional compilation. Listing 10.1 shows this code.

Listing 10.1   DataTune.Vbp   Setting Up the API Calls

```
Option Explicit

#If Win32 Then
    Declare Function GetPrivateProfileString Lib "kernel32" Alias
"GetPrivateProfileStringA" (ByVal lpApplicationName As String,
ByVal lpKeyName As Any, ByVal lpDefault As String, ByVal
lpReturnedString As String, ByVal nSize As Long, ByVal lpFileName
As String) As Long
    Declare Function WritePrivateProfileString Lib "kernel32" Alias
"WritePrivateProfileStringA" (ByVal lpApplicationName As String,
lpKeyName As Any, ByVal lpString As Any, ByVal lplFileName As
String) As Long
    Declare Function WritePrivateProfileSection Lib "kernel32"
Alias "WritePrivateProfileSectionA" (ByVal lpAppName As String,
ByVal lpString As String, ByVal lpFileName As String) As Long
#Else
    'GetPrivateProfileString
    Declare Function GetPrivateProfileString Lib "Kernel" (ByVal
lpApplicationName As String, ByVal lpKeyName As Any, ByVal
lpDefault As String, ByVal lpReturnedString As String, ByVal nSize
As Integer, ByVal lpFileName As String) As Integer
    'WritePrivateProfileString
    Declare Function WritePrivateProfileString Lib "Kernel" (ByVal
lpApplicationName As Any, ByVal lpKeyName As Any, ByVal lpString As
Any, ByVal lplFileName As String) As Integer
#End If

Public Sub IniWrite(Section As String, Item As String, ByVal _
    StrValue As String, IniFile As String)
Dim Checkit As Integer

Checkit = WritePrivateProfileString(Section, Item, StrValue, _
    IniFile)

End Sub
Public Function IniRead(Section As String, Item As String, _
    Default As String, IniFile As String) As String
Dim TheReturn As String * 255
Dim Checkit As Integer

Checkit = GetPrivateProfileString(Section, Item, Default, _
    TheReturn, Len(TheReturn), IniFile)
IniRead = TheReturn

End Function
```

III

Database Optimization

We read the .INI file's ISAM section with the code in listing 10.2. The code in listing 10.3 writes the ISAM section.

Listing 10.2 DataTune.Vbp Reading the .INI File's ISAM Section

```
Case 7 'Open & Read INI
    Text1(2) = IniRead("ISAM", "MaxBufferSize", "512", Text1(1))
    Text1(3) = IniRead("ISAM", "ReadAheadPages", "16", Text1(1))
    Text1(4) = IniRead("ISAM", "PageTimeout", "5", Text1(1))
    Text1(5) = IniRead("ISAM", "LockPageTimeout", "5", Text1(1))
    Text1(6) = IniRead("ISAM", "IdleFrequency", "0", Text1(1))
    Text1(7) = IniRead("ISAM", "LockRetry", "20", Text1(1))
    Text1(8) = IniRead("ISAM", "CommitLockRetry", "10", Text1(1))
```

Listing 10.3 DataTune.Vbp Writing the ISAM Section

```
Case 4 'Ini Save
    IniWrite "ISAM", "MaxBufferSize", Text1(2), Text1(1)
    IniWrite "ISAM", "ReadAheadPages", Text1(3), Text1(1)
    IniWrite "ISAM", "PageTimeout", Text1(4), Text1(1)
    IniWrite "ISAM", "LockPageTimeout", Text1(5), Text1(1)
    IniWrite "ISAM", "IdleFrequency", Text1(6), Text1(1)
    IniWrite "ISAM", "LockRetry", Text1(7), Text1(1)
    IniWrite "ISAM", "CommitLockRetry", Text1(8), Text1(1)
```

NOTE If you're testing in the development environment, you must change the Vb.Ini file in the Windows directory. If you're running your application, you should either change Vb.Ini or name your file *appname*.Ini and save it to the Windows directory for the changes to have an effect.

Testing the Effect of Jet Tuning

Testing Jet tuning is a laborious process. You can't just change the .INI file and then test the effects. You must force the engine to reinitialize itself by restarting all applications that have loaded the Jet DLLs. If you're testing and debugging at the same time in VB, you must change the Vb.Ini file and then restart VB, reload your application, and run your benchmark. But if your objective is to squeeze the last ounce of performance from the Jet engine, you can achieve some slight improvements by tuning the engine.

The DataTune project includes a simple test routine that loads a list box from the Address table of the test database. In this section, we'll run this test against the original database, TestSet.Mdb, with 200 records, as well as with TestSet2.Mdb, with 2,500 address records (see fig. 10.2). We'll adjust the `MaxBufferSize` and `ReadAheadPages` parameters, starting with the default value, and then halving and doubling the default (except for `ReadAheadPages`, where the default is also the minimum value).

Fig. 10.2
Testing the tuning effect with DataTune.Vbp.

This test will serve *only as an illustration of the process*. You should absolutely *never* ever try to read anything into the results of this test. Jet tuning, by its nature, is even more highly dependent on individual circumstances than normal database operations. When tuning Jet, you're optimizing on the far margins of VB. Always test against live data, in the quantities you expect, in the manner in which your routine will operate, and on a machine with features similar to your users' typical hardware configuration.

That said, the routine I'll use to illustrate the process is quite simple. I simply created a dynaset from the address table and populated the list box sequentially from the first field in the dynaset (see listing 10.4).

Listing 10.4   DataTune.Vbp   Creating a Dynaset and Populating the List Box

```
Dim foo As Integer
Dim MyDyna As Dynaset
Set MyDyna = MyDb.CreateDynaset("Select * from Address")
Select Case Index 'Test Options
Case 0
    BeginTime "Read Dynaset to List", TIME_DEBUG
    'Operation
```

(continues)

Listing 10.4 Continued

```
        List1.Clear
        Do Until MyDyna.EOF
            List1.AddItem MyDyna.Fields(0)
            MyDyna.MoveNext
        Loop
        EndTime
        MyDyna.Close
    End Select
```

As you can see in tables 10.1 and 10.2, the results aren't that encouraging about the possible benefits from tuning Jet, but then I didn't try complex scenarios and didn't adjust many of the parameters. The little I did do showed that I could speed the sequential read by about 10 percent by increasing the ReadAheadPage count on the 2,500-record TestSet2.Mdb database. The best trial on the smaller TestSet.Mdb database, though, came from cutting the MaxBufferSize parameter to half of the default value.

Table 10.1 Reading the Dynaset to a List Box (2,500 Records)

Seconds	Activity/Graph
	MaxBufferSize = 256, ReadAheadPages = 16
22.056	
	MaxBufferSize = 512, ReadAheadPages = 16
22.159	
	MaxBufferSize = 1024, ReadAheadPages = 16
23.623	
	MaxBufferSize = 256, ReadAheadPages = 32
22.261	
	MaxBufferSize = 512, ReadAheadPages = 32
20.694	
	MaxBufferSize = 1024, ReadAheadPages = 32
22.043	

In no instance were the gains in dynaset processing anywhere near the advantage previously gained by using DAO table objects. The lesson to learn here is that you can do lots of things to speed data access within VB. Using appropriate data access objects and devising efficient storage structures will return much more speed for your programmer productivity buck.

However, when operating at the margins, it may be worth your while to investigate tuning Jet. There may be situations where your particular optimization problem responds better to Jet tuning than any other method. But that would be the exception, not the rule. In almost every case, you will get a better return on your time investment by reworking your DAO operations or queries, instead of getting in the INI trenches.

Table 10.2 Reading the Dynaset to a List Box (200 Records)

Seconds	Activity/Graph
	MaxBufferSize = 256, ReadAheadPages = 16
0.726	
	MaxBufferSize = 512, ReadAheadPages = 16
0.850	
	MaxBufferSize = 1024, ReadAheadPages = 16
0.923	
	MaxBufferSize = 256, ReadAheadPages = 32
0.769	
	MaxBufferSize = 512, ReadAheadPages = 32
0.767	
	MaxBufferSize = 1024, ReadAheadPages = 32
0.736	

From Here...

Refer to the following chapters for related information:

■ Review Chapter 7, "Speeding Database Operations," Chapter 8, "More Database Speed," and Chapter 9, "Improving SQL Performance," for more details on optimizing databases.

■ See Chapter 11, "Eliminating the Jet Engine by Using File I/O," for information on replacing Jet with sequential file processing.

III

Database Optimization

Chapter 11

Eliminating the Jet Engine by Using File I/O

Programs just seem to get bigger as time goes by. Early in my programming days, I had 4K of RAM to work with (not to mention having to walk 3 miles in the snow to get to the CPU... <g>). Today, 4M isn't nearly enough RAM. And a single VB4 distributable can easily require 2M to 4M of disk space and can grow to much, much more.

Of course, RAM prices keep falling, hard drive space is cheap, and so are floppy disks. But if, for example, you're hoping to make a living from shareware distribution of your software, remember that an inverse relationship will exist between the size of your program's files and the number of users who will download them. The speed in which a popup utility—or any program, for that matter—will load is decreased by the volume of the DLLs it must read into memory. Therefore, we all need to take a close look at ways to reduce our distributable and executable size.

There are a number of measures you can take to control the size of your programs and distributables. You can reduce or eliminate the OLE controls in your project, because each one adds at least 40K to 90K. You can create your own reporting mechanism using the VB Print method or CodeBank's QuikReport subroutines rather than Crystal Reports. You can also use runtime formatted reusable forms to cut .EXE size.

Or you can eliminate the Jet database engine from your project. With VB4, the files required by the Jet engine—whether 16 or 32 bit—require more than one megabyte of space. The bound lists, grids, and other controls that you might use with Jet require even more. And .MDB files are relatively large compared to the raw data contained within them.

We'll examine a number of issues and techniques in this chapter, including

- How to decide to eliminate Jet

- Alternative methods for storage arrays and file I/O record structures

- Techniques for creating test sets

- Implementing a drill-down list

- Issues when editing file I/O records

- Making bulk changes to a file

Deciding Whether File I/O Is Appropriate

There's no doubt that eliminating the Jet engine is a radical decision, not to be made lightly. By giving it up, you lose DAOs and SQL. You won't have the ability to sort data with indexes or Order By clauses. You'll no longer be able to refer to data by field name or use Seeks, Finds, or bookmarks to locate records. Referential integrity, database field validation, and security will all be gone. There's a reason, you see, why the database DLLs are so large: They do a lot.

But much of the critical functionality of the Jet engine *can* be replaced by using VB's built-in sequential file I/O mechanisms, appropriate controls and application architecture, and a few intelligent subroutines.

Part of the decision to eliminate Jet must be based on need:

- What's your motivation for doing away with Jet?

- How many hoops are you willing to leap through?

- How much time are you willing to spend to achieve a minimum level of functionality without the engine?

Only you can answer these questions.

From a technical point of view, however, I can suggest some criteria for database designs that may translate readily to file I/O without completely eliminating all hope for programmer productivity. Of course, these aren't hard-and-fast rules, nor are they necessarily technical requirements or limitations imposed by VB. After all, if you want to, you can write indexing mechanisms or even an SQL parser in VB. (Just don't ask me to do it!) The following guidelines can, however, provide issues to consider when deciding to eliminate Jet.

Small Data Sets

First, the data sets should be relatively small, probably fewer than 500 records. Many of the operations, such as loading a sorted list box, that you'll perform in a manageable file I/O application will require that all your records be loaded into memory.

Static Data Sets

Second, the data requirements should be well defined and relatively stable. With Jet, you can to a great degree evolve your database design as you go—by adding fields or indexes here and there, and by creating new tables and relationships as you discover new normalization opportunities. But what's relatively easy to do with DAOs is painful to implement in file I/O systems. Almost everything must be explicitly coded, as you'll see in the examples in this chapter. So unless you have a complete understanding of the data requirements of your application, you might be well advised to create a Jet-driven prototype first, and then replace the Jet functionality with file I/O techniques.

Simple Database Structures

Third, you shouldn't try to convert highly complicated database designs— with, for example, numerous relationally linked tables or complicated ordering schemes—to file I/O. While you certainly can emulate referential integrity with file I/O, it's always going to be more painful than with Jet, because you have to code and debug it yourself.

Simple Retrieval Needs

Fourth, your application should have relatively simple retrieval needs. A good example is a drill-down interface, where all the record identifiers are loaded into a list box, and the user edits the full record by clicking the desired entry in the list box.

On the other hand, if you're creating a management analysis system, where you must answer the question, "How many blue widgets did we sell in Kansas during the summer?" you'd better stick to Jet. It's relatively easy to design a query-builder mechanism that lets the user ask this question with Access SQL, but it's much more difficult to accomplish with code-based logic in file I/O.

Working with the FileIO Project

If your project falls within these parameters and you have a reason not to use Jet, you might want to consider using Visual Basic's file-handling commands and functions. We'll examine the programmer productivity, maintenance, and performance issues of file I/O with a project called FileIO.Vbp, which you'll find on the CD in the \Chap11 directory.

FileIO is deliberately kept simple on the theory that if you need "advanced" features, such as indexing, you'll probably achieve greater productivity by using VB's database features. This project establishes the data structures, reads the data into memory, and then edits, displays, and orders data using the memory-based structures. When users exit the system, they're prompted to save their changes, which will write out the entire database.

The project is a simple drill-down data maintenance application, using an interface similar to the ones you tested in the earlier database chapters. FileIO contains two forms and one basic code module. The first form, frmLook, contains a list box, which you will populate with the names in a sample address file. The second form, frmEdit, is called by selecting an item from the list, and allows users to view and change the record. You can see the design-time forms in figure 11.1.

Fig. 11.1
The FileIO lookup and edit forms in design mode.

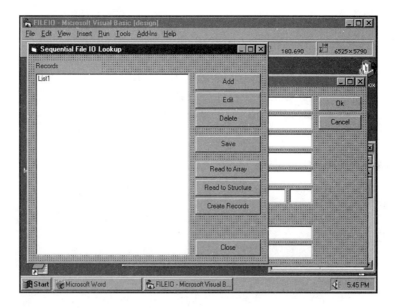

Using Storage Arrays and Record Structures

File I/O mechanics require that you pay more attention to some of the details than when using VB's database features. A good case in point is the storage structure for your data, internal and external. We'll look at two options:

- In the first case, the data is stored in a classic basic sequential file, with fields delimited by commas, records delimited by carriage returns, and strings embedded in quotations. The program reads the file into a variant array by using the `Input#` command, and writes it using the `Write#` command.

- The second method stores the data in random file structures in a fixed-length binary format. The program uses a `Type` declaration to create a file I/O record structure and performs reads and writes using `Get#` and `Put#`.

As you can see from the declarations for the internal structures in listing 11.1, the methods result in quite different declarations. The implications of each method permeate every section of the code. Type structures must always be addressed by tokenized field name, specified at design time, and compiled in. You don't have the option of using a pointer or string, as in `MyDynaset.Fields(0)` or `MyDynaset("MyField")`. This increases the amount of hard-coding you must do, reduces your opportunities to create reusable code, and makes maintenance more complex.

The internal variant array approach is more flexible but results in much less readable code. In some cases, you'll still need to hard-code your variables, but to a lesser degree than with storage based on `Type` structures.

Listing 11.1   FileIO.Vbp   Internal Structure Declarations

```
Public Type Address
    FirstName As String * 20
    LastName As String * 20
    Company As String * 30
    Address1 As String * 40
    Address2 As String * 40
    City As String * 25
    State As String * 2
    Zip As String * 10
    Country As String * 20
    Phone1 As String * 16
End Type
```

(continues)

III

Database Optimization

Listing 11.1 Continued

```
'address structure array
Global gAddrStruc() As Address

'alternative variant array
Global gAddrVar() As Variant

'Messages back from edit
Global gCancel As Integer
Global gChanged As Integer

'Messages to Edit
Global gStorageMode As Integer '0=Structure, 1=variant array
Global gEditMode As Integer '0-Add,1-Edit,2-Delete
Global gItemIndex As Integer
```

Figures 11.2 and 11.3 show how data is stored using the two methods.

Fig. 11.2

Sample output
from variant array,
in Notepad.

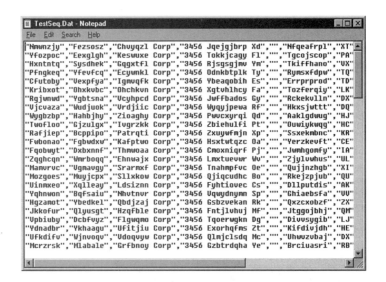

NOTE The type structure requires almost twice as much disk storage space, because it stores fixed-length fields with strings right-padded with spaces. Because you'll typically specify more space for fields such as FirstName than you expect the average name to use, significant additional space requirements will result.

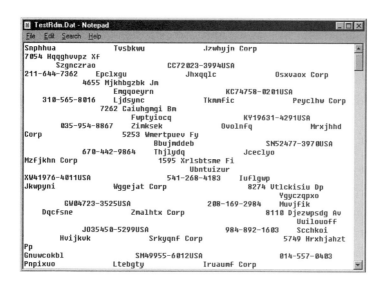

Fig. 11.3
Sample output
from type
structure, in
Notepad.

Creating Test Sets

As in the database projects, FileIO has an automated test set generator. However, the format and quantities for the test data are hard-coded, as you can see in the `RdmTestSet()` function code in listing 11.2. The routine uses the `MakeRdmText()` function and generates 100 records for each file format.

Listing 11.2 FileIO.Vbp Generating Test Records

```
Function RdmTestSet() As Integer
On Error Resume Next
Dim foo As Integer
Screen.MousePointer = 11
'Create 100 Records for Random File
ReDim gAddrStruc(99) As Address
For foo = 0 To 99    ' Loop 5 times.
    gAddrStruc(foo).FirstName = MakeRdmText(0, "Xxxxxxx")
    gAddrStruc(foo).LastName = MakeRdmText(0, "Xxxxxxx")
    gAddrStruc(foo).Company = MakeRdmText(0, "Xxxxxxx Corp")
    gAddrStruc(foo).Address1 = MakeRdmText(0, "#### Xxxxxxxxx Xx")
    gAddrStruc(foo).Address2 = ""
    gAddrStruc(foo).City = MakeRdmText(0, "Xxxxxxxxx")
    gAddrStruc(foo).State = MakeRdmText(0, "XX")
    gAddrStruc(foo).Zip = MakeRdmText(0, "#####-####")
    gAddrStruc(foo).Country = "USA"
    gAddrStruc(foo).Phone1 = MakeRdmText(0, "###-###-####")
Next foo
gStorageMode = 0
foo = SaveMe()
```

(continues)

III

Database Optimization

Listing 11.2 Continued

```
'Create 100 Records for Sequential file
ReDim gAddrVar(9, 99)
For foo = 0 To 99
    gAddrVar(0, foo) = MakeRdmText(0, "Xxxxxxx")
    gAddrVar(1, foo) = MakeRdmText(0, "Xxxxxxx")
    gAddrVar(2, foo) = MakeRdmText(0, "Xxxxxxx Corp")
    gAddrVar(3, foo) = MakeRdmText(0, "3456 Xxxxxxxxx Xx")
    gAddrVar(4, foo) = ""
    gAddrVar(5, foo) = MakeRdmText(0, "Xxxxxxxxx")
    gAddrVar(6, foo) = MakeRdmText(0, "XX")
    gAddrVar(7, foo) = MakeRdmText(0, "#####-####")
    gAddrVar(8, foo) = "USA"
    gAddrVar(9, foo) = MakeRdmText(0, "###-###-####")
Next foo
gStorageMode = 1
foo = SaveMe()
Screen.MousePointer = 0
End Function


Public Function MakeRdmText(MaskOrLen As Integer, Mask As String)
'MaskOrLen: 0 = mask is format, 1 = val(mask) is len of rdm text
Dim foo As Integer, WorkText As String, Length As Integer
Dim WorkChar As String
If MaskOrLen = 0 Then
    Length = Len(Mask)
Else
    Length = Val(Mask)
End If
For foo = 1 To Length
    If MaskOrLen = 1 Then
        WorkText = WorkText & Chr$(Int(Rnd * 26 + 65))
    Else
        WorkChar = Mid$(Mask, foo, 1)
        Select Case WorkChar
        Case "#"
            WorkText = WorkText & Format$(Int(Rnd * 9.9999))
        Case "X"
            WorkText = WorkText & Chr$(Int(Rnd * 26 + 65))
        Case "x"
            WorkText = WorkText & Chr$(Int(Rnd * 26 + 97))
        Case Else
            WorkText = WorkText & WorkChar
        End Select
    End If
Next foo
MakeRdmText = WorkText
End Function
```

The button that activates the test set routine, `Command1(5)`, is invisible by default because you'll create test sets only during the design phase. To create a new test set, simply change the button's `Visible` property before running, or call it from the debug window by typing **Command1_Click 5**. Existing data files will be deleted and replaced with new ones.

Loading a Sorted Drill-Down List

The first function of a drill-down interface is to display a pick list so that users can select the record to view or edit (see fig. 11.4). To do this in your architecture, you must read the records to memory and then add them to a list box. The test databases are loaded only when you click the appropriate command button. This allows more precise measuring and weighing of the alternative methods. Of course, in a production application, you would want to use only one method and would probably read the file at startup.

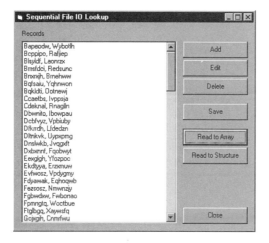

Fig. 11.4
Reading data into the pick list form.

Reading a Sequential File to a Variant Array

First, let's examine the mechanism for loading a variant array from a sequential file. Listing 11.3 shows the complete code to read the sequential file. The code performs these steps:

1. It `ReDims` the array, arranging the indexes so that we can expand the number of records with `ReDim Preserve` later. (`ReDim Preserve`, as you may recall, works only with the last index of an array.)

III

Database Optimization

2. It opens the file TestSeq.Dat for input.

3. It loops through the file, reading records with the Input# command and increasing the array as necessary.

4. Because ReDim Preserve takes a fair amount of time, the routine uses the command every 10 records (rather than every record) and rectifies its sizing when it reaches the end of the file.

Listing 11.3 FileIO.Vbp Reading the Sequential File

```
Function ReadVariant() As Integer
ReDim gAddrVar(9, 10)
Dim foo As Integer
Screen.MousePointer = 11
' Open file for random access.
Open App.Path & "\TestSeq.Dat" For Input As #1
foo = -1
Do Until EOF(1)    ' Loop
    foo = foo + 1
    If UBound(gAddrVar, 2) < foo Then
        ReDim Preserve gAddrVar(9, foo + 10)
    End If
    Input #1, gAddrVar(0, foo), gAddrVar(1, foo),_
        gAddrVar(2, foo), gAddrVar(3, foo),_
        gAddrVar(4, foo), gAddrVar(5, foo),_
        gAddrVar(6, foo), gAddrVar(7, foo),_
        gAddrVar(8, foo), gAddrVar(9, foo)
Loop
ReDim Preserve gAddrVar(9, foo)
Close #1
Screen.MousePointer = 0
End Function
```

Reading a Random File to a Record Structure

The random file read routine in listing 11.4 is quite similar to the sequential read function. Although you could use random file structures to read record by record, and thus keep all data on disk, I recommend that you keep it simple and read all records into memory.

The read routine is hard-coded to fill the address structure array, gAddrStruc. Unlike the variant array, you can fill the entire record by simply specifying the structure variable rather than each individual field.

Listing 11.4   FileIO.Vbp   The Random File Read Routine

```
Function ReadStructure() As Integer
ReDim gAddrStruc(0) As Address   ' Declare variable.
Dim HoldMe As Address, foo As Integer
Screen.MousePointer = 11
' Open file for random access.
Open App.Path & "\TestRdm.Dat" For Random As #1_
    Len = Len(gAddrStruc(0))
foo = -1
Do Until EOF(1)    ' Loop
    foo = foo + 1
    If UBound(gAddrStruc) < foo Then
        ReDim Preserve gAddrStruc(foo + 10)
    End If
    Get #1, foo + 1, gAddrStruc(foo)
Loop
ReDim Preserve gAddrStruc(foo - 1)
Close #1
Screen.MousePointer = 0
End Function
```

The file-open logic uses an open random type, which requires that the size of the record structure variable be specified.

Writing to the List Box

After the arrays are filled, we can add the last and first names to a list box. Because file I/O has no native ordering logic, we need to set the list box Sorted property to true so that the list box will order the records for us. We could always write or adapt a sort routine, of course, but why bother when the list box can do the job for us? We've got enough to do!

So that we can retrieve the full record data, the code in listing 11.5 sets a pointer back to the array in the list box's ItemData collection. Because the list is sorted, we don't automatically know the list box index for an added item. However, we can find the index of the last item added to a list box in the NewIndex property, as long as we check the index before doing another operation, such as a RemoveItem. We can then store the array pointer in the NewIndex location of the ItemData array. If the list indexes later change (because of adds or deletes), the list box will synchronize the ItemData array automatically.

III

Database Optimization

Listing 11.5 FileIO.Vbp   The *WriteList( )* Function

```
Function WriteList(lst As Object) As Integer
Dim foo As Integer
Screen.MousePointer = 11
lst.Clear
Select Case gStorageMode
Case 0
    For foo = 0 To UBound(gAddrStruc)
        lst.AddItem Trim$(gAddrStruc(foo).LastName) & ", " _
            & gAddrStruc(foo).FirstName 'Write record to file.
        lst.ItemData(lst.NewIndex) = foo 'Store Location, _
            since ListBox is sorted
    Next foo
Case 1
    For foo = 0 To UBound(gAddrVar, 2)
        lst.AddItem gAddrVar(1, foo) & ", " & gAddrVar(0, foo)
        lst.ItemData(lst.NewIndex) = foo 'Store Location, _
            since listbox is sorted
    Next foo
End Select
Screen.MousePointer = 0
End Function
```

File Load Performance

When you run the routine, you find that while the sequential file/variant array structure might offer a little more flexibility, the type structure/random file method provides significantly greater speed (see table 11.1). In fact, random file read/list loading is just as fast as the same operation performed with DAO table objects, as tested in the earlier database chapters. And because the data is now stored in a RAM array, additional retrievals in this session, for reporting or editing, will be almost instantaneous. The implication is that performance isn't a significant factor in choosing whether to use database or file I/O data storage types.

Table 11.1 Reading Data to a List Box

Seconds	Bits	Activity/Graph
		Read 100 sequential records into variant array
0.893	16	
1.290	32	
		Read 100 random records into type structure array
0.590	16	
1.551	32	

Editing Considerations

Now that the data is loaded into the pick list, you need to provide methods for changing the data, adding new records, and deleting records. Because you're implementing a drill-down interface, you'll need a separate edit form (see fig. 11.5). In project FileIO.Vbp, the edit form is called frmEdit.

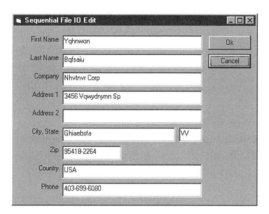

Fig. 11.5
Use the Sequential File IO Edit form to edit file I/O data.

Calling the Edit Form

The command buttons in the lookup form call the frmEdit form. These command buttons are part of a control array, where button 0 equals add, 1 equals edit, and 2 equals delete. In the case of an add, you just set the global variable gEditMode to equal 0. If you're changing a record, you need to also specify the pointer to the selected record in the array, which you do by setting a global variable, gItemIndex, to the ItemData value that you set up when you read the records. Listing 11.6 shows the code for calling the edit form.

>
>
> You need to pass this index on to the edit form, so it will know whether to add a new record or edit a selected record.

III

Database Optimization

Listing 11.6 FileIO.Vbp Calling the Edit Form

```
Case 0 'add
    gEditMode = Index
    frmEdit.Show 1
    If gCancel = False Then
        Checkit = AppendList(List1)
    End If
    EndTime
```

(continues)

Listing 11.6   Continued

```
Case 1 'edit
    BeginTime "Edit Call to Edit Form Display - Storage: " _
        & gStorageMode, TIME_DEBUG
    gEditMode = Index
    If List1.ListIndex < 0 Then Exit Sub
    gItemIndex = List1.ItemData(List1.ListIndex)
    frmEdit.Show 1
    If gCancel = False Then
        List1.RemoveItem List1.ListIndex
        Checkit = AppendList(List1)
    End If
    EndTime 'time to store record and hide window
```

Displaying the Record

After the edit form is displayed, you need to load the appropriate data into
the text controls. You do this in the form Activate event so that you can use
the Hide method on the form, for speedier form display.

If the edit mode is 0, or add, you blank the controls. Using a control array
requires just three lines of code. Changing a record requires more, however.

The routine in listing 11.7 also needs to be concerned about which storage
method you're using—variant or type arrays—so check the gStorageMode
global variable and use the appropriate logic.

Listing 11.7   FileIO.Vbp   Loading the Data into the Text Controls

```
Private Sub Form_Activate()
Dim foo As Integer
If gEditMode = 0 Then 'add
    For foo = 0 To 9
        Text1(foo) = ""
    Next foo
Else
    If gStorageMode = 0 Then
        Text1(0) = gAddrStruc(gItemIndex).FirstName
        Text1(1) = gAddrStruc(gItemIndex).LastName
        Text1(2) = gAddrStruc(gItemIndex).Company
        Text1(3) = gAddrStruc(gItemIndex).Address1
        Text1(4) = gAddrStruc(gItemIndex).Address2
        Text1(5) = gAddrStruc(gItemIndex).City
        Text1(6) = gAddrStruc(gItemIndex).State
        Text1(7) = gAddrStruc(gItemIndex).Zip
        Text1(8) = gAddrStruc(gItemIndex).Country
        Text1(9) = gAddrStruc(gItemIndex).Phone1
    Else
        For foo = 0 To 9
            Text1(foo) = gAddrVar(foo, gItemIndex)
```

```
        Next foo
    End If
End If
EndTime 'Time to show Record
End Sub
```

Because FileIO.Vbp's text control array indexes are synchronized with the variant array indexes, it can easily load the variant data in a simple loop. Type structure display, however, must be hard-coded for each instance.

As you might expect, because they work from data in RAM, both display methods are very fast (see table 11.2). From the time a user clicks the edit command button to the time the form is ready to edit is about a quarter of a second with either storage method, once the form is loaded and hidden. Although variant array loading seems to have a slight speed advantage, the difference isn't significant.

Table 11.2 Displaying a Record in an Edit Form

Seconds	Bits	Activity/Graph
		Edit Call to Edit Form Display - Storage: Variant
0.248	16	
0.412	32	
		Edit Call to Edit Form Display - Storage: Type
0.262	16	
0.428	32	

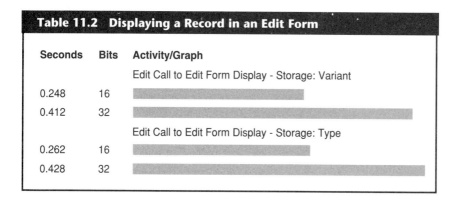

Saving the Edited Record

Since we're processing the data from RAM, we need to perform three steps to save changes:

- Store the changes in our RAM arrays

- Update the pick list

- Write the data out to file

You save the data only to RAM as you go along because saving to disk would detract from performance. At the end of the session, or by user request, you can save the data to file. The lookup form is responsible for updating the pick list, if necessary.

We'll look at those steps in a moment. For now, you just need to save the data to RAM. If you're changing a record, simply reverse the logic used to display the record. Again, type structure processing must be hard-coded for each variable field.

If you're adding a record, you need to create a new array element, which you can do with ReDim Preserve. Since you resized the array to exactly match the number of records when you read the data file, you can use the UBound() function to determine the new record's index.

Notice that you also set two global flags: gChanged to true and gCancel to false. gChanged will later indicate that the OK button has been clicked during the edit session, implying a record change. The gCancel flag is used to signal the lookup form's list update logic.

The code in listing 11.8 demonstrates how I implemented saving records after an edit.

Listing 11.8   FileIO.Vbp   Saving the Edited Record

```
BeginTime "Duration from Edit Save to Redisplay - Storage: "_
        & gStorageMode, TIME_DEBUG
gChanged = True
If gEditMode = 0 Then
    If gStorageMode = 0 Then
        ReDim Preserve gAddrStruc(UBound(gAddrStruc) + 1)
        gItemIndex = UBound(gAddrStruc)
    Else
        ReDim Preserve gAddrVar(9, UBound(gAddrVar, 2) + 1)
        gItemIndex = UBound(gAddrVar, 2)
    End If
End If
If gStorageMode = 0 Then
    gAddrStruc(gItemIndex).FirstName = Text1(0)
    gAddrStruc(gItemIndex).LastName = Text1(1)
    gAddrStruc(gItemIndex).Company = Text1(2)
    gAddrStruc(gItemIndex).Address1 = Text1(3)
    gAddrStruc(gItemIndex).Address2 = Text1(4)
    gAddrStruc(gItemIndex).City = Text1(5)
    gAddrStruc(gItemIndex).State = Text1(6)
    gAddrStruc(gItemIndex).Zip = Text1(7)
    gAddrStruc(gItemIndex).Country = Text1(8)
    gAddrStruc(gItemIndex).Phone1 = Text1(9)
Else
    For foo = 0 To 9
        gAddrVar(foo, gItemIndex) = Text1(foo)
    Next foo
End If
gCancel = False
Me.Hide
```

Again, as table 11.3 shows, there's a slight edge in processing time in favor of variant arrays. And again, the speed difference isn't significant enough to matter.

Table 11.3 Saving an Edited Record		
Seconds	**Bits**	**Activity/Graph**
		Duration from Edit Save to Redisplay - Storage: Variant
0.248	16	
0.646	32	
		Duration from Edit Save to Redisplay - Storage: Type Structure
0.262	16	
0.658	32	

Updating the Lookup List

As we saw in the edit save code in listing 11.8, the edit form sets a global flag to indicate whether the lookup form's pick list needs to be updated. The code in listing 11.9 updates the pick list with the changes. If it's adding a record, the lookup form calls the function AppendList(), which adds the item to the list box and saves the ItemData pointer. If it's editing, the lookup form first removes the old entry and then calls AppendList().

Listing 11.9   FileIO.Vbp   Updating the Pick List in the Lookup Form

```
Function AppendList(lst As Object) As Integer
Dim foo As Integer
Select Case gStorageMode
Case 0
    lst.AddItem Trim$(gAddrStruc(gItemIndex).LastName) & ", "_
        & gAddrStruc(gItemIndex).FirstName ' Write record to file.
Case 1
    lst.AddItem gAddrVar(1, gItemIndex) & ", " & gAddrVar(0,_
        gItemIndex)
End Select
'Store Location, since ListBox is sorted
lst.ItemData(lst.NewIndex) = gItemIndex
lst.ListIndex = lst.NewIndex
End Function
```

III

Database Optimization

Deleting Records

If the user wants to delete a record, there's really no need to display the edit form. However, the list and storage array must have elements removed to keep them synchronized. You can implement this in several ways. The code in listing 11.10 takes a brute-force approach: it copies all array elements from the deleted record over the previous record, and then deletes the last element by resizing the array. The array is thus always current.

Listing 11.10   FileIO.Vbp   A Brute-Force Approach to Deleting Records

```
Function DeleteRec(Item As Long)
Dim foo As Integer, foobar As Integer

Select Case gStorageMode

'Structure
Case 0
    For foo = Item To UBound(gAddrStruc) - 1
        gAddrStruc(foo) = gAddrStruc(foo + 1)
    Next foo
    ReDim Preserve gAddrStruc(UBound(gAddrStruc) - 1)

'Variant Array
Case 1
    For foo = Item To UBound(gAddrVar, 2) - 1
        For foobar = 0 To 9
            gAddrVar(foobar, foo) = gAddrVar(foobar, foo + 1)
        Next foobar
    Next foo
    ReDim Preserve gAddrVar(9, UBound(gAddrVar, 2) - 1)

End Select
End Function
```

You can add a flag or an array element to indicate that a record was deleted, and then skip records where the deleted flag is true when displaying pick lists or saving records. A large number of deletes performed before a save/read operation, however, might increase the size of the array in uncontrollable ways. This approach takes a little longer but offers the advantage of code simplicity, particularly in that other routines need to be concerned only with whether the data exists in the array.

Although this method is written for simplicity, not optimization, it's still reasonably fast, as table 11.4 shows. When you delete the first record in the list, you can realign the remaining 99 records in about a third of a second. Variants are somewhat slower than type structures, in this instance.

Table 11.4 Deleting Records from RAM

Seconds	Bits	Activity/Graph
		Delete Record from Array - Storage: Variant Array
0.375	16	▬▬▬▬▬▬▬▬
0.947	32	▬▬▬▬▬▬▬▬▬▬▬▬▬▬▬
		Delete Record from Array - Storage: Type Structure
0.352	16	▬▬▬▬▬▬▬
0.963	32	▬▬▬▬▬▬▬▬▬▬▬▬▬▬▬

Saving Changes to a File

Because you're processing the changes in RAM, you're going to need a separate mechanism for saving the changes to file. Most users are accustomed to taking this step with PC programs, but it's usually unnecessary with database programs based on the Jet engine because by default all record changes are written interactively.

Writing the Data to a File

Writing the data again requires two methods: one for sequential files and one for random data. The SaveMe() function completely rewrites the file, which would be unnecessary for random files, except that there's no delete flag or change flag for individual records. If records were deleted, we would either have to implement the delete flag, or figure out a mechanism to purge records at the end of file (if we want to avoid duplicate or blank records). However, because this solution is oriented to small data sets and code simplicity, the routine in listing 11.11 just takes the brute-force method again: delete the entire file, and then write a new instance of it.

Random files are opened as Random, and sequential are opened for Output. Output effectively creates a new file. Once the file is opened, you use Put# with random records and Write# with sequential records.

Listing 11.11 FileIO.Vbp   Rewriting the Data to a File

```
Function SaveMe() As Integer
Dim foo As Integer
Screen.MousePointer = 11
Select Case gStorageMode
```

(continues)

III

Database Optimization

```
Listing 11.11   Continued

'Random
Case 0
    Kill App.Path & "\TestRdm.Dat"
    Open App.Path & "\TestRdm.Dat" For Random As #1 Len _
        = Len(gAddrStruc(0))
    For foo = 0 To UBound(gAddrStruc)
        Put #1, foo + 1, gAddrStruc(foo) ' Write record to file.
    Next foo
    Close #1

'Sequential
Case 1
    Kill App.Path & "\TestSeq.Dat"
    Open App.Path & "\TestSeq.Dat" For Output As #1
    For foo = 0 To UBound(gAddrVar, 2)
        Write #1, gAddrVar(0, foo), gAddrVar(1, foo),_
            gAddrVar(2, foo), gAddrVar(3, foo), gAddrVar(4, foo),_
            gAddrVar(5, foo), gAddrVar(6, foo), gAddrVar(7, foo),_
            gAddrVar(8, foo), gAddrVar(9, foo)
    Next foo
    Close #1

End Select
Screen.MousePointer = 0
End Function
```

As table 11.5 shows, the performance is quite good, despite the brute-force
nature of the method. Either method takes less than a quarter of a second for
100 records. Users will expect some time to be taken in writing changes (since
you don't write without users requesting or approving it), so a quarter of a
second is as good as instantaneous in human interface terms.

Table 11.5   Saving Records to Disk

Seconds	Bits	Activity/Graph
		Changed Array - 100 Records - Sequential
0.220	16	
0.592	32	
		Changed Array - 100 Records - Random
0.233	16	
0.506	32	

Testing for Changes on Exit

If the user closes the program, the program must check to see whether changes need to be saved. As you may recall, the gChanged flag is set by the edit form. The CheckChange() function, shown in listing 11.12, tests the gChanged value and then queries the user as to whether to save the data, abandon the changes, or cancel the program exit (see fig. 11.6).

Listing 11.12   FileIO.Vbp   Testing for Changes When the User Exits

```
Function CheckChange() As Integer
On Error Resume Next
Dim Checkit As Integer
If gChanged Then
    Checkit = MsgBox("Data has been changed. Do you wish to save _
        the changes?", vbQuestion + vbYesNoCancel, "Data has
Changed")
    Select Case Checkit
    Case 6 'yes
        Checkit = SaveMe()
        gChanged = False
    Case 2 'Cancel
        CheckChange = False
        Exit Function
    End Select
End If
If Err = 0 Then
    CheckChange = True
Else

    CheckChange = False
End If
End Function
```

This routine should be called and handled from the Close button *and* the form's QueryUnload event (the latter to handle the user exiting from the control box menu or toolbar exit button).

NOTE

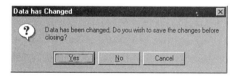

Fig. 11.6
Prompting for save on exit.

Database Optimization

From Here...

For more information on some of the subjects brought up in this chapter, refer to these chapters:

- Chapter 7, "Speeding Database Operations," and Chapter 8, "More Database Speed," cover Jet database operations.

- For more information on SQL, see Chapter 9, "Improving SQL Performance."

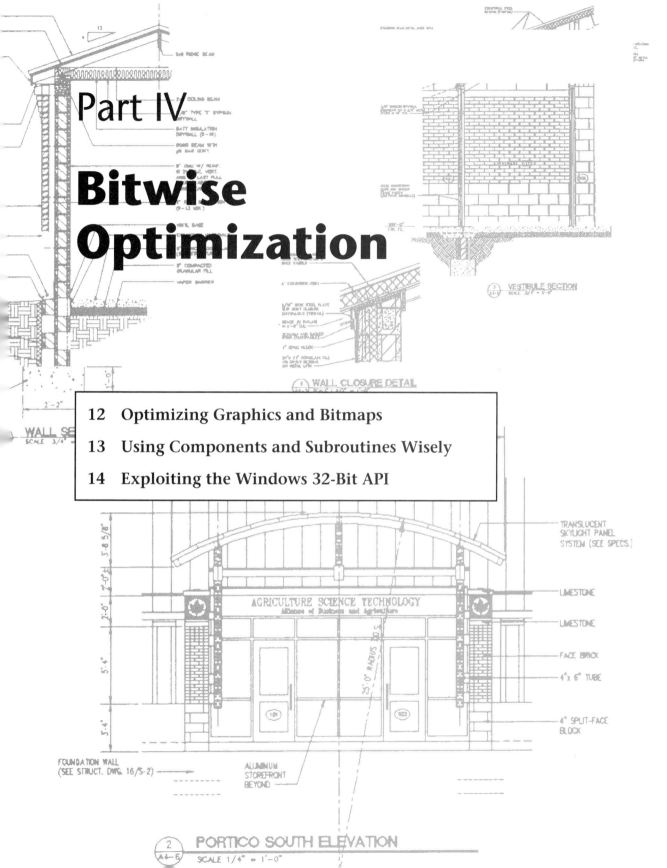

Part IV

Bitwise Optimization

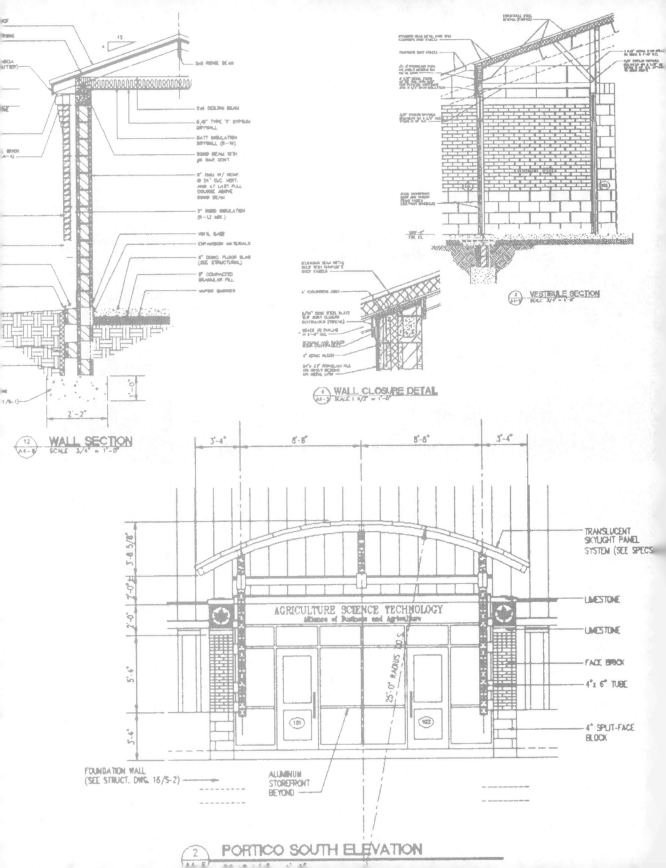

WALL SECTION
SCALE 3/4" = 1'-0"

WALL CLOSURE DETAIL
SCALE 1 1/2" = 1'-0"

VESTIBULE SECTION
SCALE 3/4" = 1'-0"

AGRICULTURE SCIENCE TECHNOLOGY
Alliance of Business and Agriculture

TRANSLUCENT
SKYLIGHT PANEL
SYSTEM (SEE SPECS)

LIMESTONE

LIMESTONE

FACE BRICK

4" x 6" TUBE

4" SPLIT-FACE
BLOCK

FOUNDATION WALL
(SEE STRUCT. DWG. 16/S-2)

ALUMINUM
STOREFRONT
BEYOND

25'-0" RADIUS TO S

PORTICO SOUTH ELEVATION

Chapter 12

Optimizing Graphics and Bitmaps

Perhaps no single task is more challenging for computers than handling today's sophisticated graphics displays. Graphics can be resource intensive, CPU intensive, and—in the case of bitmaps—disk I/O intensive.

In one sense, everything that Windows does is graphical because it is, after all, a graphical user interface. Most graphics work, however, occurs so far behind the scenes that we don't even think of the operations as graphical. Displaying text in a text box or label, for example, is thought of as assigning values to a control. Form background colors are simply properties. Scrolling a list box is under user control and requires no thought or code. In fact, we can't do much of anything to speed or slow these types of operations, intrinsic to Windows as they are.

However, we can control another class of graphical operations. We can use graphical methods, API calls, and functions to draw shapes, lines, or text on some Windows objects. We can load bitmaps, metafiles, or icons into other objects. What's more, we can manipulate this functionality in a variety of ways by using different objects, methods, properties, or API calls.

This chapter explains how you can

- Investigate the graphical controls to determine their suitability for given tasks

- Assess the different graphics methods using various properties and objects, and compare their speed and flexibility with their API equivalents

- Test different approaches to displaying and manipulating bitmap images

Graphic Controls: Lightweights, Heavyweights, and No-Weights

VB4 offers three built-in objects for image display and manipulation. The first two are VB's standard graphics controls—the picture box and the image control, both of which can be used to display bitmaps, metafiles, or icons.

A picture box is a heavyweight graphic control and consumes a greater proportion of resources than a "lightweight" image control displaying the same picture. This is because picture boxes have more functionality than image controls. You may use graphics methods, such as Draw, Circle, Print, and the new PaintPicture method. A picture box can also function as a container for other controls. On the other hand, an image control can resize bitmaps by using its Stretch property, which a picture box can't do.

The third graphical control actually isn't a control at all, but is the form itself. Forms can do many of the things that picture boxes can do with graphics: they support graphic methods, they can act as containers, and they have a Picture property for displaying graphics files. Moreover, forms use no additional resources because you have to have a form anyway, making them a no-weight graphical control. However, a form can't automatically size itself to a bitmap or save a metafile or icon as a bitmap. If an image is loaded with the Picture property, the picture always appears in the upper left corner of the form, which may not be the desired location.

Graphics Control Properties

The first issue I'll address with graphics controls is some basic property settings common to forms and picture boxes. Two properties may have a material impact on graphics performance and resource usage: AutoRedraw and ClipControls.

As you may know, AutoRedraw makes the results of graphics methods persistent—that is, if you cover and then uncover a graphic created with AutoRedraw set to true, it will redisplay automatically. Windows achieves this feat by making a copy of the bitmap image in memory, which it then refers to when it needs to repaint the form. If AutoRedraw is false, then when VB repaints a form or a portion of the form, it doesn't remember what graphics are there, and they're effectively erased.

`ClipControls` affects how a form or object is painted. If `ClipControls` is true, then before repainting, Windows checks for non-graphical areas (such as controls) and tells itself not to paint those portions of the form or object. It repaints the entire object, except for these clip regions, even if only a portion of it was uncovered. If `ClipControls` is false, Windows paints only the uncovered areas but doesn't consider placement of controls, leaving it up to the controls to display themselves.

So what real effect do these properties have on performance? GrafProp.Vbp, which is found in the \Chap12 directory on the CD provided with this book, has several benchmark tests to measure graphics performance with various control settings. Note that although you can adjust `AutoRedraw` at will, `ClipControls` can be set only at design time. By using the `Line` method and two PictureBoxes (one with `ClipControls` set to true and one set to false), GrafProp can examine the properties by themselves and in combination.

AutoRedraw

The first benchmark uses the `Line` method to paint a picture box—first with `AutoRedraw` set to true (see listing 12.1), then with `AutoRedraw` set to false (see listing 12.2). Figure 12.1 shows the project running.

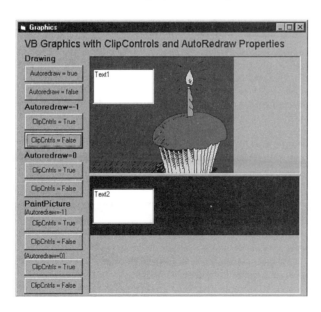

Fig. 12.1
The Graphics properties form in GrafProp.Vbp.

IV

Bitwise Optimization

Listing 12.1 GrafProp.Vbp Painting a Picture Box with _AutoRedraw_ Set to True

```
Case 0
    Picture1.AutoRedraw = True
    Picture1.ForeColor = &HFF&
    BeginTime "VB Line Method - Autoredraw = True", TIME_DEBUG
    For foo = 0 To PicHeight
        Picture1.Line (0, foo)-(PicWidth, foo)
    Next foo
    EndTime
```

Listing 12.2 GrafProp.Vbp Painting a Picture Box with _AutoRedraw_ Set to False

```
Case 1
    Picture1.AutoRedraw = False
    Set Picture1.picture = Nothing
    Picture1.ForeColor = &HFF0000
    BeginTime "VB Line Method - Autoredraw = False", TIME_DEBUG
    For foo = 0 To PicHeight
        Picture1.Line (0, foo)-(PicWidth, foo)
    Next foo
    EndTime
```

As table 12.1 shows, drawing with AutoRedraw set to false is more than twice as fast as using AutoRedraw to create a persistent image. However, if you run the test yourself, you'll see an interesting phenomenon: When AutoRedraw is false, you'll see each line as it's being drawn. The lines are obviously being drawn down the control. Of course, you must repaint the graphic each time the form is painted, because the image isn't persistent. On the other hand, with AutoRedraw set to true, the changes seem to snap to the picture box all at once, although after a greater delay.

Table 12.1 _AutoRedraw_ Settings with Graphic Methods

Seconds	Bits	Activity/Graph
		VB Line Method - AutoRedraw = True
0.179	16	
0.399	32	
		VB Line Method - AutoRedraw = False
0.082	16	
0.193	32	

These differences in display behavior mean that you need to think about the user's perception of speed as well as raw display times. Sometimes, depending on individual situations, you may want to opt for the slower benchmark time. One example of this would be if you were using graphics methods to draw a clickable control, such as a command button. It's disconcerting to the user to actually see such an object being constructed.

ClipControls

Two picture boxes are used to test `ClipControls`: one with `ClipControls` set to true and one with the property set to false. It's necessary to use two controls, rather than simply change the property of one control, because `ClipControls` can be set only at design time. To give `ClipControls` something to clip, a text box is placed on each picture control.

The code in listing 12.3 tests graphics performance with `ClipControls` set to true and `AutoRedraw` set to false. The test case in listing 12.4 sets both `ClipControls` and `AutoRedraw` to false. The code in listing 12.5 sets both `ClipControls` and `AutoRedraw` to true. The last test code, in listing 12.6, sets `ClipControls` to false and `AutoRedraw` to true.

Listing 12.3 GrafProp.Vbp Setting *ClipControls* to True and *AutoRedraw* to False

```
Case 2
    Set Picture1.picture = Nothing
    Picture1.AutoRedraw = False
    Picture1.ForeColor = &HFF&
    BeginTime "VB Line Method - ClipControls = True", TIME_DEBUG
    For foo = 0 To 100
        Picture1.Line (0, foo)-(PicWidth, foo)
    Next foo
    EndTime
```

Listing 12.4 GrafProp.Vbp Setting *ClipControls* and *AutoRedraw* to False

```
Case 3
    Set Picture2.picture = Nothing
    Picture2.AutoRedraw = False
    Picture2.ForeColor = &HFF0000
    BeginTime "VB Line Method - ClipControls = False", TIME_DEBUG
    For foo = 0 To 100
        Picture2.Line (0, foo)-(PicWidth, foo)
    Next foo
    EndTime
```

IV

Bitwise Optimization

Listing 12.5 GrafProp.Vbp Setting *ClipControls* and *AutoRedraw* to True

```
Case 4
    Set Picture1.picture = Nothing
    Picture1.AutoRedraw = True
    Picture1.ForeColor = &HFF&
    BeginTime "VB Line Method - ClipControls = True", TIME_DEBUG
    For foo = 0 To 100
        Picture1.Line (0, foo)-(PicWidth, foo)
    Next foo
    EndTime
```

Listing 12.6 GrafProp.Vbp Setting *ClipControls* to False and *AutoRedraw* to True

```
Case 5
    Set Picture2.picture = Nothing
    Picture2.AutoRedraw = True
    Picture2.ForeColor = &HFF0000
    BeginTime "VB Line Method - ClipControls = False", TIME_DEBUG
    For foo = 0 To 100
        Picture2.Line (0, foo)-(PicWidth, foo)
    Next foo
    EndTime
```

As you can see in table 12.2, the test shows that there's little or no advantage to adjusting ClipControls settings as far as performance is concerned. With AutoRedraw set to true, performance is identical whether ClipControls is true or not. When AutoRedraw is false, the picture with ClipControls set to false draws more quickly—about twice as fast. However, as you can see in figure 12.2, the image is corrupted because the text control is overwritten by the graphic! This probably isn't a great result.

PaintPicture and Properties

VB4 introduces a new graphics method: PaintPicture. It's similar to the GDI BitBlt() and StretchBlt() functions and, in fact, requires many of the same parameters, including ROP (Raster OPeration code). However, you don't have to make a GDI declaration. The same method handles straight copies and stretch manipulations, and `PaintPicture`—since it's a built-in keyword—is more "bulletproof" than the equivalent GDI calls.

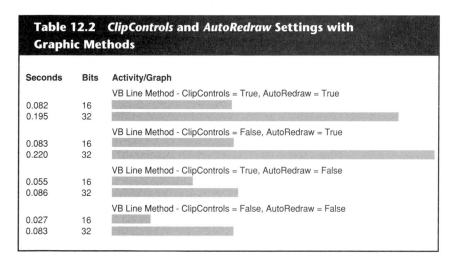

Table 12.2 *ClipControls* and *AutoRedraw* Settings with Graphic Methods

Seconds	Bits	Activity/Graph
		VB Line Method - ClipControls = True, AutoRedraw = True
0.082	16	
0.195	32	
		VB Line Method - ClipControls = False, AutoRedraw = True
0.083	16	
0.220	32	
		VB Line Method - ClipControls = True, AutoRedraw = False
0.055	16	
0.086	32	
		VB Line Method - ClipControls = False, AutoRedraw = False
0.027	16	
0.083	32	

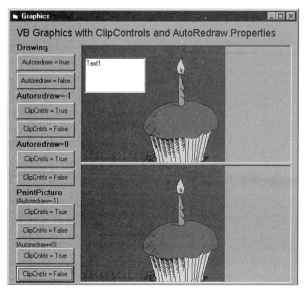

Fig. 12.2
Problems when
`ClipControls`
equals false.

Let's duplicate the control-properties tests using PaintPicture to see whether the results from the Line method test are similar across graphics methods. The version of GrafProp.Vbp on the CD, in the \Chap12 directory, already contains these changes. Figure 12.3 shows the test in action.

Fig. 12.3

The GrafProp form using PaintPicture.

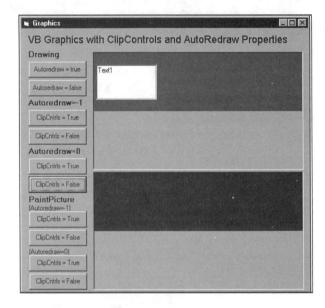

The code in listing 12.7 tests PaintPicture with both ClipControls and AutoRedraw set to true. The code in listing 12.8 sets ClipControls to false, while AutoRedraw is true. In the case shown in listing 12.9, ClipControls is true, but AutoRedraw is false. And for a last test, both properties are set to false (see listing 12.10).

Listing 12.7 GrafProp.Vbp *PaintPicture* with *ClipControls* and *AutoRedraw* Set to True

```
Case 6
    Set Picture1.picture = Nothing
    Picture1.AutoRedraw = True
    Picture1.ForeColor = &HFF&
    BeginTime "VB PaintPicture - ClipControls = True, AutoRedraw _
        = True", TIME_DEBUG
    For foo = 0 To 100 Step 10
        Picture1.PaintPicture Picture3.picture, foo, 0
    Next foo
    EndTime
```

**Listing 12.8 GrafProp.Vbp *PaintPicture* with *ClipControls*
Set to False and *AutoRedraw* Set to True**

```
Case 7
    Set Picture2.picture = Nothing
    Picture2.AutoRedraw = True
    Picture2.ForeColor = &HFF0000
    BeginTime "VB PaintPicture - ClipControls = False, AutoRedraw _
      = True", TIME_DEBUG
    For foo = 0 To 100 Step 10
        Picture2.PaintPicture Picture3.picture, foo, 0
    Next foo
    EndTime
```

**Listing 12.9 GrafProp.Vbp *PaintPicture* with *ClipControls*
Set to True and *AutoRedraw* Set to False**

```
Case 8
    Set Picture1.picture = Nothing
    Picture1.AutoRedraw = False
    Picture1.ForeColor = &HFF&
    BeginTime "VB PaintPicture - ClipControls = True, AutoRedraw _
      = False", TIME_DEBUG
    For foo = 0 To 100 Step 10
        Picture1.PaintPicture Picture3.picture, foo, 0
    Next foo
    EndTime
```

**Listing 12.10 GrafProp.Vbp *PaintPicture* with *ClipControls*
and *AutoRedraw* Set to False**

```
Case 9
    Set Picture2.picture = Nothing
    Picture2.AutoRedraw = False
    Picture2.ForeColor = &HFF0000
    BeginTime "VB PaintPicture - ClipControls = False, AutoRedraw _
      = False", TIME_DEBUG
    For foo = 0 To 100 Step 10
        Picture2.PaintPicture Picture3.picture, foo, 0
    Next foo
    EndTime
```

The results in table 12.3 are very similar to those from the Line method. Pictures where AutoRedraw equals false paint more quickly than those where AutoRedraw equals true, but the speed margin isn't as great—about 40 percent faster. Adjusting `ClipControls` has no significant effect on performance but, once again, the picture box with both `AutoRedraw` and `ClipControls` set to false displays a corrupted image. The conclusion is clear: Consider `AutoRedraw`, but don't bother with `ClipControls`. You'll find better ways to enhance performance later in the chapter.

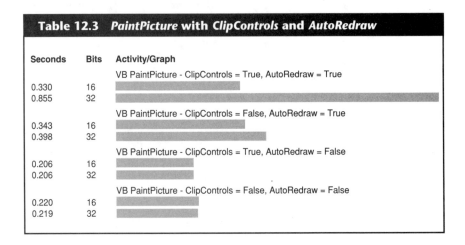

Table 12.3 *PaintPicture* **with** *ClipControls* **and** *AutoRedraw*

Seconds	Bits	Activity/Graph
		VB PaintPicture - ClipControls = True, AutoRedraw = True
0.330	16	
0.855	32	
		VB PaintPicture - ClipControls = False, AutoRedraw = True
0.343	16	
0.398	32	
		VB PaintPicture - ClipControls = True, AutoRedraw = False
0.206	16	
0.206	32	
		VB PaintPicture - ClipControls = False, AutoRedraw = False
0.220	16	
0.219	32	

Graphics Control Performance

The next test examines the differences in performance of picture boxes, images, and forms using the `Line` method and the `Picture` property with GrafCtl.Vbp, which you can find on the CD in the \Chap12 directory. Figure 12.4 shows the project running.

Of course, you can't use the `Line` method with an image box—this lightweight control doesn't support graphics methods. But where there's a will, there's a way. GrafCtl.Vbp uses a *scratchpad* technique. The project uses several forms, including the main benchmark form and a form called frmScratchPad, which contains nothing but a picture control (see fig. 12.5). Scratchpad is never displayed, just loaded, and contains no code. It's an invisible area that you can use for drawing and loading graphics in the background, which can then be transferred to wherever they need to go. You can use it in several ways to enhance a control's functionality and to speed certain operations.

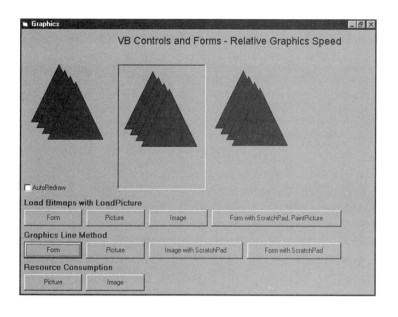

Fig. 12.4
The graphics
methods test in
GrafCtl.Vbp.

Fig. 12.5
The scratchpad
form in
GrafCtl.Vbp.

Graphic Methods Speed

To make the graphics tests a little more interesting, let's use a subroutine that
creates a shape that's not normally on the VB shape palette (neither with the
Shape control nor graphics methods): an isosceles triangle. The subroutine, in
a fit of originality, is called `Triangle`. `Triangle` is a simple routine that uses
the `Line` method to draw a triangular shape within a specified rectangle (see
listing 12.11). The apex (point) of the triangle is at the center of the top line
of the rectangle, while the bottom of the rectangle forms the base of the triangle. After drawing the body of the triangle, the subroutine then outlines
the triangle in a separate color, if desired. `Triangle` is one of the CodeBank
subroutines, and in this project is in a module called Triangle.Bas, in the
\Chap12 directory.

Listing 12.11 Triangle.Bas The *Triangle* Subroutine

```
Sub Triangle(obj As Object, Left As Single, Top As Single, Width _
    As Single, Height As Single, Color As Long, Bordercolor As Long)
'Just a simple triangle shape routine. Will draw over other
'graphics, but not controls.
Dim foo As Integer
Dim HoldColor As Long
Dim Right As Integer
Dim Bottom As Integer
Dim Center As Integer
Center = Left + (Width / 2)
Right = Left + Width
Bottom = Top + Height
HoldColor = obj.ForeColor
'paint the triangle body
obj.ForeColor = Color
For foo = 1 To Height
    obj.Line (Center - foo / 2, foo + Top)-Step(foo, 0)
Next foo
'outline the triangle
obj.Line (Left, Bottom)-(Right, Top + Height), Bordercolor
obj.Line (Left, Bottom)-(Center, Top), Bordercolor
obj.Line (Center, Top)-(Right, Bottom), Bordercolor
'restore
obj.ForeColor = HoldColor
End Sub
```

This test compares the speed of the Line graphics method on both a form and a picture box. It also uses the scratchpad to generate the same graphic and then transfers it to an image control using the Image property. Finally, it creates the graphic on the scratchpad and uses PaintPicture to transfer it to the form. (This last method may seem like a strange thing to do, since you can draw anywhere on the form anyway, but its purpose will become clear later.)

In the code shown in listing 12.12, the Triangle subroutine writes directly to the form. The code in listing 12.13 writes to a picture box. In the code in listing 12.14, Triangle draws on the scratchpad, then transfers the image to the image control. In listing 12.15, Triangle draws on the scratchpad, then transfers the image to the form using the PaintPicture method:

Listing 12.12 GrafCtl.Vbp Writing Directly to the Form

```
Case 4
    Me.picture = Nothing
    DoEvents
    Me.ScaleMode = 3 'pixels for code simplicity
```

```
BeginTime "Graphics Methods on Form", TIME_DEBUG
For foo = 0 To 3
    Triangle Me, 20 + 10 * foo, 60 + 10 * foo, 100, 100, _
        &H80&, &H0&
Next foo
DoEvents
EndTime
Me.ScaleMode = 1 ' back to twips
```

Listing 12.13   GrafCtl.Vbp   Writing to a Picture Box

```
Case 5
    Picture1.picture = Nothing
    DoEvents
    Picture1.ScaleMode = 3 'pixels for code simplicity
    BeginTime "Graphics Methods on Picture", TIME_DEBUG
    For foo = 1 To 4
        Triangle Picture1, 10 * foo, 10 * foo, 100, 100, &H80&, _
            &H0&
    Next foo
    DoEvents
    EndTime
    Picture1.ScaleMode = 1 ' back to twips
```

Listing 12.14   GrafCtl.Vbp   Drawing, then Transferring the Image to the Image Control

```
Case 6
    frmScratchPad.Picture1.picture = Nothing
    Image1.picture = Nothing
    DoEvents
    'pixels for code simplicity
    frmScratchPad.Picture1.ScaleMode = 3
    BeginTime "Graphics Methods on Image (Using ScratchPad)", _
      TIME_DEBUG
    For foo = 1 To 4
        Triangle frmScratchPad.Picture1, 10 * foo, 10 * foo, 100, _
            100, &H80&, &H0&
    Next foo
    Image1.picture = frmScratchPad.Picture1.Image
    DoEvents
    EndTime
    frmScratchPad.Picture1.ScaleMode = 1 ' back to twips
```

Listing 12.15 GrafCtl.Vbp Drawing, then Transferring the Image to the Form

```
Case 7
    frmScratchPad.Picture1.picture = Nothing
    Me.picture = Nothing
    DoEvents
    'pixels for code simplicity
    frmScratchPad.Picture1.ScaleMode = 3
    BeginTime "Graphics Methods on Form (Using ScratchPad, _
        PaintPicture)", TIME_DEBUG
    Picture1.Enabled = False
    For foo = 1 To 4
        Triangle frmScratchPad.Picture1, 10 * foo, 10 * foo, 100, _
            100, &H80&, &H0&
    Next foo
    frmScratchPad.Picture1.picture = frmScratchPad.Picture1.Image
    Me.PaintPicture frmScratchPad.Picture1.picture, 7560, 900
    DoEvents
    EndTime
    frmScratchPad.Picture1.ScaleMode = 1
```

As you can see in tables 12.4 and 12.5, the Line method is much faster when used with picture controls than when drawn directly on a form. That's because picture boxes are optimized for graphics, whereas forms are optimized as containers. Using the scratchpad to create graphics to transfer to an image control is always faster than drawing them on the form. If AutoRedraw is needed, it's even faster to draw the graphic on an invisible picture control and then transfer the graphic to the image control than to draw directly on an otherwise identical picture box.

Table 12.4 *Line* Method Speed by Control Type (*AutoRedraw* Equals False)

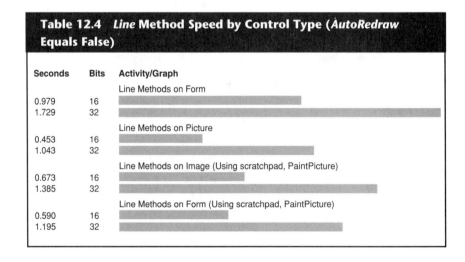

Seconds	Bits	Activity/Graph
		Line Methods on Form
0.979	16	
1.729	32	
		Line Methods on Picture
0.453	16	
1.043	32	
		Line Methods on Image (Using scratchpad, PaintPicture)
0.673	16	
1.385	32	
		Line Methods on Form (Using scratchpad, PaintPicture)
0.590	16	
1.195	32	

IV

Bitwise Optimization

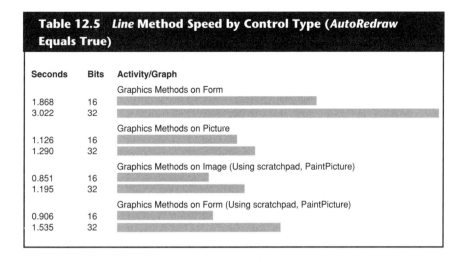

Seconds	Bits	Activity/Graph
		Graphics Methods on Form
1.868	16	
3.022	32	
		Graphics Methods on Picture
1.126	16	
1.290	32	
		Graphics Methods on Image (Using scratchpad, PaintPicture)
0.851	16	
1.195	32	
		Graphics Methods on Form (Using scratchpad, PaintPicture)
0.906	16	
1.535	32	

Table 12.5 *Line* **Method Speed by Control Type (***AutoRedraw* **Equals True)**

Drawing on the scratchpad and then transferring the graphic to the form may have seemed like redundant processing. After all, unlike images, the form control is quite capable of being drawn on. But the test shows that the scratchpad/PaintPicture method is 33 percent faster when AutoRedraw is false and more than twice as fast when AutoRedraw is true. Although you're painting each bit twice (once to the scratchpad and then again to the form), only one graphics method operation—PaintPicture—is being carried out on the relatively slow form object.

Relative Bitmap Display Speed

Although graphics methods are powerful tools, you'll want to use predrawn bitmaps for more sophisticated graphics. By necessity, loading and displaying bitmaps is relatively intensive and slow because of the sheer amount of binary data needed to represent a color for each pixel.

This section examines how quickly the different graphics controls load and display bitmaps. Figure 12.6 shows the graphics form in action.

I'll run four tests in this set. First, I'll load the test bitmap into the form, picture control, and image control's Picture property using the LoadPicture() function. The weakness of the LoadPicture() technique is that you have no control over the placement of the graphic; it will always appear flush in the upper left corner of the form or control. This isn't a tremendous problem with picture and image controls since you can move them around at will, but you rarely want a graphic to appear in a form's upper left corner. So I'll use the scratchpad form in a new way—to load the bitmap into the scratchpad picture control and then copy it to the desired location on the form using PaintPicture.

Fig. 12.6

The bitmap
LoadPicture test
in GrafCtl.Vbp.

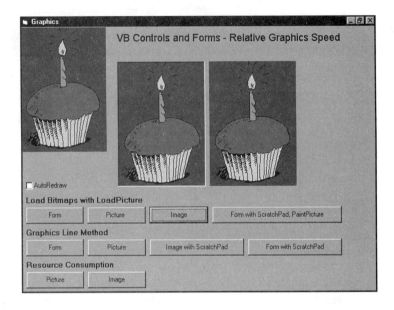

The first section of code, in listing 12.16, loads the bitmap to the form. The section of code in listing 12.17 loads the bitmap to a picture control. In listing 12.18, the code loads the bitmap to an image control. The code in listing 12.19 uses the invisible picture box in frmScratchPad to load the bitmap, and then transfers the image to the form using the PaintPicture method.

Listing 12.16 GrafCtl.Vbp Loading the Bitmap to the Form

```
sBmpFile = App.Path & "\bdaycake.Bmp"
Select Case Index
Case 0
    Me.picture = Nothing
    DoEvents
    BeginTime "Load Bitmap to Form.Picture with LoadPicture ", _
      TIME_DEBUG
    Me.picture = LoadPicture(sBmpFile)
    DoEvents
    EndTime
```

Listing 12.17   GrafCtl.Vbp   Loading the Bitmap to a Picture Control

```
Case 1
    Picture1.picture = Nothing
    DoEvents
    BeginTime "Load Bitmap to Picture1.Picture with _
      LoadPicture ", TIME_DEBUG
    Picture1.picture = LoadPicture(sBmpFile)
    DoEvents
    EndTime
```

Listing 12.18   GrafCtl.Vbp   Loading the Bitmap to an Image Control

```
Case 2
    Image1.picture = Nothing
    DoEvents
    BeginTime "Load Bitmap to Image1.Picture with LoadPicture ", _
      TIME_DEBUG
    Image1.picture = LoadPicture(sBmpFile)
    DoEvents
    EndTime
```

Listing 12.19   GrafCtl.Vbp   Using the ScratchPad and then Transferring the Image

```
Case 3
    frmscratchpad.Picture1.picture = Nothing
    Me.picture = Nothing
    DoEvents
    BeginTime "Load Bitmap to Form.Picture using Scratchpad for _
      Positioning", TIME_DEBUG
    frmscratchpad.Picture1.picture = LoadPicture(sBmpFile)
    Form1.PaintPicture frmscratchpad.Picture1.picture, 7560, 900
    DoEvents
    EndTime
```

Tables 12.6 and 12.7 display the results of the test. Notice that AutoRedraw actually has no effect on the persistence of a bitmap loaded into the picture property; it's always persistent and equally fast. However, as before, picture controls display more quickly than forms. Interestingly, picture controls also load bitmaps faster than image controls, although not by a tremendous margin.

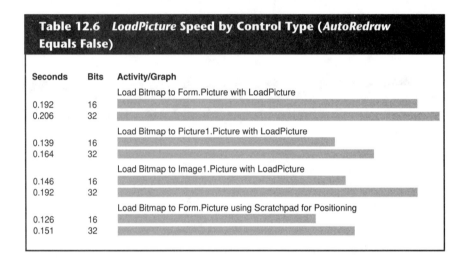

Table 12.6 *LoadPicture* **Speed by Control Type (*AutoRedraw* Equals False)**

Seconds	Bits	Activity/Graph
		Load Bitmap to Form.Picture with LoadPicture
0.192	16	
0.206	32	
		Load Bitmap to Picture1.Picture with LoadPicture
0.139	16	
0.164	32	
		Load Bitmap to Image1.Picture with LoadPicture
0.146	16	
0.192	32	
		Load Bitmap to Form.Picture using Scratchpad for Positioning
0.126	16	
0.151	32	

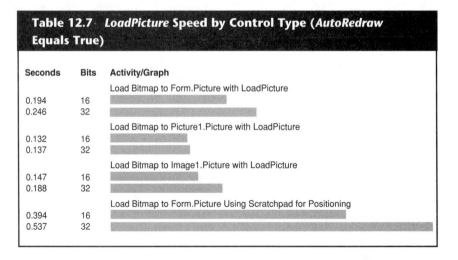

Table 12.7 *LoadPicture* **Speed by Control Type (*AutoRedraw* Equals True)**

Seconds	Bits	Activity/Graph
		Load Bitmap to Form.Picture with LoadPicture
0.194	16	
0.246	32	
		Load Bitmap to Picture1.Picture with LoadPicture
0.132	16	
0.137	32	
		Load Bitmap to Image1.Picture with LoadPicture
0.147	16	
0.188	32	
		Load Bitmap to Form.Picture Using Scratchpad for Positioning
0.394	16	
0.537	32	

Using the scratchpad to load and copy a bitmap to the form is the fastest method but also is the slowest—depending on whether AutoRedraw is true. If AutoRedraw is false, it's only marginally faster than using a picture control; on the other hand, if AutoRedraw is true, it's three times slower. Also, note that

`AutoRedraw` affects the persistence of a bitmap loaded with scratchpad; if `AutoRedraw` is false, the bitmap won't repaint if you obscure it and then uncover that region of the form.

Resource Usage

Resource usage, as you've seen in earlier chapters, isn't as much of an issue in Windows 95 as in Windows 3.1 because of the increased amount of 32-bit resource areas in Windows 95. This doesn't mean that resources are infinite, however. This section makes a quick comparison of the relative resource requirements of picture and image controls.

Image controls, as you know, are lightweight controls. They have fewer features and less functionality than picture controls but are supposed to be somewhat faster and consume fewer resources. You've seen in the preceding sections that speed improvements with the image control are marginal or nonexistent for the test bitmaps. Now let's test resource usage.

GrafCtl.Vbp has two more forms: ResPic and ResImg. These forms are the same size, contain virtually identical code, and have the same controls, except that ResPic has 10 picture controls, whereas ResImg has 10 image controls. I'll test resource usage before and after loading each form to see what usage an empty control has. I'll then load each control with the sample bitmap to test resource usage while displaying a graphic. Figure 12.7 shows the ResPic form.

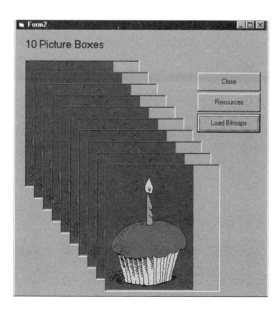

Fig. 12.7
The ResPic form for the GrafCtl.Vbp project.

This test shows that GDI usage is almost identical with both controls (see table 12.8). Empty picture controls consume a little more in the way of resources than image controls, but once filled, the GDI free percentage is identical. In any case, displaying 10 bitmaps in either control consumes only 2 percent of available GDI resources. On the other hand, image controls don't use any measurable user resource space, while 10 loaded picture controls reduce user space by just 2 percent.

Table 12.8	Resource Usage of Pictures and Images	
Seconds	**Activity/Graph**	
	GDI: 79% User: 84%	Resources Before Picture Form Display
79.000		
	GDI: 78% User: 82%	Resource Use: 10 Empty Picture Boxes
78.000		
	GDI: 76% User: 82%	Resource Use: 10 Picture Boxes with Bitmaps
76.000		
	GDI: 79% User: 84%	Resources Before Image
79.000		
	GDI: 79% User: 84%	Resource Use: 10 Empty Image Controls
79.000		
	GDI: 76% User: 84%	Resource Use: 10 Image Controls with Bitmaps
76.000		

Tuning VB Drawing Methods

As you've seen earlier in this chapter, you'll get better results in most cases by using picture controls for your graphics than other controls. Nonetheless, there's still optimization work to do. The VB graphics methods may seem straightforward—and indeed they are—but the different ways to implement them may affect performance. The following sections will test different ways to speed graphics methods using GrafMeth.Vbp, which you can find in the \Chap12 directory on the CD. Figure 12.8 shows the GrafMeth main form.

Setting Coordinates

You can specify coordinates for the Line method in two ways. For example, you can make a line 5 pixels long, starting at pixel 20, by specifying the coordinates (20,20)-(25,20) or by specifying the start point and telling VB how far to go, as in (20,20)-Step(5,0).

The first test determines whether any speed difference is associated with these two methods of specifying coordinates. Listing 12.20 shows the code that explicitly specifies coordinates. The code in listing 12.21 uses the Step keyword to set coordinates.

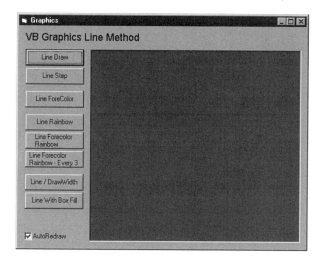

Fig. 12.8
The GrafMeth
project's main
form.

Listing 12.20   GrafMeth.Vbp   Explicitly Specifying Coordinates

```
Case 0
    BeginTime "VB Line Method -(X1,Y1)-(X2,Y2)(Autoredraw = " & _
      Picture1.AutoRedraw & ")", TIME_DEBUG
    For foo = 0 To PicHeight
        Picture1.Line (0, foo)-(PicWidth, foo), &HFF&
    Next foo
    EndTime
```

**Listing 12.21   GrafMeth.Vbp   Using the *Step* Keyword
to Set Coordinates**

```
Case 1
    BeginTime "VB Line Method - Step (Autoredraw = " & _
      Picture1.AutoRedraw & ")", TIME_DEBUG
    For foo = 0 To PicHeight
        Picture1.Line (0, foo)-Step(PicWidth, 0), &HFFFF&
    Next foo
    EndTime
```

Table 12.9 makes the results clear: There *is* no difference. (Although this may
not seem to help much, I report, as before, negative as well as positive results
so that at least you don't have to worry about testing it yourself.)

Table 12.9 Alternate Coordinate Specification Methods

Seconds	Bits	Activity/Graph
		VB Line Method -(X1,Y1)-(X2,Y2) (AutoRedraw = True)
1.180	16	
1.414	32	
		VB Line Method - Step (AutoRedraw = True)
1.195	16	
1.386	32	
		VB Line Method -(X1,Y1)-(X2,Y2) (AutoRedraw = False)
0.975	16	
1.168	32	
		VB Line Method - Step (AutoRedraw = False)
0.989	16	
1.223	32	

Color Settings

Let's examine a more profitable area: color settings. Most of VB's graphics methods allow you to either specify the color to draw or use the default forecolor for the object. I'll test whether this makes a difference by using the Line method.

The first case, in listing 12.22, explicitly sets the color to use to draw the lines. Case 2, shown in listing 12.23, draws the lines using the default color, which is the object's ForeColor.

Listing 12.22 GrafMeth.Vbp Explicitly Setting the Color

```
Case 0
    BeginTime "VB Line Method -(X1,Y1)-(X2,Y2)(Autoredraw = " & _
      Picture1.AutoRedraw & ")", TIME_DEBUG
    For foo = 0 To PicHeight
        Picture1.Line (0, foo)-(PicWidth, foo), &HFF&
    Next foo
    EndTime
```

Listing 12.23 GrafMeth.Vbp Drawing the Lines Using the Default Color

```
Case 2
    Picture1.ForeColor = &HFF0000
    BeginTime "VB Line Method - Using Default ForeColor _
      (AutoRedraw = " & Picture1.AutoRedraw & ")", TIME_DEBUG
    For foo = 0 To PicHeight
        Picture1.Line (0, foo)-(PicWidth, foo)
    Next foo
    EndTime
```

Color settings turn out to make a huge difference. As table 12.10 shows, drawing in the default color is almost five times faster when AutoRedraw is true and more than five times faster when AutoRedraw is false. You can see what the form looks like after the test in figure 12.9.

Table 12.10		Using Default Color Specification Methods	
Seconds	**Bits**	**Activity/Graph**	
		VB Line Method - Explicit Color (AutoRedraw = True)	
1.180	16		
1.455	32		
		VB Line Method - Using Default ForeColor (AutoRedraw = True)	
0.234	16		
0.577	32		
		VB Line Method - Explicit Color (AutoRedraw = False)	
0.975	16		
1.208	32		
		VB Line Method - Using Default ForeColor (AutoRedraw = False)	
0.178	16		
0.261	32		

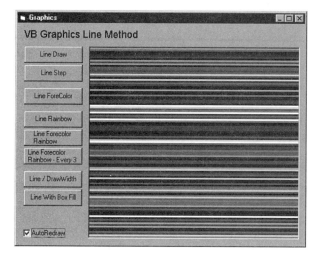

Fig. 12.9
Random rainbow of colors.

Of course, using default color settings as shown in the preceding test doesn't really accomplish much. If you want to create a solid background, you would just set the BackColor property. But does the speed come from not changing the color setting with each iteration, or is it because setting a picture control's ForeColor property is faster than the technique the Line method uses?

If the benefit does derive from simply not setting a color, how often could you reset the ForeColor property and still gain speed improvements? In other words, you'll often want to draw more than one line on a form. If you're using a graphics method to provide 3-D shading to objects, for example, you'll want two dark and two light lines for each object. What would happen if you did all the dark lines first and then the light lines by using the picture ForeColor property?

I added the following code to the GrafMeth.Vbp project. The code section in listing 12.24 resets the color randomly for each line, and draws the color using the Line method's explicit color setting. The code clip in listing 12.25 also sets the color randomly for each line, but works by changing the picture control's ForeColor property. The last code segment, shown in listing 12.26, resets the picture control's property every three lines.

Listing 12.24 GrafMeth.Vbp   Using the *Line* Method's Explicit Color Setting

```
Case 3
    BeginTime "VB Line Method - Random Explicit Colors _
        (Autoredraw = " & Picture1.AutoRedraw & ")", _
        TIME_DEBUG
    For foo = 0 To PicHeight
        Picture1.Line (0, foo)-Step(PicWidth, 0), QBColor(Rnd * 15)
    Next foo
    EndTime
```

Listing 12.25 GrafMeth.Vbp   Changing the Picture Control's *ForeColor* Property

```
Case 4
    BeginTime "VB Line Method - Rainbow Resetting Forecolor _
        (Autoredraw = " & Picture1.AutoRedraw & ")", _
        TIME_DEBUG
    For foo = 0 To PicHeight
        Picture1.ForeColor = QBColor(Rnd * 15)
        Picture1.Line (0, foo)-Step(PicWidth, 0)
    Next foo
    EndTime
```

Listing 12.26   GrafMeth.Vbp   Resetting the Control's Property Every Three Lines

```
Case 5
    BeginTime "VB Line Method - Reset Color Every 3 Lines _
    (Autoredraw = " & Picture1.AutoRedraw & ")", TIME_DEBUG
    For foo = 0 To PicHeight Step 3
        Picture1.ForeColor = QBColor(Rnd * 15)
        For foobar = 0 To 2
            Picture1.Line (0, foo + foobar)-Step(PicWidth, 0)
        Next foobar
    Next foo
    EndTime
```

As you can see in table 12.11, resetting the ForeColor property for every line is even slower than using explicit colors. On the other hand, using the same forecolor as few as three times will double the speed over using the explicit color setting.

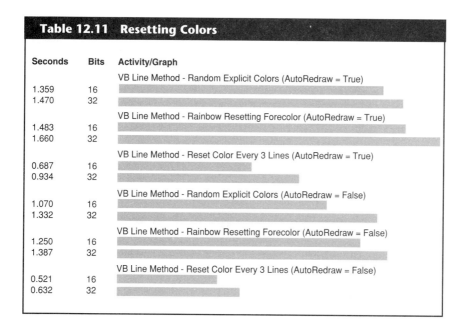

Table 12.11   Resetting Colors

Seconds	Bits	Activity/Graph
		VB Line Method - Random Explicit Colors (AutoRedraw = True)
1.359	16	
1.470	32	
		VB Line Method - Rainbow Resetting Forecolor (AutoRedraw = True)
1.483	16	
1.660	32	
		VB Line Method - Reset Color Every 3 Lines (AutoRedraw = True)
0.687	16	
0.934	32	
		VB Line Method - Random Explicit Colors (AutoRedraw = False)
1.070	16	
1.332	32	
		VB Line Method - Rainbow Resetting Forecolor (AutoRedraw = False)
1.250	16	
1.387	32	
		VB Line Method - Reset Color Every 3 Lines (AutoRedraw = False)
0.521	16	
0.632	32	

IV

Bitwise Optimization

DrawWidth vs. Box Fill

Drawing lines is only one of the functions of the Line method. You can also use it to create rectangles or to fill areas. You'll examine rectangles later in the chapter, so for now let's look at two methods you could use to create thicker lines, for graphic situations where a one-pixel line seems too light.

The first way is to adjust the control's DrawWidth property. By default, DrawWidth specifies lines that are one pixel wide. By increasing the value, you can make your lines thicker. For horizontal and vertical lines, you can achieve the same result by specifying that the Line method create a filled box. One important difference: DrawWidth specifies a radius, and thus the ends of the line are curved. Line with Box Fill will create sharply rectangular lines.

I added the following code to the GrafMeth project, which you'll find on the CD in the \Chap12 directory. Figure 12.10 shows the project after executing the new code.

Fig. 12.10

Area fill methods.

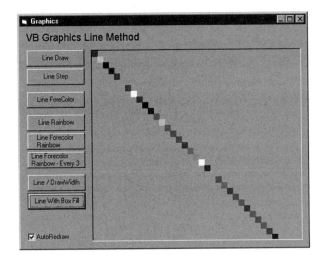

The first code clip, in listing 12.27, shows how I drew the line with a larger picture control DrawWidth setting.

Listing 12.27 GrafMeth.Vbp Using a Larger *DrawWidth* Setting

```
Case 6
    Picture1.DrawWidth = 10
    Picture1.ForeColor = QBColor(Rnd * 15)
    BeginTime "VB Line Method - DrawWidth = 4 (Autoredraw = " &
        Picture1.AutoRedraw & ")", TIME_DEBUG
```

```
    For foo = 0 To PicHeight Step 10
        Picture1.ForeColor = QBColor(Rnd * 15)
        Picture1.Line (foo, foo)-Step(10, 0)
    Next foo
    EndTime
    Picture1.DrawWidth = 1
```

The code in listing 12.28 shows the use of the Line method with the Box Fill option. Notice that you enable Box Fill by specifying the parameter BF following the color setting. If you're using default colors, as shown here, you would need to include an extra comma to indicate a null color choice.

Listing 12.28 GrafMeth.Vbp Using the *Line* Method with the Box Fill Option

```
Case 7
    Picture1.ForeColor = QBColor(Rnd * 15)
    BeginTime "VB Line Method - Box Fill (Autoredraw = " &
        Picture1.AutoRedraw & ")", TIME_DEBUG
    For foo = 0 To PicHeight Step 10
        Picture1.ForeColor = QBColor(Rnd * 15)
        Picture1.Line (foo, foo)-Step(10, 10), , BF
    Next foo
    EndTime
```

As you can see in table 12.12, the Line with Box Fill technique for creating thicker lines works about 20 percent more quickly than adjusting the DrawWidth property. However, remember that it's effective only for horizontal or vertical lines, so its use is limited; DrawWidth, on the other hand, affects even angled lines.

Table 12.12 Area Fill: *DrawWidth* vs. Box Fill

Seconds	Bits	Activity/Graph
		VB Line Method - DrawWidth = 10 (AutoRedraw = True)
0.261	16	
0.469	32	
		VB Line Method - Box Fill (AutoRedraw = True)
0.204	16	
0.261	32	
		VB Line Method - DrawWidth = 10 (AutoRedraw = False)
0.219	16	
0.261	32	
		VB Line Method - Box Fill (AutoRedraw = False)
0.164	16	
0.222	32	

API Drawing Functions

When you're faced with a difficult optimization problem, it often pays to examine the API. If there's an alternative API function for the task at hand, it will almost always perform more quickly than the VB equivalent.

Unfortunately, the API functions are often a little more difficult to work with, because VB methods often combine the functions of several API calls in one simple command. API calls are sometimes error-prone in ways that equivalent VB commands aren't. This is because VB will usually return a syntax or trappable runtime error if you provide an incorrect parameter, while API calls can generate a GPF if you don't have everything set up just right. You should be sure to save your project often when experimenting with API calls.

The API drawing functions are a case in point. While you've seen how to speed up graphics operations by five times or more by using picture controls, setting AutoRedraw to false when appropriate, and/or using the default color setting, you haven't achieved order-of-magnitude improvements. You can do better; use the GrafAPI.Vbp project to compare several VB graphics methods to their equivalent API functions. You can find GrafAPI.Vbp on the CD in the \Chap12 directory.

Declarations

The API functions I'll examine are in different DLLs in Windows 3.1 and Windows 95 and, in some cases, the function names and/or parameters have been changed. Thanks to VB4's conditional compilation, however, a single set of source can be used for both 32- and 16-bit development. The declarations GrafAPI uses are shown in listing 12.29.

Listing 12.29 GrafAPI.Vbp GrafApi's Declarations

```
Type RECT
    left As Integer
    top As Integer
    right As Integer
    bottom As Integer
End Type
Type POINT
    x As Long
    y As Long
End Type

#If win32 = True Then
    Declare Function FloodFill Lib "gdi32" (ByVal hDC As Long,
ByVal x As Long, ByVal y As Long, ByVal crColor As Long) As Long
    Declare Function Ellipse Lib "gdi32" (ByVal hDC As Long, ByVal
```

```
X1 As Long, ByVal Y1 As Long, ByVal X2 As Long, ByVal Y2 As Long)
As Long
    Declare Function Rectangle Lib "gdi32" (ByVal hDC As Long,
ByVal X1 As Long, ByVal Y1 As Long, ByVal X2 As Long, ByVal Y2 As
Long) As Long
    Declare Function RoundRect Lib "gdi32" (ByVal hDC As Long,
ByVal X1 As Long, ByVal Y1 As Long, ByVal X2 As Long, ByVal Y2 As
Long, ByVal X3 As Long, ByVal Y3 As Long) As Long
    Declare Function MoveToEx Lib "gdi32" (ByVal hDC As Long, ByVal
x As Long, ByVal y As Long, lpPoint As POINT) As Long
    Declare Function LineTo Lib "gdi32" (ByVal hDC As Long, ByVal x
As Long, ByVal y As Long) As Long
#Else
    Declare Function LineTo Lib "GDI" (ByVal hDC As Integer, ByVal
x As Integer, ByVal y As Integer) As Integer
    Declare Function MoveTo Lib "GDI" (ByVal hDC As Integer, ByVal
x As Integer, ByVal y As Integer) As Long
    Declare Function Rectangle Lib "GDI" (ByVal hDC As Integer,
ByVal X1 As Integer, ByVal Y1 As Integer, ByVal X2 As Integer,
ByVal Y2 As Integer) As Integer
    Declare Function RoundRect Lib "GDI" (ByVal hDC As Integer,
ByVal X1 As Integer, ByVal Y1 As Integer, ByVal X2 As Integer,
ByVal Y2 As Integer, ByVal X3 As Integer, ByVal Y3 As Integer) As
Integer
    Declare Function Ellipse Lib "GDI" (ByVal hDC As Integer, ByVal
X1 As Integer, ByVal Y1 As Integer, ByVal X2 As Integer, ByVal Y2
As Integer) As Integer
    Declare Function FloodFill Lib "GDI" (ByVal hDC As Integer,
ByVal x As Integer, ByVal y As Integer, ByVal crColor As Long) As
Integer
#End If
```

Avoiding *PSet*

Before analyzing these API functions, let's review some other graphics methods. As you may recall from the case study in Chapter 6, "Strategies to Improve Algorithms," much of our speed improvement when tuning the algorithm came from using API calls. The API call SetPixel(), which sets a single pixel to an RGB color, worked 10 times more quickly than the equivalent VB method, PSet. The GetPixel() API call, which retrieves the current color of a pixel, was more than twice as fast as Point. If you haven't read Chapter 6 and need to do pixel manipulations, check it out.

Snappier Lines

Much of this chapter has focused on how to get the most out of the Line method. But did it get to the point where it can compete with the API call LineTo()? The first benchmarks in GrafAPI.Vbp will test it out. Figure 12.11 shows the test running.

Fig. 12.11
Line drawing with
GrafAPI.

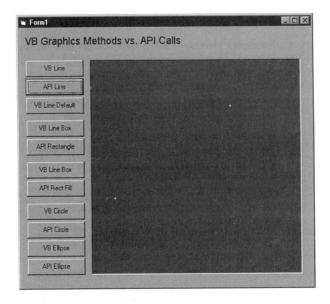

With the `Line` method, you specify four coordinates for the line to define the beginning and ending X and Y points. The API `LineTo()` function, however, allows you to enter only the ending point of the line; it always draws from the `CurrentX` and `CurrentY` coordinates. Therefore, to specify both ends of the line, you must use the `MoveTo()` or `MoveToEx()` functions, or set the `CurrentX` and `CurrentY` properties. Also, `LineTo()` always paints using the current or default forecolor.

The following code tests the API call against the `Line` method using explicit and default colors. The first code section, shown in listing 12.30, uses the `Line` method with explicit color setting. The code in listing 12.31 tests the `LineTo()` API call. Listing 12.32 shows the code that tests the VB `Line` method using the picture control's `ForeColor` (which we saw in the preceding section was much faster).

Listing 12.30 GrafAPI.Vbp Using the *Line* Method with Explicit Color Setting

```
Case 0
    BeginTime "VB Line Method", TIME_DEBUG
    For foo = 0 To PicHeight
        Picture1.Line (0, foo)-(PicWidth, foo), &HFF0000
    Next foo
    EndTime
```

Listing 12.31   GrafAPI.Vbp   Testing the *LineTo()* Call

```
Case 1
    BeginTime "API LineTo Function", TIME_DEBUG
    PicHdc = Picture1.hDC
    Picture1.ForeColor = &HFF
    For foo = 0 To PicHeight
        'win32
        #If win32 Then
            CheckLong = MoveToEx(PicHdc, 0, foo, CheckPoint)
        #Else
            CheckLong = MoveTo(PicHdc, 0, foo)
        #End If
        Checkit = LineTo(PicHdc, PicWidth, foo)
    Next foo
    Picture1.Refresh
    EndTime
```

Listing 12.32   GrafAPI.Vbp   Using the *Line* Method with the Picture Control's *ForeColor*

```
Case 2
    BeginTime "VB Line using Default Forecolor", TIME_DEBUG
    Picture1.ForeColor = &HFF00&
    For foo = 0 To PicHeight
        Picture1.Line (0, foo)-(PicWidth, foo)
    Next foo
    EndTime
```

As table 12.13 shows, the API LineTo() function speeds line drawing almost nine times over the Line method using explicit colors. Even the faster line technique, using default colors, is almost three times slower than the API call. If you're drawing a lot of single-pixel-width lines, LineTo() is definitely the way to go.

Table 12.13   The VB *Line* Method vs. the API *LineTo()* Call

Seconds	Bits	Activity/Graph
		VB Line Using Explicit Color
1.319	16	
2.280	32	
		VB Line Using Default Forecolor
0.453	16	
0.700	32	
		API LineTo() Function
0.155	16	
0.399	32	

Quicker Rectangles

It's quite possible that you'll draw more rectangles than lines. Windows is a very rectangular environment, after all, and many of the common shadings that you might want to apply will be on rectangular objects. However, in VB you use the Line method to draw rectangles as well as lines. The API is a little more sensible: The function to draw a rectangle is called Rectangle(). Figure 12.12 shows the GrafAPI.Vbp form running the test code.

Fig. 12.12
The results when using the Windows API to draw rectangles.

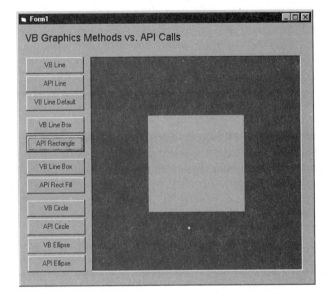

You specify the coordinates of the rectangle for the Rectangle() function by using the bounding coordinates (left, top, right, and bottom). The rectangle is always drawn using the object's ForeColor property. There's no Fill modifier for the Rectangle() call as there is for Line, so you'll fill the rectangle using the FloodFill() API function.

You must also specify the device context handle (hDC) for the control object to be drawn on. hDCs are subject to change and, in fact, change with some regularity in Windows. Consequently, you shouldn't cache the hDC until the last second. But if you're conducting multiple writes, you should cache it just before starting the writes, as looking up the hDC takes a fair amount of time.

The first code example, shown in listing 12.33, tests the speed of the VB Line method when drawing boxes. (Notice that the last parameter used in the call is just B, rather than BF for Box fill. BF draws a solid filled rectangle; B draws just the outline.) The code in listing 12.34 demonstrates how I tested Rectangle().

IV

Bitwise Optimization

Listing 12.33 GrafAPI.Vbp Drawing Boxes with the VB *Line* Method

```
Case 3 'VB Boxes
    Picture1.ForeColor = &HFF0000
    BeginTime "VB Line Box", TIME_DEBUG
    For foo = 0 To 100
        Picture1.Line (foo, foo)-(PicWidth - foo, PicHeight _
            - foo), , B
    Next foo
    EndTime
```

Listing 12.34 GrafAPI.Vbp Drawing Boxes with the *Rectangle()* API Call

```
Case 4 'API Boxes
    BeginTime "API Rectangle Function", TIME_DEBUG
    Picture1.ForeColor = &HFF&
    PicHdc = Picture1.hDC
    For foo = 0 To 100
        Checkit = Rectangle(PicHdc, foo, foo, PicWidth - foo, _
            PicHeight - foo)
    Next foo
    Picture1.Refresh 'need with autoredraw
    EndTime
```

The code in listing 12.35 uses the Line method again, but this time to fill the box. Because Rectangle() doesn't have a fill parameter, the FloodFill() function is used to draw the filled area in listing 12.36.

Listing 12.35 GrafAPI.Vbp Filling Boxes with the *Line* Method

```
Case 5 'VB Box Fill
    BeginTime "VB Box Fill", TIME_DEBUG
    Picture1.ForeColor = &HFF0000
    For foo = 0 To 100
        Picture1.Line (foo, foo)-(foo + 100, foo + 100), , BF
    Next foo
    EndTime
```

Listing 12.36 GrafAPI.Vbp Filling Boxes with the *FloodFill()* Call

```
Case 6 'API Boxes
    BeginTime "API Rectangle and FloodFill", TIME_DEBUG
    Picture1.ForeColor = &HFF&
```

(continues)

Listing 12.36 Continued

```
PicHdc = Picture1.hDC
Picture1.FillColor = &HFF&
Picture1.FillStyle = 0 'solid
For foo = 0 To 100
    Checkit = Rectangle(PicHdc, foo, foo, foo + 101, foo + 101)
    Checkit = FloodFill(Picture1.hDC, foo + 1, foo + 1, &HFF&)
Next foo
Picture1.FillStyle = 1 'trans
Picture1.Refresh
EndTime
```

The Rectangle() results, seen in table 12.14, aren't as encouraging as those created with the LineTo() function. Although the API call is faster when creating a box outline, it isn't faster by as much—only about a third. And for the first time, the API calls were slower when filling the rectangle than when using the Line method with Box Fill modifiers. The culprit here is the FloodFill() function, which is pretty slow because it looks at each pixel before it draws it to see whether it has reached the edge of the area it's supposed to fill.

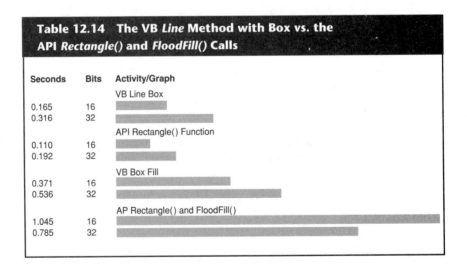

Table 12.14 The VB *Line* Method with Box vs. the API *Rectangle()* and *FloodFill()* Calls

Seconds	Bits	Activity/Graph
		VB Line Box
0.165	16	
0.316	32	
		API Rectangle() Function
0.110	16	
0.192	32	
		VB Box Fill
0.371	16	
0.536	32	
		AP Rectangle() and FloodFill()
1.045	16	
0.785	32	

Faster Circles

The Circle method and the Ellipse() API function are studies in contrast. In fact, they're a true case study in how two programmers who are trying to implement a given task may create diametrically different solutions. The VB Circle method and the API Ellipse() function both are used to create circles

IV

and ellipses. You specify the size of a `Circle` method graphic by specifying the radius. You specify the size of an `Ellipse()` graphic by specifying the points of the rectangle that bound the graphic. With `Circle`, you create an ellipse by specifying an aspect ratio. With `Ellipse()`, you adjust the aspect by altering the coordinates of your bounding rectangle.

The amazing thing is that they both create the exact same output. Of course, the `Circle` method can fill its circle, whereas `Ellipse()` just creates an outline. `Circle` can also generate a pie slice and has some other nice functionalities.

I'll test the techniques by creating circles and ellipses, again in GrafAPI.Vbp. Figure 12.13 shows the test form.

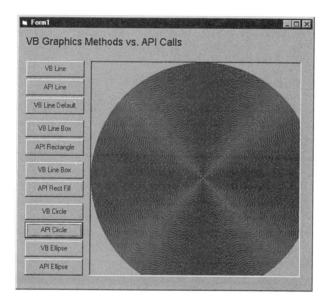

Fig. 12.13
Creating circles and ellipses.

The picture box must be refreshed after the API calls, since `AutoRedraw` is true in this project. VB's `Circle` method refreshes itself automatically.

The code in listing 12.37 demonstrates using the VB `Circle` method when drawing a circle. The code in listing 12.38 tests the `Ellipse()` API function when drawing a circle.

Listing 12.37 GrafAPI.Vbp Drawing a Circle with the *Circle* Method

```
Case 7 'VB Circle
    BeginTime "VB Circle Method", TIME_DEBUG
    Picture1.ForeColor = &HFF0000
    For foo = 0 To 200
        Picture1.Circle (200, 200), foo
    Next foo
    EndTime
```

Listing 12.38 GrafAPI.Vbp Drawing a Circle with the API *Ellipse()* Function

```
Case 8 'API Ellipse - Circle
    BeginTime "API Ellipse Function - Circular", TIME_DEBUG
    PicHdc = Picture1.hDC
    Picture1.ForeColor = &HFF&
        For foo = 0 To 200
        Checkit = Ellipse(PicHdc, 200 - foo, 200 - foo, 201 + foo, _
            201 + foo)
    Next foo
    Picture1.FillStyle = 1 'trans
    Picture1.Refresh
    EndTime
```

The code in listing 12.39 checks the VB Circle method when drawing an ellipse. The code in listing 12.40 tests the Ellipse() API function when drawing an ellipse.

Listing 12.39 GrafAPI.Vbp Drawing an Ellipse with the *Circle* Method

```
Case 9 'VB circle ellipse
    BeginTime "VB Circle Method to Ellipse", TIME_DEBUG
    Picture1.ForeColor = &HFF0000
    For foo = 0 To 200
        Picture1.Circle (200, 200), foo, , , , 0.5
    Next foo
    EndTime
```

Listing 12.40   GrafAPI.Vbp   Drawing an Ellipse with the
***Ellipse()* Function** ·

```
Case 10 'API Ellipse
    BeginTime "API Ellipse - Elliptical", TIME_DEBUG
    PicHdc = Picture1.hDC
    Picture1.ForeColor = &HFF&
    For foo = 0 To 200
        Checkit = Ellipse(PicHdc, 200 - foo, 200 - foo \ 2, 201 _
            + foo, 201 + foo \ 2)
    Next foo
    Picture1.FillStyle = 1 'trans
    Picture1.Refresh
    EndTime
```

As you might expect, the API calls are faster than the `Circle` method by 25 to 30 percent, as table 12.15 shows. But they aren't so dramatically better as to make their use a no-brainer, considering the functionality given up. More speed improvement comes from using the default `ForeColor` and limiting `DoEvents` than by the changed function. However, if you have a process that's drawing a lot of circles, you might find `Ellipse()` a worthwhile substitute.

Table 12.15   The VB *Circle* Method vs. the API *Ellipse()* Call

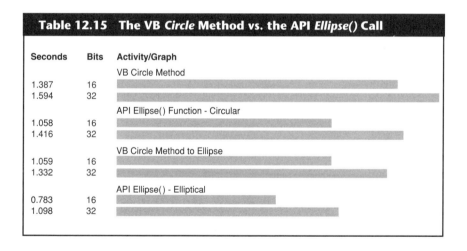

Seconds	Bits	Activity/Graph
		VB Circle Method
1.387	16	
1.594	32	
		API Ellipse( ) Function - Circular
1.058	16	
1.416	32	
		VB Circle Method to Ellipse
1.059	16	
1.332	32	
		API Ellipse( ) - Elliptical
0.783	16	
1.098	32	

Text Methods

You might not think that a chapter on graphics would have a text section, but in the world of Windows, text is a highly graphical element. The Print method is used to draw text onto an object and is indeed considered to be a graphics method. While text or label controls display text based on strings of ANSI characters with formatting beyond our control, printing text in a picture box or on a form is quite a bit more involved.

Speeding Up Textmetrics

When manually formatting and printing text, one of the most common needs is to calculate textmetrics for the strings to be output. (By *textmetrics*, I mean the width and height of characters, words, or lines of text.) VB has two handy methods for determining this information: TextWidth and TextHeight. You pass them a string as a parameter, and they return the relevant data in the scale of the object (twips, pixels, and so forth).

Width and height measurements are also handled by the 16-bit API function GetTextExtent() or the 32-bit GetTextExtentPointA() function. However, the 16-bit function returns both measurements in a single long, which must be split into low and high integers and decoded. In other words, it uses the first two bytes to store height information and the second two bytes to store width. The 32-bit call is friendlier, storing the returns in separate integers in a SIZE structure. Both calls also return only pixels, so you should always set the scalemode of your object to 3 (pixels).

You'll find the code for these tests in the TextMeth.Vbp project, in the \Chap12 directory of the CD. Figure 12.14 shows the form when running.

Listing 12.41 shows the API declares used in the TextMeth.Vbp project.

Listing 12.41   TextMeth.Vbp   The API Declarations

```
#If Win32 Then
    'Declare Function GetTextExtent Lib "gdi32" (ByVal hdc As
Integer, ByVal lpString As String, ByVal nCount As Integer) As Long
    'Declare Function GetTextExtentExPoint Lib "gdi32" Alias
"GetTextExtentExPointA" (ByVal hdc As Long, ByVal lpszStr As
String, ByVal cchString As Long, ByVal nMaxExtent As Long, lpnFit
As Long, alpDx As Long, lpSize As SIZE) As Long
    Declare Function TextOutA Lib "gdi32" (ByVal hdc As Integer,
ByVal X As Integer, ByVal Y As Integer, ByVal lpString As String,
ByVal nCount As Integer) As Integer
    Type SIZE
      cx As Integer
      cy As Integer
```

```
    End Type
    Declare Function GetTextExtentPoint Lib "gdi32" Alias
"GetTextExtentPoint32A" (ByVal hdc As Long, ByVal lpszString As
String, ByVal cbString As Long, lpSize As SIZE) As Long
#Else
    Declare Function GetTextExtent Lib "GDI" (ByVal hdc As Integer,
ByVal lpString As String, ByVal nCount As Integer) As Long
    Declare Function TextOut Lib "GDI" (ByVal hdc As Integer, ByVal
X As Integer, ByVal Y As Integer, ByVal lpString As String, ByVal
nCount As Integer) As Integer
#End If

Global TextSize As SIZE
```

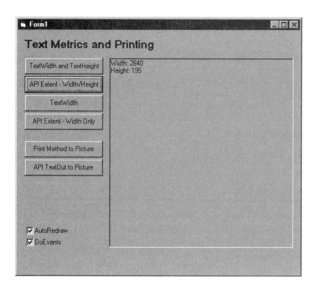

Fig. 12.14
The textmetrics
display.

The code in listing 12.42 returns the textmetrics information using the VB
`TextWidth` and `TextHeight` methods. The code in listing 12.43 tests the performance of `GetTextExtent()`.

Listing 12.42 TextMeth.Vbp   Using *TextWidth* and *TextHeight*

```
Case 0
    BeginTime "TextWidth/Height (Autoredraw = " & _
        Picture1.AutoRedraw & ")", TIME_DEBUG
    For foo = 1 To 1000
        TxtWidth = Picture1.TextWidth(TestString)
        TxtHeight = Picture1.TextHeight(TestString)
    Next foo
    EndTime
    Picture1.Print "Width: " & TxtWidth
    Picture1.Print "Height: " & TxtHeight
```

Listing 12.43 TextMeth.Vbp Using the *GetTextExtent()* Function

```
Case 1
    BeginTime "API Text Extent (Autoredraw = " & _
      Picture1.AutoRedraw & ")", TIME_DEBUG
    For foo = 1 To 1000
        #If Win32 Then
            lExtent = GetTextExtentPoint(PicHdc, TestString, _
              Len(TestString), TextSize)
            TxtWidth = TextSize.cx
            TxtHeight = TextSize.cy
        #Else
            lExtent = GetTextExtent(PicHdc, TestString, _
              Len(TestString))
            TxtWidth = (lExtent And &HFFFF&) * TwipsX
            TxtHeight = ((lExtent And &HFFFF0000) \ &HFFFF&) _
              * TwipsY
        #End If
    Next foo
    EndTime
    Picture1.Print "Width: " & TxtWidth
    Picture1.Print "Height: " & TxtHeight
```

Sometimes, you'll only need the width of a string. The code in listing 12.44 tests the speed of VB when just using the TextWidth method. In the case shown in listing 12.45, the height information isn't decoded, since only the width is needed.

Listing 12.44 TextMeth.Vbp Using *TextWidth* to Get a String's Width

```
Case 2
    BeginTime "TextWidth Only (Autoredraw = " & _
        Picture1.AutoRedraw & ")", TIME_DEBUG
    For foo = 1 To 1000
        TxtWidth = Picture1.TextWidth(TestString)
    Next foo
    EndTime
    Picture1.Print "Width: " & TxtWidth
```

Listing 12.45 TextMeth.Vbp Using *GetTextExtent()* to Get the Width

```
Case 3
    BeginTime "API Text Extent - Width (Autoredraw = " & _
        Picture1.AutoRedraw & ")", TIME_DEBUG
    For foo = 1 To 1000
        #If Win32 Then
```

```
        lExtent = GetTextExtentPoint(PicHdc, TestString, _
          Len(TestString), TextSize)
        TxtWidth = TextSize.cx
    #Else
        lExtent = GetTextExtent(PicHdc, TestString, _
          Len(TestString))
        TxtWidth = (lExtent And &HFFFF&) * TwipsX
    #End If
Next foo
EndTime
Picture1.Print "Width: " & TxtWidth
```

Despite the bitwise Ands and division necessary to decode GetTextExtent()'s long return value, GetTextExtent() is much faster than TextWidth and TextHeight, as table 12.16 shows. The 16-bit GetTextExtent() is 13 times faster when calculating both values. The 32-bit function, GetTextExtentPoint(), is also faster than VB, but by only about 3 times. If you need only width information, it's almost 16 times faster! Of course, as you can see in the preceding code listings, you have to iterate a thousand times to obtain meaningful statistics, and TextWidth/TextHeight returned results in less than a second in 16-bit mode even with a thousand iterations. But if you're writing a word-wrap function, you may find yourself calculating thousands or even tens of thousands of widths, and the savings do add up.

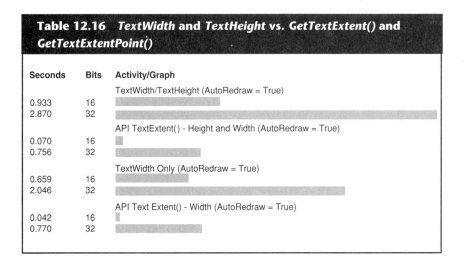

Table 12.16 *TextWidth* and *TextHeight* vs. *GetTextExtent()* and *GetTextExtentPoint()*

Seconds	Bits	Activity/Graph
		TextWidth/TextHeight (AutoRedraw = True)
0.933	16	
2.870	32	
		API TextExtent() - Height and Width (AutoRedraw = True)
0.070	16	
0.756	32	
		TextWidth Only (AutoRedraw = True)
0.659	16	
2.046	32	
		API Text Extent() - Width (AutoRedraw = True)
0.042	16	
0.770	32	

Faster Text Display

Now that you've measured the text, you need to show it to the user. Obviously, the way to do that with VB is the Print method. Print simply prints text to the location set by the object's CurrentX and CurrentY coordinates and in the object's selected font. If you list several strings, it will concatenate them. If the strings are separated by commas, it will print them flush left in tab zones. If you separate items or conclude the output with a semicolon, Print adjusts CurrentX to the position immediately following the last character but won't change the CurrentY location. Otherwise, Print issues a carriage return/line feed, incrementing CurrentY to a position directly below the current line based on TextHeight, and resetting CurrentX to 0.

The API equivalent of Print is TextOut(). TextOut() prints text to a specified position using the object's font. But it doesn't have columnar options and doesn't change CurrentX or CurrentY. If you're printing labels, TextOut()'s capability to specify your x and y positions in the call is very useful. On the other hand, Print manages some of the positioning work for you if you're writing large amounts of text, as in a word-wrap/display function.

But what are the speed issues? I added more benchmark code to TextMeth.Vbp to test TextOut() against Print. Figure 12.15 shows what the output looks like.

Fig. 12.15
Printing text with
TextMeth.Vbp.

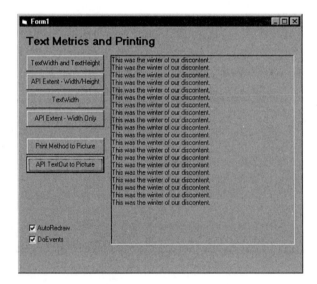

The first code section, in listing 12.46, uses the Print method to print a test string. The code in listing 12.47 tests TextOut().

Listing 12.46 TextMeth.Vbp Printing a String with the *Print* Method

```
Case 4
    BeginTime "Print Method (Autoredraw = " & Picture1.AutoRedraw _
        & ")", TIME_DEBUG
    Picture1.ScaleMode = 1
    For foo = 0 To 19
        Picture1.CurrentY = foo * 195
        Picture1.Print TestString
        If Check2 = 1 Then DoEvents
    Next foo
    DoEvents
    EndTime
```

Listing 12.47 TextMeth.Vbp Printing a String with the *TextOut()* Function

```
Case 5
    BeginTime "Text Out API (Autoredraw = " & Picture1.AutoRedraw _
        & ")", TIME_DEBUG
    Picture1.ScaleMode = 3
    PicHdc = Picture1.hdc
    For foo = 0 To 19
        #If Win32 Then
            Checkit = TextOutA(PicHdc, 0, foo * 13, TestString, _
                Len(TestString))
        #Else
            Checkit = TextOut(PicHdc, 0, foo * 13, TestString, _
                Len(TestString))
        #End If
        If Check2 = 1 Then DoEvents
    Next foo
    'If AutoRedraw must force repaint
    If Check1 = 1 Then Picture1.Refresh
    DoEvents
    Picture1.ScaleMode = 1
    EndTime
```

The first test run showed an amazing speed difference (see table 12.17)—TextOut() was five times faster! But look closely at the code above. There is a DoEvents in the code for both display mechanisms. Since the routines print multiple lines, in a loop, that means VB is giving the control time to repaint itself after every print or TextOut() call. After removing DoEvents, TextOut()

still had a significant performance advantage (it was twice as fast), but the big news is that removing the DoEvents caused the Print method display to be eight times faster than before (see table 12.18). The fastest TextOut() was an astounding 45 times faster than the slowest Print method, meaning that it's quite possible to achieve more than significant improvements in text speed if you haven't done everything just so.

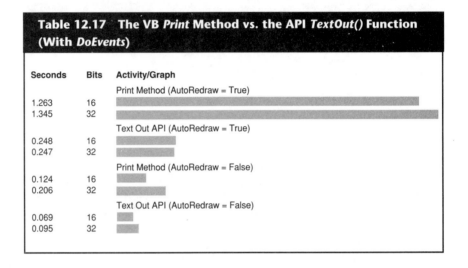

Table 12.17 The VB *Print* Method vs. the API *TextOut()* Function (With *DoEvents*)

Seconds	Bits	Activity/Graph
		Print Method (AutoRedraw = True)
1.263	16	
1.345	32	
		Text Out API (AutoRedraw = True)
0.248	16	
0.247	32	
		Print Method (AutoRedraw = False)
0.124	16	
0.206	32	
		Text Out API (AutoRedraw = False)
0.069	16	
0.095	32	

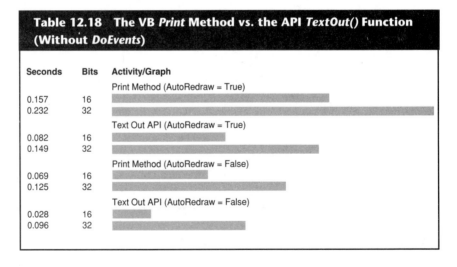

Table 12.18 The VB *Print* Method vs. the API *TextOut()* Function (Without *DoEvents*)

Seconds	Bits	Activity/Graph
		Print Method (AutoRedraw = True)
0.157	16	
0.232	32	
		Text Out API (AutoRedraw = True)
0.082	16	
0.149	32	
		Print Method (AutoRedraw = False)
0.069	16	
0.125	32	
		Text Out API (AutoRedraw = False)
0.028	16	
0.096	32	

Bitmaps and VB4

Today's interfaces are getting more and more graphical. If you create commercial or shareware software, you know that users are expecting more pizzazz than ever with bitmap metaphorical interfaces and multimedia features. The old gray screens just seem dull. This is even becoming true in the commercial world.

Fortunately, it isn't too difficult to add some pizzazz. But it does consume clock cycles. The same user who curls his lip at a 3-D gray screen will complain bitterly if screen response isn't snappy.

Design-Time or Runtime Loading

If you're creating a form that needs a background bitmap or contains static picture boxes to be used as control buttons or hot-spot indicators, you can choose whether to load the graphic at runtime or design time.

If you place your bitmaps in the form or control at design time, they're embedded into the executable, so you have fewer files to distribute. Plus, they're impervious to change, unless you allow it, even if a user has a resource editor. However, what's the impact on load times?

GrafBmp.Vbp, located in the \Chap12 directory on the CD, has two forms, each with a auto-sizable picture box. Form2 contains a preloaded bitmap; Form3 loads a bitmap from the App.Path directory at load time in the load event (see fig. 12.16). Stylistically, the forms will seem identical to the end user.

Fig. 12.16
Loading bitmap graphics files in GrafBmp.Vbp.

The code in listing 12.48 loads the forms to illustrate the performance differences between the two methods.

Listing 12.48   GrafBmp.Vbp   Loading the Two Forms

```
Case 0
    BeginTime "Show Form with Design Time Loaded Bitmaps", _
        TIME_DEBUG
    Form2.Show
    DoEvents
    EndTime
Case 1
    BeginTime "Show Form with Run Time Loaded Bitmaps", TIME_DEBUG
    Form3.Show 'reads bmp in load event
    DoEvents
    EndTime
```

The test results in table 12.19 show that neither method has a significant statistical advantage. The form containing the preloaded bitmap seems to load slightly more quickly, but not enough to make a real difference. This means that you're free to use either method without concerns that you might be sacrificing performance.

Table 12.19   Design or Runtime Bitmap Loading

Seconds	Bits	Activity/Graph
		Show Form with Design-Time Loaded Bitmaps
1.396	16	
2.685	32	
		Show Form with Runtime Loaded Bitmaps
1.324	16	
2.872	32	

PaintPicture vs. BitBlt() and StretchBlt()

A common method to handle bitmaps is to load them offline on a scratchpad form, or preload them in an artform and then Blt them into the proper position with BitBlt() or StretchBlt()—often manipulating them along the way. I'll compare the speed of VB's new PaintPicture method, which is intended to replace BitBlt() and StretchBlt(), to see whether API equivalents provide better performance. Figure 12.17 shows the test form in GrafBmp.Vbp while running the Blt tests.

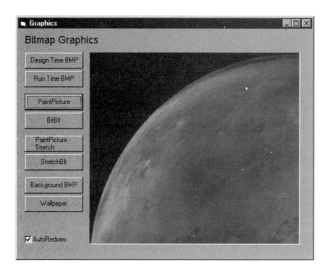

Fig. 12.17
Running a Blt test
in GrafBmp.Vbp.

The first case uses the PaintPicture method to simply copy a bitmap from
one picture control to another (see listing 12.49). The code in listing 12.50
copies the bitmap with the BitBlt() API call.

**Listing 12.49   GrafBmp.Vbp   Copying from One Control to
Another with *PaintPicture***

```
Case 2
    Load Form2
    BeginTime "PaintPicture to Copy BMP (Autoredraw = " & _
        Picture1.AutoRedraw & ")", TIME_DEBUG
    Picture1.PaintPicture Form2.Picture1.picture, 0, 0
    DoEvents
    EndTime
    Unload Form2
```

**Listing 12.50   GrafBmp.Vbp   Copying from One Control to
Another with *BitBlt()***

```
Case 3
    Load Form2
    BeginTime "BitBlt to Copy BMP (Autoredraw = " & _
        Picture1.AutoRedraw & ")", TIME_DEBUG
    checkit = BitBlt(Picture1.hDC, 0, 0, _
        Form2.Picture1.ScaleWidth, _
        Form2.Picture1.ScaleHeight, _
        Form2.Picture1.hDC, 0, 0, &HCC0020)
```

(continues)

Listing 12.50 Continued

```
If Check1 = 1 Then Picture1.Refresh
DoEvents
EndTime
Unload Form2
```

The code in listing 12.51 uses the PaintPicture method to copy the bitmap.
The code in listing 12.52 uses StretchBlt() to resize and copy the bitmap.

Listing 12.51 GrafBmp.Vbp Copying the Bitmap with *PaintPicture*

```
Case 4
    Load Form2
    BeginTime "PaintPicture to Stretch BMP (Autoredraw = " & _
        Picture1.AutoRedraw & ")", TIME_DEBUG
    Picture1.PaintPicture Form2.Picture1.picture, 0, 0, _
        Picture1.ScaleWidth, Picture1.ScaleHeight
    DoEvents
    EndTime
    Unload Form2
```

**Listing 12.52 GrafBmp.Vbp Copying and Resizing the Bitmap
with *StretchBlt()***

```
Case 5
    Load Form2
    BeginTime "StretchBlt to Copy BMP (Autoredraw = " & _
        Picture1.AutoRedraw & ")", TIME_DEBUG
    checkit = StretchBlt(Picture1.hDC, 0, 0, _
        Picture1.ScaleWidth, Picture1.ScaleHeight, _
        Form2.Picture1.hDC, 0, 0, _
        Form2.Picture1.ScaleWidth, _
        Form2.Picture1.ScaleHeight, &HCC0020)
    If Check1 = 1 Then Picture1.Refresh
    DoEvents
    EndTime
    Unload Form2
```

Surprisingly, PaintPicture is much faster than BitBlt() and StretchBlt() (see
tables 12.20 and 12.21)! Normally, of course, API equivalents are at least a
little faster than the VB command. But in the case of PaintPicture, VB's designers have obviously played some tricks, and the happy result is significantly improved performance—and over functions that were pretty fast to
begin with!

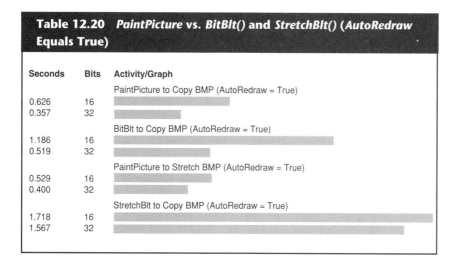

Table 12.20 *PaintPicture* vs. *BitBlt()* and *StretchBlt()* (*AutoRedraw Equals True*)

Seconds	Bits	Activity/Graph
		PaintPicture to Copy BMP (AutoRedraw = True)
0.626	16	
0.357	32	
		BitBlt to Copy BMP (AutoRedraw = True)
1.186	16	
0.519	32	
		PaintPicture to Stretch BMP (AutoRedraw = True)
0.529	16	
0.400	32	
		StretchBlt to Copy BMP (AutoRedraw = True)
1.718	16	
1.567	32	

Table 12.21 *PaintPicture* vs. *BitBlt()* and *StretchBlt()* (*AutoRedraw Equals False*)

Seconds	Bits	Activity/Graph
		PaintPicture to Copy BMP (AutoRedraw = False)
0.130	16	
0.096	32	
		BitBlt to Copy BMP (AutoRedraw = False)
0.567	16	
0.480	32	
		PaintPicture to Stretch BMP (AutoRedraw = False)
0.215	16	
0.123	32	
		StretchBlt to Copy BMP (AutoRedraw = False)
1.496	16	
1.579	32	

PaintPicture is almost twice as fast as BitBlt() in a straight copy to a picture control where AutoRedraw is set to true, whereas PaintPicture's sizing options are three times faster than StretchBlt()! With AutoRedraw set to false, the savings are even greater—PaintPicture is four times faster than BitBlt() and seven times faster than StretchBlt()! If you have existing BitBlt() or StretchBlt() code, you should immediately check to see whether you can use PaintPicture instead.

Backgrounds and Wallpaper

The next test is unlike most of the benchmarks I've run: I'll compare apples and oranges in this one. The task is to create a background for the form that's jazzier than the usual gray background. We'll take two approaches: loading a large bitmap into the form's picture, and tiling a small bitmap across the form using the PaintPicture method and the Wallpaper subroutine from the CodeBank library (in the \Vcb directory on the CD). Figure 12.18 shows the form after it has been wallpapered.

Fig. 12.18

Sample wallpaper.

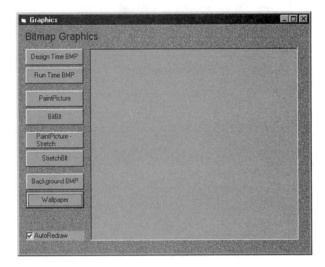

Each approach has stylistic advantages: The large bitmap is clearly a picture, which is essential for a metaphorical interface, whereas the wallpaper is simply texture that lends some roughness to the form. Wallpaper, because it repeats a small bitmap, is much less I/O intensive and results in smaller distributables. But what's the difference in performance?

The code in listing 12.53 loads a large bitmap to make the form background. The code in listing 12.54 tiles a small bitmap by calling the Wallpaper subroutine. The Wallpaper subroutine is shown in listing 12.55.

Listing 12.53   GraphBmp.Vbp   Loading a Large Bitmap to Make the Form Background

```
Case 6
    Me.picture = Nothing
    DoEvents
    BeginTime "Load Large Form Background BMP (Autoredraw = " _
      & Picture1.AutoRedraw & ")", TIME_DEBUG
```

```
Me.picture = LoadPicture(App.Path & "\MrsObs.Bmp")
DoEvents
EndTime
```

Listing 12.54   GraphBmp.Vbp   Tiling a Small Bitmap

```
Case 7
    Me.picture = Nothing
    DoEvents
    BeginTime "Create Form Wallpaper BMP (Autoredraw = " _
      & Picture1.AutoRedraw & ")", TIME_DEBUG
    Wallpaper Me, "", Picture2
    DoEvents
    EndTime
```

Listing 12.55   GraphBmp.Vbp   The *Wallpaper* Subroutine

```
Sub Wallpaper(Obj As Object, Bmp As String, SourceObj As Object)
On Error Resume Next
Dim foo As Integer, foobar As Integer
Dim HoldMode As Integer, HoldMode2 As Integer
Dim sHeight As Integer, sWidth As Integer
Dim h As Integer, v As Integer
If Len(Trim$(Bmp)) > 0 Then
    SourceObj.AutoSize = True
    SourceObj.picture = LoadPicture(Bmp)
End If
If Err <> 0 Then Exit Sub
HoldMode = Obj.ScaleMode
HoldMode2 = SourceObj.ScaleMode
Obj.ScaleMode = 1
SourceObj.ScaleMode = 1
sWidth = SourceObj.ScaleWidth
sHeight = SourceObj.ScaleHeight
h = Obj.ScaleWidth \ sWidth
v = Obj.ScaleHeight \ sHeight
For foo = 0 To h
    For foobar = 0 To v
        Obj.PaintPicture SourceObj.picture, foo * sWidth, _
            foobar * sHeight
    Next foobar
Next foo
Obj.ScaleMode = HoldMode
SourceObj.ScaleMode = HoldMode2
End Sub
```

Table 12.22 shows the performance of the two methods. When AutoRedraw is true, loading the large bitmap is slightly faster than tiling the small bitmap in 16-bit mode, while the opposite is true in 32-bit mode. If AutoRedraw is false, however, using `Wallpaper` is more than twice as fast as loading the large background file in 16-bit mode, and four times faster in 32-bit mode.

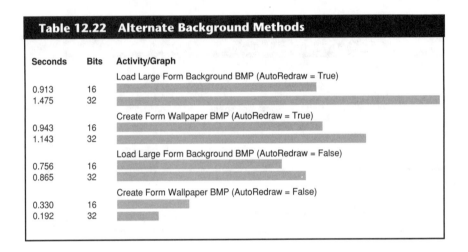

Table 12.22		Alternate Background Methods
Seconds	**Bits**	**Activity/Graph**
		Load Large Form Background BMP (AutoRedraw = True)
0.913	16	
1.475	32	
		Create Form Wallpaper BMP (AutoRedraw = True)
0.943	16	
1.143	32	
		Load Large Form Background BMP (AutoRedraw = False)
0.756	16	
0.865	32	
		Create Form Wallpaper BMP (AutoRedraw = False)
0.330	16	
0.192	32	

From Here...

For related information, see the following chapters:

- To review a practical example of optimizing a graphical subroutine, see the `Emboss3D` case study in Chapter 6, "Strategies to Improve Algorithms."

- For an example of graphics methods using custom controls and VB code, see Chapter 13, "Using Components and Subroutines Wisely."

- See Chapter 14, "Exploiting the Windows 32-Bit API," for more information on using the Windows API.

Chapter 13

Using Components and Subroutines Wisely

The key to programmer productivity is code reusability. This was the promise and rationale behind the object-oriented programming (OOP) revolution. But the promise of productivity gains remained largely unfulfilled for many programmers until Visual Basic came along with a less ambitious but more accessible object paradigm: *component programming*.

Component programming with VBXs revolutionized Windows programming and spawned a whole new industry. Components, with their encapsulated properties, methods, and events, proved not only to increase programmer productivity greatly, but also became an effective method of providing increased speed and functionality not readily obtainable with VB's interpreted language.

With VB4, Microsoft revised its custom control architecture from the proprietary 16-bit VBX model to an open specification based on OLE. OLE custom controls are available in 16- or 32-bit flavors. VB4's 16-bit mode still supports VBXs, but there will be no 32-bit VBX specification.

OLE custom controls have been well publicized. However, other paths to code reusability aren't as well known. VB4's new OLE object classes and OLE Automation Server technology provide a whole new way for VB programmers to encapsulate, share, and reuse code. Finally, there's the tried-and-true Visual Basic source library approach. New library management tools, such as CodeBank, eliminate many of the headaches associated with using library modules.

In this chapter, you look at the following:

- The performance characteristics of OLE and VBX custom controls

- A comparison of the performance of custom controls with the equivalent functionality written in Visual Basic

- The performance of various VB code architectures

- Basic routines written for the new object class and Automation Server methods, and their performance contrasted with the more traditional source library architecture

OLE Controls vs. VBXs

In one sense, the discussion of whether OLE controls are better or worse than VBXs is moot because there is no 32-bit VBX specification. If you plan to create 32-bit programs with VB and want to take advantage of VB's component architecture, you have no choice but to use OLE controls. On the other hand, you can still use VBXs in 16-bit applications running under Windows 3.x and Windows 95. Since Windows 3.1 will be with us for some time, the issue is worth considering.

Comparing the PictureClip Control to the PicClip VBX

This section compares size and performance issues of OLE controls and VBXs. You'll use VB4's PictureClip OCX control and contrast it with the PicClip VBX that shipped with VB3.

If you aren't familiar with them, PicClip and PictureClip take a bitmap file and divide it into cells. The bitmap can have multiple columns and rows. You can address and manipulate the cells individually using the control. The benefit of the control is that it allows you to package a number of identically sized bitmaps into a single file, thus speeding up load times and reducing resource consumption while maintaining ease of use in addressing the cells. VB includes a snazzy animated demonstration of a spinning top, called RedTop.Vbp, in the \Vb\Samples\PicClip directory.

I chose the PictureClip/PicClip components for this test for several reasons. Although you can use the control to generate some nice effects, it really doesn't have too much embedded functionality. If you give the matter some thought, all that's really happening here is some arithmetic to determine cell coordinates, and then BitBlting to segment the cells on demand. Since it's a relatively simple control, the speed of operation can be more directly attrib-uted to the control architecture than to the underlying code. This also means that you can emulate the control's functionality pretty completely in VB code, giving a good baseline comparison. (But more on that in the next section.)

Also, the PicClip/PictureClip functionality lends itself readily to bench-marking—especially when used in an animated sequence. It would be much more difficult to assess the speed of a common dialog control, for example, because human intervention is required to end the task. A PicClip animation can be easily looped as many times as needed to obtain accurate data.

TestTop.Vbp: The PicClip Animation Test Project

The test project for this section, TestTop.Vbp, is based on the RedTop.Vbp project that's bundled with the VB Professional and Enterprise editions. TestTop takes a bitmap with 18 animation cells in a six-column-by-three-row matrix and displays them one after the other to simulate the appearance of a spinning top. Microsoft's RedTop.Vbp demonstration places the animation events within a timer loop to obtain a more consistent spin rate. This, of course, would invalidate benchmarks, so I removed the timer subroutines and placed the animation code calls in a loop in the command button-click event. You'll find TestTop.Vbp in the \Chap13 directory of the CD included with the book. Figure 13.1 shows the TestTop form running.

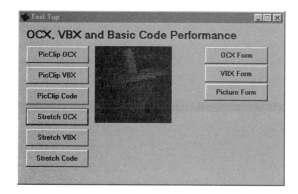

Fig. 13.1
The TestTop main form, running a PicClip animation.

If you load TestTop.Vbp into Visual Basic, VB will ask if you want to upgrade PicClip.Vbx to "the newer version," which is the 16-bit PictureClip OLE con-trol. Be sure to answer no, or else the benchmark routines will be invalidated because there will be no VBX controls to test against. Of course, if you don't have VB3 or have removed the VB3 VBXs from your system, you won't be able to edit this project at all. In that case, you'll just have to rely on the 16-bit results presented in the book.

We'll also test a 32-bit version of TestTop.Vbp, called TstTop32.Vbp, which uses the 32-bit PictureClip OLE control. We can't test VBXs there, but we'll use this data to compare 32-bit OLE control performance to 16-bit operations.

Control Size and Resource Issues

The first issue to address is the size and resources required by the controls. The PicClip VBX provided with VB3 was a pretty lean control—it required only 15K of disk space. The OLE PictureClip controls are larger—the 16-bit version needs 45K, and the 32-bit version requires just over 50K. As OLE controls go, these are still pretty compact, but if you include a variety of controls in your projects, you may find your distributable and load size increasing rapidly.

Resources aren't as great an issue with Windows 95 as they are in Windows 3.x. The resource tests run on TestTop show no difference in resource usage with OLE controls as opposed to VBX controls. However, OLE controls are larger and have greater RAM requirements.

Custom Control Performance

As indicated before, RedTop executes in a subroutine called by a timer control in the original sample project. I've removed the calling code from the timer subroutine and placed all the code in a loop to see how the controls perform when pushed to their limits. The command-button code loops determine the appropriate cell for the animation and then loads the cell from the OCX and VBX controls, respectively. The test is iterated 100 times.

To make things more interesting, the OLE control and the VBX have been set up to write to a picture box or to an image control. The image control is over-sized, and the Stretch property of the image control is set to true so that the top will be displayed in a much larger size.

Listing 13.1 shows the code used to benchmark operations of the PictureClip OCX control. The code to run the PicClip.VBX animation is very similar to the code used with the OCX, as listing 13.2 shows.

Listing 13.1   TestTop.Vbp   Benchmarking the PictureClip Control Performance

```
Case 0 'OCX
    BeginTime "OLE Custom Control PicClip Animation _
        - 100 Frames", TIME_DEBUG
    picture1.Visible = True
    y = 0
    For foo = 1 To 100
        ' Advance animation one frame
        y = y + 1
        If y = 18 Then
            y = 0
        End If
        picture1.picture = PictureClip1.GraphicCell(y)
        DoEvents
    Next foo
    EndTime
```

Listing 13.2   TestTop.Vbp   Running the PicClip Animation

```
Case 1 'VBX
    BeginTime "VBX PicClip Animation - 100 Frames", TIME_DEBUG
    picture1.Visible = True
    For foo = 1 To 100
        ' Advance animation one frame
        y = y + 1
        If y = 18 Then
            y = 0
        End If
        picture1.picture = picClip1.GraphicCell(y)
        DoEvents
    Next foo
    EndTime
```

If we want a larger animation, we assign the PictureClip image to an image box with the Stretch property set to true (see listing 13.3). Stretching the VBX image is accomplished just as with the OCX, as listing 13.4 shows.

Listing 13.3   TestTop.Vbp   Assigning the PictureClip Control to an Image Box

```
Case 3 'Stretch OCX
    BeginTime "OLE Custom Control PicClip Stretch - 100 Frames", _
        TIME_DEBUG
    picture1.Visible = False
```

(continues)

Listing 13.3 Continued

```
    For foo = 1 To 100
        ' Advance animation one frame
        y = y + 1
        If y = 18 Then
            y = 0
        End If
        image1.picture = PictureClip1.GraphicCell(y)
        DoEvents
    Next foo
    EndTime
```

Listing 13.4 TestTop.Vbp Stretching the VBX Image

```
    Case 4 'Stretch VBX
        BeginTime "VBX PicClip Animation Stretch - 100 Frames", _
            TIME_DEBUG
        picture1.Visible = False
        For foo = 1 To 100
            ' Advance animation one frame
            y = y + 1
            If y = 18 Then
                y = 0
            End If
            image1.picture = picClip1.GraphicCell(y)
            DoEvents
        Next foo
        EndTime
```

The performance figures are interesting (see tables 13.1 and 13.2). The VBX control is about 20 percent faster than the 16-bit OLE control when writing to the picture control, for a time savings of a little more than three-tenths of a second. When stretching to the image control, the percentage of improvement is much less, but the time saved is again about three-tenths of a second. Since the image control is performing the stretching, this simply serves to validate the results: The VBX PicClip control performs the simple `BitBlt()` function about three-thousandths of a second faster per iteration. The speed difference is just barely perceivable when viewing the animation, but it *is* perceivable.

Table 13.1 OLE Controls vs. VBX PicClip: Animating a Picture Control

Seconds	Activity/Graph
	16-Bit OLE Custom Control PicClip Animation - 100 Frames
1.593	
	VBX PicClip Animation - 100 Frames
1.263	
	32-Bit OLE Custom Control PicClip Animation - 100 Frames
1.649	

Table 13.2 OLE Controls vs. VBXs: Stretching an Animation to an Image

Seconds	Activity/Graph
	16-Bit OLE Custom Control PicClip Animation Stretch - 100 Frames
2.953	
	VBX PicClip Animation Stretch - 100 Frames
2.595	
	32-Bit OLE Custom Control PicClip Animation Stretch - 100 Frames
3.090	

Of course, you can look at these results in two ways, assuming that they held true for all OLE controls versus their VBX counterparts. Some people think it's a shame that OLE controls are even a little slower than VBXs. Others may be relieved that OLE controls at least come close, and that their performance is roughly comparable to VBXs.

Nonetheless, more analysis needs to be performed before anyone can be too relieved.

The Impact of OLE and VBX at Form Load Time

You've previously seen that the number of controls on a form can significantly affect the time required to load and display the form. Part of the speed and resource differential depended on whether the controls were heavy-weights or lightweights. So it's reasonable to ask whether there's any difference in the overhead needed to load an OLE control compared to a VBX.

In this section, we'll test the issue using the same OCX and VBX forms that were used to examine resource usage, but a timing call will be added. To establish a baseline, we'll also test load a form containing 10 picture controls. As you can see in figure 13.2, each form is identical, except for the type of controls placed on it. Each form has 10 controls. All controls are design-time loaded with the bitmap files.

Fig. 13.2

The OLE, VBX, and Picture control forms in design mode, showing identical setups.

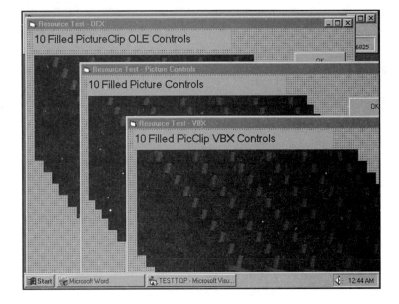

Load performance provides some disappointing results (see table 13.3). Forms with OLE PictureClip controls load much more slowly than those with PicClip VBXs. In fact, the VBX form loads over twice as fast as the OLE control form. Moreover, the real time isn't insignificant—the form with the OLE controls required almost 2 full seconds longer to display. Interestingly enough, though, the form with the VBX controls loaded even more quickly than the form with standard picture controls, although both of them loaded much more quickly than the OLE control form.

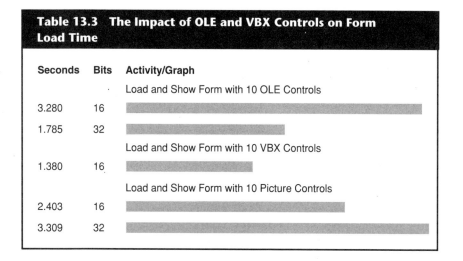

Table 13.3   The Impact of OLE and VBX Controls on Form Load Time

Seconds	Bits	Activity/Graph
		Load and Show Form with 10 OLE Controls
3.280	16	
1.785	32	
		Load and Show Form with 10 VBX Controls
1.380	16	
		Load and Show Form with 10 Picture Controls
2.403	16	
3.309	32	

However, TstTop32 (the 32-bit version of this project) was a different story. The form with picture controls took considerably longer to load and display than the PictureClip OLE Control form. Although the statistics aren't reflected here, the OLE form took considerably longer to load the first time—more than 4.5 seconds, much slower than the first load of picture control form. In successive iterations, the OLE load time greatly decreased. The picture control form stayed more constant in load time; although it showed a small performance increase, its overall average was significantly slower than the 32-bit OLE control form.

Custom Controls vs. VB Code

There are several reasons to use custom controls. They can add substantial functionality to a project with little or no coding effort. Some Windows API functions can be manipulated only with controls, because VB can't execute callback functions. Further, the design-time interface for most controls is easy to understand and use.

Also, because custom controls are written in C or C++, you might expect to achieve superior performance from a compiled control as opposed to interpreted Visual Basic code.

But is this always true? We'll examine the performance of a CodeBank subroutine, `PicClipCode`, which—from a user's point of view—implements exactly the same features as the PictureClip and PicClip controls. However, the subroutine uses the `PaintPicture` method internally to draw to a picture control, rather than load a bitmap to the control's picture property. If `AutoRedraw` is set to false, the bitmap wouldn't be persistent—that is, it wouldn't refresh itself if covered and then uncovered. But because the animation routine will constantly refresh the control anyway, this isn't terribly important.

Another internal difference results from the fact that `PaintPicture` can't be used on a control that doesn't support graphics methods. So rather than enlarge the cell using the image control's `Stretch` property, the subroutine must enlarge the picture control and then stretch the bitmap to the picture control with `PaintPicture`.

The subroutine in listing 13.5 extracts a numbered cell from the top bitmap. The bitmap must be stored in a picture control with `AutoSize` set to true. You'll find the full source in the \Chap13 directory, in TestTop.Bas.

NOTE If the `Init` parameter is set to true or if cell coordinates haven't previously been calculated, the subroutine will calculate the cell coordinates based on the size of the picture box and the numbers of rows and columns specified.

Listing 13.5 TestTop.Bas Extracting a Numbered Cell from the Top Bitmap

```
Public Sub PicClipCode(Dest As Object, Src As Object, Cols As _
    Integer, Rows As Integer, Cell As Integer, Init As Integer)
Static Cellwidth As Integer, CellHeight As Integer
Static PicWidth As Integer, PicHeight As Integer

    'do setup if needed
    If Cellwidth = 0 Or Init = True Then
        Cellwidth = Src.Width / Cols
        CellHeight = Src.Height / Rows
        PicWidth = Dest.Width
        PicHeight = Dest.Height
        Exit Sub
    End If
    'Paint
    Dest.PaintPicture Src.picture, 0, 0, PicWidth, PicHeight, _
        (Cell Mod Cols) * Cellwidth, (Cell \ Cols) * _
        CellHeight, Cellwidth, CellHeight
    DoEvents

End Sub
```

The subroutine is called in the same fashion as the controls, with a 100-iteration loop. Listing 13.6 shows the code from the TestTop form that calls the subroutine and performs the timings.

Listing 13.6 TestTop.Frm Calling the *PicClipCode* Subroutine

```
Case 2 'Call Code Sub
    BeginTime "VB Codex Subroutine PicClip Animation - 100 _
        Frames", TIME_DEBUG
    picture1.Visible = True
    PicClipCode picture1, Picture2, 6, 3, 0, True
    For foo = 1 To 100
        ' Advance animation one frame
        y = y + 1
        If y = 18 Then
            y = 0
        End If
        PicClipCode picture1, Picture2, 6, 3, y, False
        'Note: DoEvents in sub
    Next foo
    EndTime
```

The code in listing 13.7 calls the subroutine as before, but with parameters that cause the PaintPicture method to stretch the bitmap.

Listing 13.7 TestTop.Frm Calling the Subroutine with Stretch Parameters

```
Case 5 'Code Sub
    BeginTime "VB Codex Subroutine PicClip Animation - Stretch - _
        100 Frames", TIME_DEBUG
    picture1.Visible = True
    picture1.Height = image1.Height
    picture1.Width = image1.Width
    PicClipCode picture1, Picture2, 6, 3, 0, True
    For foo = 1 To 100
        ' Advance animation one frame
        y = y + 1
        If y = 18 Then
            y = 0
        End If
        PicClipCode picture1, Picture2, 6, 3, y, False
        'Note: DoEvents in sub
    Next foo
    EndTime
```

The results, as shown in tables 13.4 and 13.5, are more than a little surprising: The VB code is twice as fast as the OLE control and 70 percent faster than the VBX control! Of course, this example actually has very little interpreted code; the functionality of the controls and the subroutine are provided mainly by using the Windows API to BitBlt a portion of the source image to the destination picture. Nevertheless, the code routine has to calculate the cell coordinates and then use the PaintPicture method to copy the cell.

Table 13.4   VB Animation Subroutine vs. Equivalent OCX and VBX PicClip Control

Seconds	Bits	Activity/Graph
		OLE Custom Control PicClip Animation - 100 Frames
1.703	16	
1.649	32	
		VBX PicClip Animation - 100 Frames
1.387	16	
		Visual CodeBank Subroutine PicClip Animation - 100 Frames
0.783	16	
0.897	32	

Table 13.5   Subroutine vs. Equivalent OCX and VBX PicClip Control: Stretching the Bitmap Image

Seconds	Bits	Activity/Graph
		OLE Custom Control PicClip Animation Stretch - 100 Frames
2.925	16	
3.090	32	
		VBX PicClip Animation Stretch - 100 Frames
2.609	16	
		Visual CodeBank Subroutine PicClip Animation Stretch - 100 Frames
1.332	16	
1.415	32	

There's one significant difference between the methods, which accounts for the speed differential: Since this test is animation, the destination picture control didn't need the AutoRedraw property. The PictureClip and PicClip controls, however, both write to the Picture property of the destination picture box, which is by its nature persistent. PaintPicture, however, produces only a persistent bitmap if AutoRedraw is set to true. If you set AutoRedraw to true, the PicClipCode subroutine's performance degrades significantly—to the point where it would be slower than the OLE control—whereas the VBX and OLE controls' performance doesn't degrade significantly.

Subroutines, Functions, and Inline Code

One of Visual Basic's leading features is its capability to increase programmer productivity with reusable code components packaged in controls. When you're using components, such as OLE controls and VBXs, you really have little flexibility in your approach. You place the form on the control, set the properties, and use whatever functions the control designer built into the control. That's the tradeoff for the ease of use of controls.

VB code procedures represent the opposite side of reusable code: You can organize and place them just about any way and anywhere you want. It's up to you, but you'll have to make the decisions and usually exert more coding effort.

The following sections will analyze performance of different procedure architectures and methods using a test project called FunSub.Vbp, which you'll find on the CD in the \Chap13 directory.

Procedure Architecture

Visual Basic procedures—subroutines, functions, or even inline code sections—can have a number of different architectures. VB code performance isn't just a matter of efficient coding and elegant algorithms. You can place the same code in two locations in your project and have very different performance results.

VB offers several architectural options for code placement:

- You can forego using reusable functions and subroutines, and place the code within an event procedure on a form. This is known as *inline code*.

- You can place the functions or subroutines in the general section of a form. This makes the subroutine private to the form—that is, only the form may call the subroutine.

- You can place the routines in a code module. The functions can be public or private. Public procedures can be called from anywhere in your application, whereas private ones can be called only from other procedures in the same module.

FunSub.Vbp demonstrates these procedure architecture options. Figure 13.3 shows the subroutine test form from FunSub.Vbp.

Fig. 13.3
The subroutine test form demonstrates different procedure architectures.

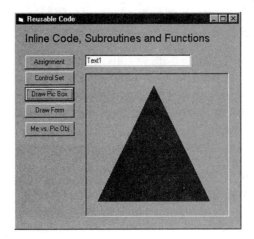

Assignment
You'll begin testing procedure architectures with the simplest example possible: an assignment of an integer value from one variable to the other. Variable assignments are among the fastest VB operations, so this test will isolate the time required to call functions and subroutines very well. They're also very simple, as you can see from the following code.

Listing 13.8 shows the test code for the inline code architecture. The code in listing 13.9 illustrates calling a function or subroutine local to the form. In listing 13.10, the code calls a function and subroutine in a public basic module.

Listing 13.8   FunSub.Vbp   The Inline Code

```
BeginTime "Inline Code", TIME_DEBUG
For foo = 0 To 20000
    foobar = foo
Next foo
EndTime
```

Listing 13.9   FunSub.Vbp   The Form Function Code

```
BeginTime "Form Function Code", TIME_DEBUG
For foo = 0 To 20000
    foobar = FormAssignFun(foo)
Next foo
EndTime

BeginTime "Form Subroutine Code", TIME_DEBUG
For foo = 0 To 20000
    FormAssignSub foo, foobar
Next foo
EndTime
```

Listing 13.10   FunSub.Vbp   The Form Subroutine Code

```
BeginTime "Module Function Code", TIME_DEBUG
For foo = 0 To 20000
    foobar = ModAssignFun(foo)
Next foo
EndTime

BeginTime "Module Subroutine Code", TIME_DEBUG
For foo = 0 To 20000
    ModAssignSub foo, foobar
Next foo
EndTime
```

This code shows the local assignment function (the public module function is essentially identical):

```
Function FormAssignFun(foo As Integer) As Integer
FormAssignFun = foo
End Function
```

The subroutine syntax is slightly different from the function, since the assigned value must be returned through the second parameter:

```
Sub ModAssignSub(foo As Integer, foobar As Integer)

foobar = foo

End Sub
```

To obtain significant results, you have to repeat the loop 20,000 times, which should provide an indication that you're not going to be talking about significant time differences on individual calls. However, as you can see in table 13.6, these tests do show that, when looped 20,000 times, form and module procedures can take about a half second longer to execute—a performance difference of 10 times! In 32-bit mode, the differences aren't quite as extreme, but inline code is still considerably faster. As you've seen in other examinations of VB code constructs, VB code and architectures are inherently pretty fast, but if you repeat them often enough, the speed difference will become apparent.

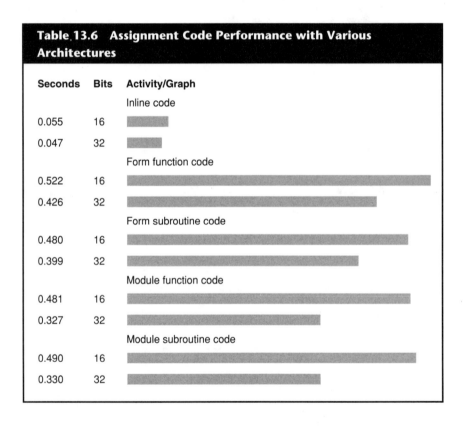

Table 13.6 Assignment Code Performance with Various Architectures

Seconds	Bits	Activity/Graph
		Inline code
0.055	16	
0.047	32	
		Form function code
0.522	16	
0.426	32	
		Form subroutine code
0.480	16	
0.399	32	
		Module function code
0.481	16	
0.327	32	
		Module subroutine code
0.490	16	
0.330	32	

Control Setting

The next architectural test performs a more time-consuming task: setting the text property of a text control. This requires a visual update to a control rather than an entirely internal operation, like the assignment test. That means that this test will tell us less about the isolated time required by different architectures but perhaps more about how those architectures will impact real-world tasks.

In this test you'll also examine another alternative: conducting loop operations within the subroutine. In other words, rather than call the subroutine repeatedly, you call it once and tell the subroutine how many iterations to perform. In the test project, FunSub.Vbp, this code is executed by clicking the second command button, labeled *Control Set*.

The inline code is straightforward, as listing 13.11 shows. In listing 13.12, the form subroutine is passed the control as an object. The module subroutine call is similar to the form subroutine call (see listing 13.13).

Listing 13.11   FunSub.Vbp   The Inline Code

```
BeginTime "Inline Code", TIME_DEBUG
For foo = 0 To 100
    Text1 = foo
    DoEvents
Next foo
EndTime
```

Listing 13.12   FunSub.Vbp   The Form Subroutine Code

```
BeginTime "Form Subroutine Code", TIME_DEBUG
For foo = 0 To 100
    FormTextSub foo, Text1
    DoEvents
Next foo
EndTime
```

Listing 13.13   FunSub.Vbp   The Module Subroutine Code

```
BeginTime "Module Subroutine Code", TIME_DEBUG
For foo = 0 To 100
    ModTextSub foo, Text1
    DoEvents
Next foo
EndTime
```

Listing 13.14 shows how to call the subroutine that performs its loops within the subroutine, so it is called only once. Listing 13.14 also shows how the subroutine that loops internally is coded.

Listing 13.14 FunSub.Vbp   Calling the Subroutine and Looping

```
BeginTime "Module Subroutine - Repeat Code", TIME_DEBUG
ModTextAllSub Text1, 100
EndTime

Sub ModTextAllSub(TxtCtl As Control, Iterations As Integer)
Dim foo As Integer
For foo = 0 To Iterations
    TxtCtl = foo
    DoEvents
Next foo
End Sub
```

As table 13.7 shows, the comparison is quite different when you try to ac-complish real work in the routine. Although inline code is still faster, the performance difference is marginal compared to the variations in the assign-ment test. Placing the loop within the subroutine eliminated any speed dif-ference. Of course, you can't always do this, but if you can, you'll get better speed.

Table 13.7 Setting Control Properties with Various Code Architectures

Seconds	Bits	Activity/Graph
		Inline code
1.250	16	
2.225	32	
		Form subroutine code
1.345	16	
2.280	32	
		Module subroutine code
1.346	16	
2.308	32	
		Module subroutine - repeat code
1.250	16	
2.225	32	

Table 13.8 shows the results if we duplicate the subroutine looping method using the assignment logic from the preceding section. The test duplicates the

control setting results. This proves that nothing is inherently slow about code within a subroutine. Rather, it's the subroutine call that's slow—the interface between form code and module code.

Table 13.8	**Assigning Values to a Variable Within a Subroutine**	
Seconds	**Bits**	**Activity/Graph**
		Inline code
0.055	16	
0.055	32	
		Module subroutine code
0.490	16	
0.330	32	
		Module subroutine - repeat code
0.069	16	
0.056	32	

Assume Nothing

The procedure looping tests conducted in the preceding section showed that there's no difference in speed between code executing in a code module and code executing in an event. But with VB, things aren't always as they initially appear. This section is titled "Assume Nothing" because it's an important philosophy to take to optimization. For example, you can't assume, just because I ran a test setting the properties of a text box, that setting a label control will produce equivalent results—so you don't have to test your own code. If you need convincing on this issue, just read the following sections.

Triangle Inline Code vs. the *Triangle* Subroutine

To continue the architectural tests, let's compare two methods of drawing on a form and a picture box to create a triangle shape. You'll use the `Triangle` subroutine that was introduced in a code module in Chapter 12, "Optimizing Graphics and Bitmaps." And you'll duplicate its functionality in a command button-click event on the form. This test will again be conducted using FunSub.Vbp from the \Chap13 directory on the CD.

Listing 13.15 shows the code to draw a triangle. Listing 13.16 shows how I duplicated the `Triangle` subroutine in inline code, once to draw on a picture box and once to draw directly on the form.

Listing 13.15 FunSub.Vbp Drawing a Triangle

```
Sub Triangle(obj As Object, Left As Single, Top As Single, Width _
    As Single, Height As Single, Color As Long, Bordercolor As Long)
'Just a simple triangle shape routine. Will draw
'over other graphics, but not controls.
Dim foo As Integer
Dim HoldColor As Long
Dim Right As Integer
Dim Bottom As Integer
Dim Center As Integer
Center = Left + (Width / 2)
Right = Left + Width
Bottom = Top + Height
HoldColor = obj.ForeColor
'paint the triangle body
obj.ForeColor = Color
For foo = 1 To Height
    obj.Line (Center - foo / 2, foo + Top)-Step(foo, 0)
Next foo
'outline the triangle
obj.Line (Left, Bottom)-(Right, Top + Height), Bordercolor
obj.Line (Left, Bottom)-(Center, Top), Bordercolor
obj.Line (Center, Top)-(Right, Bottom), Bordercolor
obj.ForeColor = HoldColor
End Sub
```

Listing 13.16 FunSub.Vbp Duplicating the Triangle Subroutine in Inline Code

```
Case 2
    BeginTime "Triangle Inline Code on Picture", TIME_DEBUG
    Left = 20
    Top = 20
    Width = 200
    Height = 200
    Center = Left + (Width / 2)
    Right = Left + Width
    Bottom = Top + Height
    'paint the triangle body
    Picture1.ForeColor = &HFF&
    For foo = 1 To Height
        Picture1.Line (Center - foo / 2, foo + Top)-Step(foo, 0)
    Next foo
    'outline the triangle
    Picture1.Line (Left, Bottom)-(Right, Top + Height), &H0&
    Picture1.Line (Left, Bottom)-(Center, Top), &H0&
    Picture1.Line (Center, Top)-(Right, Bottom), &H0&
    DoEvents
    EndTime

Case 3 'form draw
    Me.ScaleMode = 3
    Picture1.Visible = False
```

```
DoEvents
BeginTime "Triangle Inline Code on Form", TIME_DEBUG
Left = 100
Top = 100
Width = 200
Height = 200
Center = Left + (Width / 2)
Right = Left + Width
Bottom = Top + Height
'paint the triangle body
Me.ForeColor = &HFF&
For foo = 1 To Height
    Me.Line (Center - foo / 2, foo + Top)-Step(foo, 0)
Next foo
'outline the triangle
Me.Line (Left, Bottom)-(Right, Top + Height), &H0&
Me.Line (Left, Bottom)-(Center, Top), &H0&
Me.Line (Center, Top)-(Right, Bottom), &H0&
DoEvents
EndTime
Me.Cls
DoEvents

'Sub on form
BeginTime "Triangle Subroutine Code on Form", TIME_DEBUG
Triangle Me, 100, 100, 200, 200, &HFF&, &H0&
DoEvents
EndTime
```

The code follows the rules for module code speed that were developed earlier—loops are contained within the subroutine. As you can see in table 13.9, when you run the code against a picture control, all is well: Performance is virtually identical in 16-bit mode, while in 32-bit mode, the inline code has a slight edge in performance. But when you test the subroutine against a form, the inline code—compared to the same subroutine—is significantly faster. In fact, as table 13.10 shows, it's almost three times faster in both 16- and 32-bit modes.

Why would drawing on a form in a subroutine be so much slower? I don't know what causes this behavior. Something deep inside VB is clearly not optimized, or perhaps it needed to be kludged because of a messaging problem or other consideration. Only VB's designers can really answer this question, and they're not talking.

The lesson to be learned from this drawing example is that you can assume nothing in optimization. VB has so many permutations and possibilities that you can rely on very few hard-and-fast rules to apply to all situations. As I've said before, you should approach optimization as though it were a science experiment: assume nothing, test everything, and listen to what your results tell you.

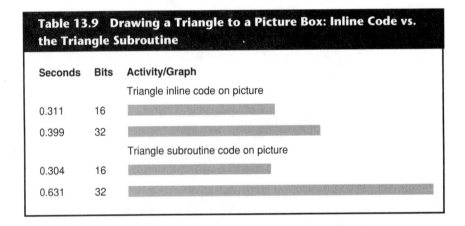

Table 13.9 Drawing a Triangle to a Picture Box: Inline Code vs. the Triangle Subroutine

Seconds	Bits	Activity/Graph
		Triangle inline code on picture
0.311	16	
0.399	32	
		Triangle subroutine code on picture
0.304	16	
0.631	32	

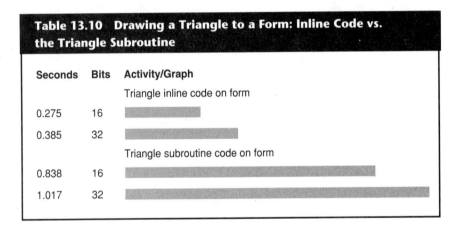

Table 13.10 Drawing a Triangle to a Form: Inline Code vs. the Triangle Subroutine

Seconds	Bits	Activity/Graph
		Triangle inline code on form
0.275	16	
0.385	32	
		Triangle subroutine code on form
0.838	16	
1.017	32	

Module-to-Control Communications

The disparity between inline and subroutine code performance will be investigated from a different angle in this section. Rather than perform a graphic method on the controls, you'll have inline code and a subroutine read the form and picture control Height property. After all, graphics methods take a fair amount of time. Reading a property, while also time-consuming, is more like a variable assignment: It's all internal and thus should reflect architectural differences that we want to examine.

The code in listing 13.17 uses inline code to read the form's Height property. The routine obtains form height using a module-based function in listing 13.18.

Listing 13.17   FunSub.Vbp   Obtaining Form Height with Inline Code

```
Case 4 'return heights
    BeginTime "Form Height - Me, Inline Code", TIME_DEBUG
    For foo = 0 To 1000
        foobar = Me.Height
    Next foo
    EndTime
    DoEvents
```

Listing 13.18   FunSub.Vbp   Obtaining Form Height Using a Module-Based Function

```
BeginTime "Form Height - Me, ObjFunction", TIME_DEBUG
foobar = ObjHeight(Me, 1000)
EndTime
DoEvents
```

Then, in listing 13.19, the procedures are duplicated for picture boxes.

Listing 13.19   FunSub.Vbp   Obtaining Picture Box Height

```
BeginTime "Pic Height - Picture1, Inline Code", TIME_DEBUG
For foo = 0 To 1000
    foobar = Picture1.Height
Next foo
EndTime
DoEvents

BeginTime "Pic Height - Picture1, ObjFunction", TIME_DEBUG
foobar = ObjHeight(Picture1, 1000)
EndTime
DoEvents
```

Listing 13.20 shows the ObjHeight() function, which is called to obtain both form and picture box heights.

Listing 13.20   FunSub.Vbp   Obtaining Form and Picture Box Height

```
Function ObjHeight(Obj As Object, Iterations As Integer) As Long
Dim foo As Integer, foobar As Long
For foo = 1 To Iterations
    foobar = Obj.Height
Next foo
ObjHeight = foobar
End Function
```

Although the operation had to be iterated 1,000 times to get significant results, you can see that there are delays in communications between form module and a code module (see table 13.11). When the subroutine attempted to read form height, the subroutine took 10 times as long to get results as inline code. When the target was a picture control, which seems to have better communication skills than forms, the subroutine still took three times as long as code within the form.

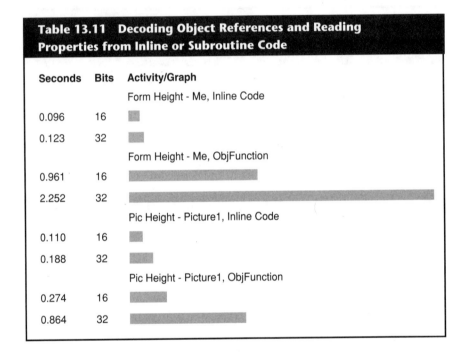

Table 13.11 Decoding Object References and Reading Properties from Inline or Subroutine Code

Seconds	Bits	Activity/Graph
		Form Height - Me, Inline Code
0.096	16	
0.123	32	
		Form Height - Me, ObjFunction
0.961	16	
2.252	32	
		Pic Height - Picture1, Inline Code
0.110	16	
0.188	32	
		Pic Height - Picture1, ObjFunction
0.274	16	
0.864	32	

The design implication here is that if you can read properties outside loops, you'll gain much greater performance, and the performance will be even better if you can construct your algorithms to at least do your property reads within form-based code.

OLE Automation Servers and Object Classes

One of VB4's more exciting aspects is that it allows you to create OLE Automation Servers with VB. These servers can be registered and then used by any application that supports OLE Automation. You can design and implement your own object classes, properties, and methods. Reusable VB code and forms can be compiled and then distributed with complete security. While you can't quite create custom controls with VB, OLE Automation Servers are the next best thing.

When creating 32-bit OLE Automation Servers, you can even compile them to run as in-process servers, meaning that the running server code shares executable space with the calling application. In-process servers run much more quickly than out-of-process servers. To make your server in-process, don't compile your project by choosing Make Exe from the VB File menu. Instead, choose the next option, Make OLE DLL (OLE DLL is the somewhat disingenuous term that Microsoft has selected for in-process OLE servers).

The big question, as far as this book is concerned, is how do they perform compared to projects that use pure VB code and code libraries?

A Matter of Gravity: The OLE Test Project

You'll test the performance of OLE Automation Servers against project-based VB code by using the Gravity.Vbp and GravTest.Vbp sample projects included with VB4. You'll find the modified versions of these projects on the CD in the \Chap13 directory. Gravity is the server, and GravTest provides the user interface. When GravTest is run, it instantiates the Gravity object, which will be used to calculate the effect of gravity on a ball that's "thrown" by the user. The initial velocity and angle of attack of the ball is determined by the user. The routine then loops until the ball passes beyond the right or bottom edges of the screen.

For the test, there'll just be a few changes to the code. First, the original project uses a timer loop to slow down and average out the display of points along the throw. The test project removes the code in the timer routine and replaces it with a private subroutine, Gravloop. Also, I've placed an additional command button on the form that sets a flag to trigger the calculation of the ball's position using inline code instead of referencing the OLE Automation Object. Plus, I added some code to the form to calculate gravitational effects without calling the server as well as some benchmarking code.

Since this project simulates the effect of gravity on a thrown ball over time, the time required for each method to complete the throw will be exactly the same. However, the number of times each routine will calculate positions, draw a ball, and repeat will vary according to the efficiency of the method.

The benchmark calculations in GravTest massage the number of iterations that each method can perform before the throw is completed to provide a statistic measuring the length of time required by 100 calls. You can also observe the efficiency by seeing how much the circles representing the ball overlap. The more they overlap, the more the routine has calculated, drawn, and then reiterated.

The code in listing 13.21 shows how the routines to throw the ball are set up. GravTest's Gravloop subroutine does the actual calculation or server calls (see listing 13.22).

Listing 13.21 GravTest.Vbp Setting Up the Routines

```
Private Sub Command1_Click(index As Integer)
    If index = 0 Then
        Runtype = "OLE Server Object"
    Else
        Runtype = "Inline Code"
    End If
    oT.throw dblStartXVelocity, -dblStartYVelocity
    Iterations = 0
    dblStartTime = CDbl(timeGetTime()) / 1000
    Timer1.Interval = 1
    Timer1.Enabled = True
    Command1(0).Enabled = False
    Command1(1).Enabled = False
    Label1.Visible = False
    Label2.Visible = False
    Shape1.Visible = False
    Me.Cls
    Me.Circle (dblStartDistance, dblStartHeight), 100

End Sub
```

Listing 13.22 GravTest.Vbp Making the Calculations

```
Private Sub Gravloop()
    Dim dblNow As Double
    Dim dblHeight As Double
    Dim dblDistance As Double
    Dim mtti As Long
Do
    mtti = timeGetTime() ' TimerCount mtti
    Iterations = Iterations + 1
```

```
dblNow = CDbl(mtti) / 1000
If Runtype = "OLE Server Object" Then
    'OLE Server Call to compute effect of gravity
    dblHeight = oT.Height(dblNow)
    dblDistance = oT.distance(dblNow)
Else
    'Inline Code to compute gravitational effect on velocity
    dblElapsed = dblNow - dblStartTime
    dblDistance = dblElapsed * dblStartXVelocity
    dblHeight = (-dblStartYVelocity) * dblElapsed - 16 * _
        dblElapsed * dblElapsed
End If
' When the ball travels off the screen, stop drawing, and beep.
If (dblStartHeight - dblHeight < Me.ScaleHeight) And _
        (dblStartDistance + dblDistance < Me.ScaleWidth) Then
    Me.Circle (dblStartDistance + dblDistance, dblStartHeight _
        - dblHeight), 100
Else
    dblElapsed = dblNow - dblStartTime
    Command1(0).Enabled = True
    Command1(1).Enabled = True
    Label1.Visible = True
    Label2.Visible = True
    Shape1.Visible = True
    Beep
    Debug.Print "Iterations to Complete Throw with " & _
        Runtype & ": " & Iterations
    Debug.Print Format$(100 / Iterations * dblElapsed, _
        "##0.0000") & "        Required Per 100 Call _
        Iterations with " & Runtype
    Exit Sub
End If
Loop
End Sub
```

Performance

As you could probably deduce from figures 13.4 and 13.5, the inline code example could draw many more circles in the same amount of time than the OLE Server in 16-bit mode. In fact, as table 13.12 shows, the 16-bit VB inline code could complete 25 times as many operations. The 16-bit OLE server, on the other hand, required almost two-tenths of a second per cycle. For many tasks, that would be far too much time. When running in 32-bit mode, the in-process server performed much better relative to the VB subroutine, but still was twice as slow as VB code.

Fig. 13.4

The GravTest form using OLE Automation in 16-bit mode.

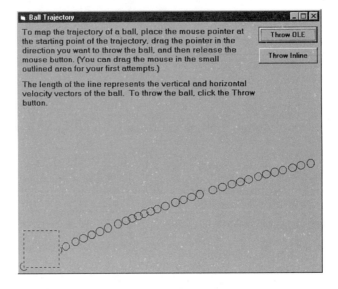

Fig. 13.5

The GravTest form using inline basic code to throw the ball. Notice the greater number of iterations, as shown by the overlapping circles.

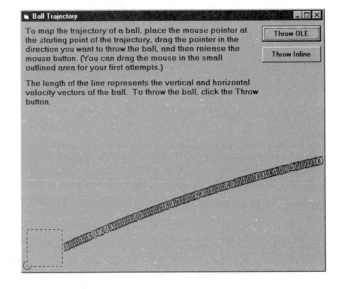

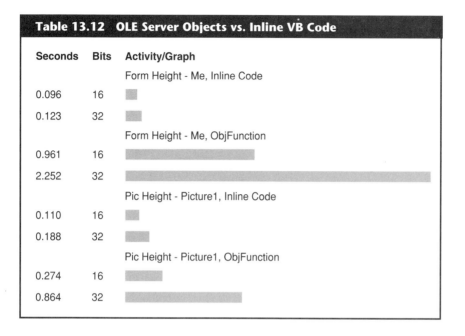

Table 13.12   OLE Server Objects vs. Inline VB Code

Seconds	Bits	Activity/Graph
		Form Height - Me, Inline Code
0.096	16	
0.123	32	
		Form Height - Me, ObjFunction
0.961	16	
2.252	32	
		Pic Height - Picture1, Inline Code
0.110	16	
0.188	32	
		Pic Height - Picture1, ObjFunction
0.274	16	
0.864	32	

From Here...

For more information, refer to these chapters:

- To review a practical example of optimizing a graphical subroutine, see the Emboss3D case study in Chapter 6, "Strategies to Improve Algorithms."

- Chapter 12, "Optimizing Graphics and Bitmaps," analyzes the VB graphics methods with various property settings and different control targets.

- For more information on using the Windows API, see Chapter 14, "Exploiting the Windows 32-Bit API."

Chapter 14

Exploiting the Windows 32-Bit API

Using the Windows API can be a great way to speed up the internals of your application. It can also reduce memory requirements and limit the number of resources that your application uses. Calling the Windows API can, at times, be very easy. However, because of its vastness, finding the information and functions to use can be very difficult.

The Windows API covers many diverse areas of functionality. Its functions range from graphic functions for drawing, copying, or moving bitmaps, to functions that totally control most aspects of Windows, including memory management.

Most API calls are directly accessible from Visual Basic, but some aren't. If you plan to call an API function that provides callback functionality or a function with a parameter that requires a pointer to a function to be passed, you'll have to use some intermediate method. Many third-party companies supply callback OLE controls that provide the functionality needed for calling these callback functions.

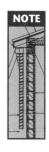

NOTE

The first thing to remember is not to be afraid to use the API. It's a very powerful tool that can put that final polish on your applications.

But be warned: Using the API can sometimes be risky while you're learning. You may inadvertently cause access violations (formerly known as general protection faults) if you accidentally call the wrong function with the wrong information. Keep this in mind while you're programming, and *always* save your project before you run it and try to test it. I give this advice because access violations still happen to me. In fact, I even had one while writing this chapter!

In this chapter, I'll give an overview of the basics of using the Windows 32-bit API to optimize your applications. More specifically, in this chapter you learn how to do the following:

- Use the Windows 32-bit API to speed up your application

- Minimize resource usage by using the Windows API to eliminate the use of certain controls

- Speed up your network applications by using compressed data files

How Visual Basic Uses the API

Since Visual Basic is a Windows application, it's written in C++ using the Windows API. Many of the built-in functions, properties, and methods of Visual Basic objects are really just calls that are passed from your Visual Basic program to the underlying operating system. Directly calling these functions bypasses much of the overhead involved with setting a property in Visual Basic or calling a method on an object. For example, if you have a list box on a form and do the following,

```
List1.Clear
```

then Visual Basic executes this code by using the API function SendMessage() to send the message LB_RESETCONTENT to the list box. You could replace this code with your own appropriate SendMessage() code and thus bypass the overhead of the Visual Basic method. That code might look something like this:

```
Private Declare Function SendMessage Lib "user32" Alias
"SendMessageA" (ByVal hwnd As Integer, ByVal msg As Integer, ByVal
wp As Integer, ByVal lp As Long) As Long

b = SendMessage(List1.hWnd, &H184, 0, 0)
```

The time savings from this would be negligible because to send the message, you have to write code that accesses the hWnd property on the list box object. If you were clearing this list box thousands of times in an application, the SendMessage() API would make a small difference in overall execution speed. If there's an API call to do something like this, you should investigate to find out whether the speed or efficiency of your application could improve by using it.

16-Bit API vs. 32-Bit API

If you're converting your applications from 16-bit to 32-bit, you may face some issues when converting your API calls for Win16 to calls for Win32. Win32 changes, adds, and deletes some of the 16-bit calls that were available under 16-bit versions of Windows. For example, if you used the 16-bit API function LZCopyFile(), it's no longer recommended for Win32. Its replacements are the LZOpenFile() and LZCopy() API functions.

If you used any of the 16-bit communication API functions, you're in for quite a shock. This API set has changed drastically under Win32. If you have to keep your application so that it can compile under both 16- and 32-bit versions of Visual Basic, you'll want to use the conditional compilation statements. For most API declarations, you'll need totally different versions of the parameters, as well as a different DLL name.

Using the Alias keyword in the declare statements helps keep your actual underlying code very compatible with the 16- and 32-bit versions. As you'll see in the next section, any of the API functions that pass strings may now have two versions that can be called.

Understanding Unicode and ANSI

Before you start using the Win32 API, you need to understand a bit about ANSI, Unicode, and MBCS (Multi-Byte Character System) strings and how they relate to the Win32 API. We're all familiar with ANSI strings because they were used in the 16-bit world of Visual Basic 3.0. ANSI strings take 1 byte per character for storage. MBCS characters can be one or more bytes long.

MBCS (often called DBCS, or Double Byte Character System) is used by Windows implementations that have a character set exceeding 255 characters. These implementations, such as Windows J (Japanese-language Windows) or Chinese Windows, use MBCS to represent their character set.

Most characters in Windows J, for example, are 2 bytes long. With MBCS strings, you may have one byte representing the letter *A* and then two bytes representing a Japanese *Kanji* character. To Windows, ANSI and MBCS strings are identical. You can pass an ANSI or an MBCS string to most functions.

Unicode is a string representation that contains 16 bits (2 bytes) per character. All characters, including our standard alphabet, take up 2 bytes of storage. Now for a little bad news: The Win32 API has ANSI and Unicode versions of most function calls that accept strings. In most cases, this really isn't an issue because Visual Basic passes string information to DLLs as ANSI strings. But it becomes important when you're writing your declare statements; you need to make sure that you use the ANSI versions of the functions.

The ANSI versions of a function call are appended with the letter A. The example in the preceding section calls `SendMessage()`. If you look at the declare statement, `SendMessage()` is an alias of `SendMessageA()`. Unicode functions are appended with the letter W, for wide characters. The Unicode version of `SendMessage()` is `SendMessageW()`.

Now that the Unicode and ANSI issues are out of the way, let's examine ways to actually use the API to speed up our applications.

Common Dialogs

Most applications that allow loading, saving, or using disk files usually use the Windows common dialogs to get file names and paths that the user wants to use. Using common dialogs is a good way to reuse resources because Windows always has the common dialog library loaded (ComDlg32.Dll). Many programmers think that to use the common dialogs from Visual Basic, you have to use the Common Dialog OLE custom control (ComDlg32.Ocx) that comes with Visual Basic. This isn't necessarily true.

The Common Dialog control that comes with Visual Basic makes it easier for some programmers to get the functionality of the dialogs easily, quickly, and modularly into their application. To tune the performance of your application, however, you should use as few custom controls as possible. Most of the common dialog routines in the Win32 API can be called directly from Visual Basic.

Put the code shown in listing 14.1 in a Visual Basic form to bring up the File Open common dialog.

 This sample has the code in the `Form_Click()` event, so after you run the example, click the form to make the common dialog appear.

Listing 14.1 Sample02.Vbp Using the File Open Common Dialogs Without Using a Custom Control

```
Private Type OPENFILENAME
        lStructSize As Long
        hwndOwner As Long
        hInstance As Long
        lpstrFilter As String
        lpstrCustomFilter As String
        nMaxCustFilter As Long
        nFilterIndex As Long
        lpstrFile As String
        nMaxFile As Long
        lpstrFileTitle As String
        nMaxFileTitle As Long
        lpstrInitialDir As String
        lpstrTitle As String
        flags As Long
        nFileOffset As Integer
        nFileExtension As Integer
        lpstrDefExt As String
        lCustData As Long
        lpfnHook As Long
        lpTemplateName As String
End Type

Private Declare Function GetOpenFileName Lib "comdlg32.dll" Alias
"GetOpenFileNameA" (pOpenfilename As OPENFILENAME) As Long

Private Sub Form_Click()
    Dim ofn As OPENFILENAME

    ofn.lStructSize = Len(ofn)
    ofn.hwndOwner = Form1.hwnd
    ofn.hInstance = App.hInstance
    ofn.lpstrFilter = "Text Files (*.txt)" + Chr$(0) + "*.txt" _
      + Chr$(0) + "Rich Text Files (*.rtf)" + Chr$(0) + "*.rtf" _
      + Chr$(0)
    ofn.lpstrFile = Space$(254)
    ofn.nMaxFile = 255
    ofn.lpstrFileTitle = Space$(254)
    ofn.nMaxFileTitle = 255
    ofn.lpstrInitialDir = "c:\"
    ofn.lpstrTitle = "Our File Open Title"
    ofn.flags = 0

    a = GetOpenFileName(ofn)

    If (a) Then
        MsgBox "File to Open: " + Trim$(ofn.lpstrFile)
    Else
        MsgBox "Cancel was pressed"
    End If
End Sub
```

This code provides the File Open functionality without all the extra resource and memory overhead of loading the Common Dialog OLE control. There's a little more code here than you would have to use to get the file name from the OLE control. The final .EXE size varies by a few hundred bytes, however, and the amount of resources used during runtime and the distributable code size decrease quite a bit. You no longer have to distribute the 80K+ ComDlg32.Ocx file on your disks.

Some features might go away by using the API to bring up the File Open dialog. If you rely on the Help button on the dialogs, the Common Dialog control uses the `.HelpFile` property to bring up your help file when a user clicks that button.

If you want to have something similar happen when using the API, you have two choices: use a callback OLE control, or write a C DLL wrapper around the call to the Common Dialog code that handles the notification message resulting from the user clicking the Help button. Choosing the latter of those two options still beats the extra overhead of the full common dialog control. Bringing up the color selection common dialog box is very similar process but requires a small amount of additional programming because the `ChooseColor` user-defined type contains a member called `lpCustColors`. This points to an array of long integers.

Since there's no way to directly pass `lpCustColors` in Visual Basic, you send a string (allocating 4 bytes for each entry) for each of the 16 custom colors that the dialog supports. On return from the `ChooseColor()` API function call, you convert these 4 characters back into a long integer that's stored in an array of custom colors. To test the color selection dialog, add the code shown in listing 14.2 to a form.

Listing 14.2   Sample04.Vbp   Using the Color Common Dialog with a Custom Control

```
Private Type ChooseColor
        lStructSize As Long
        hwndOwner As Long
        hInstance As Long
        rgbResult As Long
        lpCustColors As String
        flags As Long
        lCustData As Long
        lpfnHook As Long
        lpTemplateName As String
End Type

Private Declare Function ChooseColor Lib "comdlg32.dll" Alias
"ChooseColorA" (pChoosecolor As ChooseColor) As Long
```

```
Private Sub Form_Click()
    Dim cc As ChooseColor
    Dim CustColor(16) As Long

    cc.lStructSize = Len(cc)
    cc.hwndOwner = Form1.hWnd
    cc.hInstance = App.hInstance
    cc.flags = 0

    cc.lpCustColors = String$(16 * 4, 0)

    a = ChooseColor(cc)

    Cls
    If (a) Then
        MsgBox "Color chosen:" & Str$(cc.rgbResult)

        'Create the custom color array based on
        'the colors passed back from the String
        For x = 1 To Len(cc.lpCustColors) Step 4
            c1 = Asc(Mid$(cc.lpCustColors, x, 1))
            c2 = Asc(Mid$(cc.lpCustColors, x + 1, 1))
            c3 = Asc(Mid$(cc.lpCustColors, x + 2, 1))
            c4 = Asc(Mid$(cc.lpCustColors, x + 3, 1))

            CustColor(x / 4) = (c1) + (c2 * 256) + (c3 * 65536) _
                + (c4 * 167772216&)
            Print "Custom Color"; Int(x / 4); "="; CustColor(x / 4)
        Next x
    Else
        MsgBox "Cancel was pressed"
    End If
End Sub
```

From this set of sample code, you should be able to work with the other common dialogs and get them implemented in code rather than use their OLE control equivalents. Microsoft will continue adding new dialogs to the common dialog controls. The more you use the code that Microsoft has written, the smaller your applications will be. Using the common dialogs in the above manner optimizes your application for speed and resource usage. Not to mention that you don't have to write so much code!

Accessing Multimedia Support

Many applications provide or use some type of multimedia support, whether or not they're really considered a multimedia application. If you play sound files (.WAV) or start a Video for Windows file (.AVI), you may benefit from using the MCI API directly.

You're now probably using the Multimedia Control Interface OLE custom control (Mci32.Ocx) in your application. Since you're again removing a custom control, your resource usage will go down—in this case, by quite a bit. The MCI control uses resources for bitmaps and has other Windows overhead as it creates an hWnd button for each button that's visible on the control. By eliminating the need for this control, you also improve your load-time performance.

To play a wave file (.WAV) by using the MCI interface, add the code shown in listing 14.3 to a form.

Listing 14.3   Sample03.Vbp   Playing a .WAV File Without Using the MCI Custom Control

```
Private Declare Function mciSendString Lib "winmm.dll" Alias
"mciSendStringA" (ByVal lpstrCommand As String, ByVal
lpstrReturnString As String, ByVal uReturnLength As Long, ByVal
hwndCallback As Long) As Long

Private Sub Form_Click()
    Dim ReturnString As String
    ReturnString = Space$(255)
    a = mciSendString("play d:\win95\media\tada.wav", _
      ReturnString, Len(ReturnString), 0)
End Sub
```

The mciSendString() API call can provide most of the functionality of the MCI OLE control—minus the graphical interface, of course. With a few lightweight image controls and some mouse-handling code, you'll have a workalike version of the MCI without all the associated overhead.

You may still need to do some additional work to get all the functionality of the OLE control. You also may need to do some subclassing (using a subclassing or callback control) to get specific notification messages, if needed, by your application.

For further information on what commands are available through the mciSendString() API call, see the Windows Multimedia help file that's included with the Win32 SDK, or look in the appropriate Win32 user's manual. Supported devices include—but aren't necessarily limited to—sound files

(.WAV), MIDI, Mixer, Video Disc/VCR, and Digital Video (.AVI). Using the above multimedia programming techniques can cut your resource and memory usage greatly.

Optimizing Disk Access and File Copying

If your application copies or moves files from one location to another, you should be aware of a few Win32 API calls. In the past, I either used the Shell command to do a DOS copy, or I opened the file for binary access with the Visual Basic OPEN command and copied byte by byte to the destination file. Both methods work, but both are slower than using the appropriate Win32 API call.

Using *CopyFile()* to Speed Up File Copying

The CopyFile() API function takes a source file name and a destination file name and copies one file to the other. A third parameter tells the function whether it should fail if the destination file already exists. Since you don't have the overhead of starting a shelled process or of going through the file a byte at a time, CopyFile() is much faster. CopyFile() is the most highly optimized method for copying files (see table 14.1).

Table 14.1 Copying a 1M File: Shell of DOS *Copy* vs. *CopyFile()*	
Seconds	**Activity/Graph**
	Shell to DOS Copy Test
1.649	
	CopyFile API Test
0.070	

The code in listing 14.4 compares two functions used to copy files. The Shell() function is used to start a DOS copy command and the CopyFile() function is used for comparison. It uses a file in the root directory of C called Junk.Fil. It copies this file to Junk1.Fil, Junk2.Fil, Junk3.Fil, Junk4.Fil, and Junk5.Fil.

Listing 14.4 Sample05.Vbp Comparing *CopyFile()* to *Shell()* of DOS Copy to Copy a File

```
Private Declare Function CopyFile Lib "kernel32" Alias "CopyFileA"
(ByVal lpExistingFileName As String, ByVal lpNewFileName As String,
ByVal bFailIfExists As Long) As Long

Private Sub Form_Click()

BeginTime "Shell to Dos Copy", 1
    For x = 1 To 5
        a = Shell("command.com /c copy c:\junk.fil c:\junk" + _
        Trim$(Str$(x)) + ".fil")
    Next x
    EndTime

    BeginTime "CopyFile test", 1
    For x = 1 To 5
        a = CopyFile("c:\junk.fil", "c:\junk" + Trim$(Str$(x)) _
        + ".fil", False)
    Next x
    EndTime

    If a Then
        'Successful
    Else
        'Failed
    End If
End Sub
```

Using *MoveFile()* to Quickly Move Files Between Directories

The MoveFile() function works in a similar manner. It takes two parameters: a source path\file name and a destination path\file name. Rather than copy the file, it moves a file from one directory to another or changes the name of a file or directory. This saves time because, rather than do a copy and then a delete on a file, you can just move the file to the appropriate path.

MoveFile() has one limitation: You can't move files across volumes (drives). You'll still have to use the CopyFile() function to do this. However, in the example shown in listing 14.5, I've written code that moves a file called C:\Junk\Test.Doc to C:\Junk1\Test.Doc. Calling the MoveFile() function just changes the directory entries to map the file to the new location. This means that even huge files are "moved" instantly to their new location. It's not necessary to copy individual bytes.

IV

Listing 14.5 Sample06.Vbp   Moving a File Across Directories Using the *MoveFile()* API Function

```
Private Declare Function MoveFile Lib "kernel32" Alias "MoveFileA"
(ByVal lpExistingFileName As String, ByVal lpNewFileName As String)
As Long

Private Sub Form_Click()
    a = MoveFile("c:\junk\test.doc", "c:\junk1\test.doc")
    If a Then
        MsgBox "File moved!"
    Else
        MsgBox "Error. File not moved!"
    End If
End Sub
```

Using *MoveFileEx()* with Windows NT

If your application will run only under Windows NT, you have a third option for moving files: MoveFileEx() is an NT version of the MoveFile() API function that provides some additional functionality. It has the original two parameters of the MoveFile() function—the source and destination path\file names—and it adds an additional dwFlags parameter, which specifies a specific action to be taken during the move of the file (see table 14.2).

This function works only under Windows NT!

Table 14.2 Valid *dwFlags* Parameters for Windows NT's *MoveFileEx()* Function

Parameter	Purpose
MOVEFILE_REPLACE_EXISTING	Replaces a file if it exists
MOVEFILE_COPY_ALLOWED	Allows moving across volumes (drives)
MOVEFILE_DELAY_UNTIL_REBOOT	Moves the file after the next reboot

The MOVEFILE_COPY_ALLOWED flag tells MoveFileEx() to simulate a move across volumes by calling the CopyFile() API function and then the DeleteFile() API function.

The MOVEFILE_DELAY_UNTIL_REBOOT flag can be useful if you don't want the file moved until the user reboots the machine and restarts the operating system. This is useful if the file that you want to move is going to replace a file that the operating system or an application is using.

To test the example, you'll have to change the path and file names so that they point to valid files. Put the code shown in listing 14.6 in a form to test the move of a file across volumes.

Listing 14.6   Sample07.Vbp   Moving a File Across Volumes Using the *MoveFile()* API Function

```
Private Declare Function MoveFileEx Lib "kernel32" Alias
"MoveFileExA" (ByVal lpExistingFileName As String, ByVal
lpNewFileName As String, ByVal dwFlags As Long) As Long
Private Const MOVEFILE_REPLACE_EXISTING = &H1
Private Const MOVEFILE_COPY_ALLOWED = &H2
Private Const MOVEFILE_DELAY_UNTIL_REBOOT = &H4

Private Sub Form_Click()
    ' This function will ONLY work correctly
    ' under Windows NT!
    a = MoveFileEx("c:\junk\test.doc", "c:\test.doc", _
      MOVEFILE_COPY_ALLOWED)
    If a Then
        MsgBox "File moved!"
    Else
        MsgBox "Error. File not moved!"
    End If
End Sub
```

Faster Graphic Drawing Using the Windows API

The VB Form and the PictureBox control contain methods that allow you to draw graphics onto their display services. These methods, such as PSet, Circle, Line, and so forth, have the extra overhead of a method set for each drawing operation that you do on the object. Calling these methods over and over slows down the application that's doing the drawing.

Using the Win32 API can again get a speed boost. First, let's look at the Visual Basic PSet method. It's the method that sets a pixel on a form, picture box, or the printer objects to a specific color (see table 14.3).

Table 14.3	*PSet* vs. *SetPixel()*	
Seconds	**Activity/Graph**	
	PSet Test	
0.673	███████████████████████████████	
	SetPixel Test	
0.224	████████████	

The Win32 API function is called `SetPixel()`. It takes an `hDC`, an x coordinate (`int`), a y coordinate (`int`), and a color reference (`COLORREF`).

> The default mapping mode, when you get an `hDC` from a form using `form.hDC`, is in pixels. If you want to work in twips, you have to set the mapping mode of the `hDC` returned from `Form1.hDC` by using the `SetMapMode()` API call.

In my example, I set the mapping mode of the VB form to pixels by setting the `ScaleMode` property. This causes the `PSet` method on that form object to use pixels as its unit measurement. The declare for the `SetPixel()` API call is as follows:

```
Private Declare Function SetPixel Lib "gdi32" (ByVal hdc As Long,
ByVal x As Long, ByVal y As Long, ByVal crColor As Long) As Long
```

The code shown in listing 14.7 shows the difference between using `PSet` and `SetPixel()`.

Listing 14.7 Sample08.Vbp Benchmarking *PSet* and *SetPixel()*

```
Form1.ScaleMode = vbPixels      '3

BeginTime "PSet Test", 1

For y = 1 To 100
    For x = 1 To 1000
        Form1.PSet (x, y)
    Next x
Next y

EndTime

Form1.Cls

BeginTime "SetPixel Test", 1
hdc1 = Form1.hdc
For y = 1 To 100
    For x = 1 To 1000
        a = SetPixel(hdc1, x, y, 0)
    Next x
Next y
EndTime
```

Bitwise Optimization

IV

The next test is of the `Circle` method as compared to the `Ellipse()` API function call. The speed difference on these two isn't as great as on the `SetPixel()`/`PSet` test. However, if you're drawing thousands or millions of circles, every millisecond saved may count (see table 14.4). The sample code shown in listing 14.8 draws 1,000 circles using both the VB method and the API call.

Table 14.4   The *Circle* Method vs. the *Ellipse()* API Function

Seconds	Activity/Graph
	Circle Method
1.488	▓▓▓▓▓▓▓▓▓▓▓▓▓▓▓▓▓▓▓▓▓▓▓▓▓▓▓▓▓▓▓▓▓
	Ellipse API
1.059	▓▓▓▓▓▓▓▓▓▓▓▓▓▓▓▓▓▓▓▓▓▓▓

NOTE   When using the API calls for `Ellipse()` and—later in this chapter—`Rectangle()`, the API draws up to, but not including, the bottom right coordinates specified. To make this consistent with the Visual Basic commands, you have to adjust these numbers accordingly.

Listing 14.8   Sample09.Vbp   Benchmarking the *Ellipse()* API and *Circle* Method

```
Private Declare Function Ellipse Lib "gdi32" (ByVal hdc As Long,
ByVal X1 As Long, ByVal Y1 As Long, ByVal X2 As Long, ByVal Y2 As
Long) As Long

Private Sub Form_Click()

    Form1.ScaleMode = vbPixels    '3

    BeginTime "Circle Method Test", 1

    For x = 1 To 1000
        Form1.Circle (200, 200), 100
    Next x

    EndTime

    Form1.Cls

    BeginTime "Circle API Test", 1
    hdc1 = Form1.hdc
    For x = 1 To 1000
        Call Ellipse(hdc1, 100, 100, 300, 300)
```

```
        Next x

    EndTime

End Sub
```

The next test uses the Visual Basic Line method to draw a series of lines. To simulate this method by using the API, you actually have to use two different API calls: MoveToEx() and LineTo().

MoveToEx() moves the current position to a specified X,Y coordinate. The LineTo() method draws a line from the current X,Y position to the X,Y position specified by the parameters in the call. It also returns a point structure that contains the last starting position. Notice that even though we're making two different API calls, this procedure is still nearly three times as fast as using the Visual Basic Line method (see table 14.5). The sample code in listing 14.9 shows the use of both the VB method and the API function call.

Listing 14.9 Sample10.Vbp Benchmarking the *Line* Method and the *LineTo()* API Function

```
Private Declare Function LineTo Lib "gdi32" (ByVal hdc As Long,
ByVal x As Long, ByVal y As Long) As Long

Private Type POINTAPI
        x As Long
        y As Long
End Type

Private Declare Function MoveToEx Lib "gdi32" (ByVal hdc As Long,
ByVal x As Long, ByVal y As Long, lpPoint As POINTAPI) As Long

Private Sub Form_Click()

    Dim lpPoint As POINTAPI
    Form1.ScaleMode = vbPixels     '3

    BeginTime "Line Method Test", 1

    For x = 1 To 250 Step 10
        For y = 1 To 100
            Form1.Line (0, 0)-(x, y)
        Next y
    Next x

    EndTime

    Form1.Cls

    BeginTime "LineTo API Test", 1
    hdc1 = Form1.hdc
```

(continues)

Listing 14.9   Continued

```
        For x = 1 To 250 Step 10
            For y = 1 To 100
                Call MoveToEx(hdc1, 0, 0, lpPoint)
                Call LineTo(hdc1, x, y)
            Next y
        Next x

        EndTime

    End Sub
```

Table 14.5   The VB *Line* Method vs. the *MoveToEx()/LineTo()* API Functions

Seconds	Activity/Graph
	Line Method
0.430	████████████████████████████████
	MoveToEx()/LineTo() API
0.172	██████████████

The next test involves drawing a rectangle. Visual Basic uses the Line method to draw a rectangle, while the Win32 API uses the Rectangle() function. The code in listing 14.10 compares the method and the API function call by drawing 1,000 rectangles. Table 14.6 shows the results.

Listing 14.10   Sample11.Vbp   Benchmarking the *Line* Method (to Draw Rectangles) and the *Rectangle()* API Function

```
    Private Declare Function Rectangle Lib "gdi32" (ByVal hdc As Long,
    ByVal X1 As Long, ByVal Y1 As Long, ByVal X2 As Long, ByVal Y2 As
    Long) As Long

    Private Sub Form_Click()

        Form1.ScaleMode = vbPixels    '3

        BeginTime "Rectangle (using Line Method) Test", 1

        For x = 1 To 1000
            Form1.Line (100, 100)-(200, 200), , BF
        Next x

        EndTime

        Form1.Cls
```

```
        BeginTime "Rectangle API Test", 1
        hdc1 = Form1.hdc
        For x = 1 To 1000
            Call Rectangle(hdc1, 100, 100, 200, 200)
        Next x

        EndTime

    End Sub
```

Table 14.6 *Rectangle* **(Using** *Line* **Method) vs. the** *Rectangle()*
API Call

Seconds	Activity/Graph
	Line Method (using BF for rectangle)
0.625	
	Rectangle API
0.109	

Network Speedups

Many installations of applications today in corporate America have software packages installed on local area network (LAN) servers. One way to enhance the performance of your applications loaded on LAN servers is to put the components that are used most often on a user's local hard drive. (This may not always be possible, however, because of system management issues or physical limitations, such as lack of drive space.)

Installing the shared components on a local drive is often a very good way of speeding up your application. When designing your application, keep in mind that you'll have to include a smart setup application that gives users the option of putting the specific files on their local systems instead of on the server. Some applications, such as Microsoft Office, allow users to specify where they want the shared components to be installed when running the setup application. Installing these shared components on a local drive greatly enhances the performance of the applications that use those components.

There are also ways, using the Windows API functions, to improve performance when your application is running over a network. One of these techniques involves the loading of bitmaps.

Loading large, decompressed bitmaps over a network-shared drive can be a very slow process. One way around this is to compress your bitmaps with VB's Compress.Exe utility, and then use the Windows API to decompress these files in real time over the network to a new temporary file name on a local drive. Next, you load the bitmap. Finally, you delete the temporary file when it's no longer needed.

To accomplish this, use the LZOpenFile(), LZCopy(), and LZClose() Win32 API functions. LZOpenFile() opens the file handles of the source and destination files. It also internally calls the LZInit() API function, which allocates memory buffers that are used during the decompression of the source file. LZCopy() takes a source and destination file handle and decompresses the source into the destination file. LZClose() closes the file handles and cleans up the memory buffers that were allocated by the LZOpenFile() call.

Loading the compressed file speeds up because only the compressed bitmap data—not the entire decompressed file—travels across the network. The load process from the local disk is usually a very speedy process. This technique can speed up an application by more than 75 percent, depending on the size and compressibility of the bitmap data.

Depending on your disk caching, you can also see a performance difference even when loading from a local hard drive for the first time. Once the decompressed bitmap is in cache memory, however, the load time is much faster for it. The bitmap I used for the test was 1,921,078 decompressed bytes and 269,983 bytes in its compressed form. You, of course, will have to change the path and file names to match your drive configurations.

In my example, drive C is the local drive and drive J is the network drive, as listing 14.11 shows.

Listing 14.11   Sample13.Vbp   Using the Compressed Files and the LZ Functions to Speed Up Network Access

```
Private Const OFS_MAXPATHNAME = 128

' OpenFile() Structure
Private Type OFSTRUCT
        cBytes As Byte
        fFixedDisk As Byte
        nErrCode As Integer
        Reserved1 As Integer
        Reserved2 As Integer
        szPathName(OFS_MAXPATHNAME) As Byte
End Type

Private Const OF_READ = &H0
Private Const OF_WRITE = &H1
Private Const OF_READWRITE = &H2
Private Const OF_SHARE_COMPAT = &H0
Private Const OF_SHARE_EXCLUSIVE = &H10
Private Const OF_SHARE_DENY_WRITE = &H20
```

```
Private Const OF_SHARE_DENY_READ = &H30
Private Const OF_SHARE_DENY_NONE = &H40
Private Const OF_PARSE = &H100
Private Const OF_DELETE = &H200
Private Const OF_VERIFY = &H400
Private Const OF_CANCEL = &H800
Private Const OF_CREATE = &H1000
Private Const OF_PROMPT = &H2000
Private Const OF_EXIST = &H4000
Private Const OF_REOPEN = &H8000

Private Declare Function LZCopy Lib "lz32.dll" (ByVal hfSource As
Long, ByVal hfDest As Long) As Long
Private Declare Function LZOpenFile Lib "lz32.dll" Alias
"LZOpenFileA" (ByVal lpszFile As String, lpOf As OFSTRUCT, ByVal
style As Long) As Long
Private Declare Sub LZClose Lib "lz32.dll" (ByVal hfFile As Long)

Private Sub Form_Click()

    Dim fhSource As Long
    Dim fhDest As Long
    Dim ofsSource As OFSTRUCT
    Dim ofsDest As OFSTRUCT

    BeginTime "LZCopy to load bitmap", 1

    fhSource = LZOpenFile("j:\huge.bm_", ofsSource, OF_READ Or _
      OF_SHARE_DENY_NONE)
    fhDest = LZOpenFile("c:\hugetmp.bmp", ofsDest, OF_CREATE Or _
      OF_SHARE_DENY_NONE)
    'If no error occurred
    If ofsSource.nErrCode = 0 And fhDest > 0 Then
        lzerr = LZCopy(fhSource, fhDest)
        If lzerr < 0 Then
            LZClose (fhSource)
            LZClose (fhDest)
            MsgBox "LZCopy Error occurred"
            Exit Sub
        End If
    Else
        MsgBox "Error occured opening source file"
        Exit Sub
    End If

    LZClose (fhSource)
    LZClose (fhDest)
    Picture1.Picture = LoadPicture("c:\hugetmp.bmp")
    Kill "c:\hugetmp.bmp"

    EndTime

    'Test loading the same decompressed bitmap
    Picture1.Picture = LoadPicture("")
    BeginTime "Loading 2mb bitmap directly", 1
    Picture1.Picture = LoadPicture("j:\huge.bmp")
    EndTime
End Sub
```

As you can see in table 14.7, this technique can make quite a difference in load times. These were tested on a network that had little activity, so if you're running on a network with a heavy load, this may make an even bigger difference.

Table 14.7 Using the *LZExpand()* API to Load Bitmaps	
Seconds	**Activity/Graph**
	Using LoadPicture( ) with Decompressed Bitmap
3.680	
	Using LZCopy( ) with Compressed Bitmap
2.328	

You can also shell to Compress.Exe and use the LZExpand() API to enhance performance or increase disk space for your applications. If certain static portions of your programs or databases are rarely needed, keep them in a compressed state. When they're needed, decompress them to a temporary file, use them, and—when finished—delete them. This keeps your disk space usage to a minimum.

From Here...

For more information, refer to these chapters:

- Chapter 12, "Optimizing Graphics and Bitmaps," analyzes the VB graphics methods with various property settings and different control targets.

- For an example of graphics methods using custom controls and VB code, see Chapter 13, "Using Components and Subroutines Wisely."

Index

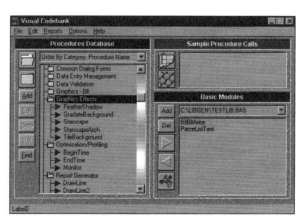

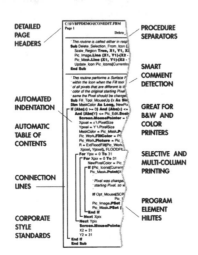
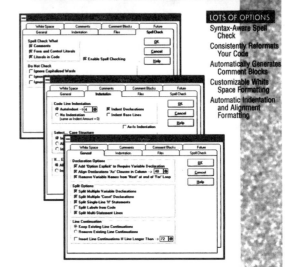

Complete and Return this Card
for a *FREE* Computer Book Catalog

Thank you for purchasing this book! You have purchased a superior computer book written expressly for your needs. To continue to provide the kind of up-to-date, pertinent coverage you've come to expect from us, we need to hear from you. Please take a minute to complete and return this self-addressed, postage-paid form. In return, we'll send you a free catalog of all our computer books on topics ranging from word processing to programming and the internet.

Mr. ☐ Mrs. ☐ Ms. ☐ Dr. ☐

Name (first) ☐☐☐☐☐☐☐☐☐☐☐ (M.I.) ☐ (last) ☐☐☐☐☐☐☐☐☐☐☐☐☐☐☐☐☐

Address ☐☐☐☐☐☐☐☐☐☐☐☐☐☐☐☐☐☐☐☐☐☐☐☐☐☐☐☐☐☐☐☐☐☐

City ☐☐☐☐☐☐☐☐☐☐☐☐ State ☐☐ Zip ☐☐☐☐☐☐☐☐☐☐

Phone ☐☐☐ ☐☐☐ ☐☐☐☐ Fax ☐☐☐ ☐☐☐ ☐☐☐☐

Company Name ☐☐☐☐☐☐☐☐☐☐☐☐☐☐☐☐☐☐☐☐☐☐☐☐☐☐☐☐☐☐

E-mail address ☐☐☐☐☐☐☐☐☐☐☐☐☐☐☐☐☐☐☐☐☐☐☐☐☐☐☐☐☐☐

Please check at least (3) influencing factors for purchasing this book.

Front or back cover information on book .... ☐
Special approach to the content .... ☐
Completeness of content .... ☐
Author's reputation .... ☐
Publisher's reputation .... ☐
Book cover design or layout .... ☐
Index or table of contents of book .... ☐
Price of book .... ☐
Special effects, graphics, illustrations .... ☐
Other (Please specify): _____ ☐

How did you first learn about this book?

Saw in Macmillan Computer Publishing catalog .... ☐
Recommended by store personnel .... ☐
Saw the book on bookshelf at store .... ☐
Recommended by a friend .... ☐
Received advertisement in the mail .... ☐
Saw an advertisement in: _____ ☐
Read book review in: _____ ☐
Other (Please specify): _____ ☐

How many computer books have you purchased in the last six months?

This book only .... ☐   3 to 5 books .... ☐
2 books .... ☐   More than 5 .... ☐

4. Where did you purchase this book?

Bookstore .... ☐
Computer Store .... ☐
Consumer Electronics Store .... ☐
Department Store .... ☐
Office Club .... ☐
Warehouse Club .... ☐
Mail Order .... ☐
Direct from Publisher .... ☐
Internet site .... ☐
Other (Please specify): _____ ☐

5. How long have you been using a computer?

☐ Less than 6 months   ☐ 6 months to a year
☐ 1 to 3 years   ☐ More than 3 years

6. What is your level of experience with personal computers and with the subject of this book?

	With PCs	With subject of book
New	☐	☐
Casual	☐	☐
Accomplished	☐	☐
Expert	☐	☐

Source Code ISBN: 0-7897-0206-1

7. Which of the following best describes your job title?

Administrative Assistant .... ☐
Coordinator .... ☐
Manager/Supervisor .... ☐
Director .... ☐
Vice President .... ☐
President/CEO/COO .... ☐
Lawyer/Doctor/Medical Professional .... ☐
Teacher/Educator/Trainer .... ☐
Engineer/Technician .... ☐
Consultant .... ☐
Not employed/Student/Retired .... ☐
Other (Please specify): _____ ☐

8. Which of the following best describes the area of the company your job title falls under?

Accounting .... ☐
Engineering .... ☐
Manufacturing .... ☐
Operations .... ☐
Marketing .... ☐
Sales .... ☐
Other (Please specify): _____ ☐

Comments: _____

_____

_____

Fold here and scotch-tape to ma

9. What is your age?

Under 20 .... ☐
21-29 .... ☐
30-39 .... ☐
40-49 .... ☐
50-59 .... ☐
60-over .... ☐

10. Are you:

Male .... ☐
Female .... ☐

11. Which computer publications do you read regularly? (Please list)

_____
_____
_____
_____
_____
_____
_____
_____
_____
_____

Licensing Agreement

By opening this package, you are agreeing to be bound by the following:

Installing the Book's Program Files

For instructions on how to install the book's program files onto your system's hard drive, refer to the ReadMe.Txt file located in the root directory of the CD-ROM.

Installing the Aardvark Applications

Pretty Printer and Polisher have their own installation routines included on the CD.

The Pretty Printer application is in the \PRETTYPR directory, and the Polisher application is in the \POLISHER directory. To install them, run their respective Setup.Exe utility.